STATISTICS
FOR EDUCATION

STATISTICS FOR EDUCATION:
With Data Processing

DAVID WHITE
Utah State University

HARPER & ROW, PUBLISHERS
New York, Evanston, San Francisco, London

Sponsoring Editor: Lane Akers
Project Editor: Cynthia Hausdorff
Designer: Jared Pratt
Production Supervisor: Valerie Klima

Library of Congress Cataloging in Publication Data

White, David.
  Statistics for education.

  Bibliography: p.
  1. Electronic data processing—Education.
2. Education—Statistics. I. Title.
LB2846.W437   370'.1'83   72-12468
ISBN 0-06-047065-8

To
WALTER R. BORG,
some of whose work
provided the
incentive for writing
this book

CONTENTS

PREFACE

This book is designed to introduce statistics to people having the following characteristics:

1. They have relatively little background in mathematics (a maximum of one year of high school algebra).
2. They are interested in being able to use a few statistical tools (as contrasted with a desire simply to know what statistics is about).
3. Their research interests are primarily educational in nature, and they are oriented toward projects involving relatively large groups of people, rather than small laboratory studies over a period of time with few subjects.
4. They would like to have the basic tools to use computer center facilities for statistical purposes.

To reach this group of people, the following techniques have been employed (the topic numbers correspond to the paragraphs above):

1. Basic arithmetic is taught at the first place in the text where it is needed; hence sections on arithmetic, elementary algebra, and some geometry are interspersed throughout the book.
2. Ability to use statistical tools is developed through the provision of appendixes containing large amounts of raw educational data collected by W. R. Borg. The student will be asked to use his statistical tools by carrying out the following steps:

   a. Translate a research problem into statistical terminology.
   b. Make a sampling plan.
   c. Collect the data, using the sampling plan (from the raw data in the appendix).
   d. Analyze the data.
   e. Interpret the data in the light of the research problem assigned.

These steps are among those any researcher must carry out in planning and executing a research project; they can be considered important parts of the so-called story problems of an applied statistics course. A heavy emphasis on story problems should enable the conscientious student to gain skill in carrying out his own research projects with some degree of statistical competence. Basic emphasis will be on the meaning to the researcher of the techniques used.

3. To maintain student interest, the text material is focused on educational problems; statistical methods are introduced as they are needed to help solve these problems. It is hoped that this approach will appeal to those whose primary interest is education rather than statistics itself. The educational data referred to earlier have been provided not only for the experience they permit, but also because of the intrinsic interest education students are likely to have in such data. Any branch of applied mathematics becomes more appealing to the nonmathematician if it is embedded in a topic he truly cares about.

4. To provide training in the use of computer center facilities, the elements of data processing are taught throughout the text at the points where the material is needed, just as for the basic arithmetic. Appendixes K–N are computer programs to use with the statistical methods covered. These are in the FORTRAN language approved by the U.S.A. Standards Institute; thus they may be used at most computer centers.

A word of advice to instructors is in order with respect to the computer program listings provided. Computer centers are different enough to make successful operation of a program on the first try a highly unusual event. Minor changes should always be expected, and the best policy is to submit your listings to one of the resident programmers before you expect to have your class use it, and to let him have the program deck punched and made operational on your equipment. Then, duplicates of his deck can be made by the computer center for distribution to the class members.

Another alternative is available if your computer center has a set of simple and easy to use statistical programs. Such a set should be accompanied by clear instructions that can be made available to your students on how to use the programs. If this is your good fortune, you can—and should—ignore the listings in the Appendix and take advantage of the programs provided by your own computer center. However, it is recommended that you avoid using programs which do many more things than your class needs. Such programs are usually more difficult to use and will tend to "turn off" beginning students who are using computer facilities for the first time.

It should be emphasized here that most of the Experiences with Data do not have a single answer. A question such as "Design and execute a project to determine the degree to which a student's morale is affected by his school" will result in as many different papers as there are class members. The student must define *morale* in terms of available measures, decide such matters as whether deviations in morale can be attributed to socioeconomic differences rather than to the schools themselves, decide on statistical techniques, collect his own data, and analyze and interpret the data. Students inevitably will differ in each of these steps; and papers which differ greatly, will often be of equally high quality. Incidentally, papers reporting projects of this kind turn out to be no more time consuming to grade conscientiously than the more conventional kind—and they are much more interesting.

The text is designed to include sufficient material for one academic year of work if the class meets twice a week and an additional weekly lab period is allotted for reports and class discussion arising from the problems in the Experiences with Data sections. Early chapters can be covered more rapidly than the later ones since the Experiences with Data play a larger role as the student progresses through the book and these problems are more time consuming.

For those who wish to use the text for one semester, Chapters 1 to 5 provide a logical set of topics if the sections marked with an asterisk are omitted. Throughout the text the asterisked sections can be omitted without affecting the continuity of the material. Chapters 6, 7, and 8 are self-contained topics; any one of these can be taken up after Chapter 5 is completed. Chapter 9 assumes that Chapters 7 and 8 have been covered. Exercises marked † are essentially sampling problems designed to familiarize students with the meaning of certain aspects of statistical inference. Exercises marked ‡ require coordination of the results by the instructor as part of a class period. This extra effort will have its reward in the increased understanding that students acquire for confidence intervals, type I and type II errors, and other concepts that the beginning student often has trouble with.

A section appears at the end of each chapter giving solutions to all problems with the exception of those marked † or ‡. Those marked with † have no fixed answer, but in some cases a sample solution is given. The reader is encouraged to use these sections; often computational short-cuts are given there that are not described in the main body of the chapter.

DAVID WHITE

ACKNOWLEDGMENTS

I am indebted to the Literary Executor of the late Sir Ronald A. Fisher, F.R.S., to Dr. Frank Yates, F.R.S., and to Oliver and Boyd, Edinburgh, for permission to reprint Tables III, IV, and V from their book *Statistical Tables for Biological, Agricultural and Medical Research*. I also wish to express gratitude to McGraw-Hill Book Co., for permission to reproduce material in Tables 16–10 and 16–19 from *An Introduction to Linear Statistical Models*, Vol. I, by F. A. Graybill; and to C. W. Dunnett and M. Sobel and *Biometrika* for permission to reproduce Table 4 from their paper "A Bivariate Generalization of Student's *t*-Distribution." Hayden Book Co. has kindly permitted the reproduction of Figures 2-5(a) and 2-5(b) from *Comprehensive Standard Programming* by J. N. Haag; I am indebted to John Wiley and Sons, Gads Forlag, and Skandinavisk Aktuarietidskrift for permission to reproduce the table of logarithms and the normal distribution.

I wish to call particular attention to the effectiveness of the editorial staff at Harper & Row. Editorial recommendations have been uniformly good; and the speed with which production details were completed has been especially appreciated. My association with the company has been a distinct pleasure.

The final version of the manuscript was typed with much patience and attention to detail by Nola White, Ann White, and Susan Walk, and the answers to the problems in the first six chapters were worked out by Ann White and Lorraine Flynn; I am most grateful to them for their efforts. I owe my greatest debt of gratitude to my wife, Thelma, who has provided constant support through the years during which this book has been in preparation.

STATISTICS
FOR EDUCATION

CHAPTER 1
RANDOM SAMPLING
WITH MATHEMATICAL
PRELIMINARIES

The goal of this book is to make statistics useful and interesting for the student who is pursuing a career in education. Statistical techniques are important tools for educational research and for decision-making at the district level. One of the ways in which we can learn to use these tools is through the study of specific educational problems in a quantitative setting—this is the approach of this text. In this chapter you will be introduced to a research project that is of current educational interest. Data from this project will be used throughout the book to explain the proper use of statistical techniques.

The topics covered in this chapter are (1) how to obtain a random sample; and (2) a review of the mathematics needed for this text. The random sampling comes first, so that you will have some concrete experiences with educational data to apply your symbols to; then the mathematics can be related to these experiences.

Some hints to the student are in order here as you begin your work.

1. Answers to all exercises in a chapter are at the end of the chapter. There is no known substitute for working problems to ensure understanding; students are encouraged to (1) work the examples in the book as though they were problems; (2) do some of the problems at the end of each section.

2. There is a glossary at the end of the book giving all math symbols used in the text, how to pronounce each, and the section where it is first explained. Make a practice of referring to it, if you have forgotten the meaning of a symbol.

3. A review of all concepts and formulas introduced appears at the end of each chapter, to help you to periodically summarize the material you have read.

We next turn to a description of our educational research project. In December 1965 a report entitled "Ability Grouping in the Public Schools" by W. R. Borg appeared in the *Journal of Experimental Education*. The circumstances surrounding this study were a bit unusual; two Western school districts of comparable socioeconomic background and rural-urban characteristics were considering a change to ability grouping, such that children in any given classroom would be at the same ability level. One of the districts decided to change to ability grouping; the other elected to stay with the conventional type of classroom organization. Borg was responsible for conducting a study that obtained both social adjustment and academic achievement measures for a large proportion of the children in both districts. The goal was to detect any genuine differences between the two districts that could con-

FIGURE 1-1
Ability grouping vs. random grouping in two school districts.

Ability Grouped Students

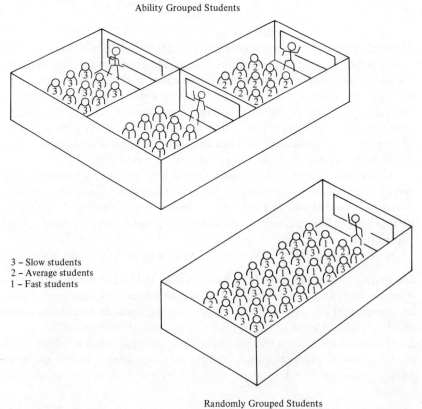

3 – Slow students
2 – Average students
1 – Fast students

Randomly Grouped Students

FIGURE 1–2

Layout of schools in two districts. (a) Students grouped randomly; (b) Students grouped by ability levels.

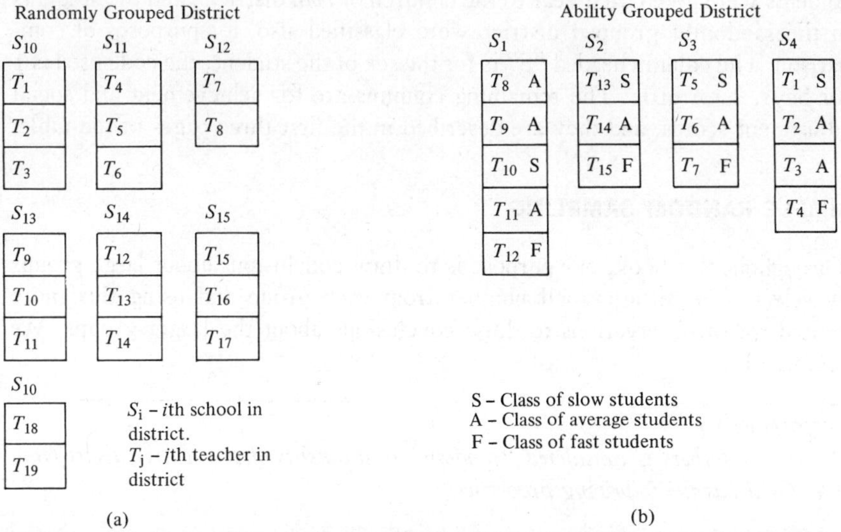

Randomly Grouped District

S_{10}	S_{11}	S_{12}
T_1	T_4	T_7
T_2	T_5	T_8
T_3	T_6	

S_{13}	S_{14}	S_{15}
T_9	T_{12}	T_{15}
T_{10}	T_{13}	T_{16}
T_{11}	T_{14}	T_{17}

S_{10}
T_{18}
T_{19}

S_i – ith school in district.
T_j – jth teacher in district

(a)

Ability Grouped District

S_1	S_2	S_3	S_4
T_8 A	T_{13} S	T_5 S	T_1 S
T_9 A	T_{14} A	T_6 A	T_2 A
T_{10} S	T_{15} F	T_7 F	T_3 A
T_{11} A			T_4 F
T_{12} F			

S – Class of slow students
A – Class of average students
F – Class of fast students

(b)

ceivably be due to ability grouping, and also to determine whether these differences were large enough to be meaningful in the educational sense.

Part of the "raw" data (the original measurements) appears in Table A of the Appendix; a brief consideration of it will be useful at this point. At the beginning of Table A is an explanation of the meaning of the data in the body of the table; we will find these pages useful later.

The table itself is divided into two parts, one for each of two different school districts. The classes in the first district (starting on page AR1) were organized in the conventional manner—that is, there are approximately equal numbers of bright, average, and slower children in each classroom. We will call this the "randomly grouped" district. The children in the second district (beginning on page AA1) were grouped according to ability. Their achievement scores for the preceding year were used as a basis for dividing them into three groups: (1) above average, (2) average, and (3) below average children. Each class taught in this district had children from only one classification; this will be termed the "ability grouped" district. The students were all in the fifth grade, 447 of them in the ability grouped district, and 544 in the set of randomly grouped students from the other district. Figure 1–1 is an illustration of the situation for a few of the classrooms in the two districts; Figure 1–2 illustrates the actual arrangement diagramatically presenting an overview of the entire set of data provided in the text.

Now turn to page AR1 of Appendix Table A. This is the set of data for the 25 children from one classroom. Each row corresponds to one child; each column corresponds to a particular type of information. The first four columns contain sampling numbers, which will be explained later. The next column, headed PL, gives the pupil level for each child; 1 for above average, 2 for average, and 3 for below average. Note that the tests used for classifying the students were given each year to the children of *both* districts, and the students in the randomly grouped district were classified also, for purposes of comparison. The column headed "S" is for the sex of the student; the code used is 1 for boys, 2 for girls. The remaining columns are for achievement and social adjustment scores, and they are described in the first three pages of the table.

SIMPLE RANDOM SAMPLING

Throughout this book, our purpose is to draw conclusions about large groups by selecting a certain small number from each group and using this more limited set of observations to draw conclusions about the larger groups. We begin with

---

DEFINITION 1.1
A list of numbers is considered "random" if it consists of consecutive digits from 0 to 9 and has the following properties:

1. *There is no systematic way in which the digits are written: that is, a given digit cannot be predicted from preceding digits.*
2. *In the list, the digits occur with relatively equal frequencies.*

Appendix Table B is a list of this type; it will be used throughout the text. It is designed to give numbers of the type that could be obtained, were one to put 10 bingo-type disks, numbered 0 to 9 in a hat, and draw one out, record it, replace it, and repeat this process thousands of times. This set was generated on a computer, to save labor. The list can be used to generate larger numbers by considering the table as a set of consecutive numbers, each containing three digits, for example, so that beginning at the upper left-hand corner of the first page of Table B and going down, we get 041, 504, 947, . . . , instead of 0, 5, 9.

We now describe how to use this list to select observations at random from a large group. Let the larger group be Part I of Table A (the randomly grouped fifth grade students). Note that each student has been assigned an identification number from 1 to 544. To allow each ID number to appear, we must use consecutive sets of three digits each. To illustrate, we begin at the top left-hand corner of the first page of Table B and work down. On reaching the bottom, we return to the top of the page, using the next three digits, and continue in this fashion. Numbers greater than 544 *and numbers that have already been chosen* are ignored. From this procedure comes the list in Table 1–1. Note that in the table the number 246 (fourth from the end) was deliberately changed to illustrate the ignoring of ID numbers already selected; we are pretending that 246 actually occurred where 130 is.

TABLE 1-1
Selection of a Random Sample of Size 10 from 544 Students, without Replacement

NUMBER IN TABLE OF RANDOM NUMBERS	NUMBERS SELECTED	NUMBERS IGNORED	REASON FOR IGNORING
041	41		
504	504		
947		947	Greater than 544
602		602	Greater than 544
595		595	Greater than 544
855		855	Greater than 544
021	21		
246	246		
746		746	Greater than 544
987		987	Greater than 544
383	383		
372	372		
752		752	Greater than 544
146	146		
483	483		
354	354		
246		246	Already selected
709		709	Greater than 544
778		778	Greater than 544
447	447		

DEFINITION 1.2
The method of selecting students from a list in the manner described above is called "simple random sampling without replacement."

DEFINITION 1.3
If the foregoing method of selecting students is changed to allow numbers already selected to be selected again, the procedure is called "simple random sampling with replacement."

When the method outlined in Definition 1.3 is used, ID numbers already selected are not ignored but are included as many times in the list as they appear, as though they were separate individuals.

EXERCISES

1.1 Select a simple random sample without replacement of ten students from the ability grouped population and make a list of the STEP science scores for each of these students. Obtain the average STEP science score.

1.2 Do the same for the randomly grouped students.

1.3 Can you draw any conclusions from your two random samples about the relative merits of random grouping and ability grouping with respect to science achievement? Describe your reasoning.

The reasoning for the preceding type of activity needs to be discussed at this stage. When a researcher arrives at the point at which students must be selected for a given study, he needs to set down some ground rules for selection. If these rules include some decision-making on the part of the researcher himself about specific people to be included, the project can be jeopardized simply because it is so difficult to prevent personal bias from creeping into such judgments. The researcher may reason, "That subject is not typical; we had better not use him," when in fact he really means that the person under consideration may help to take the results in what, for him, is the "wrong" direction. Other researchers may deliberately lean over backward to keep from doing this and pick subjects who would be less likely to send the results "their" way. One safe way of selecting subjects, so that the selection is indifferent with respect to the results, is that described in this section. This type of procedure protects a research project from the personal biases of those who are carrying it out; this book is built around methods of selection of random samples and the types of analyses that can be carried out when these methods are followed.

SOME ARITHMETIC PRELIMINARIES

Before we go on to further discussions of statistics, we shall review the arithmetic rules we will need for this text.

Arithmetic Operations

Table 1–2 gives the standard arithmetic symbols and their meaning. Note that in an expression involving exponentiation, multiplication, and addition, one

TABLE 1–2

Standard Notation for Arithmetic Symbols

USUAL NOTATION	MEANING
$3 + 2$	The sum of 3 and 2
3×2	The product of 3 and 2
7^2	7×7—the "square" of 7
7^3	$7 \times 7 \times 7$—the "cube" of 7
$3 \times 2 + 7$	The product of 3 and 2 plus 7
	Note: Multiplication is carried out before addition, unless otherwise specified by use of parentheses
$3 \times (2 + 7)$	Add 2 and 7, then multiply by 3
	Note: The parentheses mean: Do whatever is indicated in the parentheses *first;* then perform the remaining operations
$3^2 \times 12$	Square 3, then multiply by 12
	Note: Exponentiation (squaring or raising to a higher power) is carried out *before* multiplication, unless otherwise indicated by use of parentheses
$(3 \times 12)^2$	Multiply 3 by 12, then square the result
$5^2 \times 4 + 3^2 + 7 \times 9$	Square first, multiply next, add last
$7 - 4$	Subtract 4 from 7
$7/4$	7 divided by 4
$\sqrt{13}$	The square root of 13

raises terms to a power first, then multiplies, and finally adds. Or, in the same sequence, one obtains the square root, divides, and lastly, subtracts. Examine Table 1–2 before doing the following exercises.

EXERCISE

1.4 Obtain numerical values for the following quantities:

    a. $6^3 + 3 \times 2^2 \times 4 + (7 \times 3)^2$ b. $(2 \times 3)^2 \times 5 + 6 \times (4 + 2)$

    c. $3 \times (7 + 2)^2 + (9 \times 2)^4$ d. $2 \times 3^2 \times 5 + 6 \times 4 + 2$

    e. $3 \times 7 + 2^2 + 9 \times 2^4$

Some Common Arithmetic Laws

When we are considering expressions involving parentheses, frequently we want to rewrite them in an alternative, equal form without parentheses. Consider

(1.1) $$7 \times (3 + 2)$$

We will find that this expression is exactly equal to

(1.2) $$7 \times 3 + 7 \times 2$$

where now we carry out the multiplication first, addition second. In general, we have

(1.3) $$a \times (b + c) = a \times b + a \times c$$

We summarize laws of this type in Table 1–3 on the next page. The student should become familiar with these laws, which will help him avoid the trivial arithmetic errors that many who are not mathematicians are prone to make.

EXERCISES

1.5 Obtain numerical values for the following expressions:

    a. $7 \times (2 + 6); \quad 7 \times 2 + 7 \times 6$

    b. $(2 + 6)^2; \quad 2^2 + 2 \times 2 \times 6 + 6^2$

    c. $(3 \times 4 \times 2)^2; \quad 3^2 \times 4^2 \times 2^2$

1.6 Obtain the equivalent form of the following expressions:

    a. $(1 + 3)^2$ b. $(2 + 6)^2 \times 3$ c. $(2 + 4)^2 + 9 \times (2 \times 3)^2$

Square Roots

DEFINITION 1.4

The "square root" of a number (call the original number c) is another number, which, when multiplied by itself, gives the original number. This is denoted by $\sqrt{c}$.

TABLE 1-3

Description of Some Arithmetic Laws

EXAMPLE	MEANING	GENERAL FORM
$7 \times (2 + 3) =$ $7 \times 2 + 7 \times 3$	LHS:* Add 2 and 3 first, then multiply by 7 RHS:* Multiply 7×2 and 7×3 first, then add	$a \times (b + c) =$ $a \times b + a \times c$
$(2 \times 4)^2 = 2^2 \times 4^2$	LHS: Multiply 2 and 4 first, then square result RHS: Square 2 and 4 first, then multiply	$(a \times b)^2 = a^2 \times b^2$
$(2 \times 3 \times 7)^2 = 2^2 \times 3^2 \times 7^2$	LHS: Take the product first; then square RHS: Square each term first, then multiply	$(a \times b \times c)^2 = a^2 \times b^2 \times c^2$
$(2 + 5)^2 =$ $2^2 + 2 \times 2 \times 5 + 5^2$	LHS: Add first, then square RHS: Square first term, *multiply the product of both terms by two*, square the second term; add all results	$(a + b)^2 =$ $a^2 + 2 \times a \times b + b^2$
$3 \times 7 = 7 \times 3$	LHS: Add 7 3 times RHS: Add 3 7 times	$a \times b = b \times a$
$3 + 7 = 7 + 3$	Order of writing terms in a sum does not affect the results	$a + b = b + a$
$(3 \times 2) \times 7 = 3 \times (2 \times 7)$	LHS: Multiply 3 by 2 then multiply result by 7 RHS: Multiply 2 by 7 then multiply by 3	$(a \times b) \times c = a \times (b \times c)$
$(3 + 2) + 7 = 3 + (2 + 7)$	LHS: Add 3 and 2 then add result to 7 RHS: Add 2 and 7, then add result to 3 *Note:* This rule is called the associative law; i.e., the order of combining numbers does not matter if the operations that are being performed are all the same	$(a + b) + c = a + (b + c)$

* LHS is left-hand side; RHS is right-hand side.

EXAMPLE   If $c = 9$, $\sqrt{c} = 3$; that is, $3^2 = 3 \times 3 = 9$.

EXAMPLE   The number 1.414 is approximately equal to the square root of 2, for, $(1.414)^2 = 1.999396 \cong 2$. (The symbol $\cong$ means approximately equal to.)

When no tables are available, we seek a simple method of obtaining the square root of a number. First note that if one divided a number by its square root, the answer again will be the square root. For example, if we divide 2 by 1.414 we get 1.4142, which is close to 1.414. Our procedure will be to guess what the square root is, and divide the number by our guess. If the guess is very accurate, the answer will be very close to the guess. If the guess is too low, the answer will be too high, and a guess that is too high will produce an answer that is too low. We average the guess and the answer to get a new guess, which will be more accurate. This procedure is repeated until the result of dividing the number by the guess is very close to the guess. This usually takes only three or four steps for the accuracy commonly needed, not more than a minute's time on a desk calculator.

As an example, let us find the square root of 10. Since 3 is the square root of 9, we try 3.2 as our first guess for the square root of 10. Dividing 3.2 into 10 gives 3.125; 3.2 is a little high. Averaging 3.2 and 3.125 gives 3.1625; we try this as our new guess and get 3.16205 as our new answer. Multiplying 3.162 by itself as a check gives 9.998244, which is close enough for many practical purposes.

EXERCISES

1.7 Obtain the square root of 5.671, accurate to the nearest hundredth.

1.8 Obtain the square root of 0.6359, accurate to three places to the right of the decimal.

1.9 Obtain the square root of 23.72, correct to the nearest hundredth.

Fractions

We begin our discussion of fractions by considering addition; we use pieces of pie to illustrate our points. In Figure 1–3, two pies are divided into six pieces each. In the first pie, the shaded area represents one-sixth of the pie; we denote this as

(1.4) $\qquad\qquad\qquad \frac{1}{6}$ or $\quad 1/6$

Next suppose we add two such sixths of pie together; this is

(1.5) $\qquad\qquad \frac{1}{6} + \frac{1}{6} = 2 \times \frac{1}{6} = \frac{2}{6}$ or $\quad 2/6$

Each of these forms is acceptable.

FIGURE 1–3
Addition of fractions.

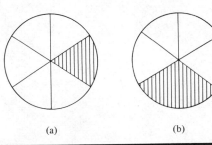

(a)   (b)

The same method of adding holds, no matter what fraction of the pie is used, *as long as all fractions being added are the same.* Hence

(1.6) $\frac{1}{7} + \frac{1}{7} + \frac{1}{7} = \frac{3}{7}$ or $1/7 + 1/7 + 1/7 = 3/7$

We shall sometimes want to add terms that represent different fractions, such as

(1.7) $\frac{2}{6} + \frac{3}{7} = 2/6 + 3/7 = 1/6 + 1/6 + 1/7 + 1/7 + 1/7$

Before we begin on this, however, we need to concern ourselves with multiplication of fractions.

Multiplication of Fractions

The simplest way to acquaint oneself with this type of problem is in an intuitive way; for example, we consider Figure 1–4(a), which represents $\frac{1}{2} \times \frac{1}{4}$.

We are used to thinking of $\frac{1}{2}$ as something divided in two. The lightly shaded area represents $\frac{1}{4}$; and cutting this in half clearly results in the cross-hatched area, which is $\frac{1}{8}$ of the pie. Hence

(1.8) $\dfrac{1}{4} \times \dfrac{1}{2} = \dfrac{1 \times 1}{4 \times 2}$ or $1/4 \times 1/2 = 1/(4 \times 2)$

In a similar way, we define the multiplication of any two fractions $1/a \times 1/b$ to be $1/(a \times b)$; the results obtained in this fashion can be seen to be consistent by noting that in Figure 1–4(b) where $\frac{1}{7}$ of a pie is subdivided into 6 parts, one of these subdivisions is $\frac{1}{42}$ of the pie since there are 6×7 such subdivisions in the entire pie. Hence $\frac{1}{7} \times \frac{1}{6} = \frac{1}{42}$, and so on. We next consider fractions of the type $\frac{1}{7} \times \frac{2}{6}$; this one is

(1.9) $\frac{1}{7} \times (2 \times \frac{1}{6})$

We note that $\frac{1}{7}$ of two pie sixths would have to be twice the size of $\frac{1}{7}$ of one pie

---

FIGURE 1–4
Graphic description of fraction products.

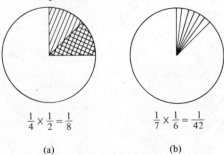

$\frac{1}{4} \times \frac{1}{2} = \frac{1}{8}$ $\frac{1}{7} \times \frac{1}{6} = \frac{1}{42}$

(a)   (b)

sixth. But this is the same as saying that

(1.10) $$\tfrac{1}{7} \times (2 \times \tfrac{1}{6}) = 2 \times \tfrac{1}{42} = \tfrac{2}{42}$$

In a similar way,

(1.11) $$\tfrac{3}{7} \times \tfrac{2}{6} = (3 \times \tfrac{1}{7}) \times (2 \times \tfrac{1}{6}) =$$
$$(3 \times 2) \times (\tfrac{1}{7} \times \tfrac{1}{6}) = 6 \times \tfrac{1}{42} = \tfrac{6}{42}$$

In general, we can obtain a rule for multiplying two fractions by using the following definition:

DEFINITION 1.5
In the fraction a/b, a is termed the "numerator" and b is the "denominator."

To multiply two fractions, use the product of the numerators for the new numerator; similarly, use the product of the denominators for the new denominator. In symbols,

(1.12) $$\frac{a}{b} \times \frac{c}{d} = \frac{a \times c}{b \times d} \qquad \text{or} \qquad (a/b) \times (c/d) = (a \times c)/(b \times d)$$

EXERCISE
1.10 Multiply the following sets of fractions, with answers correct to 2 places to the right of the decimal:

a. $\tfrac{3}{7} \times \tfrac{2}{6}$ b. $(4/9) \times (3.17/2.01)$ c. $\left(\dfrac{6.72}{0.91}\right) \times \left(\dfrac{0.67}{3.88}\right)$

Division of Fractions

We need to look at problems of the type $\tfrac{2}{3}$ divided by $\tfrac{5}{8}$. We begin with 6 divided by $\tfrac{1}{2}$. Now, 6 pies divided by 2 is equivalent to asking, "How many groups of two pies each can I obtain from six pies?" As illustrated in Figure 1–5, we obtain 3 such groups.

Replacing 2 by $\tfrac{1}{2}$ in this argument, we ask, "How many groups of one-half pie each can I obtain from six pies?" Figure 1–6 on the following page illustrates the point; there are 12 such groups.

FIGURE 1–5
Division of 6 by 2.

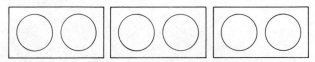

FIGURE 1–6
Division of 6 by $\frac{1}{2}$.

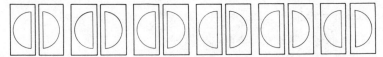

Apparently we come out with the correct answer if we multiply by 2, or, in other terms, if we invert the fraction (replace $\frac{1}{2}$ with $\frac{2}{1}$) and then multiply. In general, this is the case, and we have the following rule:

$$(1.13) \qquad \frac{a}{b} \Big/ \frac{c}{d} = \frac{a}{b} \times \frac{d}{c} = \frac{a \times d}{b \times c}$$

EXERCISE
1.11 In the following problems divide the first fraction by the second and express the answer in fractional form:

a. $\frac{3}{5}; \frac{11}{13}$ b. $\frac{6}{8}; \frac{15}{10}$ c. $\frac{x}{\sigma}; \frac{s}{\sigma}$

Addition of Fractions

Before adding fractions, we need to make one more observation. If we multiply $\frac{1}{3}$ by 3, we will surely get 1; three thirds of a pie make a whole pie, seven sevenths of a pie make a whole pie, and so on. Hence, in general,

$$(1.14) \qquad c \times \frac{1}{c} = \frac{c}{c} = c/c = 1$$

Further, if we multiply a fraction by 1, we do not change its value, for any number times one gives the same number again. We use the preceding facts to add

$$(1.15) \quad \frac{1}{3} + \frac{1}{2} = \frac{1}{3} \times 1 + \frac{1}{2} \times 1 = \frac{1}{3} \times \frac{2}{2} + \frac{1}{2} \times \frac{3}{3} = \frac{2}{6} + \frac{3}{6} = \frac{5}{6}$$

A picture of this operation is Figure 1–7. By dividing both the one-half pie and

FIGURE 1–7
Adding fractions of a pie.

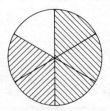

FIGURE 1-8
The improper fraction $\frac{7}{6}$.

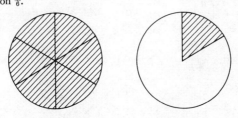

the one-third pie into pie-sixths, we were able to obtain both pieces of pie in terms of the same pie fraction; then the rules in Table 1–3 hold and the result is easy to get.

The next question is, "How did we know what numbers to multiply each fraction by?" The answer is that we must find some number that is a multiple of both denominators (as small as possible) and use this as a guide. For example, 6 is a multiple of both 2 and 3; we multiply 2 by 3 to get 6 and 3 by 2 to get 6. We could have used 12 as well, although the result would have been a little more cumbersome. That is,

$$(1.16) \qquad \tfrac{1}{2} + \tfrac{1}{3} = \tfrac{1}{2} \times \tfrac{6}{6} + \tfrac{1}{3} \times \tfrac{4}{4} = \tfrac{6}{12} + \tfrac{4}{12} = \tfrac{10}{12}$$

This answer is also correct since

$$(1.17) \qquad \frac{10}{12} = \frac{5 \times 2}{6 \times 2} = \frac{5}{6} \times \frac{2}{2} = \frac{5}{6} \times 1 = \frac{5}{6}$$

and the right-hand term is the previous answer. As a second example we have

$$(1.18) \quad \frac{2}{7} + \frac{6}{3} = \frac{2}{7} \times \frac{3}{3} + \frac{6}{3} \times \frac{7}{7} = \frac{2 \times 3}{7 \times 3} + \frac{6 \times 7}{7 \times 3} = \frac{6}{21} + \frac{42}{21} = \frac{48}{21}$$

Note that there is nothing wrong with having the numerator larger than the denominator; $\frac{7}{6}$, for instance, can be represented as in Figure 1–8. Such fractions are called *improper fractions*. For us however, they are perfectly proper and respectable.

EXERCISE
1.12   Evaluate the following fractions:
      a. $\frac{1}{3} + \frac{7}{8}$ b. $\frac{7}{9} + \frac{8}{3}$ c. $\frac{1}{16} + \frac{2}{10} + \frac{3}{5}$

Powers and Square Roots of Fractions

We note, first, that

$$(1.19) \qquad \left(\frac{3}{7}\right)^2 = \frac{3}{7} \times \frac{3}{7} = \frac{3 \times 3}{7 \times 7} = \frac{3^2}{7^2}$$

Hence to square a fraction, we simply divide the square of the numerator by the square of the denominator. In general, this gives

(1.20) $$\left(\frac{a}{b}\right)^2 = \frac{a^2}{b^2} \quad \text{or} \quad (a/b)^2 = a^2/b^2$$

Next we consider $\sqrt{\dfrac{a}{b}} = \sqrt{a/b}$. We submit that this is $\sqrt{a}/\sqrt{b}$, for if we square this, we get

(1.21) $$\frac{\sqrt{a}}{\sqrt{b}} \times \frac{\sqrt{a}}{\sqrt{b}} = \frac{\sqrt{a} \times \sqrt{a}}{\sqrt{b} \times \sqrt{b}} = \frac{a}{b}$$

which is the desired result.

EXERCISE

1.13   Obtain the square roots of the following quantities correct to 2 places to the right of the decimal.

    a. $3.621/9.732$ b. $\frac{9}{4} \times (3.067)$ c. $\frac{80}{27}$

This completes the preliminary review of arithmetic operations; other topics, such as the use of negative numbers, will be introduced later. We now turn to some elementary algebra.

ALGEBRAIC EXPRESSIONS

This section will consider in detail how we use letters to represent unknown numbers. Applications in statistics will be emphasized.

Subscripts and Summation Signs

Sometimes we may need a formula for calculating an average, when we do not know what numbers will have to be used. We then use letters to represent the unknown numbers. For example, if we wished a formula for the average of five numbers, we could write

(1.22) $$(a + b + c + d + e)/5$$
$$\text{or} \quad (1/5) \times (a + b + c + d + e)$$
$$\text{or} \quad \frac{a + b + c + d + e}{5}$$

However, suppose we have 100 numbers to average; there are not enough letters in the alphabet to go around, and even if there were, writing 100 letters would be a tedious process. So we look for another way of writing what we mean by the average.

Consider a random sample of five students, selected from the district whose students were randomly grouped, as in Table 1–4.

Next let x_{432} be the STEP score for student number 432, x_{096} be that for student 096, and so on. The number on the lower right-hand side of the x is called a *subscript*, and it simply identifies the student the score is for. It should be emphasized that the subscript has no relationship to the score itself; it simply distinguishes one score from another. Thus we have $x_{432} = 239$, $x_{096} = 269$, $x_{171} = 254$, and so on. The formula for the average can then be written as

$$(1.23) \qquad (x_{432} + x_{096} + x_{171} + x_{173} + x_{301})/5$$

We still have a problem, however; the next time a sample is selected, the ID numbers will change, and our notation does not provide for that yet. So renumber the ID's, letting x_1 be the score for the first student selected, x_2 be that for the second student, and so on, so that the numbers correspond to the "new" ID numbers listed in Table 1–4, Then the average can be written as

$$(1.24) \qquad (x_1 + x_2 + x_3 + x_4 + x_5)/5$$

Still, we are in trouble; suppose we now wish to write the average of 100 numbers; it will take about 10 lines simply to write the formula. We need a more compact way of doing this, which is made possible by the introduction of the symbol Σ. This is the capital Greek letter *sigma*, which is used to stand for "the sum of." Then we write

$$(1.25) \qquad x_1 + x_2 + x_3 + x_4 + x_5 = \sum_{i=1}^{5} x_i$$

where now the subscript i is used with the letter x to show that it does not remain constant; the terms just below and above the Σ are the lower and upper limits of the subscript, and it is assumed that the subscript takes on all integral (whole number) values between 1 and 5. Expression 1.25 is read as "the sum of x sub i, as i goes from 1 to 5".

Now we can write out the average of 100 numbers as

$$(1.26) \qquad \sum_{i=1}^{100} \frac{x_i}{100}$$

TABLE 1–4

Random Sample of Five Students

ID NO.	STEP SCIENCE SCORE	NEW ID NO.
432	239	1
096	269	2
171	254	3
173	279	4
301	261	5

in just as compact form as

(1.27)
$$\sum_{i=1}^{5} \frac{x_i}{5}$$

was written.

Next suppose we do not even know how many numbers will be used in the average. We need a formula that can be used to describe the average when the number of observations has not been determined. We let n be the number of observations, and we write

(1.28)
$$\frac{1}{n}\sum_{i=1}^{n} x_i = \left(\sum_{i=1}^{n} x_i\right)/n$$

for the average of n observations.

From here on, we are going to use a dot instead of $\times$ to represent multiplication, since the old symbol will get mixed up with the x_i's.

To illustrate the use of the summation, let $x_1 = 3$, $x_2 = 1$, and $x_3 = 5$. Then

(a)
$$\sum_{i=1}^{3} x_i = x_1 + x_2 + x_3 = 3 + 1 + 5 = 9$$

(b)
$$\sum_{i=1}^{3} (2x_i + 7 + x_i{}^2) = (2 \cdot 3 + 7 + 3^2)$$
$$+ (2 \cdot 1 + 7 + 1^2) + (2 \cdot 5 + 7 + 5^2)$$
$$= 22 + 10 + 42 = 74$$

(c)
$$\sum_{i=1}^{3} x_i{}^2 = 3^2 + 1^2 + 5^2 = 35$$

(d)
$$\left(\sum_{i=1}^{3} x_i\right)^2 = (3 + 1 + 5)^2 = 9^2 = 81$$

Note that the parentheses in the last expression indicate that addition is to be carried out *first*, rather than after the observations have been squared, as was done in expression c.

EXERCISE

1.14. Let

$$x_1 = 3, \quad x_2 = 1, \quad x_3 = 5$$
$$x_4 = 4, \quad x_5 = 6, \quad x_6 = 4 \ .$$

Calculate the following quantities:

a. $\displaystyle\sum_{i=1}^{3} x_i$ b. $x_1{}^2 + x_2{}^2 + x_3{}^2$ c. $2x_1 + 2x_2 + 2x_3$ d. $\displaystyle\frac{1}{5}\sum_{i=1}^{5} x_i$

e. $\displaystyle\left(\sum_{i=1}^{5} x_i\right)/5$ f. $\displaystyle\sum_{i=1}^{6} x_i{}^2$ g. $\displaystyle\left(\sum_{i=1}^{6} x_i\right)^2$

NEGATIVE NUMBERS

Often one is interested not in a number itself, but in that number's deviation from the average. For example, an IQ of 110 is meaningful because we know that 100 is average, and then 110 really means 10 points above the average. Hence 110 corresponds to $+10$, while 100 is neither above or below average but corresponds to 0.

What we really did in the preceding paragraph was to compute $x - 100$; that is, $110 - 100 = +10$, $90 - 100 = -10$, $100 - 100 = 0$, and so on. To learn how to operate with numbers of this type, consider Figure 1–9, which is a graphic picture of addition of the two numbers, 15 and 10. Letting that part of the scale to the right of zero represent the positive numbers, and that to the left of zero correspond to the negative numbers, we can add 15 and 10 together by drawing an arrow from zero to 15, to represent the first number, while the tail of the arrow corresponding to second number is placed at the tip of the first arrow. The tip of the second arrow reaches to 25. To subtract 10 from 15, we again place the tail of the 10 arrow touching the tip of the 15 arrow, but the 10 arrow now points in the opposite direction, as in Figure 1–10.

Next, if we subtract 15 from 10, we obtain a negative number as in Figure 1–11; we get $10 - 15 = -5$. Hence, if a is larger than c, then $c - a$ is a negative number.

FIGURE 1–9
Addition of 15 and 10.

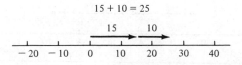

FIGURE 1–10
Subtraction of 10 from 15.

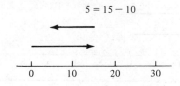

FIGURE 1–11
Subtraction of 15 from 10.

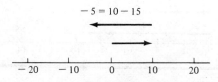

EXERCISE
1.15   Obtain numerical values for the following expressions:
       a.   7 − 11   b.   12 − 11   c.   2 − 9   d.   3 − 3

To multiply numbers, we note that 2 · 5 means 5 + 5, whereas 5 · 2 means 2 + 2 + 2 + 2 + 2. Graphs of both operations are seen in Figure 1–12.

Next we consider the meaning of multiplication of a positive number by a negative one: −2 · 5 means to subtract 5 twice, whereas −5 · 2 means to subtract 2 five times. These procedures are diagrammed in Figure 1–13. Now, we still want −5 · 2 to be equal to 2 · −5, so we interpret 2 · −5 to mean that we add −5 twice (see Figure 1–13). Similarly, 5 · −2 means to add −2 five times.

Now it certainly should be that 5 · 2 − 5 · 2 = 0, for adding 2 five times and then subtracting 2 five times should bring us back to the starting point as in Figure 1–14. Furthermore, it should be that −(5 · −2) + 5 · −2 = 0, since one is the negative of the other. Since 5 · −2 moves to the left, we must conclude that −(5 · −2) must go to the right; otherwise we would not return to zero. This implies that −(5 · −2) = +10 (see Figure 1–14). Now, −(5 · −2) = −1 · (5 · −2) = (−1 · 5) · −2 = −5 · −2. Hence −5 · −2 = +10, so that the product of two negative numbers is a positive number.

FIGURE 1–12
Multiplication of 2 and 5.

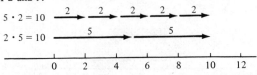

FIGURE 1–13
Multiplication of −2 and 5, and −5 and 2.

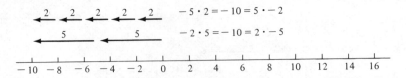

FIGURE 1–14
Diagramming addition, then subtraction.

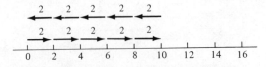

We summarize the preceding pages: If X and Y are positive, we have:

$$X \cdot Y \quad \text{is positive}$$
$$-X \cdot Y \quad \text{is negative}$$
$$X \cdot -Y \quad \text{is negative}$$
$$-X \cdot -Y \quad \text{is positive}$$

In particular, this means that a negative number squared is positive; $(-3)^2 = 9$, and so on.

EXERCISES

1.16   Obtain the following quantities:

    a. $-2 \cdot 6$ b. $-15 \cdot -17$ c. $7 \cdot -13$

    d. $-6 \cdot -1$ e. $0 \cdot -3$ f. $0 \cdot 7$

1.17   Take the set of ten observations drawn from the randomly grouped students in Exercise 1.1 and

    a. Subtract the mean of the ten observations from each of the observations; list the ten new values thus obtained.

    b. Add up the resulting ten new values.

    c. Square each of the ten new values and add up the squares.

1.18   Using the subscript notation write a formula for what you did in (b) above. Let the ten scores be $x_1, x_2, x_3, \ldots, x_{10}$.

1.19   Do the same for (c) above in subscript notation.

INEQUALITIES

Algebraic expressions need not involve an equality. Instead of having

(1.29) $X + Y = 4$

for instance, we may have

(1.30) $X + Y < 4$

This expression means that the sum of X and Y is *less than* 4. An easy way to remember the meaning is to note that the pointed end of the symbol $<$ is next to the quantity we wish to be smaller; the larger or open end is next to the larger quantity.

    Consistent with this notation, we also can reverse the symbol, and use the notation

(1.31) $X + Y > 4$

to mean that the sum of X and Y is *greater than* 4. We summarize this in Definition 1.6.

DEFINITION 1.6
The symbols < and > will be used between two quantities; these terms mean that the element next to the pointed end is less than that next to the open end. Similarly, ≤ and ≥ mean that the element next to the pointed end is less than or equal to the element next to the open end.

EXAMPLE Usually in statistics inequalities are used to assist in making decisions. For example, "Change to the new textbook if the average achievement score of 100 people sampled from the population is greater than 83," is translated to "Change to the new textbook if

$$(1.32) \qquad \bar{x} > 83$$

where $\bar{x}$ represents the average score." One calculates $\bar{x}$ and makes the decision on the basis of its numerical value. Figure 1–15 shows all values for $\bar{x}$ that are greater than 83.

FIGURE 1-15
A set of inequalities.

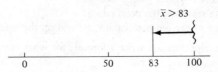

EXAMPLE One may subtract a constant from the quantity being investigated before obtaining the inequality. That is, instead of having $\bar{x} > 83$, we may have

$$(1.33) \qquad \bar{x} - 50 > 83 - 50 \qquad \text{or} \qquad \bar{x} - 50 > 33$$

Note that in this case, whenever $\bar{x} < 83$, $\bar{x} - 50 < 33$; and conversely. For if $\bar{x} = 84 > 83$ then $\bar{x} - 50 = 34 > 33$; and if $\bar{x} - 50 = 34 > 33$, then $\bar{x} = 84 > 83$. We can formulate this notation into

RULE 1 FOR INEQUALITIES
If $X < Y$, then adding or subtracting a constant from both sides of an expression leaves the inequality unchanged; that is, if $X < Y$, then

$$(1.34) \qquad X + C < Y + C \qquad \text{and} \qquad X - C < Y - C$$

EXERCISES
1.20 Write inequality statements for each of the following pairs of numbers:
  a. 15.78; 5.23   b. 3.90; −6.18
  c. −1.67; −3.21   d. 3.27; $(3.27)^2$
  e. .87; $(.87)^2$ f. −.23; $(.23)^2$
  g. −.23; −$(.23)^2$

1.21 Describe the set of values for X which satisfy the following inequalities, using a diagram for each inequality:

    a. $X + 50 < 10$ b. $X - 3 < 7$

    c. $X + 11 > -2$ d. $X - 11 > 8$

Frequently, more than one inequality will be used to describe a set of values. For example, X may be *between* 3 and 7. Figure 1–16 illustrates the situation, and it is described by the expression $3 < X < 7$. Actually this expression is equivalent to

(1.35) $\qquad\qquad\qquad 3 < X \qquad$ and $\qquad X < 7$

If we were to require that X *not* be in this area, we would write

(1.36) $\qquad\qquad\qquad X < 3 \qquad$ or $\qquad X > 7$

and the diagram would be as in Figure 1–17.

The conjunction *or* is used instead of *and* because both statements cannot hold simultaneously.

EXERCISE

1.22 Draw diagrams to describe the sets of values, X, which satisfy the following inequalities:

    a. $-3 < X < -1$ b. $-2 < X < 1$

    c. $0 < X < 83$ d. $0 < X - 5 < 15$

    e. $-1 < X - (-2) < 2$

Sometimes in the text we will wish to divide (or multiply) some unknown quantity by a constant. An example of this is the division of the sample mean

FIGURE 1–16
A double inequality.

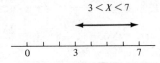

FIGURE 1–17
A double inequality.

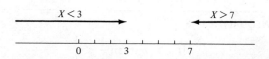

$\bar{x}$ by a certain quantity, which we will call C. We will then need inequalities in the following form: Let $C = 5$.

(1.37) $\qquad\qquad \bar{x} < 83 \qquad$ or $\qquad 5\bar{x} < 5 \cdot 83 = 415$

As before, we note that

(1.38) $\qquad\qquad$ if $\quad \bar{x} < 83$, then $5\bar{x} < 5 \cdot 83 = 415$

for

$\qquad\qquad$ if $\quad \bar{x} = 82 < 83$, then $5 \cdot 82 < 5 \cdot 83$

and

$\qquad\qquad$ if $\quad \bar{x} = 84 > 83$, then $5 \cdot 84 > 5 \cdot 83$

We must be cautious with this rule, however; if $C = 2$ and we multiply each side by -2, we get $\bar{x} < 83$, but

(1.39) $\qquad\qquad -2\bar{x} > -2 \cdot 83$

As an example, let $\bar{x} = 82$. Then

$$-2(82) = -164 > -2 \cdot 83 = -166$$

We summarize these results in

RULE 2 FOR INEQUALITIES
If $X < Y$, and if C is a positive constant, we have

(1.40) $\qquad\qquad CX < CY \qquad$ and $\qquad -CX > -CY$

EXERCISES
1.23 Write inequality statements for the new pairs of numbers in Exercise 1.20, if each number of the pair is multiplied by:
$\qquad$ a. 3 $\quad$ b. -2

1.24 Draw diagrams to describe the set of values X which satisfy the following inequalities:
$\qquad$ a. $-2X < 13$ $\quad$ b. $-X + 3 < 19$ $\quad$ c. $3X - 2 > 10$
$\qquad$ d. $-2(X + 1) < 17$ $\quad$ e. $\dfrac{(X - 5)}{7} < 2$ $\quad$ f. $\dfrac{X + 3}{2} > 4$
$\qquad$ g. $\dfrac{3(X - 5)}{2} < 6$ $\quad$ h. $\dfrac{2X}{5} + 7 > -1$ $\quad$ i. $\dfrac{2X + 7}{5} > -1$

We have one final rule for inequalities which will sometimes be used; this is

---

RULE 3 FOR INEQUALITIES

(1.41) $\qquad\qquad$ If $a > b$, then $\dfrac{1}{a} < \dfrac{1}{b}$

Since $1/a$ and $1/b$ are called the *reciprocals* of a and b, we can say that inequalities are reversed when taking reciprocals, just as they are when multiplying by a negative number.

It is easy to see why Rule 3 is true; "if $8 > 3$, then $\frac{1}{8} < \frac{1}{3}$," constitutes an example. We know from experience that the reciprocal of a larger number is smaller than that of a small number.

The same law holds for fractions; for example,

(1.42) $\frac{3}{8} < \frac{7}{16}$ so $\frac{8}{3} > \frac{16}{7}$

Here the result is less obvious; we express the rule in general form:

(1.43)   If $\dfrac{a}{b} < \dfrac{c}{d}$, then $\dfrac{b}{a} > \dfrac{d}{c}$

EXERCISE

1.25   Obtain inequalities for the following pairs of numbers and for their reciprocals:
   a.. $\frac{9}{10}$; $\frac{1}{2}$ b.   8.312; 8.310   c. $\frac{15}{14}$; $\frac{17}{16}$

LOGARITHMS
Rationale for the Use of Logs

Logarithms (*logs*) are a device for simplifying numerical calculations. Specifically, they are used to reduce multiplication and division to a process of adding and subtracting, as described in this section. We will find that to each number corresponds another number, called the *logarithm* of the first number, and that different numbers always have different logs.

We begin by reviewing some rules about exponents. We have

(1.44) $2^3 = 2 \cdot 2 \cdot 2$ and $5^4 = 5 \cdot 5 \cdot 5 \cdot 5$ and so on

In general,

(1.45) $a^n = a \cdot a \cdot \cdots \cdot a$

where there are n factors, each equal to a. Now, let $a = 10$, in order to simplify computations. We can construct Table 1–5 with 10^n in one column and the number corresponding to it in the other. Note that since we are always using the same number to raise to a power, we can omit it and simply use the power itself, as in the third column of Table 1–5 on page 24.

We next observe that if we wish to deal only with the powers of 10, we can multiply numbers by adding the exponents.

EXAMPLE

(1.46) $100 \cdot 1000 = 10^2 \cdot 10^3 = (10 \cdot 10) \cdot (10 \cdot 10 \cdot 10)$
              $= 10 \cdot 10 \cdot 10 \cdot 10 \cdot 10 = 10^{2+3} = 10^5$

TABLE 1-5

Powers of 10

POWERS OF 10	CORRESPONDING NUMBER	EXPONENT
10^1	10	1
10^2	100	2
10^3	1,000	3
10^4	10,000	4
10^5	100,000	5

That is, we begin with $100 \cdot 1000$ and instead of multiplying directly, we do the following:

1. Reduce each number to a power of 10 (i.e., $100 = 10^2$, $1000 = 10^3$).
2. Add the powers $(2 + 3 = 5)$.
3. Look up the number corresponding to the sum of the powers (that is, 100,000 corresponds to the power 5, which is the sum of 2 and 3).

In the last procedure, we have reduced multiplication to a process of addition and table checking.

EXERCISE
1.26 Extend Table 1–5 for exponents up to and including 11, and then multiply the following terms, using the table to look up the log and then adding.
   a. 10 and 10,000   b. 1000 and 10,000
   c. 10,000 and 1000   d. $(10,000)^2$
   e. 1000 and 100,000

Referring to Table 1.5, we have the following definition:

DEFINITION 1.7
If $Y = 10^n$, then n is termed "the logarithm of Y to the base 10."

EXAMPLE The number $1000 = 10^3$, so the logarithm of 1000 to the base 10 is 3.

EXERCISE
1.27 Using your extended table from the preceding problem, obtain the following:
   a. The logarithm (or log) of 10,000 to the base 10.
   b. The log of 1,000,000 to the base 10.

The term "to the base 10" is usually dropped, and we simply say the log of 1,000,000, the log of 10,000, and so on.

Multiplication Using Logs

Clearly, what we have done thus far is not adequate; no one deals only with a number of the form 10, 100, 1000, and so on, and we have to be able to work with arbitrary numbers if the method is to be practical. We note that thus far we only used integers for logs; it seems reasonable that if 1 is the logarithm of 10 and 2 is the logarithm of 100, then a number between 1 and 2 should in fact be the logarithm of a number between 10 and 100. This suggests that we consider powers of 10 which are not integers but fractions; we now investigate this possibility.

First note that we wish to preserve the property of adding logs to get the log of the product; in this light,

$$(1.47) \qquad X^{1/2} \cdot X^{1/2} = X^{1/2+1/2} = X$$

Hence $X^{1/2}$ must be interpreted as the square root of X. Also,

$$(1.48) \qquad X^{1/3} \cdot X^{1/3} \cdot X^{1/3} = X^{1/3+1/3+1/3} = X$$

so that $X^{1/3}$ must be the cube root of X, and in general, $X^{1/n}$ must be some number which, when multiplied by itself n times gives X, that is, $X^{1/n}$ is the nth root of X. This is sometimes denoted as $\sqrt[n]{X}$. Now,

$$(1.49) \qquad X^{3/2} = X^{1/2} \cdot X^{1/2} \cdot X^{1/2} = (X^{1/2})^3$$

That is, take the square root of X and raise the result to the power 3.

In general, we have

$$(1.50) \qquad X^{n/m} = X^{1/m} \cdot X^{1/m} \cdot \cdots \cdot X^{1/m}$$

That is, take the mth root of X and raise the result to the power n to get $X^{n/m}$.

You have learned how to obtain the logarithm of a number. Next you will be asked to find the number which corresponds to a given log.

EXERCISES

1.28 If a logarithm is $\frac{1}{2}$, it corresponds to the number $10^{1/2}$. Calculate $10^{1/2}$.

1.29 If a logarithm is $\frac{5}{2}$, it corresponds to $10^{5/2}$. Calculate $10^{5/2}$ by raising $10^{1/2}$ to the fifth power.

1.30 Multiply $10^{1/2}$ by $10^{5/2}$.

1.31 Let n be the sum of the logs of $10^{1/2}$ and $10^{5/2}$. What number corresponds to n? This number should be close to the answer for Exercise 1.30.

Table C in the Appendix is a short table of logarithms. The work of calculating the logarithms for all numbers from 1 to 10 is given there. As we shall shortly see, this table will be sufficient for calculating numbers in any other range. Just now, however, we wish to provide some practice at using logs.

Suppose we wish to multiply 2.78 and 3.15 (we are somewhat limited in our problems at the moment; we want the answer to be between 1 and 10). We use exactly the same procedure as we did when multiplying 100 and 10,000:

1. Reduce each number to a power of 10 (look up logs—the log of 2.78 is .4441 and the log of 3.15 is .4983. This means that $10^{.4441} = 2.78$ and $10^{.4983} = 3.15$).

2. Add the powers (add the logs):

$$(2.78) \cdot (3.15) = (10^{.4441}) \cdot (10^{.4983}) = 10^{.4441 + .4983} = 10^{.9424}.$$

3. Look up the number corresponding to the sum of the powers (look up the number corresponding to the sum of the logs). The logarithms are in the *body* of the table; we look up .9424—the number corresponding to it is 8.757. To get the last digit of 8.757, note that .9424 is between 9420 and 9425, and the log for 9420 is 8.75. The section to the right of the table tells us that for that line, an increase of .0004 in the log (.9420 to .9424) corresponds to changing 8.75 to 8.757.

If we calculate $(2.78) \cdot (3.15)$ using a desk calculator or directly, we get 8.7570; although the answer is exact in this case, this is not always so. Next, suppose we want to find $(2.78) \cdot (3.15) \cdot (1.01)$; here three numbers are involved. We simply add three logs instead of two, by looking up the log of 1.01, which is .0043. The log of the product of the three numbers is then $.9424 + .0043 = .4441 + .4983 + .0043 = .9467$, and the number corresponding to the sum is 8.844, which is close to 8.84451, the exact number.

EXERCISE

1.32 Using the log table (Appendix Table C), multiply the following sets of numbers, using logs, and verify your results on a desk calculator.

      a. 2.762, 1.09   b. 4.003, 1.632   c. 1.630, 2.065, 1.876

We now wish to extend our use of logs to numbers greater than 10. Consider the logarithm of 18.3; we can rewrite 18.3 as $10 \cdot (1.83)$. But using the table we find that this is $10 \cdot 10^{.2625} = 10^1 \cdot 10^{.2625}$, so that the logarithm of 18.3 is 1.2625. Next, suppose we have a large logarithm, say 2.1803; the range of logs is from 0 to 1, so we let $2.1803 = 2 + .1803$. What number does this logarithm correspond to? Now we remember our definition; if $Y = 10^n$, then n is the log of Y, so $10^{2.1803} = 10^{2 + .1803} = 10^2 \cdot 10^{.1803} = Y$. Now we look up the number whose log is .1803, multiply it by 10^2 to get 151.5 as the number whose log is 2.1803.

The basic rules in the foregoing procedure are:

1. To obtain the log of a large number, express it as a number between 1 and 10 times some power of 10, where the power is a whole number. Then look up the log of the number between 1 and 10, and add the whole number to it, to get the final logarithm.

2. To find a number corresponding to a logarithm which is out of the range of those given in the body of the table, divide the log into its integer and decimal parts. Look up the number corresponding to the decimal part of the log; then multiply this number by 10 raised to the integer.

3. To find the log of a number of more than four digits, drop all but the first four digits from the left, replacing them with zeros. Round the fourth digit up if the fifth digit is 5 or more. The result will be less accurate, but more exhaustive log tables will be needed to get greater accuracy. For instance, if we want the log of 632,381.5, we look up the log of 632,400.00.

EXERCISES

1.33 Find the logarithms of the following numbers:
   a. 63.2981   b. 1294.6
   c. 128.2   d. 1,623,419

1.34 Find the numbers whose logarithms are equal to the following values:
   a. 6.3121   b. 0.9903
   c. 4.0017   d. 1.6021

1.35 Multiply the following sets of numbers together, first using logs and then using a desk calculator:
   a. 33.17; 1.83   b. 695.2; 327.9; 28.1
   c. 68,632; 8,962   d. 92,862; 6,401

Division Using Logs

Note that up to this point we have not considered logarithms of numbers less than 1; before we can, we need to concern ourselves with division using logs. If we have two numbers, X and Y, and wish to obtain $X \div Y = X/Y$, we proceed as follows: $X = 10^n$, and $Y = 10^m$, and

$$(1.51) \qquad X/Y = 10^n/10^m$$

For a moment, let n and m be integers. Then if $n = 5$ and $m = 3$,

$$(1.52) \qquad 10^n/10^m = 10^5/10^3 = \frac{10 \cdot 10 \cdot 10 \cdot 10 \cdot 10}{10 \cdot 10 \cdot 10}$$

We cancel the 10's in the denominator with three of those in the numerator to get $10 \cdot 10 = 10^{5-3} = 10^2$. In fact, we subtracted the power of the lower number in the fraction from that of the upper number. This same rule holds in general, whether or not the logs are whole numbers, so that $10^n/10^m = 10^{n-m} = X/Y$. But n was the log of X, and m was the log of Y. Hence to get the log of a fraction, we subtract the log of the lower number from the log of the upper number so that $\log (X/Y) = \log X - \log Y$.

Now we can obtain the logarithm of a number between 0 and 1, for instance. The log of .5 equals the log of $5/10 = \log 5 - \log 10 = \log 5 - 1$. This will be a negative number. We get

(1.53) $$\log .5 = \log 5 - 1 = .6990 - 1$$

It is easier to leave the logarithm in such a form than to calculate it directly, as $.6990 - 1 = -.3010$.

As a convention, we require the negative part of the term to be a multiple of 10 to simplify computations, so we add 9 and subtract 9 to get

(1.54) $$.6990 - 1 = 9.6990 - 10$$

This is a standard form for a negative log, and we proceed to use it.

EXAMPLE Multiply 6.23 by .07.

$$\log 6.23 = 0.7945$$
$$\log .07 = \log (7/10^2) = \log 7 - \log 10^2$$
$$= \log 7 - 2$$
$$= 0.8451 - 2$$
$$= 8.8451 - 10$$

Now we add the logs as usual:

$$\log 6.23 = 0.7945$$
$$\log .07 = \underline{8.8451 - 10}$$
$$9.6396 - 10$$

The number whose log is $9.6396 - 10$ is the same as that number whose log is $0.6396 - 1$. This number is $10^{.6369-1} = 10^{.6396}/10^1 = 4.361/10 = .4361$.

In practice, we do not go through all these steps; we simply remember the following rules:

1. If the log is positive and the number to the left of the decimal is k, then there are $k + 1$ digits to the left of the decimal in the corresponding number.
2. If the log is negative, a 9 means the first nonzero digit of the answer goes just to the right of the decimal; 8 means put a zero to the right of the decimal before the first nonzero digit of the answer; 7 means put two zeros; and so on.

EXAMPLE Calculate .693/.009.

$$\log .693 = 9.8408 - 10$$
$$\log .009 = \underline{7.9543 - 10}$$
$$1.8865 - 10 - (-10)$$
$$= 1.8865$$

The number corresponding to the logarithm 1.8865 is 7.7

1.36 Calculate the following quantities, using first logarithms and then a desk calculator:
- a. $832.1/698.2$ b. $1632.2 \cdot 738.5$
- c. $.0631 \cdot .000078$ d. $16.3/19.8$

In conclusion, we return briefly to expression 1.47: There we noted that $X^{1/2}$ is the square root of X. This gives us a new way of obtaining square roots. Since

$$X^{1/2} \cdot X^{1/2} = X$$

we know that

$$\log X^{1/2} + \log X^{1/2} = \log X$$
$$2 \log X^{1/2} = \log X$$
$$\log X^{1/2} = \tfrac{1}{2} \log X$$

That is, if we wish the log of the square root of X, we simply divide the log of X by 2.

EXAMPLE Obtain $\sqrt{9.831}$.

$$\log 9.831 = 0.9926$$
$$\tfrac{1}{2} \log 9.831 = 0.4963$$

The corresponding number is 3.135.

EXAMPLE Obtain $\sqrt{.6731}$.

$$\log .6731 = 9.8281 - 10$$

Add and subtract 10, so that the negative number will be 10 again after division by 2:

$$\log .6731 = 19.8281 - 20$$
$$\tfrac{1}{2} \log .6731 = 9.9141 - 10$$

The corresponding number is 0.8206.

EXERCISE
1.37 Obtain the square roots of the numbers in Exercises 1.7, 1.8, 1.9, and compare the results with the earlier answers.

INTERPOLATION

One problem encountered in working with tables is that the number we need to look up usually is not exactly equal to any number in the table; it lies somewhere between two of them. We need to develop a procedure for using a table when this is the case. For instance, in discussing multiplication using logs, we used the log table (Appendix Table C), which provides an interpolation table in the right-hand margin. Suppose, now, we disregard it, and do the interpolating ourselves. We there found $2.78 \cdot 3.15$ gave us a logarithm of .9424, and we wished to know what number corresponds to it. Now, 9424 lies between 9420 and 9425, which are the numbers in the table; .9420 corresponds to 8.75, and .9425 to 8.76; hence .9424 must go with a number somewhere between these two values. Our rule is to add to 8.75 the same percentage of the distance between 8.75 and 8.76, that .9424 is between .9420 and .9425. Now, .9424 is 80 percent of that distance; that is, $(.9424 - .9420)/(.9425 - .9420) = .80$. So, we add to 8.75, .8 of the distance between 8.75 and 8.76, to get 8.758 as our interpolated value.

We seek a general formula for use in interpolating. Let x be the number we begin with, and y be the number that corresponds to it in some table; y is the number we are seeking. In the table, x lies between a_1 and a_2, and the table gives numbers c_1 and c_2, corresponding to them. Then y lies between c_1 and c_2 and we have (if $a_1 < a_2$ so that $c_1 < c_2$):

$$(1.55) \qquad y = c_1 + \frac{(x - a_1)}{(a_2 - a_1)} \cdot (c_2 - c_1)$$

Again using our example,

$$x = .9424$$

with

$$a_1 = .9420 \quad \text{and} \quad a_2 = .9425$$

so that

$$c_1 = 8.75 \quad \text{and} \quad c_2 = 8.76$$

$$(1.56) \qquad y = 8.75 + \frac{(.9424 - .9420)}{(.9425 - .9420)} (8.76 - 8.75)$$

$$= 8.75 + (.8)(.01) = 8.758$$

EXERCISE

1.38 Ignoring the interpolation table, find the logarithms of the following numbers; in each case, list the values for a_1, a_2, c_1, c_2, x, and y.

    a. 57.28   b. 103.2

    c. 691.7   d. 399.9

Note that in (b), your interpolated value differs more from that given in the right-hand margin of Table C than do the values for (a) (c), and (d). The more refined procedure used in the table is needed most in the range of logarithm values near unity.

SOLUTIONS TO EXERCISES

1.4
- a. 705
- b. 216
- c. 105,219
- d. 116
- e. 169

1.5
- a. 56; 56
- b. 64; 64
- c. 576; 576

1.6
- a. $1^2 + 2 \times 1 \times 3 + 3^2$
- b. $2^2 \times 3 + 2 \times 2 \times 6 \times 3 + 6^2 \times 3$
- c. $2^2 + 2 \times 2 \times 4 + 4^2 + 9 \times 2^2 \times 3^2$

1.7
2.38

1.8
.797

1.9
4.87

1.10
- a. $\frac{1}{7}$
- b. .70
- c. 1.28

1.11
- a. $\frac{39}{55}$
- b. $\frac{1}{2}$
- c. x/s

1.12
- a. $\frac{29}{24}$
- b. $\frac{31}{9}$
- c. $\frac{69}{80}$

1.13
- a. .61
- b. 2.63
- c. 1.72

1.14
- a. 9
- b. 35
- c. 18
- d. $\frac{19}{5}$
- e. $\frac{19}{5}$
- f. 103
- g. 529

1.15
- a. -4
- b. 1
- c. -7
- d. 0

1.16
- a. -12
- b. 255
- c. -91
- d. 6
- e. 0
- f. 0

1.18
$$\sum_{i=1}^{10} (x_i - \bar{x})$$

1.19
$$\sum_{i=1}^{10} (x_i - \bar{x})^2$$

1.20
- a. $15.78 > 5.23$
- b. $3.90 > -6.18$
- c. $-1.67 > -3.21$
- d. $3.27 < (3.27)^2$
- e. $.87 > (.87)^2$
- f. $-.23 < (.23)^2$
- g. $-.23 < -(.23)^2$

1.21

a. $x < -40$

b. $x < 10$
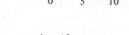

c. $x > -13$
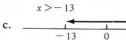

d. $x > 19$
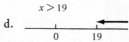

1.22

a.
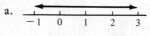

b.
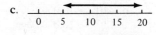

c.

d.
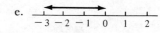

e.

1.23

a. $47.34 > 15.69$; $-31.56 < -10.46$ b. $11.70 > -18.54$; $-7.80 < 12.36$

c. $-5.01 > -9.63$; $3.34 < 6.42$ d. $9.81 < 32.0787$; $-6.54 > -21.3858$

e. $2.61 > 2.2707$; $-1.74 < -1.5138$ f. $-.69 < .1587$; $.46 > -.1058$

g. $-.69 < -.1587$; $.46 > .1058$

1.24

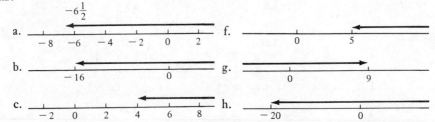

1.25

a. $\frac{9}{10} > \frac{1}{2}$; $\frac{10}{9} < 2$ b. $8.312 > 8.310$; $.12031 < .12034$

c. $\frac{15}{14} > \frac{17}{16}$; $\frac{14}{15} < \frac{16}{17}$

1.26

POWERS OF 10	CORRESPONDING NUMBER	EXPONENT
10^6	1,000,000	6
10^7	10,000,000	7
10^8	100,000,000	8
10^9	1,000,000,000	9
10^{10}	10,000,000,000	10
10^{11}	100,000,000,000	11

1.26 (continued)   **1.27**   **1.28**

a. $10^5 = 100,000$ a. 4 $A = \sqrt{10} = 3.1623$

b. $10^7 = 10,000,000$ b. 6

c. $10^7 = 10,000,000$

d. $10^8 = 100,000,000$

e. $10^8 = 100,000,000$

1.29   **1.30**   **1.31**

$\sqrt{10^5} = 316.23$ 1000.014 $n = \frac{1}{2} + \frac{5}{2} = 3$; 1000 cor-

responds to 10^3

1.32
a. 3.011
b. 6.533
c. 6.314

1.33
a. 1.8014
b. 3.1123
c. 2.1078
d. 6.2104

1.34
a. 2,052,000 (answer falls halfway between 1 and 2; halfway is rounded up to 2)
b. 9.779
c. 10,040
d. 40.0

1.35
a. 60.7; 60.7011
b. 6,406,000; 6,405,565.848
c. 615,000,000; 615,079,984
d. 594,400,000; 594,409,662

1.36
a. 1.192; 1.19177885992
b. 1,203,000; 1,205,379.70
c. .000004921; .0000049218
d. .8234; .823232

1.37
a. 2.382
b. .7974
c. 4.871

1.38
a. 1.7580
b. 2.0136
c. 2.8399
d. 2.6020

CHAPTER 2
POPULATIONS AND
THEIR PROPERTIES

The main concept of this chapter is best expressed in terms of a problem: we wish to know something about a large group of people, termed a *population;* we propose to make measurements on a small group called a *sample,* to help us learn something about the large group from which the sample was selected.

Generally our first step is to define carefully the large group we wish to learn about. The definition should be good enough to enable us to tell whether any given person is in the population or not. This is not always an easy task; for example, how does one go about defining the population of all Democrats or Republicans who reside in a given state if the state does not require party registration?

We begin our discussion by establishing a formal definition for a population:

DEFINITION 2.1
A group of people, animals, or other objects are termed the elements of a "population" if the elements have some characteristic in common that permits identification of an arbitrary element as being in, or not in, the group.

As examples, we may wish to obtain information about the people who live in Los Angeles; these comprise the Los Angeles *population.* We may also be interested in all fourth-grade children from certain school districts, or all nonwed mothers living in a given state. The population need not consist of people, but may be the collection of all schools in a state, or all private industries employing ten or more people, and so on. In Table A of the Appendix are data for two populations, (1) randomly grouped and (2) ability grouped fifth-grade children from certain school districts.

We have thus discussed a *random sample* (in Chapter 1) and now the *population* from which a random sample is drawn. The process of coming to conclusions about the population on the basis of measurements made on the sample is commonly called *statistical inference*, and we will learn how to do this in such a manner as to control the percentage of times we draw wrong conclusions.

In this chapter, we will discuss the kinds of meaningful questions that can be asked about a population. In the next chapter, we will consider methods of answering some of the questions.

POPULATION PARAMETERS

Population parameters are certain characteristics of a population that can be calculated when numerical measurements are possible for each member of that population. If a numerical measurement made on a population element is called an observation, we may want to ask the following questions:

1. Where are most of the observations?
2. How are they distributed?

Population parameters are intended to help answer such questions. The following material provides a graphical procedure to help us study these problems.

Frequency Distributions

It is sometimes profitable to use a graphic procedure for describing where the observations in a population are located. The result of one such procedure is called a *frequency histogram*. We construct a frequency histogram by drawing a graph in which the *x*-axis (the horizontal scale) is used for the scores—we will use the STEP science scores—and the *y*-axis (the vertical scale) is used to denote the number of people who fall into a given scoring range. We use the STEP science scores for the randomly grouped students to illustrate the result in Figure 2–1. Scores are missing for 10 students, so that a total of 534 students is available. We seldom have the entire population plotted and charted as this one is; in practice we must select, in some fashion, a few of the members of the population and attempt to draw conclusions about the entire population from the few that we have.

Next we wish to concern ourselves with the question, What percentage of students gets a score ≥ 270? We are interested in percentages because of the information we learn about the relative position of people with a given score. For example, in the histogram we have just constructed, there are 115 students with scores ≥ 270. If there are 130 students in the study, 270 is a poor score; if there are 1000 students, 270 is a good score. In the first case, $115/130 = .885$, so 88.5 percent of the students got a score better than 270. In the second case, $115/1000 = .115$, and 11.5 percent got a better score. Thus percentages give a better feel for what a histogram can tell us than do the original numbers.

FIGURE 2-1
Frequency histogram, STEP science scores, randomly grouped fifth-grade students.

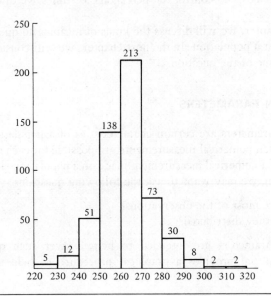

FIGURE 2-2
Relative frequency histogram, STEP science scores, randomly grouped fifth-grade students.

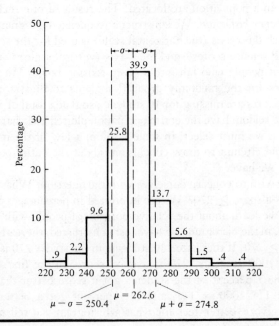

TABLE 2-1

Relative Frequency Distribution of STEP Science Scores
for Randomly Grouped Fifth-Grade Students

INTERVAL	PERCENTAGE IN INTERVAL
220–229	.9
230–239	2.2
240–249	9.6
250–259	25.8
260–269	39.9
270–279	13.7
280–289	5.6
290–299	1.5
300–309	.4
310–319	.4

In Figure 2–2 we reconstruct the histogram to show percentages instead of actual numbers; we call this a *relative frequency histogram*. From this histogram we can construct a table which gives, for each interval of score values in Figure 2–2, the percentage of people whose scores lie in the interval. For example, 12 scores lie in the interval from 230 to 239, so that the percentage of such scores is $(12/534) \cdot 100 = 2.2$. The results for all such intervals are given in Table 2–1.

This brings us to

DEFINITION 2.2

A set of pairs of table entries, the first of each pair giving the score value interval for a frequency histogram and the second giving the percentage of scores in the interval, is called a "relative frequency distribution."

EXERCISES

2.1 The following data present the frequency distribution for the ability grouped students. Compare it, using the same scale, with that for the randomly grouped students. Construct the frequency histogram.

210–219	0
220–229	10
230–239	25
240–249	63
250–259	136
260–269	135
270–279	49
280–289	18
290–299	2
300–309	3
310–319	3
	444

2.2 Construct a graph of the relative frequency distribution for the ability grouped students.

The Population Mean

Frequency histograms give us a better feel for what a population "looks like." We seek some numerical measures to describe the properties of a population, and begin with

---

DEFINITION 2.3
If a population consists of N members, then x_i is defined as measurement x, made on the ith member. Such a measurement is called an "observation."

Thus there may be 352 people in a population—and on the ith person we can obtain, for instance, (1) his IQ score x_i, (2) his GPA y_i, (3) his height z_i, and so on. The purpose of the foregoing definition is to distinguish between x_i, y_i, z_i and the members of the population on which these measurements are made; we can make many measurements on the same population member.

DEFINITION 2.4
The "population mean" for x is defined as

$$(2.1) \qquad \mu = \frac{1}{N} \sum_{i=1}^{N} x_i$$

where N is the number of items in the population and x_i is the observation for the ith term. (μ is a Greek letter, pronounced "mew.")

It is conventional in statistics to denote quantities calculated from populations with Greek symbols. The corresponding sample values use Roman symbols. If, for instance, we had a sample mean (the average of the values from a random sample), we would denote this with an italic Roman letter. Furthermore, we usually denote the size of the random sample with a lower case n. Hence the sample mean has a different formula and a different symbol to represent it. We use

$$(2.2) \qquad \bar{x} = \frac{1}{n} \sum_{i=1}^{n} x_i \qquad (\bar{x} \text{ is pronounced "x-bar")}$$

The population mean usually is close to what we think of as the middle of a population, and it is sometimes called a "measure of central tendency." In the case of the populations of Table A (Figure 2–1), the population means are 262.6 and 258.8 for the STEP science scores of the randomly grouped and ability grouped students, respectively.

2.3 Draw a vertical dotted line for the mean on the relative frequency histogram of the ability grouped students, using the STEP science scores of Table A.

The Population Variance

Consider a very simple and small population of three observations, say 7, 13, and 4, illustrated with triangles in Figure 2–3. Here the population mean is $\mu = 8$. Consider another population, 7, 8, 9 (illustrated with circles in Figure 2–3), whose mean is also 8. The average ($\mu = 8$) describes the "middle" of the population in both cases. There is a way in which the populations are dissimilar, however—consider the "spread" between the observations. Let us try a few different ways of measuring this spread.

1. Adding the differences from the mean of each of the observations does not help. For we get

$$(2.3) \qquad \begin{matrix} 7 - 8 = -1 & 7 - 8 = -1 \\ 13 - 8 = +5 & 8 - 8 = 0 \\ 4 - 8 = \underline{-4} & 9 - 8 = \underline{+1} \\ 0 & 0 \end{matrix}$$

2. Using the "size" of the number without its sign is somewhat better. Then, letting $|x|$ represent the size of x, we get

$$(2.4) \qquad \begin{matrix} |\,7 - 8| = 1 & |7 - 8| = 1 \\ |13 - 8| = 5 & |8 - 8| = 0 \\ |\,4 - 8| = \underline{4} & |9 - 8| = \underline{1} \\ 10 & 2 \end{matrix}$$

However, this measure has embarrassing properties for mathematicians: the mathematics involved in solving some kinds of problems is too unwieldy. So we try another measure, which has been found to be more tractable, mathematically speaking. We use the *square* of the differences from the mean:

$$\begin{matrix} (7 - 8)^2 = 1 & (7 - 8)^2 = 1 \\ (13 - 8)^2 = 25 & (8 - 8)^2 = 0 \\ (4 - 8)^2 = \underline{16} & (9 - 8)^2 = \underline{1} \\ 42 & 2 \end{matrix}$$

FIGURE 2–3
Two small populations, graphically illustrated.

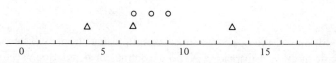

FIGURE 2–4
A larger population, graphically illustrated.

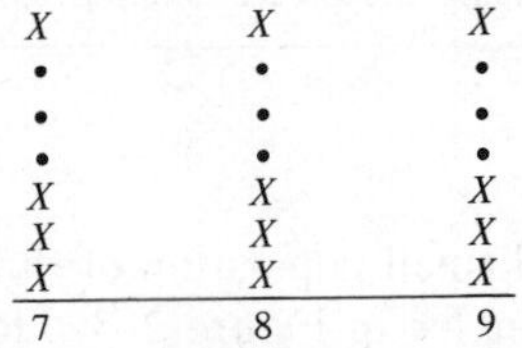

```
   X          X          X
   •          •          •
   •          •          •
   •          •          •
   X          X          X
   X          X          X
   X          X          X
 ─────────────────────────────
   7          8          9
```

We still have a problem. To illustrate it, consider a new population with 25 observations at the point 7, 25 at the point 8, and 25 at 9 (Figure 2–4). The measure of the spread will then be obtained as follows. We first calculate the population mean:

$$\mu = \frac{(25 \cdot 7) + (25 \cdot 8) + (25 \cdot 9)}{(3 \cdot 25)}$$

$$= \frac{25 \cdot (7 + 8 + 9)}{(3 \cdot 25)}$$

$$= \frac{25 \cdot (7 + 8 + 9)}{3 \cdot 25}$$

$$= \frac{24}{3} = 8$$

The spread will then be

$$(7 - 8)^2 + (7 - 8)^2 + \cdots + (7 - 8)^2$$
$$+ (8 - 8)^2 + (8 - 8)^2 + \cdots + (8 - 8)^2$$
$$+ (9 - 8)^2 + (9 - 8)^2 + \cdots + (9 - 8)^2$$
$$= 25(7 - 8)^2 + 25(8 - 8)^2 + 25(9 - 8)^2 = 50$$

The results of these calculations are summarized in Figure 2–5.

Surely the population with 75 observations each 7, 8, or 9 ought to have no more spread than the population with 3 observations at 7, 8, or 9, and it ought to have less than that with observations at 4, 7, and 13. The measure of spread should not depend on the number of observations in the population. To correct this problem, we can divide our measure by the number of observations in the population. This formula would be written as

$$(2.5) \qquad \sum_{i=1}^{N} \frac{(x_i - \mu)^2}{N}$$

We still may make one more modification. Calculations will be simplified if we divide by $N - 1$ instead of N. So we define our population variance to be in accordance with

FIGURE 2-5

Comparison of three populations, illustrating the concept of variance.

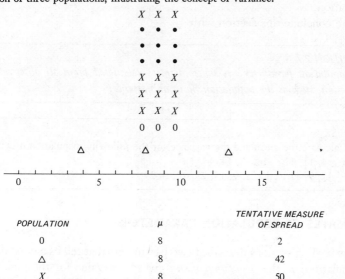

POPULATION	μ	TENTATIVE MEASURE OF SPREAD
0	8	2
△	8	42
X	8	50

DEFINITION 2.5

If x_i is the ith measurement made on a population of size N, so that we obtain the observations $x_1, x_2, \ldots, x_N$, then

$$\sigma^2 = \frac{1}{N-1} \sum_{i=1}^{N} (x_i - \mu)^2$$

is termed "the population variance" for the observations.

The left-hand symbol in Definition 2.5 is the lower case Greek letter sigma,* which we have squared. We next introduce

---

DEFINITION 2.6

If a set of x_i are defined as in Definition 2.5, then

$$\sigma = \sqrt{\frac{1}{N-1} \sum_{i=1}^{N} (x_i - \mu)^2}$$

which is called the "population standard deviation" for the observations.

---

* Many authors do not make this last modification, and define

$$\sigma^2 = \frac{1}{N} \sum_{i=1}^{N} (x_i - \mu)^2$$

The definition used here is adopted for pedagogical reasons; the statistical properties are simplified, and a single formula applies for all variances considered in the text.

For many frequency distributions encountered in practice, the two score values $\mu + \sigma$ and $\mu - \sigma$ include about two-thirds of all the scores in the population.

We conclude this section with

DEFINITION 2.7
A "population parameter" is some quantity calculated from all observations of a population, such as the population mean or variance.

EXERCISE
2.4   Calculate the mean and the variance for the following population measurements:
    a. 4, 11, 12   b. 7, 14, 15
    c. 7, 9, 11   d. 5, 9, 15, 23, 17, 6, 29

ESTIMATES OF POPULATION PARAMETERS

The preceding sections described two parameters that tell us a good deal about a population: μ, the *population mean*, gives us a value for the middle of the population; σ, the *population standard deviation*, when used with the mean, tells where most of the observations are. That is, we can construct an interval whose limits are σ units above and σ units below the mean; this interval includes about two-thirds of the observations in the population. We should think of μ as a *place*, and of σ as a *distance*. The dotted lines in Figure 2–2 illustrate these parameters.

The problem that we face in practice is that we never—or at most very rarely—know the values for μ and σ. To obtain these we would need to measure each element in the population, and most often we cannot afford to do this. Consequently, we must select a *random sample* from the population, and obtain what we hope are good estimates of μ and σ from the sample.

The Population of Sample Means

Typically, we will use the mean of a random sample, $\bar{x}$, to estimate the population mean, μ. Since we need to know how close $\bar{x}$ is likely to be to μ, we will next examine the properties of $\bar{x}$.

One thing we can do is examine the relative frequency histogram for $\bar{x}$. To do this we must obtain many random samples, obtaining an $\bar{x}$ for each sample and making a histogram for the $\bar{x}$'s (not for the observations from which the $\bar{x}$'s were computed). In Figure 2–6 we have done this for 1000 random samples, each with ten observations. The mean for each sample was computed using the STEP science scores from the population of randomly grouped children, giving 1000 sample means in all. Note that although there are only 534 original scores, we can obtain far more than this number of sample means—in fact, we could obtain millions of them, each different. However, 1000 will do for our purposes. This population is different from the original one in several ways. First, the

FIGURE 2-6
Means from 1000 samples, each sample with 10 observations. (Compare with original population, Figure 2–2.)

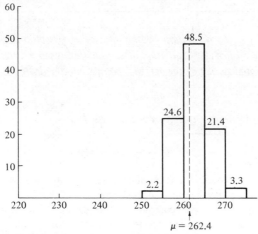

means are clustered closer together than are the original observations; this implies that the variance is smaller. In fact, it is 14.46, compared with 149.2 for the original population. However, the mean, 262.4, is essentially unchanged, being compared with the original mean of 262.6. We can formalize these results as follows:

DEFINITION 2.8
The population of sample means is defined relative to some original population from which the samples are drawn and is the collection of means of all samples which can be drawn from the original population.

DEFINITION 2.9
The population mean of the sample means is defined as the average of all sample means in the population of Definition 2.8. The symbol used for this is $\mu_{\bar{x}}$, pronounced "mew sub-x bar".

Our observation that the mean of the sample means did not change much from that of the original observations can now be formalized.

THEOREM 2.1
$\mu_{\bar{x}} = \mu$. *In words, this theorem says that the average for the population of sample means is the same as that for the original observations.*

Next, consider the variance for the 1000 sample means. It is smaller than that of the original population; in fact, we can obtain a formula that relates the two quantities. If we multiply the variance of the sample means by 10 (the sample size), we get 144.6, which is close to the value of the original variance. This property is general, and we have

---

THEOREM 2.2

Let x_1, x_2, . . . , x_n be a random sample of size n from some population with variance equal to σ^2. Then the population of sample means has a variance, $\sigma_{\bar{x}}^2$, which is approximately equal to that of the original population divided by n. In symbols,

$$(2.6) \qquad\qquad \sigma_{\bar{x}}^2 \cong \sigma^2/n$$

Note: the symbol $\cong$ means "is approximately equal to".

EXERCISES

†2.5   Select 10 random samples, each of size 4, from the population of randomly grouped children and obtain the mean of the STEP science scores *for each sample*. You should then have 10 numbers, one corresponding to each of your samples. Obtain the mean, the variance, and the standard deviation of these 10 numbers.

‡2.6   Compile the results of Exercise 2.5 with those of the other members of your class and construct a relative frequency histogram for all sample means obtained. Compute the mean, the variance, and the standard deviation of these numbers. (The number of means should be ten times the number of class members.)

The Population of Sample Variances

Analogous to the use of sample means to estimate the population mean, we will use the sample variance to estimate the population variance. We begin by defining it.

DEFINITION 2.10

Let x_1, x_2, . . . , x_n be a random sample of size n from some population. Then the sample variance, s^2, is defined as

$$(2.7) \qquad\qquad s^2 = \frac{1}{n-1} \sum_{i=1}^{n} (x_i - \bar{x})^2$$

To illustrate the definition, we compare (2.7) with the formula for σ^2. We have

$$(2.8) \qquad\qquad \sigma^2 = \frac{1}{N-1} \sum_{i=1}^{N} (x_i - \mu)^2$$

Put into words (2.8) means "subtract the population mean from each observation, square each result, add, and divide by one less than the number in the population." The verbal description for (2.7) can be obtained from the fore-

FIGURE 2-7
Variances from 1000 samples, each sample with 10 observations.

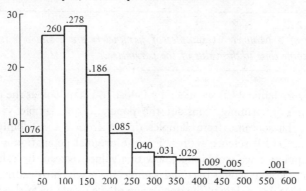

going sentence by replacing the word *population* wherever it appears with the word *sample*. Do exactly the same with the numbers; in each case the only difference is that you are using a sample instead of the population. Note that an italic Roman letter characterizes the sample variance, whereas a Greek letter is used for the population variance. Figure 2-7 gives the relative frequency histogram for the variances calculated from the 1000 random samples previously obtained. There is much less consistency between sample variances than there is between sample means. It is quite likely that we will encounter sample variances as small as 50 and as large as 300, even though the population variance is 149.2. However, the average of all the sample variances turns out to be very close to the population variance—147.4. We summarize this below:

DEFINITION 2.11
The population of sample variances is defined relative to some original population from which the samples are drawn and is the collection of variances of all samples that can be drawn from the original population.

THEOREM 2.3
The population of sample variances has a mean, μ_{s^2}, which is equal to the variance of the original population. In symbols,

$$(2.9) \qquad \mu_{s^2} = \sigma^2$$

Unbiased Estimates

In the light of the foregoing we can now provide a useful set of definitions:

DEFINITION 2.12
A "statistic" is a formula for calculating a single number from a set of observations.

Examples of statistics are $\bar{x}$ and s^2. There are many more of these, some of which will be encountered in this text.

DEFINITION 2.13
An estimate of a parameter (examples of parameters are μ and σ^2) is a statistic designed to come close to the value of the parameter.

One way to define what we mean by "close to" is to look at the population of statistics. For example, consider the population of sample variances in Figure 2–7. These came from samples drawn from the randomly grouped district, using STEP science scores. For the original population σ^2 is 149.2, although in practice we would not know this value. Instead, by calculating s^2 from the sample, we would have *one* sample from which to estimate σ^2. We would hope that the middle of the population of s^2's would be fairly close to σ^2. If we define "middle" as the average of all the estimates, then our hope is realized—that is, the average of all possible values for s^2, called μ_{s^2} (pronounced ("mew subess-squared"), will be equal to σ^2. In symbols, $\mu_{s^2} = \sigma^2$, as previously given in (2.7).

DEFINITION 2.14
A statistic is termed an "unbiased estimate" for a population parameter if the population mean for the statistic is equal to the parameter.

Thus, the first examples we have of unbiased estimates are $\bar{x}$ as an unbiased estimate of μ (since $\mu_{\bar{x}} = \mu$) and s^2 as an unbiased estimate of σ^2 (since $\mu_{s^2} = \sigma^2$).

CUMULATIVE FREQUENCY DISTRIBUTIONS

We next wish to introduce a frequency histogram derived from the type of histogram introduced previously. If we want to discuss the number of people (or percentage of people) whose STEP science scores are *less than* a certain level (as we often wish to do), we are then concerned with what are commonly called *percentile scores*. We frequently would like to know if a certain student did better than 95 percent of his colleagues—or better than only 5 percent of them, and so on. We can draw a graph to illustrate this by including in each column all people whose scores were *equal to or less than* the score for that column. In this situation, an individual's score will be included in more than one column; in fact, it will be included in every column with a score higher than his own. We illustrate in Figure 2–8, using the data of Figure 2–1.

It is now a simple matter to estimate the number of people who score less than a specified number. For example, there are 522 people whose STEP

FIGURE 2–8
Cumulative frequency histogram, STEP science scores, fifth-grade randomly grouped students.

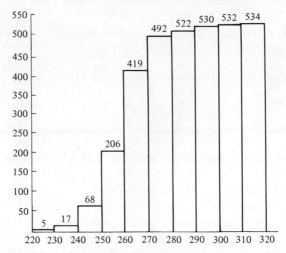

science score is less than 290. There are approximately

$$419 + (492 - 419) \cdot \left(\tfrac{4}{10}\right) = 447.4$$

people who score less than 274. This result is obtained by noting:

1. There are 419 students whose scores are less than 270.
2. In the interval from 270 to 279 inclusive, the people whose scores are less than 274 are those whose scores are one of the numbers 270, 271, 272, 273, or approximately four-tenths of the number with scores in the interval.

FIGURE 2–9
Relative cumulative frequency histogram for data of Figure 2–8.

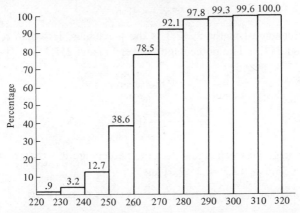

TABLE 2-2

List of STEP Science Score Values, With the Percentage
of Students With Scores Less Than Each Value

SCORE VALUE	PERCENTAGE VALUE	SCORE VALUE	PERCENTAGE VALUE
220	.0	280	92.1
230	.9	290	97.8
240	3.2	300	99.3
250	12.7	310	99.6
260	38.6	320	100.0
270	78.5		

The number of people with scores less than 274 is the sum of (1) and (2) above.

If we wish the percentages of people with scores less than a specified number, we can construct a "relative" cumulative frequency histogram, as in Figure 2-9 by dividing the height of each column by the total number of people in the population. This graph is often the most informative of all for practical purposes. For instance, we can now construct a table containing a list of score values and with each value a corresponding entry showing the percentage of students whose scores were less than that value, as in Table 2-2. Many statistical tables for frequency distributions commonly encountered in practice are of this type. Let us now illustrate this idea.

EXAMPLE

Using the relative cumulative frequency histogram of Figure 2-9, calculate the percentage of observations whose values are less than 257.3.

SOLUTION   We know 257.3 lies between 250 and 260. If we let $c_4 = 250$ and $c_5 = 260$ (see Figure 2-10), then

$$\% < c_4 = 12.8$$
$$\% < c_5 = 38.6$$

The total percentage less than 257.3 is the percentage less than c_4 plus that between c_4 and 257.3. The percentage between c_4 and 257.3 is

(2.10)
$$\frac{257.3 - c_4}{c_5 - c_4} \cdot (\% \text{ between } c_4 \text{ and } c_5)$$

$$\frac{257.3 - c_4}{c_5 - c_4} = .73$$

and the percentage between c_4 and c_5 is the percentage less than c_5 minus that less than $c_4 = 38.6 - 12.7 = 25.9$. Thus

$$\% \text{ between } c_4 \text{ and } 257.3 = (.73)(25.9) \cong 18.9\%$$

Finally, the percentage less than 257.3 is $12.7 + 18.9 = 31.6$ percent.

FIGURE 2–10
A procedure for calculation of the percentage less than a specified value.

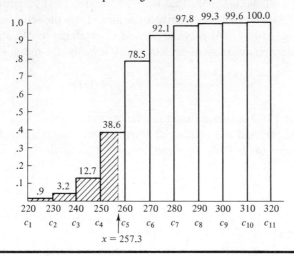

$$x = 257.3$$

EXERCISES

2.7   Using the data of Exercise 2.1, construct a cumulative frequency histogram.

2.8   Construct a relative cumulative frequency histogram from the results of the preceding exercise.

2.9   Using the data of Exercises 2.7 and 2.8, construct a statistical table, giving the percentage of scores less than each score value in the table. Use the same intervals as in Table 2–2, adding whatever additional intervals are appropriate if the range of scores is slightly different. Then obtain the percentage of scores less than 267.

2.10   For the population of STEP science scores of the randomly grouped fifth grade students $\mu = 262.6$ and $\sigma^2 = 149.2$, approximately. Calculate the two score values $\mu + \sigma$ and $\mu - \sigma$. Find the approximate percentage of scores less than $\mu + \sigma$. Also obtain the percentage less than $\mu - \sigma$. What percentage lies between these two values?

Cumulative Frequency Distributions Expressed in Terms of the Mean and Variance

Statisticians have made a practice, for reasons that will be apparent later, of expressing the score values for a population in terms of its mean and standard deviation. For example, in the case of the randomly grouped data (Figures 2–1, 2–2, 2–8, 2–9) for STEP science scores of fifth grade children, we would talk of some score value as being so many standard deviations above the mean (or below the mean, if that is appropriate). Consider the value 270 from the STEP science scores of the randomly grouped district; it is above the mean of 262.6. Further,

$$(2.11) \qquad \sigma = \sqrt{149.2} = 12.21 \qquad \text{and} \qquad \frac{(270 - 262.6)}{12.21} = .606$$

That is, 270 is .606 of a standard deviation above the mean. We know 250 is 12.6 points below the mean. We represent the fact that it is below the mean by attaching a minus sign to it. That is, -12.6 represents 12.6 points less than $\mu = 262.6$. Algebraically we subtract the mean from the score we are interested in, using $250 - 262.6$ as the method of obtaining it. We still have not determined how many standard deviations 250 is below the mean. But we have

$$(2.12) \qquad \frac{(250 - 262.6)}{12.21} = (-1.032)$$

so that 250 is 1.032 standard deviations below the mean.

In general, to find the number of standard deviations which a particular score x is above (or below) the mean, we use the formula

$$(2.13) \qquad \frac{x - \mu}{\sigma}$$

If the result is negative, the score is that many standard deviations below the mean; if it is positive, the score is above the mean.

DEFINITION 2.15
Score values expressed in the form $(x - \mu)/\sigma$ are termed "standard scores." The original scores are called "raw scores."

EXERCISE
2.11 Replace all the raw score values of Table 2–2 with standard scores, assuming that for these data $\mu = 262.6$ and $\sigma = 12.21$.

THE NORMAL FREQUENCY DISTRIBUTION

In this section we will examine a frequency distribution which is used so often that it deserves special attention. Although very few populations have exactly this distribution, a great many come close to having it. Moreover, one or two special properties of sample means depend on this distribution and make its study essential. The normal distribution has the property that score values expressed in standard form correspond to certain fixed percentages, as can be seen in Appendix D. For example, 84.13 percent of the observations are less than 1.0 standard deviations above the mean, and so on. If the relative cumulative distribution of Figure 2–9 were, in fact, normal, then the percentage of observations less than 270 should be the number corresponding to

$$\frac{(270 - 262.6)}{12.21} \cong .61$$

which is 72.91 percent.

2.12 Plot all the percentage values for Figure 2–9 that would be appropriate if the frequency distribution were normal.

If we wish to obtain the frequencies that would hold for the relative frequency distribution of Figure 2–2 if it were normal, we note that here we want the percentage of observations that lie between two raw score values, such as 260 and 270. This number is seen to be the percentage less than 270 minus the percentage less than 260. But in standard scores, this is the percentage less than

$$(2.14) \qquad \frac{270 - 262.6}{12.21} = .61$$

minus the percentage less than

$$(2.15) \qquad \frac{260 - 262.6}{12.21} = -.21$$

Now we look in Appendix Table D opposite the value .61 for the standard score and find that 72.91 percent of the observations will have a standard score of less than .61 if the population is normal. Similarly, 41.68 percent have a standard score less than $-.21$. Hence the percentage of observations *between* the standard scores is

$$(2.16) \qquad 72.91\% - 41.68\% = 31.23\%$$

as compared with 39.9 percent actually observed. We next consider two examples.

EXAMPLE
If the population mean is $\mu = 59$ and the population variance is 63, find the percentage of values less than 55.

SOLUTION   We need to express 55 as a standard score to use the tables. The standard score corresponding to x is $(x - \mu)/\sigma$. Here $x = 55$, $\mu = 59$, and $\sigma = \sqrt{63} \cong 7.94$, so that x corresponds to the standard score.

$$(2.17) \qquad \frac{x - \mu}{\sigma} = \frac{55 - 59}{7.94} = -.504 \cong -.50$$

Using Table D, we see that 31 percent of the observations in a normal distribution have a standard score less than $-.50$. This is the same as the percentage of scores less than 55, if $\mu = 59$ and $\sigma^2 = 63$. Hence the answer is 31 percent.

EXAMPLE
If the population mean is $\mu = 57$ and the population variance is 100, find the score such that 75 percent have lower scores.

SOLUTION This problem is the converse of the first example; that is, instead of having the score and being asked to find the percentage, we have the percentage and are required to find the score corresponding to it. Since Table D gives percentages corresponding to standard scores, if we look for the score that corresponds to .75, we know it will be equal to $(x - \mu)/\sigma$. That is (using Table D, and interpolating), we find that the standard score .6745 corresponds to .75 in the body of the table. But

$$(2.18) \qquad .6745 = \frac{(x - \mu)}{\sigma}$$

with $\mu = 57$ and $\sigma = 10$. Hence

$$(2.19) \qquad .6745 = \frac{(x - 57)}{10} \qquad \text{or} \qquad 63.745 = x$$

which is the answer. That is, 75 percent of the observations will have scores lower than 63.745 if $\mu = 57$ and $\sigma^2 = 100$.

EXERCISES
2.13   Plot the percentage values for Figure 2–2 that would be appropriate for each of the intervals if the distribution function were normal, with mean 262.6 and variance 149.2.

2.14   For the normal distribution,

IF THE POPULATION MEAN IS	AND THE POPULATION VARIANCE IS	FIND THE PERCENTAGE OF SCORES LESS THAN
a. 13	26	13
b. 1.5	2.1	−1.2
c. −.62	2.57	2.8
d. 631	432	568

2.15   For the same distribution,

IF THE POPULATION MEAN IS	AND THE POPULATION VARIANCE IS	FIND THE RAW SCORE VALUE (NOT STANDARD SCORE) SUCH THAT THE FOLLOWING PERCENTAGES HAVE LOWER SCORES
a. 16	9	68%
b. 381	183	25%
c. 13.5	10	33%
d. −6.2	3.8	29%

The Distribution of Sample Means

We now find we must be more careful with respect to what we assume about a frequency distribution. For many problems, the only basic assumption we make about the frequency distribution is that its variance is some finite value.

For other problems—and we will be careful at each stage to indicate *what* problems—the additional assumption that the frequency distribution is normal will be required. Just now, we wish to make this assumption and state

---

THEOREM 2.4

If the frequency distribution for a population is normal and if we consider the population of all means, $\bar{x}$, from samples of size n selected from the original population, then the following assertions hold:

    a. *The frequency distribution for the population of sample means is normal.*

    b. $\mu_{\bar{x}} = \mu$ (see Theorem 2.1).

    c. $\sigma_{\bar{x}}^2 = \sigma^2/n$.

The only thing really new in this theorem is the fact that if the original population has a normal frequency distribution, the population of sample means also has a normal frequency distribution. We note that even though the sample means have the same population mean, their variance (spread) is much smaller, so that the sample means are more accurate. In fact, for a sample mean of size 10, the variance is already one-tenth the size of the variance of the original population. Hence, it is advantageous to use sample means rather than single observations to answer questions about a population mean.

The question may well be asked, What if we don't know whether the frequency distribution for the population is or is not normal? One answer is to select a random sample of 400 or 500 members of the population and compare the observed frequency distribution with what you should have obtained if it were normal—as you did in Exercise 2.16. From experience, a distribution like that of Figure 2–2 is usually considered close enough to being normal for practical purposes. However, we often do not have the time or the money to obtain a sample large enough to check for normality of the frequency distribution. In such cases the next theorem is very useful.

THEOREM 2.5 (The Central Limit Theorem)

From a population with a finite number of elements ($N \geq 100$), consider the population of all means, $\bar{x}$, from samples of size n. Then the following assertions hold:

    a. *The frequency distribution for the population of samples means gets closer to a normal distribution as n gets larger, no matter what the form of the original distribution.*

    b. $\mu_{\bar{x}} = \mu$.

    c. $\sigma_{\bar{x}} \cong \sigma^2/n$.

From this theorem, we can justify our use of the tables for the normal distribution, no matter what the original frequency distribution is like; this is the one of the major justifications for the great emphasis on normal theory that is found in most textbooks on statistics.

FIGURE 2-11

Relative frequency histogram for 1000 sample means, each with 25 observations coming from the population of randomly grouped children, "Things in General" scores. (The original population is in Figure 2–16.)

Dashed vertical line corresponds to part (a) of Exercise 2.3.

Relative frequency histogram for times-chosen scores (TI/CH), District I (randomly grouped).

Note that the percentages above can be obtained from the answer to Exercise 2.12 by subtracting successive percentages—that is, the percentage between 240 and 250 equals the difference between 4.17 and 5.12 percent, and so on. Can you see why?

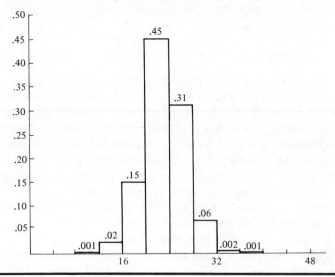

To illustrate this theorem, consider the relative frequency histogram for "Things in General" scores as given in Figure 2–16. This set of scores was obtained by considering both districts together as a single population. The distribution cannot be considered "bell shaped" and, therefore, is certainly not normal. One thousand random samples, each of size 25, were selected from this population, and a frequency histogram, using the same scale as that for Figure 2–16, was made. The result is Figure 2–11. Note that the relative frequency histogram for the sample means is more bell shaped than that of Figure 2–16. The mean of the scores in Figure 2–16 is $\mu = 27.05$ and the variance is $\sigma^2 = 282.1$. For Figure 2–11 the values are $\mu_{\bar{x}} = 27.04$ and $\sigma_{\bar{x}}^2 = 11.07$. These are close to what they are expected to be according to Theorem 2.5.

EXERCISES

‡ 2.16 Make a relative frequency histogram for the times chosen scores for the randomly grouped school district. You can do this by giving each person in the class a few classrooms to do and then combining your results in class the next day. Use 0–4, 5–9, 10–14, 15–19, etc. for class intervals.

‡ 2.17   Select 5 random samples of size 10 each and obtain the mean for each sample. Combine your results with those of the other class members and construct a frequency histogram for the means of samples of size 10. Compare this distribution with that of Exercise 2.16. What is your explanation of the results?

The Distribution of Sample Variances—Chi-Square

We have just completed a section in which two points were made:

1.   If the frequency distribution of a population is normal, then the frequency distribution for the sample means also is normal.

2.   If the population frequency distribution is *not* normal, the frequency distribution for the sample means still tends to become normal as the sample size increases; hence the assumption of normality for the original population is not too essential.

Next we come to a section in which the assumption of normality is definitely essential. We begin by assuming that a population consisting of the observations x_j where $j = 1, 2, \ldots, N$ has a normal relative frequency distribution. Let

(2.20)
$$s_i{}^2 = \frac{1}{n-1} \sum_{j=1}^{n} (x_j - \bar{x})^2$$

where $x_1, x_2, \ldots, x_j, \ldots, x_n$ is the ith random sample selected from the population. Then consider the population of statistics,

(2.21)
$$\frac{(n-1)s_i{}^2}{\sigma^2}$$

where $i = 1, 2, \ldots$. This is a set of elements, each of which is obtained by multiplying the sample variance by the sample size, less one, then dividing the result by the population variance.

We note that the term $(n-1)s^2/\sigma^2$ will always be positive, since every term in it is positive. Appendix Table E gives the relative cumulative frequency distribution for $(n-1)s^2/\sigma^2$ for different values of $n-1$ ($n-1 = f$ in the table), when the frequency distribution for the original population *is normal*. This distribution is commonly called a "chi-square" distribution.

EXERCISES

† 2.18   Select four random samples, each of size 5, from the randomly grouped students of Table A. Select each sample without replacement, but replace all items in a given sample before selecting a new sample, so that a specific observation may appear in more than one sample but not twice in the same sample. Calculate s^2 and $(n-1)s^2/\sigma^2$ for each sample, using the STEP science scores.

‡2.19   Collect all the values $(n - 1)s^2/\sigma^2$ for the entire class, and using the intervals

0–.999	5.000–5.999	10.000–10.999
1.000–1.999	6.000–6.999	11.000–11.999
2.000–2.999	7.000–7.999	12.000–12.999
3.000–3.999	8.000–8.999	13.000 and up
4.000–4.999	9.000–9.999	

calculate the relative frequency histogram for the STEP science scores. Remember that for this case $\sigma^2 = 149.2$.

We summarize the preceding results in

THEOREM 2.6
Let the relative frequency distribution for the observations $x_1, x_2, \ldots, x_n$ be normal and let them be a random sample. Define

$$(2.22) \qquad \sigma^2 = \frac{1}{N - 1} \sum_{i=1}^{N} (x_i - \mu)^2$$

$$s^2 = \frac{1}{n - 1} \sum_{i=1}^{n} (x_i - \bar{x})^2$$

Then the population of values $(n - 1)s_1^2/\sigma^2$, $(n - 1)s_2^2/\sigma^2$, $\ldots$, has the relative frequency distribution commonly denoted as "chi-square," with $n - 1$ degrees of freedom.

The terminology needs a little explanation. The term "chi-square" derives from the fact that if we have $n - 1$ score values, each sampled randomly from a normal population with zero mean and unit variance, and if we square and then add them, the population for this result will have a chi-square frequency distribution, with $n - 1$ degrees of freedom. Although this situation is not likely to be encountered in practice, and has mainly theoretical significance, the name itself is derived from this situation.

The term "degrees of freedom," referring to the divisor in

$$1/(n - 1) \sum_{i=1}^{n} (x_i - \bar{x})^2$$

has a geometric significance for theoretical statisticians but relatively little for the researcher. The term has come into common usage, however, and therefore is used in this book.

One final point needs to be made; in the preceding section we learned that as the number of observations in a sample mean increases, the relative frequency distribution for the sample means gets closer to the normal distribution, regardless of the frequency distribution of the original population. A similar conjecture for $(n - 1)s^2/\sigma^2$ does not hold; that is, we cannot assume that because we calculate s^2 from a larger sample, $(n-1)s^2/\sigma^2$ is approximately distributed as chi-square, regardless of the relative frequency distribution of the original observations; these must be normal for the theorem to hold.

We will need percentage points for the chi-squared distribution, just as we need them for the t-distribution. These are provided in Appendix Table E and for a specified percentage give the scores which have exactly that percentage to the left of the score. The appropriate degrees of freedom are found to the left of each row, while the percentages are at the head of each column.

DEFINITION 2.16
The value that has exactly $(1-\alpha)\cdot 100$ *percent of statistics coming from a chi-squared distribution with k degrees of freedom to the left of that value is defined as* $\chi^2_{(k)1-\alpha}$.

CONTINUOUS DISTRIBUTIONS

In this section, we wish to discuss an "idealization" of the relative frequency distribution introduced in this chapter. To illustrate the point, suppose we pool the students from both districts and use the SRA score "Things in General" (GEN). If from this group we select every tenth score, we obtain 99 scores, which we can compile into a relative frequency histogram, using the intervals 0–15, 16–31, 32–47, etc., finishing with ≥ 80. The result is the diagram of Figure 2–12.

Next, suppose that we divide the intervals in half, so that our limits are 0–7, 8–15, 16–23, etc.—finishing with ≥ 88. We now have 12 intervals instead of six; this frequency histogram is seen in Figure 2–13. Notice that it is a bit more "ragged" than Figure 2–12, and it may occur to us that we can fix this by using more observations, say every fourth score, which gives 247 observa-

---

FIGURE 2–12
Frequency distribution, 99 SRA scores, "Things in General," with grouping intervals 16 units wide.

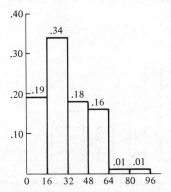

tions. This gives us the frequency histogram of Figure 2–14, which is less ragged than that of Figure 2–13. Now split the intervals again, to obtain Figure 2–15 with intervals 4 units wide. Once more, we need to use more observations; in Figure 2–16 we use every other score. Repeating the procedure again—that is, splitting the interval, and doubling the number of observations—we arrive at Figure 2–17. What we have been doing is permitting the grouping of observations in ever decreasing interval widths, in the belief that a truer picture of the relative frequencies will be obtained in this manner.

In the case used here for illustrative purposes, we can go no further, since the smallest possible interval width is a single unit. Suppose, however, that the scores are the time required to complete some task or the number of

FIGURE 2–13
Frequency distribution, 99 SRA scores, with grouping intervals 8 units wide.

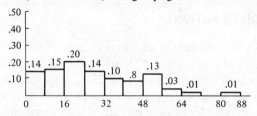

FIGURE 2–14
Frequency histogram, 247 SRA scores, with grouping intervals 8 units wide.

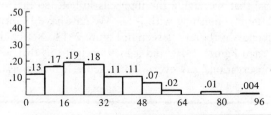

FIGURE 2–15
Frequency histogram, 247 SRA scores, with grouping intervals 4 units wide.

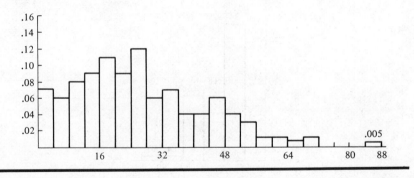

FIGURE 2–16
Frequency histogram, 495 SRA scores, with grouping intervals 4 units wide.

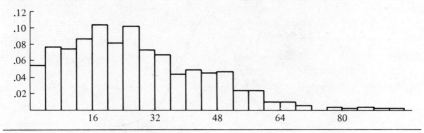

FIGURE 2–17
Frequency histogram, 991 SRA scores, with grouping intervals 2 units wide.

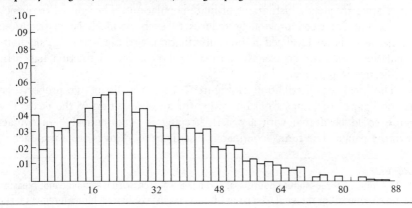

FIGURE 2–18
Idealized relative frequency histogram.

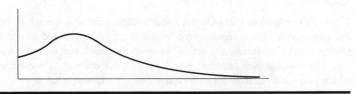

pounds of pressure that can be exerted by some student on a hand dynamometer in a physical education class. Now there is no lower limit to the number of times we can split the interval, as long as we can also add new observations.

The ultimate consequence of repeatedly splitting interval widths and doubling the number of observations is an idealized description of a population having an infinite number of observations. It is a "smooth" relative frequency histogram, which the mathematician refers to as a probability density function; an example is seen in Figure 2–18.

There is a certain advantage to such idealized distributions; calculation of probabilities frequently is easier if idealized distributions are used instead of

FIGURE 2–19
A normal probability density function.

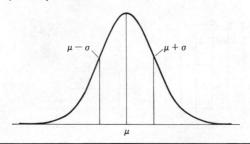

the relative frequency histograms of finite populations. The normal frequency distribution described previously reduces to such an idealized distribution; Figure 2–19 is an idealized normal distribution. Strictly speaking, no finite population can ever be exactly normal, although the distinction has little significance in practice.

The idealized distribution of Figure 2–18 has a distinctive property: it has no "gaps" or jumps from one value for an observation to the next. The figure could be drawn with a pencil, keeping it "continuously" in contact with the paper. The term "continuous distribution" derives from this fact.

EXERCISES

2.20   Obtain a three-minute hourglass, and using a watch with a second hand, measure the time required for the sand to run out of the glass. Make five such measurements, and calculate $\bar{x}$ and s^2. What, in your opinion, does the population consist of, in this case? Although you may not know its value, can you conceive of how μ ought to be calculated? How σ^2 ought to be calculated?

2.21   (Alternative to 2.21) Obtain five readings of the pressure which you can exert on a dynamometer; leave enough time between readings to avoid effects due to fatigue. Obtain $\bar{x}$ and s^2. Describe the set of observations which you consider to be the population. How would you calculate μ and σ^2? In your opinion, is the set of observations which you have calculated a true random sample? If not, what is it?

SOLUTIONS TO EXERCISES

2.1

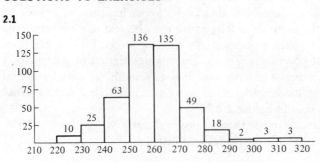

2.2

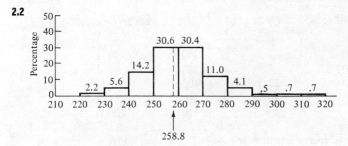

2.3 See answer to Exercise 2.2.

2.4

a. $9 = \mu$; $19 = \sigma^2$ b. $12 = \mu$; $19 = \sigma^2$

c. $9 = \mu$; $4 = \sigma^2$ d. $14.86 = \mu$; $80.14 = \sigma^2$

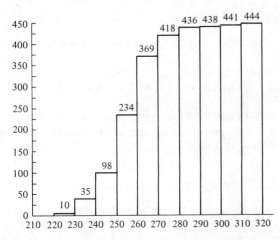

2.8

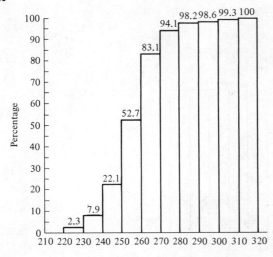

2.9

SCORE	PERCENTAGE LESS	SCORE	PERCENTAGE LESS
220	0.0	270	83.1
230	2.3	280	94.1
240	7.9	290	98.2
250	22.1	300	98.6
260	52.7	310	99.3
		320	100.0

Percentage of scores less than 267 = 52.7 + 21.3 = 74.0

2.10 (See Table 2–2 for source of numbers used below.)

$$\sigma = \sqrt{149.2} = 12.2 \qquad \mu + \sigma = 274.8; \qquad \mu - \sigma = 250.4$$

Percentage less than 274.8 = percentage less than 270 + percentage between 270 and 274.8 (see Fig. 2.9).

Percentage less than 270 = 78.5.

Percentage between 270 and 274.8 =

$$\frac{4.8}{10}(\% < 280 - \% < 270) = .48(92.1 - 78.5) = .48(13.6) = 6.53\%$$

Hence $\% < 274.8 = 78.5 + 6.5 = 85.0\%$

Similarly, the percentage less than 250.4 is $12.7 + (.04)(38.6 - 12.7) = 12.7 + 1.0 = 13.7$.

The percentage *between* 250.4 and 274.8 is the percentage less than 274.8 but *not* less than 250.4, which is the percentage less than 274.8 minus the percentage less than 250.4 = 85.0 − 13.7 = 71.3.

2.11

SCORE	STANDARD SCORE	SCORE	STANDARD SCORE
220	−3.49	270	+ .61
230	−2.67	280	+1.43
240	−1.85	290	+2.24
250	−1.03	300	+3.06
260	− .21	310	+3.88
		320	+4.70

2.12

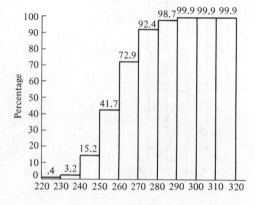

2.13

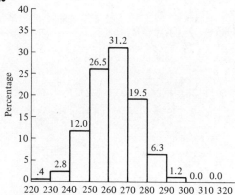

2.14

a. 50%   b. 3.14%

c. 93.4%   d. .12%

2.15

a. 17.41   b. 371.87

c. 12.11   d. −7.27

2.16

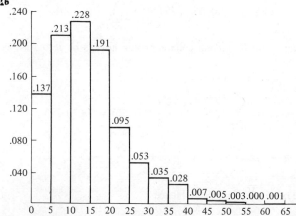

2.19 An example of a random sample selected from the randomly grouped students with s^2 and $(n-1)s^2/\sigma^2$ calculated for the STEP science scores follows.

1. Selection of the random sample.

There are 544 students, so use all random numbers < 544. Begin at bottom right-hand corner of page B5 and work up (position you start from is arbitrary).

STEP SCIENCE SCORE

044		$x_1 = 269$
698	ignore	
829	ignore	
325		$x_2 = 271$
620	ignore	
576	ignore	
059		$x_3 = 258$
331		$x_4 = 254$
394		$x_5 = 257$

2. Calculation of

$$(n - 1)s^2 = \sum_{i=1}^{n} (x_i - \bar{x})^2$$

where

$$\bar{x} = \frac{1}{n} \sum_{i=1}^{n} x_i = \frac{1}{5} (269 + 271 + 258 + 254 + 257)$$

$$= \frac{1309}{5} = 261.8$$

Layout for calculating:

		$x_i - \bar{x}$	$(x_i - \bar{x})^2$
	269	7.2	51.84
	271	9.2	84.64
	258	−3.8	14.44
	254	−7.8	60.84
	257	−4.8	23.04
Total	1309	0.0	$234.80 = \sum_{i=1}^{5} (x_i - \bar{x})^2$

The sum of the terms in the second column should always be zero (use as a check).

3. Calculation of s^2 and $(n - 1)s^2/\sigma^2$.

$$s^2 = \frac{1}{5 - 1} \sum_{i=1}^{5} (x_i - \bar{x})^2 = \frac{1}{4} (234.80) = 58.70$$

$$(n - 1)s^2 = 4s^2 = 4 \cdot \frac{1}{4} (234.80) = 234.80$$

In general, $(n - 1)s^2 = \sum_{i=1}^{n} (x_i - \bar{x})^2$. Hence

$$\frac{(n - 1)s^2}{\sigma^2} = \sum (x_i - \bar{x})^2$$

$$= \frac{234.80}{149.2}$$

$$\cong 1.574$$

Alternative procedure for step 2. There is another method for calculating $\sum_{i=1}^{n} (x. - \bar{x})^2$, which is sometimes easier to use. The procedure already given requires that we subtract $\bar{x}$ from each observation, then square the result, and finally sum the squared terms. To get the same result, we have the following formula:

$$\sum_{i=1}^{n} x_i^2 - \left(\sum_{i=1}^{n} x_i \right)^2 / n = \sum_{i=1}^{n} (x_i - \bar{x})^2$$

To explain this procedure, consider the following layout:

x_i	x_i^2
269	72,361
271	73,441
258	66,564
254	64,516
257	66,049

$$\sum_{i=1}^{n} x_i = 1309 \qquad 342,931 = \sum_{i=1}^{n} x_i^2$$

$\sum_{i=1}^{n} x_i^2 = 342,931$ is obtained by squaring each term first, then summing. (*Note:* $\bar{x}$ is not subtracted before squaring.)

$\left(\sum_{i=1}^{n} x_i\right)^2 / n = 1309^2/5 = 342,696.2$ is obtained by summing the terms first, then squaring, then dividing by n:

$$\sum_{i=1}^{n} x_i^2 - \left(\sum_{i=1}^{n} x_i\right)^2 / n = 342,931.0 - 342,696.2$$

$$= 234.8$$

Many desk calculators have features that make this new formula easier to use, and some computer programs also are more efficient if it is used.

REVIEW FOR CHAPTER 2

1. Population. Large collection (size $= N$) of people or other objects about which we wish to draw conclusions.

2. Random sample. Smaller number (size $= n$) drawn at random from the population, and used as a basis for conclusions about the population.

3. Frequency distribution.

4. Population mean. Average of the scores for all the members of the population:

$$\mu = \frac{1}{N} \sum_{i=1}^{N} x_i$$

5. Sample mean. Average of the scores for all the members of the sample:

$$\bar{x} = \frac{1}{n} \sum_{i=1}^{n} x_i$$

6. Population variance. Total of the squared differences from the population mean of all members in the population; the result divided by the population size, less one:

$$\sigma^2 = \frac{1}{N-1} \sum_{i=1}^{N} (x_i - \mu)^2$$

7. Sample variance. Total of the squared differences from the sample mean of all members in the sample; the result divided by the sample size, less one:

$$s^2 = \frac{1}{n-1} \sum_{i=1}^{n} (x_i - \bar{x})^2$$

8. Population standard deviation. The square root of the population variance:

$$\sigma = \sqrt{\frac{1}{N-1} \sum_{i=1}^{N} (x_i - \mu)^2}$$

Roughly $\frac{2}{3}$ of observations lie between $\mu - \sigma$ and $\mu + \sigma$ if the population is bell-shaped.

9. Sample standard deviation. The square root of the sample variance:

$$s = \sqrt{\frac{1}{n-1} \sum_{i=1}^{n} (x_i - \bar{x})^2}$$

10. Population of sample means. Many different samples can be drawn from the same population. If the sample mean is obtained from each of all the possible samples, the collection of all such means is the population of sample means.

11. Population of sample variances. The collection of variances, each obtained from a different member of the collection of all possible samples.

12. The population mean of the sample means. The average of all possible sample means.

13. The population variance of the sample means. The variance of all possible sample means.

14. The population mean of the sample variances. The average of all possible sample variances.

15. Relationships between 12, 13, and 14 above.

$\mu_{\bar{x}} = \mu$. That is, the mean of the sample means is the same as the mean of the population from which the samples were taken (the "original" mean).

$\sigma_{\bar{x}} \cong \sigma^2/n$. The variance of the sample means is equal to the "original" variance divided by the sample size.

$\mu_{s^2} = \sigma^2$. The average of all possible sample variances is equal to the variance of the population from which the samples were taken (the "original" variance).

16. Cumulative frequency distributions.

17. The normal frequency distribution. The cumulative frequency distribution for the normal case is in Appendix Table D.

18. The central limit theorem. The frequency distribution for sample means gets closer to the normal case as the sample size gets larger, *regardless of the nature of the original distribution.*

19. The distribution of the sample variances. Chi-square. Appendix Table E gives the cumulative percentages for the chi-square distribution.

CHAPTER 3
STATISTICAL INFERENCE
FOR ONE POPULATION

INTRODUCTION

Statistical treatment of data makes the basic assumption—at least in this book—that the researcher is attempting to answer questions about a population by analyzing a random sample selected from it. We wish first to examine the types of questions the researcher is likely to ask.

1. Questions about the "middle" of a population. We already know that the sample mean is an unbiased estimate of the population mean. However, a superintendent who has a sample mean of 280 for the STEP science scores of two classrooms used in a trial study wants to ask a further question: How close is my 280 to what I would obtain if I put the entire district on the teaching method used with these two classrooms? Perhaps we just happened to pick two bright classes.

A sociologist who has obtained scores on an innovativeness measure for a random sample of subjects from a rural county wishes to know how close the sample mean is to the population mean for the entire county.

2. Questions about the "spread," or variance, of a population. Here, the superintendent wants to know if there is a wide range of individual differences in his district—or the sociologist wishes to characterize communities on the basis of the range of innovativeness found therein. In each case, a good measure for this type of problem is the sample variance, which was found in Chapter 2 to be an unbiased estimate of the population variance. The researcher wishes to know how close the sample variance is to the population variance.

3. Questions about the limits that include a certain percentage of the population. The superintendent may wish to know what score includes the top

25 percent of his district. If he gets an estimate of this, how close is it to the correct value? The distinction between this and the preceding question is that in (2) we were interested only in the size of the spread, not in where most of the observations were. Here, we ask not only, How large is the spread? We also ask, Where are most of the scores located? As might be suspected, solutions to this problem involve both the mean and the variance.

The foregoing examples are designed to describe the kinds of questions we can ask about a population. The basic point is that a question about the middle, or average, of a population is not always a fruitful question. As an example, we may have a population with a mean income of $8000 per year. Either one of the following statements (but not both) may hold with respect to a population with a mean income of $8000.

1. Fifty-five percent of the population has an income of over $5000 per year.
2. Ninety percent of the population has an income of over $7000 per year.

Each of these statements tells us more about the population than does the fact that the mean income is $8000, since one of the meaningful aspects about income is that deviations below the mean are of more concern than deviations above it.

The point needs to be reiterated here that the questions being asked are with respect to the population of observations, not the random sample selected from it. We hope that the random sample will tell us what we want to know about the population, but we must constantly keep in mind that there is a possibility that the random sample will misinform us. The remainder of this chapter will deal with ways of determining how likely this possibility is and then of minimizing it. (There is no way of completely eliminating it.)

More Properties of Populations

We begin with some preliminary definitions.

DEFINITION 3.1
A "random variate" is the numerical value of an observation selected at random from a population.

As an example, the STEP science score of student No. 172 in the randomly grouped district is 264. If this student was selected randomly, then the number $x_{172} = 264$ is a random variate.

DEFINITION 3.2
A "random variable" is an observation selected randomly from some population whose value is not specified.

As an example, the STEP science score of the ith student (x_i) in the randomly grouped district is an example of a random variable if the student is to be selected randomly from the population.

DEFINITION 3.3
The statement "x comes from a population with mean equal to μ and variance equal to σ²" is symbolized as

(3.1) $$x \sim (\mu, \sigma^2)$$

Next consider a small population made up, for example, of ten "times-chosen" scores from the sociometric measure, randomly grouped district. These are

(3.2) $$8, 11, 37, 7, 41, 7, 37, 1, 17, 11$$

Note that for the moment we are considering these scores as a population. The mean times-chosen for this population is $17.7 = \mu$.

Now define a new population for which each observation is one of the original observations with the population mean subtracted from it. We get

(3.3) $8.0 - 17.7,$ $11.0 - 17.7,$ $37.0 - 17.7,$ $7.0 - 17.7,$ $41.0 - 17.7,$ $7.0 - 17.7,$ $37.0 - 17.7,$ $1.0 - 17.7,$ $17.0 - 17.7,$ $11.0 - 17.7$

which results in

(3.4) $-9.7, -6.7, 19.3, -10.7, 23.3, -10.7, 19.3, -16.7, -0.7, -6.7$

for our new population. By calculation, we find that the new population mean is exactly zero. This property generally holds true; the results will be part of Theorem 3.1.

Subtracting the mean from each observation is equivalent to sliding the entire population to the left, so that its center is at the point zero, as in Figure 3–1.

One point which needs to be made is that the spread, or the position of the observations relative to each other, remains the same. This can be verified by

---

FIGURE 3–1
The result of subtracting the mean from each observation in a population; X = old population, 0 = new population.

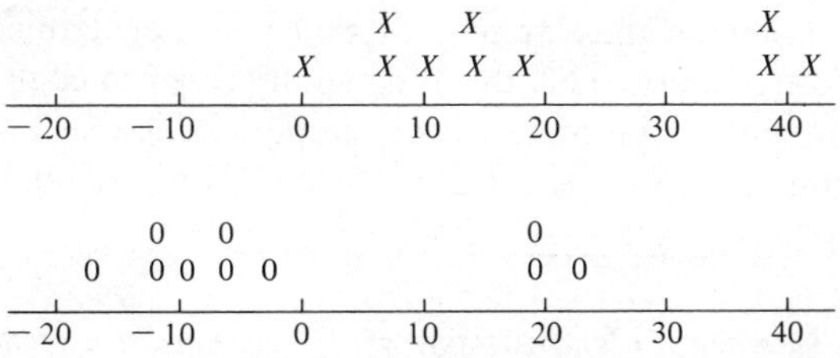

calculating σ^2 for the old and new populations, as summarized in Theorem 3.1.

THEOREM 3.1

If the population mean is subtracted from each observation in a population, a new population is generated which has a population mean of zero and the same variance. In symbols, if $x \sim (\mu, \sigma^2)$, then $x - \mu \sim (0, \sigma^2)$.

EXERCISES

3.1 Using the population scores 16, 13, 28, 9, 5, 31, 12 ("Me and Home," SRA scores from randomly grouped students) calculate μ and σ^2. Make a graph of the population like that of Figure 3–1.

3.2 Subtract μ from each observation. Calculate the new population mean and variance. Make a graph of this population.

We now return to our modified population (3.4) and divide each observation by $\sigma = \sqrt{220.01} \cong 14.833$. This gives still another population as follows:

$$(3.5) \qquad \begin{aligned} &-.654, \; -.452, \; 1.301, \; -.721, \; 1.571, \\ &-.721, \; 1.301, \; -1.126, \; -.047, \; -.452 \end{aligned}$$

The mean of these observations is still zero; Figure 3–2 is their graph compared with the population from which they were obtained.

FIGURE 3–2

The result of dividing each observation by the standard deviation when the population mean is zero. $\Delta = \mu$ subtracted and each observation divided by σ; $0 = \mu$ subtracted from each observation.

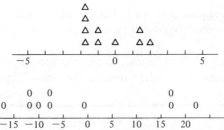

Now if we calculate the variance of this new population, we observe that it is very close to unity. That this is generally true can be proved; we will state the theorem without proof, however, simply noting that Figure 3–2 is an illustration of how division by σ modifies the spread of the observations.

THEOREM 3.2

Let a population have mean μ and variance σ^2. If we subtract μ from each observation and then divide the result by σ, a new population is generated whose mean is zero *and whose variance is 1. In symbols,*

(3.6) $$\text{if } x \sim (\mu, \sigma^2), \quad \text{then} \quad \frac{(x - \mu)}{\sigma} \sim (0, 1)$$

EXERCISES

3.3 Using the population of Exercise 3.1, subtract the mean from each observation (you have already done this in Exercise 3.2) then divide by σ. Make a graph of the new population and compare it with that for Exercise 3.2. (These should be on the same scale.)

3.4 Calculate the variance of the new population generated in Exercise 3.3.

We next consider some additional results:

DEFINITION 3.4

The statement "x comes from a normal population with mean equal to μ and variance equal to σ^2" is symbolized as

(3.7) $$x \sim N(\mu, \sigma^2)$$

THEOREM 3.3

If x comes from a normal population with mean μ and variance σ^2, then the new population generated by $(x - \mu)/\sigma$ is also normal and has zero mean and unit variance. In symbols,

(3.8) $$\text{if } x \sim N(\mu, \sigma^2), \quad \text{then} \quad \frac{(x - \mu)}{\sigma} \sim N(0, 1)$$

We now wish to review the use of Appendix Table D. Recall that this table has two types of entries: those in the first column are standard scores and represent the number of standard deviations above or below the mean, and those in the body of the table give the percentage (divided by 100) of observations less than the corresponding standard score.

All we have done in the preceding material is to convert to standard scores; that is, if x is the original score, $(x - \mu)/\sigma$ is the corresponding standard score. Thus, we have a procedure for reducing all scores to the same scaling system, regardless of their size or range. We are saying that no matter what the original scores are like, *any* standard score has zero mean and unit variance. A method for reducing most types of scores to the same units of measure has considerable merit, as we will soon see.

Probability

The concepts of probability permeate virtually all statistical work. They need to be formalized at this point. To illustrate, we begin with a very simple example. Suppose we select one observation at random from the population of randomly grouped fifth-grade children whose cumulative relative frequency histogram is Figure 2–9. We then wish to consider the percentage of times an observation will be less than 290 if the action of selecting an observation at random and then replacing it is repeated an indefinite number of times. From the histogram (Figure 2–9) we see that this value is 97.8 percent. Further, the percentage of times the observation will be less than 240 is 3.1. Hence the percentage of times it will lie between 240 and 290 is 97.8 − 3.1 = 94.7. We subtract the 3.1 percent because this represents observations that are not between the two numbers.

Next we wish to introduce notation that has become a standard part of statistical language.

DEFINITION 3.5
The "probability" that an observation from a population will lie in any interval is defined as 1/100 of the percentage of times it will lie in that interval if it has been selected randomly from the population.

Additional notation will help in our discussion of the preceding definition. Let E be a symbol for an event. For example, E may be the event, "A person selected randomly has a STEP science score less than 290," or the event, "A person selected randomly has blond hair." In the first case, the event is associated with a numerical value, and we can symbolize it as $E = (x < 290)$. In the second case, we may choose to leave E as it is without any additional symbolism.

DEFINITION 3.6
If E is an arbitrary event, we denote the probability of the event E as $P(E)$.

Using this definition, we can symbolize the examples from Figure 2–9 as

$$(3.9) \qquad P(x < 290) = .978$$
$$P(240 \leq x \leq 290) = P(x \leq 290) - P(x < 240) = .947$$

We reiterate, probabilities are most easily thought of by the beginning student as percentages and represent the percentage of times that an event occurs when a specified experiment is repeated an indefinite (actually infinite) number of times. The experiment is usually some kind of sampling procedure and almost always is random in nature. We shall see that random samples are not restricted to simple random samples; they may be what are called "stratified" samples. or "cluster" samples, or a combination of these.

A Review of the Normal Distribution

Before we discuss confidence intervals, it will be helpful to review some of the material on the normal distribution.

Suppose a population is approximately normal with mean $\mu = 262.6$ and standard deviation $\sigma = 12.2$. The population of Figure 2–2 has this set of properties. In Exercise 2.13 you were asked to calculate the probabilities that would be appropriate for each interval in Figure 2–2 if the distribution were normal. You may wish to review that exercise at this point.

Next, suppose we want to know the "raw" scores that would include 95 percent of this population if it were normal. Before, we were given raw scores and asked to calculate the percentages; now, we are given percentages and asked to calculate the appropriate raw scores. We can draw a simple diagram that describes both procedures; in either case, we use the standard scores to make the transition:

$$x = \text{raw score}$$
$$\updownarrow \qquad \text{from the formula } Z = \frac{(x - \mu)}{\sigma}$$
$$Z = \text{standard score}$$
$$\updownarrow \qquad \text{from Appendix Table D}$$
$$\text{percentages}$$
$$\text{or probabilities}$$

In order to solve this type of problem, we must know μ and σ, or estimates of them. At this stage we will assume that we know μ and σ; later we will work with the estimates. If we are given the raw scores, we convert to standard scores and look up the percentages in Appendix Table D. If we are given a percentage, we find the values for the standard scores that correspond to the percentage, again using Table D. Then we convert the standard scores to raw scores.

In the case before us, we are given the percentage (95) and asked for the raw scores within which this percentage of observation lies. We then have the situation of Figure 3–3. The value that exceeds 97.5 percent of the standard scores cuts off 2.5 percent of the scores in the right hand tail of the distribution. We call this value $Z_{.975}$. We also need to cut off 2.5 percent from the left-hand tail; the value to use is the *negative* of $Z_{.975}$, since the normal distribution is symmetric (or balanced) about the mean. Cutting off 2.5 percent from each of the two tails leaves 95 percent in the middle. Hence, if we can find $Z_{.975}$ from Table D we have the *standard scores*, which include 95 percent. Looking in Table D, we find that the standard score that exceeds 97.5 percent is $Z_{.975} = 1.96$. (You have to hunt through the body of the table—not the margins—to find this.) The standard scores are then 1.96 and -1.96; these include 95 percent of the standard scores. We have now moved from the bottom to the middle stage of our diagram. To change to raw scores we use the formula

$$(3.10) \qquad\qquad Z = \frac{(x - \mu)}{\sigma}$$

where $Z = \pm 1.96$, $\mu = 262.6$, and $\sigma = 12.2$ are given. Substituting these values in the above formula, we get

$$Z = 1.96 = \frac{x - 262.6}{12.2}$$

$$1.96(12.2) = x - 262.6$$
$$1.96(12.2) + 262.6 = x$$

for the upper limit, and in the same way,

$$-1.96(12.2) + 262.6 = x$$

for the lower limit. These are the limits shown in Figure 3–3. Formalizing all of this, we get

(3.11) $\quad .95 = P(-1.96 < Z < 1.96)$

$$.95 = P\left(-1.96 < \frac{x - 262.6}{12.2} < 1.96\right)$$
$$.95 = P[262.6 - 1.96(12.2) < x < 262.6 + 1.96(12.2)]$$
$$.95 = P(238.7 < x < 286.5)$$

Checking this result against Figure 2–2, we notice that about 92.9 percent of the observations actually lie within these limits. The discrepancy (which is not large) is due to the fact that the distribution is not exactly normal.

Now, on the basis just established we can convert any score to a standard score and then calculate the relative position of the original score. Appendix Table D gives percentages that are exceeded by any standard score. Let us consider the score 283, coming from a normal population with mean $\mu = 262.6$ and standard deviation $\sigma = 12.2$. If the population is normal, where does a person with a score of 283 stand, relative to the rest? To answer this we convert 283 to a standard score; this is

(3.12) $$Z = \frac{283 - 262.6}{12.2} = 1.67$$

The standard score 1.67 exceeds $95.252 \cong 95.2$ percent of the scores; this in turn, means that a person with a score of 283 has done better than 95.2 per-

---

FIGURE 3–3
Limits including 95 percent of the observations in an idealized normal population.

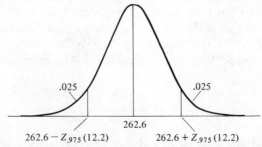

cent of his class. Note that conversion of a score to standard form does not change its position in the population. The reason is that if one raw (unconverted) score is greater than another, then the standard score for the first is also greater than the standard score for the second. Hence, if 95 percent of a set of raw scores are less than some value, when we standardize all the raw scores, including the value referred to, there will still be 95 percent of the standard scores less than the standardized value. Therefore, we can find the relative position of a raw score by finding the relative position of its standardized value.

EXERCISES

3.5 Calculate the limits in a normal population with mean 59 and standard deviation 3 which include 99 percent of the observations.

3.6 Repeat Exercise 3.5, using $\mu = 262.6$ and $\sigma = 12.2$. Compare your result with the percentage that actually lies within the calculated limits in Figure 2–2.

CONFIDENCE INTERVALS

We now turn to methods of making statements about populations when we have only a sample selected randomly from the population. We begin with

---

DEFINITION 3.7

An interval with limits calculated from a random sample (so that the limits change from one sample to the next) is called a "$100(1 - \alpha)$ percent confidence interval" for a population parameter if the percentage of times the limits will include the parameter is $100 \cdot (1 - \alpha)$.

The point needs to be emphasized that the limit or limits of the interval are the random variables, while the population parameter is fixed and is in the interval a certain percentage of the time. Here α (the Greek letter alpha) is the probability that the random interval will fail to cover the parameter.

Statements About the Population Mean

To illustrate the preceding definition, we begin with a very simple example. Suppose we select one observation at random from the population of randomly grouped fifth grade children whose relative frequency histogram is presented in Figure 2–2. Using normal theory, we have

$$(3.13) \qquad P(\mu - 1.96\sigma \leq x \leq \mu + 1.96\sigma) = .95$$

approximately, using the material of the preceding section.

Suppose, now, we know σ from past experience with similar data, but do not know μ. For example, we might know how much spread to expect

FIGURE 3–4
Simple confidence interval.

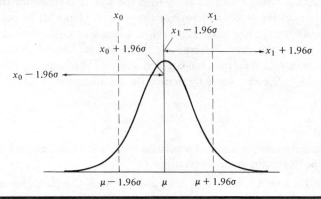

in a school district but not whether it is above or below the average in achievement. We now propose an interval, using the population of Figure 2–2 again (where $\sigma = 12.2$):

$$(3.14) \qquad [x - 1.96(12.2). \quad x + 1.96(12.2)]$$

The rationale is given in Figure 3–4; from Equation (3.13),

$$(3.15) \qquad P(\mu - 1.96\sigma \leq x \leq \mu + 1.96\sigma) = .95$$

But whenever

$$(3.16) \qquad \mu - 1.96\sigma \leq x \leq \mu + 1.96\sigma$$

it is also true that

$$(3.17) \qquad x - 1.96\sigma \leq \mu \leq x + 1.96\sigma$$

To see this, note that when $x = x_1 = \mu + 1.96\sigma$, then the lower limit of the confidence interval (which is then $x_1 - 1.96\sigma$) just touches μ. For $x_0 < x < x_1$, the interval always "covers" μ, and when $x = x_0$, the upper limit of the interval (now $x_0 + 1.96\sigma$) again barely touches μ. Thus the confidence interval covers μ whenever $x_0 \leq x \leq x_1$; and

$$(3.18) \quad P(x_0 \leq x \leq x_1) = P(\mu - 1.96\sigma \leq x \leq \mu + 1.96\sigma) = .95$$

This is an intuitive justification of the notion of a confidence interval.

EXAMPLE
Obtain a confidence interval for μ in the population of Figure 2–2, assuming that we know σ but not μ.

SOLUTION We enter the table of random numbers at the lower right hand corner of Appendix Table B, page B3, and work up, if necessary, to obtain a random number less than or equal to 544. We get 43, which results in a STEP science score of 252. Now $\sigma = 12.2$, so our confidence interval is

(3.19) $[252 - 1.96(12.2), \quad 252 + 1.96(12.2)]$ or $(228.1, 275.9)$

We can express this result by saying that our "confidence" that the interval $(228.1, 275.9)$ includes, or covers, μ is .95.

We next repeat the process, to show how the interval changes with each random sample. Continuing on page B4, we next get 323, which gives a STEP science score of 250, with a resulting interval of

(3.20) $[250 - 1.96(12.2), \quad 250 + 1.96(12.2)]$ or $(226.1, 273.9)$

Now 95 percent of such intervals will cover μ.

EXERCISES

3.7   Obtain the value Z from Table D such that:
   a. $P(\mu - Z\sigma \leq x \leq \mu + Z\sigma) = .90$ b. $P(\mu - Z\sigma \leq x \leq \mu + Z\sigma) = .99$

3.8   Suppose 269 is the STEP science score of a student selected at random from the population of randomly grouped students. Construct:
   a.   A 95 percent confidence interval for μ, assuming $\sigma = 12.2$, exactly as is done in expressions 3.19 and 3.20.
   b.   A 90 percent confidence interval for μ in the same manner as in part (a) above.

†3.9   Select one observation at random from the population of randomly grouped students, and construct a 90 percent confidence interval with it in the same manner as done in expressions 3.19 and 3.20. Repeat the process four more times.

‡3.10   Compile the results of all class members and calculate the percentage of times the interval covered the true value, 262.6, for μ.

A Confidence Interval for the Mean When the Population Standard Deviation Is Known

Next we will endeavor to be a little more practical. Generally we would be likely to select a random sample with more than one observation: we have a certain intuitive notion that it would be better to have more data. In our first example we knew the distribution was close to normal; in practice, however, we will not always know this. To resolve these problems, we rely on the central limit theorem (Chapter 2). By this theorem, we know that the population of means from samples of size n is close to normal and has the same mean as the original population. Using Theorem 2.5 (p. 53),

1. $\bar{x}$ is normally distributed so that the cumulative tables using standard scores are appropriate.

2. $\mu_{\bar{x}} = \mu$, that is, the population mean for $\bar{x}$ is the same as that we wish to draw conclusions about.

3. $\sigma_{\bar{x}}^2 = \sigma^2/n$.

In the case of the STEP science scores for the randomly grouped students $\sigma_{\bar{x}}^2 = 149.2/25 = 5.97$ and $\sigma_{\bar{x}} = 12.2/5 = 2.44$, if we have means obtained from samples of size 25 each.

We want a probability statement about the limits for $\bar{x}$, so that we can obtain a confidence interval for μ as we did in expressions (3.13) to (3.18). To arrive at such a statement, we calculate the standard score as before, except that now we have a sample of size n:

Note that the mean for $\bar{x}$ is μ, while the variance is σ^2/n. The standard deviation is $\sqrt{\sigma^2/n} = \sigma/\sqrt{n}$. Next, we go through the same procedure as before:

$\bar{x}$ = mean of raw scores

$\updownarrow$ from the formula $Z = \dfrac{\bar{x} - \mu}{\sigma/\sqrt{n}}$

Z = standard score

$\updownarrow$ from Appendix Table D

percentages
(or probabilities)

Again, we must know μ and σ to make the conversion in either direction. Note that while there is a change in the conversion formula from raw to standard scores, the standard scores themselves remain unchanged. We now want the limits, which will include 95 percent of the means (the means now take the place of the raw scores).

The upper limit for the standard score is 1.96; thus, the sample mean has reached its upper limit when.

(3.21) $$\frac{\bar{x} - \mu}{\sigma/\sqrt{n}} = 1.96$$

that is, when the mean converted to a standard score is 1.96. In our case, $\mu = 262.6$, $\sigma = 12.2$, $n = 25$. This means that the upper limit for $\bar{x}$ is

(3.22) $$\bar{x} = \mu + 1.96\sigma/\sqrt{n} = 262.6 + 1.96(12.2/5)$$

This last result was obtained by solving (3.21). In a similar fashion the lower limit for the sample means is

(3.23) $$\bar{x} = \mu - 1.96\sigma/\sqrt{n} = 262.6 - 196(12.2/5)$$

In general, we have that

(3.24) $$P\left(\mu - \frac{1.96\sigma}{\sqrt{n}} \leq \bar{x} \leq \mu + \frac{1.96\sigma}{\sqrt{n}}\right) = .95$$

Next we apply the same reasoning we used to get the results from (3.13) to (3.18). There we showed that

(3.25) $$\mu - 1.96 \leq x \leq \mu + 1.96\sigma$$

is equivalent to

(3.26) $$x - 1.96\sigma \leq \mu \leq x + 1.96\sigma$$

Now we assert that

(3.27)
$$\mu - \frac{1.96\sigma}{\sqrt{n}} \leq \bar{x} \leq \mu + \frac{1.96\sigma}{\sqrt{n}}$$

is equivalent to

(3.28)
$$\bar{x} - \frac{1.96\sigma}{\sqrt{n}} \leq \mu \leq \bar{x} + \frac{1.96\sigma}{\sqrt{n}}$$

so that the probabilities are the same. The reasoning of Figure 3–4 has already been used to justify this approach. (Mathematicians tend to prefer an algebraic proof, using the rules given in Chapter 1, which is not too difficult to obtain.)

Now note that (3.28) provides the required set of limits; the two limits are random variables that cover μ with the required probability. The general form of this result is

---

THEOREM 3.4

Let a random sample of size n be selected from a normal population for which the standard deviation, σ, is known. Further, let $-Z$ and Z be the lower and upper standard scores, which include $(1 - \alpha) \cdot 100$ percent of the observations in a normal distribution (Table D). Then,

(3.29)
$$\left(\bar{x} - Z \frac{\sigma}{\sqrt{n}}, \quad \bar{x} + Z \frac{\sigma}{\sqrt{n}} \right)$$

is a confidence interval which will cover μ with the percentage of times specified above. That is,

(3.30)
$$P\left(\bar{x} - Z \frac{\sigma}{\sqrt{n}} \leq \mu \leq \bar{x} + Z \frac{\sigma}{\sqrt{n}} \right) = 1 - \alpha$$

To calculate Z, we have $Z = Z_{1-\alpha/2}$; this is the score that cuts off $(\alpha/2) \cdot 100$ percent in the *right-hand* tail of the distribution. We illustrate the matter in Figure 3–5. If we wish a probability of $1 - \alpha$ in the middle, we need to delete

---

FIGURE 3-5
Appropriate probabilities used for a confidence interval.

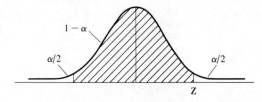

percent less than $Z = (1 - \alpha/2) \cdot 100\%$

Distribution for
the Sample Mean.

a probability of $\alpha/2$ from each tail of the distribution; then the probability of an observation being *less than* the limit for the right tail is $\alpha/2 + 1 - \alpha = 1 - \alpha/2$, as given above. Figure 3–3 also illustrates the point. We will work a problem to illustrate the use of this confidence interval.

EXAMPLE
Again using the population of Figure 2–2, obtain a random sample of size 7 and obtain a 90 percent confidence interval for the population mean, assuming $\sigma = 12.2$ but μ is not known.

SOLUTION   Using Appendix Tables B and A, we obtain the results seen in Table 3–1. Next, $1 - \alpha = .90$ so that $\alpha = .10$, and thus $1 - \alpha/2 = .95$ and $Z_{.95} = 1.645$, from Appendix Table D. Further, $\sigma = 12.2$ and $n = 7$, so that

$$\frac{\sigma}{\sqrt{n}} = \frac{12.2}{\sqrt{7}} \cong 4.61$$

Thus, by (3.30), our limits are

$$[271.3 - 1.645(4.61), \quad 271.3 + 1.645(4.61)] = [263.7, \quad 278.9]$$

Note that this time the confidence interval failed to cover the population mean. Theorem 3.4 states only that it will be covered $(1 - \alpha) \cdot 100$ percent of the time—in this case 90 percent; we happened to get one of the samples in the other 10 percent.

TABLE 3–1

Random Sample Illustrating Construction
of a Confidence Interval

RANDOM NUMBER (TABLE B, PAGE B5, TOP RIGHT, GOING DOWN)	STEP SCIENCE SCORE
186	256
958	
835	
342	287
279	291
772	
20	263
609	
274	267
984	
210	—
283	276
678	
131	259
	$\bar{x} = 271.3$
	$s^2 = 188.2$ (for future use)

It should be emphasized that, in practice, you will not know whether an interval covers μ or not; we only have a certain "degree of confidence" in our results. If we wish to increase confidence in having the interval cover the mean, we need to increase $1 - \alpha$.

EXERCISES

3.11 Suppose a random sample of 16 is selected from the population of randomly grouped children, using the STEP science scores. If $\bar{x} = 266.3$, obtain a 90 percent confidence interval for μ, assuming that $\sigma = 12.2$.

†3.12 Select a random sample of size 25 from the population of randomly grouped fifth grade children, using the STEP science scores. Obtain a 75 percent confidence interval for the population mean of these scores, assuming $\sigma = 12.2$.

‡3.13 Combine the results of all class members and determine the percentage of intervals that do not cover μ.

A Confidence Interval for the Mean When the Population Standard Deviation Is Unknown

The foregoing approach does not always give us limits for μ since we do not know σ, the population standard deviation, unless we already have much data from earlier work. We next inquire, What will happen to $(\bar{x} - \mu)/\sigma/\sqrt{n}$ if we replace the population standard deviation, σ, by the value $s = \sqrt{s^2}$? Fortunately, we know the answer to this, due to a famous result by W. S. Gosset, whose pseudonym was Student.

The cumulative distribution for

$$(3.31) \qquad \frac{\bar{x} - \mu}{s/\sqrt{n}}$$

is called the distribution for Student's t with $n - 1$ degrees of freedom. It is given in Appendix Table F and provides the percentages of terms of the form (3.31) which will be less than specified values for a given sample size. This distribution is similar to the normal distribution in that it is bell shaped with two tails and has its mean at the point zero. However, this distribution changes when the sample size changes, and the value used from the table depends on the sample size. A sample distribution is given in Figure 3–6. The symbol to be used to represent a value from the table for the t-distribution is $t_{(df)\,p}$, where df refers to the degrees of freedom, and $100p$ is the percentage of observations which are less than $t_{(df)\,p}$. In the early examples, the degrees of freedom will be one less than the sample size; that is, $df = n - 1$.

As an example, suppose that we have a sample of size 20 and wish to know the limits within which $(1 - \alpha) \cdot 100$ percent $= 95$ percent of values of the form $(\bar{x} - \mu)/(s/\sqrt{n})$ will lie. These values come from a t-distribution with 19 degrees of freedom if the observations are normal, and we need values

FIGURE 3-6
Example for Student's *t*-distribution.

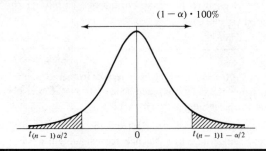

to cut off 2.5 percent of both the upper and lower tails. The values in the table thus correspond to $1 - \alpha/2$ and $\alpha/2$ by reason of Theorem 3–4. In this case, $\alpha = .05$, and we look for the values $t_{(19).975}$ and $t_{(19).025}$. But it turns out that $t_{(19).025} = -t_{(19).975}$, so that we need only look up one of these values. Using Table F, we have

$$t_{(19).975} = 2.093$$

Notice that in this table, only the percentages most commonly used are provided; the tables would be far too bulky if the entire set of percentages were provided for each degree of freedom.

From the foregoing reasoning, we see that if $n = 25$,

$$P\left[-2.06 \leq \frac{(\bar{x} - \mu)}{s/5} \leq 2.06 \right] = .95$$

where 2.06 was obtained from Table F, using the columns .025 and .975. Then, using the same reasoning as on the preceding pages,

(3.32) $$P\left(\bar{x} - \frac{2.06s}{5} \leq \mu \leq \bar{x} + \frac{2.06s}{5} \right) = .95$$

We repeat, the table now requires that we know the sample size to be used. Although the term "degrees of freedom" is misleading, it is in such common use that we will continue to use it. The distribution of $t = (\bar{x} - \mu)/(s/\sqrt{n})$ changes with the sample size, so that the limit above which a certain percentage lies depends on n. The degrees of freedom are $n - 1$, or one less than the sample size. We summarize these results in

---

THEOREM 3.5 (Student's t)
If x comes from a normal population with mean μ and variance σ^2, and if a random sample of size n is selected from it,

(3.33) $$\frac{\bar{x} - \mu}{s/\sqrt{n}}$$

follows Student's t-distribution with degrees of freedom equal to the sample size less one, and where

$$(3.34) \qquad s = \sqrt{\frac{1}{n-1} \sum_{i=1}^{n} (x_i - \bar{x})^2}$$

EXERCISES

3.14 Find:

    a. $t_{(29).95}$ b. $t_{(19).975}$

    c. $t_{(4).75}$ d. $t_{(9).10}$

3.15 Find the limits that include 99 percent of the observations from Student's *t*-distribution with 9 degrees of freedom.

3.16 If $\alpha = .10$ and $n = 25$, find:

    a. $t_{(n-1)1-\alpha/2}$ b. $t_{(n-1)\alpha/2}$

THEOREM 3.6

Let a simple random sample of size n be selected from a normal population. Further, let −t and t be the lower and upper values, which include $(1 - \alpha) \cdot 100$ percent of the observations from Student's t-distribution (Table F) with $n - 1$ degrees of freedom. Then,

$$(3.35) \qquad \left(\bar{x} - t \frac{s}{\sqrt{n}}, \quad \bar{x} + t \frac{s}{\sqrt{n}} \right)$$

is a confidence interval that will cover μ with the percentage of times specified above. That is,

$$(3.36) \qquad P\left(\bar{x} - t \frac{s}{\sqrt{n}} \le \mu \le \bar{x} + t \frac{s}{\sqrt{n}} \right) = 1 - \alpha$$

To calculate t, we have

$$t = t_{(n-1)1-\alpha/2}$$

As an example, suppose we select a random sample of size 4 from the "Concept of Self" scores, ability grouped students. The scores are 46, 43, 59, 41. Suppose we wish a 90 percent confidence interval. Then $1 - \alpha = .90$, $\alpha = .10$, and $1 - \alpha/2 = .95$, $n - 1 = 3$, so that we need

$$(3.37) \qquad t_{(3).95} = 2.35$$

from Table F. Now

$$(3.38) \qquad \bar{x} = 47.25, \quad s^2 = \tfrac{1}{3}(196.75) \cong 65.58$$

Then $s = 8.098$, $s/\sqrt{n} = 4.049$, which gives a confidence interval of

$$(3.39) \qquad 47.25 - (2.35)(4.049) \leq \mu \leq 47.25 + (2.35)(4.049)$$
$$37.73 \leq \mu \leq 65.77$$

EXERCISES

3.17 Suppose a random sample of size 9 is selected from the population of ability grouped students, using the STEP science scores, and that the observations are 258, 243, 289, 301, 267, 260, 265, 273, 278. Construct a 90 percent confidence interval for the mean, assuming that the observations come from a normal population.

†3.18 Select a random sample of size 5 from the population of ability grouped students (STEP science scores) and construct a 90 percent confidence interval for the mean, assuming that the population is normal.

†3.19 Repeat the experiment using a new sample of size 10.

‡3.20 Combine your results from Exercises 3.14 and 3.15 with those of the others in your class and calculate the percentage of times in which the confidence interval fails to cover the population mean. In what way does the increased sample size of Exercise 3.19 help you when compared with that for Exercise 3.18?

---

*PERCENTILES AND THEIR USES

The tolerance limit is closely related to the percentile or percentile rank which is so often used for interpretation of test scores. People are constantly asking not only what the score on a particular test is for a certain person, but also:

1. How did that person rank with respect to the other people who took the test?
2. How would that person rank in the population from which he was selected?

The answer to the first question can be obtained from the population sample used. The answer to the second question is a problem in statistical inference and will be treated in this section. We consider

---

DEFINITION 3.8
In a population of observations, each of which is a numerical value, the $100 \cdot p$th percentile, K_p, is that score below which $100 \cdot p$ percent of the observations are found.

We have three basic kinds of problems, using this definition, that need to be answered using a random sample selected from the population.

1. What score values correspond to certain prespecified percentile ranks?
2. What set of score values includes $(1 - \alpha) \cdot 100$ percent of the population?
3. What percentile rank does a particular score value have in the population?

We concern ourselves with these problems in the next section.

Estimation of Score Values Corresponding to Prespecified Percentile Ranks

In this section, we will assume that the population of observations is normal with mean μ and variance σ^2. Under these conditions we will obtain an estimate for K_p. We have

---

THEOREM 3.7
If a population of observations is normal, an estimate of K_p is

$$\bar{x} + \sqrt{(1 + 1/n)}\, t_{(n-1)p} \cdot s$$

This quantity has the property that the average percentage which it exceeds is $100 \cdot p$.

As an example, suppose we use the random sample used earlier with "concept of self" scores, and obtain an estimate of the twenty-fifth percentile. Then

$$(3.40) \qquad \bar{x} = 47.75, \quad s = 8.098, \quad n = 4$$
$$t_{(3).25} = -.766 \qquad \text{(from Table F)}$$

$$(3.41) \qquad K_{.25} = 47.75 + \sqrt{(1 + 1/4)}\,(-.766)(8.098)$$
$$= 47.75 - (1.118)(.766)(8.098) = 40.81$$

This procedure is found in Fraser and Guttman (1956).

Assuming that the "Concept of Self" score is a valid measure, we can now estimate that the cut-off point for the quarter of the population with the lowest self-image is 40.81. If we wish the middle 95 percent of the population, we can estimate this using the 97.5 and 2.5 percentiles, obtaining $K_{.975}$ and $K_{.025}$ as described in Theorem 3.7.

EXERCISES

3.21 A random sample of size 10 is selected from the randomly grouped students, using the times-chosen score, with the following results: 18, 6, 13, 4, 10, 19, 33, 51, 10, 0. Obtain an estimate of $K_{.10}$, the limit below which lie the 10 percent of students who are least popular.

†3.22 Sampling from the randomly grouped district, obtain an estimate of the times-chosen score for the 10 percent of the students who are least popular, using a random sample of size 25. Assume the population is normal.

†3.23 Estimate the STEP science score which exceeds 95 percent of the scores in the population of randomly grouped fifth grade children, using a random sample of size 10.

†3.24 For the same data used in Exercise 3.23, estimate the STEP science score that exceeds 5 percent of the scores. From this and the preceding exercise obtain an estimate of boundaries for the middle 90 percent of the population.

Estimation of Percentile Ranks Corresponding to a Given Score Value

In general, a good estimate of the percentile rank in the population is the percentile rank in the sample, if the sample is reasonably large, say over 25. For example, if the score whose percentile is to be estimated has 18 scores less than it and a total of 25 scores in the sample, then 18/25 is an estimate of the percentile rank.

EXERCISE

3.25 Suppose 25 scores "Me and Home" are obtained at random from the population of randomly grouped students; the scores are as follows: 23, 0, 15, 16, 6, 8, 11, 16, 7, 22, 13, 10, 9, 6, 30, 10, 8, 12, 9, 3, 2, 19, 8, 3, 19. Estimate the percentile rank for the score 12.

THE CORRELATION COEFFICIENT

Another aspect of our study of inference for one population is of considerable importance. To illustrate, note that we have a total of 13 distinct numerical measures on each student in our population of randomly grouped students. The question can be asked, If the STEP math score for a student is high, does the science score tend to be high also? One intuitively feels that if two measurements go up and down together, there is a strong relationship between them. We can ask more questions, including: Is the relationship between the STEP math and STEP science scores no higher than that between the math and social studies scores? What is the relationship between popularity (measured by the sociometric score) and achievement? The correlation coefficient was designed to answer questions of this kind; it is one procedure for measuring the strength of the relationship between two measurements made on the members of the same population.

The Scatter Diagram

A good graphical procedure for illustrating strength of relationship is commonly called the *scatter diagram*. Suppose we consider the first class among the randomly grouped students and make a chart such as Figure 3–7 on which to depict the relationship between STEP science and STEP math scores. Student No. 4 has a science score of 258 and a Math score of 238. The circle marked with a 4 corresponds to his pair of scores. Dropping vertically down from the circle indicates the student's score corresponds to 258 on the horizontal axis. Going horizontally across the diagram, we cut the vertical axis at 238. To position a circle, we need a pair of numbers, one for the horizontal and one for the vertical axis. In the same fashion, students No. 5 and 6 have the pairs (287, 263) and (254, 245), respectively. The first number in the pair (the Science score) gives the reading for the horizontal axis; the second number, for the vertical axis, is the math score.

FIGURE 3-7
Scatter diagram for STEP math and STEP science scores for the first class (teacher No. 1), randomly grouped fifth-grade students.

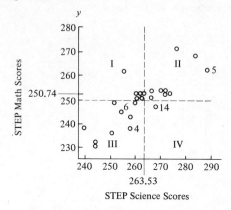

STEP Science Scores

If a score is above average on the science score (that is, to the right of the dotted line), it tends to be above average on the math score (above the dotted line) in Figure 3-7 also. That is, if a number is to the right of the vertical dotted line, it tends also to be above the horizontal dotted line. In fact, there is only one exception—the pair (267, 247), which is the set of scores for student No. 14. Similarly, most scores that are to the left of the vertical dotted line are also below the horizontal dotted line; 11 scores to the left are also below, while 6 to the left are above the horizontal line. The dotted lines divide the diagram into four quadrants; most observations, for this case, lie in quadrants II and IV.

The relationship just described is considered to be a strong relationship in the social sciences. In Figure 3-8 we are investigating the relationship between an achievement score and a score representing the student's feelings about home, Science Research Associates' "Me and Home." Although there should be some connection, we would suspect that the relationship would be less close than that between two achievement scores. We note first that a high SRA score implies poor adjustment and that if any relationship exists, it may be described by saying that poor home adjustment goes with low academic achievement. However, if one score (that for student No. 15) were deleted, it would be difficult to establish any relationship. In this case, there does not seem to be an *established* trend so that a low achievement score goes with a high (that is, poor) adjustment score. There are many low achievers with good adjustment scores (quadrant IV). Also high achievers seem to be equally balanced with respect to above average and below average adjustment scores. We say that there is not a strong relationship in Figure 3-8.

In general, a strong relationship will yield a pattern that is close to a straight line (either ascending or descending), whereas a weak relationship

FIGURE 3–8

Scatter diagram for STEP science and SRA "Me and Home" scores for the first class (teacher No. 1), randomly grouped fifth-grade students. High score on "Me and Home" indicates unfavorable adjustment.

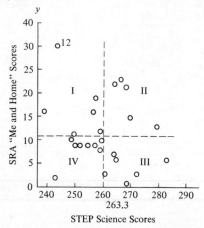

STEP Science Scores

usually results in a less well-defined, often "blotchy" pattern. A third scatter diagram involving two SRA scores gives a relationship which is weaker than that of Figure 3–7 but stronger than that of Figure 3–8. The final diagram, relating times chosen on a sociometric score with SRA's "Me and School" scores, shows a descending line of the kind encountered when high scores on one measure (times-chosen) go with low scores on the other (number of personal problems in school).

The Sample Correlation Coefficient

We now seek a method of obtaining a numerical measure for the strength of the relationship between two sets of observations. Sir Francis Galton and Karl Pearson first studied this problem a century ago; the elements of their population were families and the two measurements were height of father and height of the eldest son. They suggested a measure we will develop here. If the strength of the relationship is high, either most scores will lie in quadrants II and IV, with relatively few in I and III, or they will lie in I and III, with relatively few in II and IV, as previously indicated. The second case occurs if high values on one measure usually go with low values on the other. (We refer the reader back to the section on negative numbers in Chapter 1 if his skill with them is a bit rusty.)

At this point we modify our notation for $\bar{x}$ and use $\bar{x}_{\cdot\cdot}$. The dot is a way of indicating that the subscript in the formula for $\bar{x}$ has been summed over. This notation will be used throughout the remainder of the text; its usefulness will be apparent later.

If we consider the deviation of each observation from its mean, then the *i*th person has two scores, one for the deviation of the score on the horizontal axis from its mean ($x_i - \bar{x}$.), and another for the deviation of the score on the vertical axis ($y_i - \bar{y}$.). If the person scored above average on one of the scores and below average on the other, then the product of the two deviations will be negative, since one of the deviations is positive and the other is negative. If both deviations are either above or below average, their product will be positive.

For each circle in Figures 3–7 to 3–10, we can obtain the product of two deviations. If the circle is in quadrant I or III, the product will be negative, by the argument in the preceding paragraph; if in quadrant II or IV, the product will be positive. Suppose we add up all the products obtained as

FIGURE 3-9
Scatter diagram for two SRA scores for the first class (teacher No. 1), randomly grouped fifth-grade students. High score on either test means unfavorable adjustment.

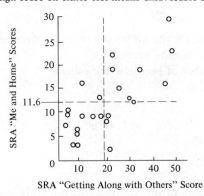

SRA "Me and Home" Scores

SRA "Getting Along with Others" Score

FIGURE 3-10
Scatter diagram for two negatively related scores on personal adjustment. Low SRA scores and high "times chosen" indicate desirable scores.

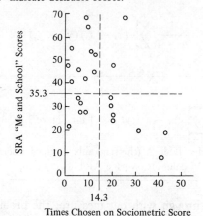

SRA "Me and School" Scores

Times Chosen on Sociometric Score

described earlier. If the relationship is strong and measures are positively related as in Figure 3–7, most products will be positive and the sum of the products should be positive. If the relationship is weak, as in Figure 3–8, about as many products will be negative as positive, and the sum should be close to zero. If the relationship is moderately strong, as in Figure 3–9, the sum should be somewhere between the first two. Finally, if the relationship is strong but inverse in the sense that low scores on one measure go with high scores on the other, as in Figure 3–10, there will be more negative products than positive, and the sum of the products will be negative.

We can write the tentative measure we are using in terms of a formula by noting that the product of the ith deviation is

$$(3.42) \qquad\qquad (x_i - \bar{x}.)(y_i - \bar{y}.)$$

and their sum is then

$$(3.43) \qquad\qquad \sum_{i=1}^{n} (x_i - \bar{x}.)(y_i - \bar{y}.)$$

where x_i = the score for the ith person on the horizontal axis
$\quad\qquad y_i$ = the same for the vertical axis
$\quad\qquad n$ = the number of people in the sample

$$\bar{x}. = \frac{1}{n} \sum_{i=1}^{n} x_i$$

$$\bar{y}. = \frac{1}{n} \sum_{i=1}^{n} y_i$$

We immediately modify this measure for the same reason that we previously modified the variance; we do not want it influenced by the number of people used. Hence we will divide by $n - 1$ as before, so that our measure becomes

$$(3.44) \qquad\qquad \frac{1}{n-1} \sum_{i=1}^{n} (x_i - \bar{x}.)(y_i - \bar{y}.)$$

EXERCISES

3.26   Calculate $\dfrac{1}{n-1} \sum_{i=1}^{n} (x_i - \bar{x}.)(y_i - \bar{y}.)$ for Figure 3–8, obtaining the data from teacher No. 1 of Appendix Table A (the randomly grouped students). This is found in the STEP/SCI and HOM columns on page AR1 (School 10, Teacher 1).

We are still not through with our measure; the problem is that we can increase the strength of the relationship simply by multiplying each score by a sufficiently large constant. This does not seem reasonable; the scatter diagrams would look exactly the same since multiplying merely changes the scale on the vertical axis. We have a strong intuitive feeling that the shape of the data indicates the strength of the relationship, and we want our measure to be independent of the scale we happen to use. So the measure must be modified once more by dividing the sum of the products (3.44) by the product of the standard deviations. This gives

$$(3.45) \qquad \frac{\dfrac{1}{n-1} \displaystyle\sum_{i=1}^{n} (x_i - \bar{x}.)(y_i - \bar{y}.)}{s_x s_y} = r$$

which is formally known as Pearson's product moment correlation coefficient.

The measure r defined in (3.45) ranges in possible values between -1 and $+1$; if $r = +1$, there is a perfect relationship; that is, given x or y, we can find exactly what the other value is. If $r = -1$, the relationship is also perfect, but it is inverse; high y scores go with low x scores. In practice, r is a random variable whose observed value lies between these limits.

A simple table layout for the correlation coefficient can be constructed as in Table 3–2. We use the correlation between STEP math and STEP science scores to illustrate. Separate columns are used for the original scores, the scores minus the sample means, and the squares and products of the third and fourth columns. The sum of the right-hand columns is divided by $n - 1$, and then by the product of the standard deviations, to obtain r. We have, from the table, $s_x^2 = 135.54$, $s_y^2 = 97.21$, and

$$s_{xy} = \frac{1}{n-1} \sum_{i=1}^{n} (x_i - \bar{x}.)(y_i - \bar{y}.) = 106.03$$

Hence

$$r = \frac{s_{xy}}{s_x s_y} = \frac{106.03}{(11.64)(9.86)} = .93$$

which is a very close relationship as measures in the social sciences go.

Note: For convenience to the reader, the measures used correspond to people in the first class of randomly grouped students. Statements about larger populations virtually always require that the measures be made on a random sample selected from the larger population. Thus the methods of the next section depend on doing what we failed to do here.

EXERCISE

3.27 Using the data of Exercise 3.34, calculate r.

TABLE 3—2

Layout for Calculation of Correlation Coefficient

STEP SCIENCE x_i	STEP MATH y_i	$x_i - \bar{x}.$	$y_i - \bar{y}.$	$(x_i - \bar{x}.)^2$	$(x_i - \bar{x}.)$ $(y_i - \bar{y}.)$	$(y_i - \bar{y}.)^2$
269	254	7.04	3.88	49.5616	27.3152	15.0544
271	253	9.04	2.88	81.7216	26.0352	8.2944
273	253	11.04	2.88	121.8816	31.7952	8.2944
258	238	−3.96	−12.12	15.6816	47.9952	146.8944
287	263	25.04	12.88	627.0016	322.5152	165.8944
254	245	−7.96	−5.12	63.3616	40.7552	26.2144
251	249	−10.96	−1.12	120.1216	12.2752	1.2544
239	238	−22.96	−12.12	527.1616	278.2572	146.8944
266	251	4.04	.88	16.3216	3.5552	.7744
266	254	4.04	3.88	16.3216	15.6752	15.0544
283	269	21.04	18.88	442.6816	397.2352	356.4544
250	236	−11.96	−14.12	143.0416	168.8752	199.3744
255	262	−6.96	11.88	48.4416	−82.6848	141.1344
267	247	5.04	−3.12	25.4016	−15.7248	9.7344
244	231	−17.96	−19.12	322.5616	343.3952	365.5744
262	253	.04	2.88	.0016	.1152	8.2944
260	251	−1.96	.88	3.8416	−1.7248	.7744
261	253	−.96	2.88	.9216	−2.7648	8.2944
258	243	−3.96	−7.12	15.6816	28.1952	50.6944
263	253	1.04	2.88	1.0816	2.9952	8.2944
244	231	−17.96	−19.12	322.5616	343.3952	365.5744
271	254	9.04	3.88	81.7216	35.0752	15.0544
262	251	.04	.88	.0016	.0352	.7744
276	272	14.04	21.88	199.1216	307.1952	478.7344
259	249	−2.96	−1.12	8.7616	3.4152	1.2544
Total 6549	6253	0.00	0.00	3252.9600	2333.1020	2544.6400
Average 261.96	250.12			135.54	97.21	106.03

The Population Correlation Coefficient

Every population whose elements have two measures also has a population correlation coefficient between the measures which is denoted by

$$(3.46) \quad \rho = \frac{\dfrac{1}{N-1} \displaystyle\sum_{i=1}^{N} (x_i - \mu_x)(y_i - \mu_y)}{\left(\sqrt{\dfrac{1}{N-1} \displaystyle\sum_{i=1}^{N} (x_i - \mu_x)^2}\right)\left(\sqrt{\dfrac{1}{N-1} \displaystyle\sum_{i=1}^{N} (y_i - \mu_y)^2}\right)}$$

where N is the population size and

$$\mu_x = \frac{1}{N} \sum_{i=1}^{N} x_i \quad \text{and} \quad \mu_y = \frac{1}{N} \sum_{i=1}^{N} y_i$$

Note that ρ, the Greek letter rho, (corresponding to r) denotes the population correlation coefficient. The formula for ρ is thus $\rho = \sigma_{xy}/\sigma_x\sigma_y$, where

$$(3.47) \qquad \sigma_{xy} = \frac{1}{N-1} \sum_{i=1}^{N} (x_i - \mu_x)(y_i - \mu_y)$$

$$\sigma_x = \sqrt{\frac{1}{n-1} \sum_{i=1}^{n} (x_i - \mu_x)^2}$$

$$\sigma_y = \sqrt{\frac{1}{n-1} \sum_{i=1}^{n} (y_i - \mu_y)^2}$$

STATISTICAL INFERENCE FOR THE POPULATION CORRELATION COEFFICIENT

We begin this discussion by noting that the problem is to learn something about ρ by the use of the sample value r. We will see that r is very close to being an unbiased estimate of ρ; that is, to a very close approximation

$$(3.48) \qquad \mu_r = \rho$$

A Confidence Interval for ρ

If the two sets of observations from a parent population are normal or close to normal, we can obtain a confidence interval for ρ using Appendix Table G. We need to know only the sample size and the value for r. Appendix Table G gives a $.95 \cdot 100$ percent confidence interval for ρ. We use the row corresponding to our value for r and the column corresponding to the appropriate sample size; the entries in the cell at the intersection of the row and column define the confidence interval. If our values are not in the table margins, we interpolate. For instance, $r = .58$ and the sample size is 25. If $r = .60$, then the confidence intervals are $(.26, .80)$. If $r = .55$, they are $(.20, .77)$. Now $r = .58$ is $\frac{3}{5}$ of the distance from $r = .55$ to $r = .60$, and we use these proportions to get $(.24, .79)$ as the appropriate 95 percent confidence interval for ρ.

EXERCISES

3.28 Suppose in a random sample of size 15, the calculated r between the times-chosen score (TI/CH) and the "Me and School" score (SCH) is $r = .32$. Obtain a 95 percent confidence interval for ρ between these two scores.

†3.29 Select a random sample of 10 students from the randomly grouped population. Obtain the correlation coefficient between the STEP science and SRA "Me and Home" scores, and use it to obtain a 95 percent confidence interval for ρ.

‡3.30   Combine your result with those of the rest of the class. The value for ρ in this case is $-.137$. Determine the percentage of times in the class when the confidence interval included ρ.

A Hypothesis Test for ρ

The first example of a hypothesis test is introduced here in an informal fashion. Suppose we wish to consider the notion that there is, in fact, no relationship at all between two measures; that is, knowledge of one measure tells us nothing about the value of the other measure. We can test this hypothesis using the following reasoning:

1. If the hypothesis is true (that is, if $\rho = 0$), we can find limits such that any value of r outside these limits is highly improbable.
2. If r falls inside the limits described above, we accept the hypothesis: $\rho = 0$.
3. If r falls outside the limits, we may accept either of two alternative conclusions:
    a. $\rho = 0$ and a highly improbable event has occurred.
    b. $\rho \neq 0$ ($\neq$ means "is unequal to").

If $\rho = 0$, it is unlikely that r will fall outside the limits; if r does fall outside the limits, we conclude that $\rho = 0$, and we say we have rejected the null hypothesis $H: \rho = 0$.

To make this test, we use Appendix Table H with the sample size, the value for r, and the probability we specify for the highly improbable event. For example, if $n = 25$ and we want the small probability to be .01, we enter the table in the row corresponding to $n = 25$ and the column for the probability at .01 and find .445. This means that if $\rho = 0$, then the probability that $r > .445$ or $r < -.445$ is .01, based on a sample size of 25. Then our rule is to accept $H: \rho = 0$ if $-.445 < r < .445$; we reject H if $r < -.445$ or $.445 < r$.

EXERCISES
3.31   Using $r = -.62$, $n = 15$ from Exercise 3.27, test the hypothesis $\rho = 0$, using $\alpha = .05$.

†3.32   Select a random sample of size 10 from the randomly grouped children. Let ρ be the population correlation between the STEP science and SRA "Me and Home" scores. Establish a rule for rejecting $H: \rho = 0$ such that the probability is .05 of rejecting the hypothesis if it is, in fact, true. Carry out the test with your sample.

‡3.33   Combine the result of your test with those of the other members of your class. Calculate the percentage of people who rejected the hypothesis.

Experiences with Data
In this section, the problems will be less structured, to give the student an opportunity to plan and carry out his own project and to learn how data

behave in the face of efforts to draw conclusions about a population. In the following problems, the student is asked to

1. Decide the measure (or measures) that are appropriate for answering the questions.
2. Decide what populations are to be considered in answering the question.
3. Determine and execute a sampling plan (this involves sample size, the sampling list, and so on).
4. Decide on the type of data analysis to use.
5. Carry out the analysis.
6. Interpret the results to answer the question originally posed.

It should be emphasized that there is no one "correct" way of answering these questions; students may arrive at conflicting answers to the same questions without being incorrect. Some of the problems are designed to point toward a need for more sophisticated tools; where you encounter a problem that has apparently not been discussed previously, attempt to "make the best" of the situation and devise methods of answering the question. Such methods may be very crude; often they will be merely visual comparison of a set of means or the like.

PROBLEMS

3.1 What are the relative performance levels of fast, average, and slow students on STEP science scores for the randomly grouped students?

3.2 Answer the same question for the ability grouped students.

3.3 The tests "Concept of Self" and "Ideal Self" were constructed by W. R. Borg and associates for the purposes of the study on ability grouping. The measures "Me and School," "Me and Home," "About Myself," "Getting Along with Others," and "Things in General" were constructed by Science Research Associates. A high score on Borg's tests indicates good social adjustment; a high score on the SRA test indicates poor adjustment. For the data available here, can you determine whether the randomly grouped students accept themselves better than they do their home environment? Defend your answer.

3.4 On the basis of the test results, what would you consider to be a normal social adjustment score for the fifth grade randomly grouped students?

3.5 Answer the same question for the ability grouped students.

3.6 Can you determine with the present data (randomly grouped students) whether individual differences have a greater effect on achievement than social adjustment? If so, do so. If not, explain why you cannot.

3.7 Are individual differences more pronounced among ability grouped students or among randomly grouped students with respect to achievement? With respect to social adjustment?

3.8 Within what limits do most children fall with respect to the number of times they were chosen on the sociometric score? (You must define what you mean by "most.")

3.9 Answer the same question for the SRA test "Me and Home."

3.10 Answer the same question for the STEP science score.

3.11 Consider the following question: Is popularity equivalent to good social adjustment among elementary school age children? Design and carry out a sampling plan to gather evidence on this point, using any measure or measures you feel will help answer this question. Analyze your data and, on the basis of the evidence, draw all conclusions you feel you can. You should describe your sampling plan and method of analysis carefully and be prepared to defend your position. (For one possible solution to this problem see page 101.)

3.12   Do students who are well adjusted at school tend to be well adjusted at home? Proceed as in the preceding problem.

3.13   Is scholastic achievement related to popularity?

SOLUTIONS TO EXERCISES

3.1

$$X\ X\ XX\ X \qquad X\ X$$

$$
\begin{array}{cccccccc}
-20 & -10 & 0 & 10 & 20 & 30 & 40
\end{array}
$$

$\mu = 16.3$

$\sigma^2 = \frac{1}{6}[(16 - 16.3)^2 + (13 - 16.3)^2 + (28 - 16.3)^2 + (9 - 16.3)^2$
$\qquad + (5 - 16.3)^2 + (31 - 16.3)^2 + (12 - 16.3)^2]$
$\qquad = \frac{1}{6}(.09 + 10.89 + 136.89 + 53.29 + 127.69 + 216.09 + 18.49)$
$\qquad = 93.9$

3.2

$$0\ \ 0\ \ 00\ 0 \qquad 0\ \ \ 0$$

$$
\begin{array}{cccccccc}
-20 & -10 & 0 & 10 & 20 & 30 & 40
\end{array}
$$

The new population is $-.3, -3.3, 11.7, -7.3, -11.3, 14.7, -4.3$

$$\mu = -.014 \cong 0 \qquad \sigma^2 = \frac{563.43}{6} = 93.9$$

3.3

$$X\ \ XX$$
$$XXXX$$

$$
\begin{array}{cccccccc}
-20 & -10 & 0 & 10 & 20 & 30 & 40
\end{array}
$$

$\sigma \cong 9.691$; the new population is $-.031, -.341, 1.207, -.753, -1.166, 1.517, -.444$

3.4

$\sigma^2 = \frac{1}{6}(.00096 + .1156 + 1.4568 + .5670 + 1.3596 + 2.3012 + .1971)$
$\qquad = .9997 \cong 1.0$

3.5

$$P(59 - Z_{.995}\sigma \le x \le 59 + Z_{.995}\sigma) = .99$$

$$-Z_{.995} \le \frac{x - 59}{3} \le Z_{.995}; \qquad Z_{.995} = 2.58$$

$$.99 = P\left(-2.58 \le \frac{x - 59}{3} \le 2.58\right)$$

$$.99 = P[59 - 2.58(3) \le x \le 59 + 2.58(3)]$$

$$.99 = P(51.26 \le x \le 66.74)$$

Hence the limits 51.26, 66.74 include 99 percent of the observations.

3.6

$.99 = (262.6 - Z_{.995}\sigma \le x \le 262.6 + Z_{.995}\sigma)$

$.99 = \left(-Z_{.995} \le \dfrac{x - 262.6}{12.2} \le Z_{.995}\right)$

$.99 = \left(-2.58 \le \dfrac{x - 262.6}{12.2} \le 2.58\right)$

$.99 = [262.6 - 2.58(12.2) \le x \le 262.2 + 2.58(12.2)]$

$.99 = (231.12 \le x \le 294.08)$

The limits 231.1, 294.1 contain 99 percent of the observations. To compare, 98.4 percent is less than 294.1, and 1.0 percent is less than 231.1. This gives $98.4 - 1.0 = 97.4$ percent between the two limits, compared with 99 percent for the idealized case.

3.7

a. $P(\mu - Z\sigma \le x \le \mu + Z\sigma) = .90;$ $Z = Z_{.95} = 1.645$

b. $P(\mu - Z\sigma \le x \le \mu + Z\sigma) = .99;$ $Z = Z_{.995} = 2.575$

3.8

a. $269 - Z_{.975}(12.2),$ $269 + Z_{.975}(12.2)$

 $269 - 1.96(12.2),$ $269 + 1.96(12.2)$

 $269 - 23.9,$ $269 + 23.9$

 $(245.1, 292.9)$ is the confidence interval.

b. $269 - Z_{.95}(12.2),$ $269 + Z_{.95}(12.2)$

 $269 - 1.645(12.2),$ $269 + 1.645(12.2)$

 $(248.93, 289.07)$ is the confidence interval.

3.9

Random sample is as follows:

$ID = 168;$ score $= 251;$ $\sigma = 12.2;$ $Z_{(.95)} = 1.645$

$[251 - 1.645(12.2), 252 + 1.645(12.2)] = (230.9, 272.1)$

3.11

The $(1 - \alpha) \cdot 100\%$ confidence interval is

$\alpha = .10$

$$\left[\bar{x} - Z_{.95}\left(\frac{\sigma}{4}\right), \ \bar{x} + Z_{.95}\left(\frac{\sigma}{4}\right)\right]$$

$$\left[266.3 - 1.645\left(\frac{12.2}{4}\right), \ 266.3 + 1.645\left(\frac{12.2}{4}\right)\right]$$

$(261.28, 271.32)$

3.12

There are four steps to this problem:

1. Select the random sample.
2. Calculate the sample mean.
3. Find the value for $Z_{1-\alpha/2}$.
4. Obtain the limits for the confidence interval.

Step 1.   Select the random sample.
Begin with Appendix page B6, top right, and go down.

ID NO.	STEP SCIENCE SCORE	ID NO.	STEP SCIENCE SCORE	ID NO.	STEP SCIENCE SCORE
223	267	254	absent*	549	ignore
962	ignore	665	ignore	71	287
825	ignore	437	253	584	ignore
856	ignore	595	ignore	494	257
308	256	282	287	366	302
306	263	343	264	301	261
339	257	097	233	871	ignore
439	276	188	231	510	252
936	ignore	374	257	219	250
657	ignore	143	261	465	267
445	273	022	271	158	269
874	ignore	449	283		
033	248	104	233		

* Take another observation.

Note the student who had a STEP science score of zero (No. 254). He was absent when the test was administered; another ID number was selected to obtain a person to take his place. Be careful in doing this; if there is reason to believe that the student was absent *because* he felt he would not do well, a better alternative would be to test that student at another time rather than treat his result as a missing observation.

Step 2.   Calculate the sample mean.
For this case it is $\bar{x} = 262.32$.
Step 3.
The requirement of the problem is $(1 - \alpha) \cdot 100 = 75$. Thus $1 - \alpha = .75$, or $\alpha = .25$. Hence $1 - \alpha/2 = .875$, and we want $Z_{.875}$. From Appendix Table D,

$$Z_{.875} \cong 1.15$$

Step 4.
Using Expression 3.40, we have

$$\bar{x} - Z_{1-\alpha/2} \frac{\sigma}{\sqrt{n}} = 262.32 - \frac{(1.15) \cdot (12.2)}{5}$$

$$= 262.32 - 2.81 = 259.51$$

$$\bar{x} + Z_{1-\alpha/2} \frac{\sigma}{\sqrt{n}} = 262.32 + \frac{(1.15) \cdot (12.2)}{5}$$

$$= 262.32 + 2.81 = 265.13$$

Hence our confidence interval for the mean is 259.51, 265.13.

3.14

a. $t_{(29) \cdot 95} = 1.699$ b. $t_{(19) \cdot 975} = 2.09$

c. $t_{(4) \cdot 75} = .741$ d. $t_{(9) \cdot 10} = -1.383$

3.15

$\alpha = .01;\ \alpha/2 = .005;\ 1 - \alpha/2 = .995$

$t_{(9).005} = -3.25;\ t_{(9).995} = 3.25$

3.16

$1 - \alpha/2 = .95$

a. $t_{(24).95} = 1.711$ b. $t_{(24).05} = -1.711$

3.17

$\bar{x} = 270.4;\ s^2 = 300.025;\ s_{\bar{x}} = 17.32/3 = 5.77;\ t_{(8).95} = 1.86$

$270.4 - 1.86(5.77) \le \mu \le 270.4 + 1.86(5.77)$

$259.67 \le \mu \le 281.13$

3.18

There are four steps to this problem:

1. Select a random sample.
2. Obtain $\bar{x}$, s^2, s.
3. Obtain $t_{(n-1)1-\alpha/2}$.
4. Calculate the limits for the confidence interval.

Step 1.

Start on Appendix page B5, line 15, column 9, work down.

ID NO.	STEP SCIENCE SCORES	ID NO.	STEP SCIENCE SCORES
855	ignore	646	ignore
886	ignore	513	269
573	ignore	394	257
797	ignore	029	254
789	ignore	224	246
193	260		

Step 2.

$x_i = 260, 269, 257, 254, 246$

$$\sum_{i=1}^{5} x_i = 1286;\quad \bar{x} = 257.2$$

$$\sum_{i=1}^{5} x_i^2 = 331{,}042$$

$$\left(\sum_{i=1}^{5} x_i\right)^2 = 1286^2 = 1{,}653{,}796$$

$$\left(\sum_{i=1}^{5} x_i\right)^2 \Big/ 5 = 330{,}759.2$$

$$\sum_{i=1}^{5} (x_i - \bar{x})^2 = \sum_{i=1}^{5} x_i^2 - \left(\sum_{i=1}^{5} x_i\right)^2 \Big/ 5$$

$$= 331042.0 - 330759.2 = 282.8 = 4s^2$$

$$s^2 = 70.7;\quad s = 8.41$$

Step 3.   Obtain $t_{(n-1)1-\alpha/2}$.
In this case, $(1 - \alpha) \cdot 100 = 90$ and $n = 5$.

$$\frac{\alpha}{2} = .05; \qquad 1 - \frac{\alpha}{2} = .95; \qquad n - 1 = 4$$

$t_{(4).95} = 2.132$

Step 4.   Calculate the limits for the confidence interval.
From Theorem 3.6, we have

$$\bar{x} + t_{(n-1)(1-\alpha/2)} \frac{s}{\sqrt{n}} = 257.2 + \frac{(2.132)(8.41)}{\sqrt{5}}$$

$$= 257.20 + 8.02 = 265.22$$

$$\bar{x} - t_{(n-1)(1-\alpha/2)} \frac{s}{\sqrt{n}} = 257.20 - 8.02 = 249.18$$

so that our confidence interval is $(249.18, 265.22)$.

3.19

Repeat the procedure for Exercise 3.18, using the increased sample size.

3.21

$$K_p = \bar{x} + \left(1 + \frac{1}{n}\right)^{1/2} t_{(n-1)p} \cdot s$$

$K_{.10} = 16.4 + (\sqrt{1.1})(-1.383)(\sqrt{229.6})$
$\qquad = 16.4 - (1.0486)(1.383)(15.1)$
$\qquad = 23.4 - 21.6 = 1.8$

3.25

The scores in order are 0, 2, 3, 3, 6, 6, 7, 8, 8, 8, 9, 9, 10, 10, 11, <u>12</u>, 13, 15, 16, 16, 19, 19, 22, 23, 30. The percentile rank for the person whose score is 12 is $15/25 = .60$.

3.26

$$\frac{1}{n-1} \sum_{i=1}^{n} (x_i - \bar{x}.)(y_i - \bar{y}.) = \frac{-374.6}{24} = -15.61$$

3.27

$$r = \frac{-15.61}{(11.64)(7.23)} \doteq -.185$$

3.28

$(-.23, .70)$

3.31

From Appendix Table H, if $n = 15$, $\alpha = .05$, we reject $H: \rho = 0$ if r is outside the limits $(-.514, .514)$. Since $r = -.62$ is indeed outside these limits, we reject H and conclude that $\rho \neq 0$.

Problem 3.11. One of many possible solutions consists of the following five steps.

Step 1. Decide on the statistical techniques.
One measure of popularity is the times-chosen score; the arbitrarily chosen measure of social adjustment is the "Me and School" score. If we say that these two measures are "equivalent," we are saying that the correlation between them is high. To examine this question, the confidence interval for ρ will be used, with a fairly large sample size of 30. (A hypothesis test for $\rho = 0$ is not considered, since the alternatives are either to accept H: $\rho = 0$ or to conclude that $\rho \neq 0$. What we need to determine is whether $\rho \geq .60$, for example, and a confidence interval is the only tool you have at present for this problem.)

Having decided on the statistical tool to use, we go onto the following steps:

Step 2. Select a random sample.
Obtain both the times chosen and the "Me and School" score for each person sampled.

Step 3. Perform calculations.
Determine

$$s_x, \quad s_y, \quad \frac{1}{n-1} \sum_{i=1}^{n} (x_i - \bar{x})(y_i - \bar{y})$$

Suppose that
$r = .369$ from step 2.

Step 4. Obtain the confidence interval for ρ.
We know $r \cong -.37$ and $n = 30$. Now we interpolate for r:

If $n = 25$

$r = -.40$	$-.68 \leq \rho \leq .00$
$r = -.37$	$-.66 \leq \rho \leq .03$
$r = -.35$	$-.65 \leq \rho \leq .05$

If $n = 50$

$r = -.40$	$-.61 \leq \rho \leq -.14$
$r = -.37$	$-.59 \leq \rho \leq -.10$
$r = -.35$	$-.57 \leq \rho \leq -.08$

Next interpolate for n:

$n = 50$	$-.59 \leq \rho \leq -.10$
$n = 30$	$-.646 \leq \rho \leq .044$
$n = 25$	$-.66 \leq \rho \leq .03$

Hence the confidence interval for ρ is $-.646 \leq \rho \leq .044$, with $r = -.37$.

Step 5. Interpret the results in the light of the question asked.
If the lower limit of the confidence interval for ρ is near .6, the original question, Is popularity equivalent to good social adjustment, can be answered by affirming that there is a high relationship. Since the best estimate for ρ is $-.37$, we do not have evidence to support the notion that there is a high relationship between popu-

larity and social adjustment. They are not equivalent concepts, at least as far as these measures are concerned.

REVIEW FOR CHAPTER 3

1. **Preliminary symbols**
   a. $X \sim (\mu, \sigma^2)$ means X comes from a population with mean $= \mu$ and variance $= \sigma^2$.
   b. $X \sim N(\mu, \sigma^2)$ means X comes from a *normal* population with mean $= \mu$ and variance $= \sigma^2$.
2. **Generation of new populations**
   a. If $X \sim (\mu, \sigma^2)$, then $X - \mu \sim (0, \sigma^2)$.
   b. If $X \sim (\mu, \sigma^2)$, then $(X - \mu)/\sigma \sim (0, 1)$.
3. **Probability using the normal distribution**
4. **$(1 - \alpha) \cdot 100$ percent confidence interval** for the mean when the standard deviation is known:

$$\bar{x} - Z \frac{\sigma}{\sqrt{n}}, \qquad \bar{x} + Z \frac{\sigma}{\sqrt{n}}$$

where n is the sample size.
Z is the value in the margin of Table D, corresponding to the value $1 - \alpha/2$ in the body of the table.
$\bar{x}$ is the sample mean.
σ is the known standard deviation.
5. **$(1 - \alpha) \cdot 100$ percent confidence interval** for the mean when the standard deviation is unknown:

$$\bar{x} - t \frac{s}{\sqrt{n}}, \qquad \bar{x} + t \frac{s}{\sqrt{n}}$$

where n is the sample size.
   t is the value in Table F for the row with $df = n - 1$ and the column with $P = 1 - \alpha/2$.
6. **The $100 \cdot p$th percentile estimate** for a normal population is

$$K_p = \bar{x} + \sqrt{1 + \frac{1}{n}} \, t_{(n-1)p} \cdot s$$

where $\bar{x}$ is the sample mean
   n is the sample size
   t is from Table F with $df = n - 1$ and the column corresponding to p.
   s is the sample standard deviation
7. **Scatter diagram.**
8. **The correlation coefficient:**

$$r = \frac{1}{n - 1} \sum_{i=1}^{n} \frac{(x_i - \bar{x}.)(y_i - \bar{y}.)}{s_x s_y}$$

is the sample correlation coefficient where

$$s_x = \frac{1}{n-1} \sum_{i=1}^{n} (x_i - \bar{x}.)^2 \quad \text{and} \quad s_y = \frac{1}{n-1} \sum_{i=1}^{n} (y_i - \bar{y}.)^2$$

Then

$$\rho = \frac{1}{n-1} \sum_{i=1}^{n} \frac{(x_i - \mu_x)(y_i - \mu_y)}{\sigma_x \sigma_y}$$

is the population coefficient and σ_x, σ_y are defined as usual

9. **Confidence interval for ρ** (Table G).
10. **Hypothesis test H: $\rho = 0$** (Table H).

CHAPTER 4
STATISTICAL
DATA PROCESSING

The objective of this chapter is to acquaint the beginning statistics student with the basics necessary to utilize data processing facilities. It is not intended as programming instruction, although a few programming statements will be introduced. The approach of this chapter is to describe briefly the major parts of high-speed computers and show the student how to use statistical programs that have already been written, which serve the needs of this book. Two programs with instructions for their use are provided here; these can be used if comparable programs are not available. It is hoped that the student will become aware of the time savings that are gained by the use of the equipment described.

HIGH-SPEED COMPUTING SYSTEMS

The term "computer" is almost a misnomer for the equipment we are discussing, for the same reason that the term "rocket" is inadequate to describe the complex aggregation of components used to boost astronauts into orbit and return them safely to earth. In the latter case the rocket must be supported by additional equipment at the launching site, an extensive communications system, and a group of highly trained personnel. In this context we speak not of a rocket or an aircraft, but of a "system" which includes not only the vehicle itself but also the support equipment and the people who are trained to operate the "hardware"; the entire system is an integrated whole.

In the same sense, the computer is but a small (and of course highly important) part of a data processing system. This system is most easily described in terms of the functional parts of the equipment:

1. Auxiliary storage media
2. Data recording equipment
3. Input-output devices
4. Central processing unit
   a. Control functions
   b. Arithmetic functions
5. Internal storage unit

The function of each of these groups of equipment can be briefly described as follows.

Auxiliary Storage Media

Information processed with high-speed equipment must be recorded on material that can be used for transferring the data to the computer, or central processing unit. These materials, or external storage media, include:

1. Cards, on which holes punched in certain positions represent numbers and/or characters
2. Magnetic tape, on which the data are recorded much as on home tape recorders.
3. Disks, on which the data are also recorded magnetically.

By external storage, we mean that the medium for recording the data is portable, and it can be completely separated from the hardware (see Figure 4–1).

Data Recording Equipment

The equipment for recording data on these media are usually designed with a typewriter-type console (Figure 4–2). In addition, a particularly useful piece of equipment for handling cards is the sorter, which can accomplish certain jobs far more inexpensively than can the computer facilities. The sorter will be discussed in detail later.

Input-Output Devices

Input-output devices are equipment designed to transfer data from the external storage media to the central equipment (input) and from the central equipment to the external storage media (output).

Often the input and output devices are incorporated into the same physical unit. Input-output devices for cards, tape, and disk appear in Figure 4–3.

(a)

(b)

(c)

FIGURE 4-2
Cardpunch equipment for recording data on external storage media. (Photo courtesy of IBM Corporation)

The Central Processing Unit (CPU)

This is the computer proper. It has two important functions:

1. When programs are written for the system, they are in the form of instructions given in sequence. Each instruction is called a *statement*, and they must be executed in the order given, for the same reason that the order in a series of arithmetic operations is important. Consequently, the computer system must be designed to keep track of the sequence of statements. This is often termed the *control function* of the central processing unit.

2. Arithmetic operations are also carried on in the CPU; data are brought

FIGURE 4-1
External storage media. (a) Data card; (b) Magnetic tape; (c) Disks with magnetic storage capacity. (Courtesy of IBM Corporation)

FIGURE 4-3
Input-output devices for cards, tape, and disk. (a) Card reader; (b) Card punch; (c) Tape drive; (d) Disk drives. (Photos courtesy of IBM Corporation)

from a storage unit to temporary storage positions within the CPU while the arithmetic operations are performed.

Internal or Core Storage Unit

This is the so-called *memory* of a computer system. It consists, usually, of thousands of tiny core magnets, each of which can have its magnetic field reversed, and each of which can be examined to determine the direction of the magnetic field at a given instant. A group of eight such cores can have many different combinations for the field direction of its members. For instance, if one field direction corresponds to 0 and the opposite direction to 1, then a string of eight cores can have a pattern such as

(4.1)   1 0 1 1 1 0 0 1

Many different numbers and characters can be represented by such patterns; such a group of cores is used to represent a single digit or character. A collection of strings, each with eight cores, can be used to form a large number or word; this is sometimes called a "core storage position."

We now have two storage places, internal and external storage. The advantage of the internal storage unit is that information can be obtained from it for processing very rapidly; its disadvantage is that it is much more expensive than the cost for the external storage media. A program can be written to use tape or disk storage during execution, if there is insufficient internal storage space for the task. This slows the program down but is less expensive,

FIGURE 4-4
Computer system, showing diagrammatic flow of information for processing.

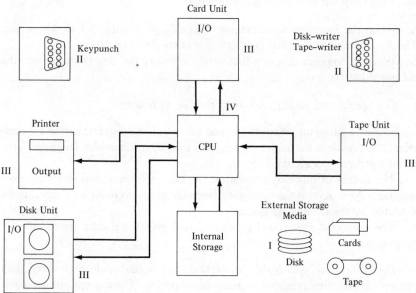

since internal storage space rents for more money than the equipment needed for tape or disk storage.

Figure 4–4 is a diagram of the component parts of a computer system.

COMPILERS

On most central processing units there are very few operations (usually about 30) that can be executed. The code for the execution of an operation is usually some combination of digits which serves to activate the hardware needed to carry out the operation. This would include addition, multiplication, and storage of data in a location. Each storage position has two numbers associated with it; the first tells where it is located (its *address*) and the second (which may be zero) is the number that has been stored at that address.

Motivation for the Use of Compilers

When the use of high-speed computers was beginning, the programmer had to include in his instructions where he wished to store his data (the exact number of the addresses); he then had to recall where he had stored it, so that he could get the data out of storage later. Further, suppose he wished to extract a square root. Arithmetically this is a long and involved process, and every time he wished to extract a square root, he had to repeat the process, possibly taking 30 to 50 instructions each time. The instructions were in what has since been termed "assembler language." This is simply a set of numeric codes which correspond to the 30 instructions that were available to the programmer. Programmers soon sought a new language that would be easier to use. One proposal was to do the following:

1. Write the language first, making it as easy as possible for people to use. The first version was called FORTRAN, for FORMULA TRANSlation.
2. Write a computer program that would translate the new language into the old assembler language.

The operational procedure would then be as follows:

1. Submit a program in FORTRAN, and use another program, called a "compiler," to translate the FORTRAN program into the "assembler language," the set of instructions executable by the machine.
2. The output of this first program is the same job translated into assembler language. Now submit the assembler language program in its own right, to be executed by the computing system.
3. The output of the second go-around will give the results desired by the programmer.

This procedure was highly successful, and it has made high-speed data processing facilities available to many more people. These steps are not obvious to the observer watching a computing system in operation, since the results of the first program are usually put on tape or disk and immediately resubmitted from there to the CPU upon completion of the translation. The process was more visible on some of the older machines, where the translation was punched out on cards and then manually put into the card input unit again, so that the observer could see what was happening. The new machines make the process almost as magical as that used for a modern dairy herd, where the milk is "untouched by human hands."

Some Technical Terms

Some technical jargon may be helpful to the reader.

Assembler Language: A set of codes corresponding to instructions that can be given sequentially, which the central processing unit is designed to execute.

Program: A set of sequentially ordered instructions designed to execute some computing task.

Compiler: The name of any program designed to translate some easier-to-use language into an assembler language.

Source Program: A program written in the easier-to-use language.

Object Program: The translation of the source program into assembler language.

FORTRAN: The name of the first successful language and compiler for scientific work. The name stands for FORmula TRANslation.

COBOL: The name of an early and successful language and compiler for business-oriented jobs. The name stands for commercial BUSINESS-oriented LANGUAGE.

USE OF A COMPUTER SYSTEM
The Basics of Program Utilization

Most data processing jobs are initiated with the use of cards rather than with tape or disk. The cards can be checked for errors before submission and, moreover, card-punching machines are less expensive. There are three sets of cards that must be filled out for each program:

1. The program itself, or "source deck." In our case, the source deck gives the formulas to be used in the statistical analysis.

2. The data cards. These are the observations obtained in the researcher's study which are to be analyzed. They are usually preceded by one or two cards that specify how many observations there are to be analyzed, how they are to be classified, and so on.

3. Systems cards. These are cards in a different language, which is usually unintelligible to most researchers. They specify the compiler to be used, the external storage units that will be needed (if any), and other information about the use of the computer center facilities. These vary from one facility to the

FIGURE 4–5

Decks to be submitted for data processing. (a) Program is not in computer center library and must be compiled; (b) program is in computer center library.

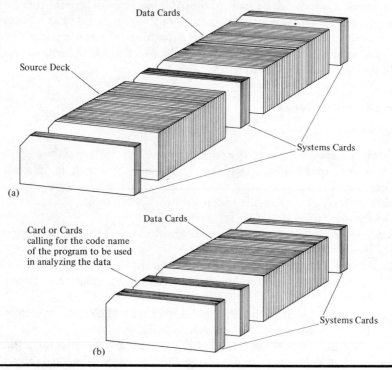

next, and they will not be discussed here. Details for these cards can be found at local computer centers. They usually are placed

a. Before the source deck
b. Between the source deck and the data
c. Following the data

Figure 4–5 is a diagram of a sample deck.

Sometimes a program is used so frequently that the computer center prefers to place the program in its library of programs which are kept available for users, without their having to submit the source deck each time. In this case a code is provided for that source deck, and the user submits (1) a systems card calling for that program, using the code, (2) other appropriate systems cards, and (3) the data deck. The deck submitted to the computer center is small, and the user is freed from having to keep a program deck on hand or worrying about its becoming dog-eared from use.

General Rules for Preparation of Data

One problem commonly encountered by research workers is entering data on cards so they may be used for later work. The cards must be useful not only for one analysis, but also for future work, where it is difficult to predict the exact way in which the data will be used. Often the first analysis of a set of data suggests other methods of analysis, and it would be very inconvenient to rework the cards by hand to make further analysis possible. A few basic rules are in order at this point.

1. Put all the data collected on cards *in their original form*, whether or not you plan to use all the data in your analysis. Let any changes (such as conversion to percentages or adjustment of scores to account for guessing) be made by the data processing unit, and have the results punched on another deck. It is also good policy to keep a duplicate of your original deck.

2. Document your data carefully, with a written description of what is entered in each column of your set of data cards. Much work is wasted by people who neglect to carry out this very simple step.

3. Use a separate card (or cards) for each sampling unit in the study and provide a code to enable the researcher to distinguish one sampling unit from the next. This is particularly important when anecdotal records are available for the sampling units.

4. If the order of the cards is important, a numbering sequence needs to be given, usually in the first or last set of adjacent columns. Then, if a deck is dropped, rearranging them in proper order requires a very few minutes on a card sorter.

Data Editing

Once the raw data are stored on cards, we may wish to modify these data prior to analysis. Or we may wish to use a program for analysis which requires that the data be in some rigid format, other than that in which we have prepared our raw data. In these cases, our conscientiousness in punching our data with a careful description of what we did will pay off. We next give a programmer a written description of how we want the data deck modified. Many computer centers have a standard program designed to "massage" data which will meet the researcher's needs with a minimum of programming effort.

Another way of solving the problems of data editing is found in some large university departments, where a programmer is hired specifically to assist social scientists in their research tasks. This is, in fact, a healthy sign; many research projects of consequence in the social sciences are the product of the work of interdisciplinary teams made up of people with diverse backgrounds. People with training in programming and quantitative methods frequently can be of help on teams of this type.

THE PREPARATION OF DATA CARDS

We now begin a more detailed description of how to prepare data for the computer. Figure 4–6 presents diagrams of the keyboards for the most

FIGURE 4–6

Keyboards for standard cardpunch equipment currently in use. (a) Keyboard of the 029 keypunch; (b) keyboard of the 026 keypunch. (Redrawn from *Comprehensive Standard Fortran Programming* by J. N. Haag, Hayden Book Company, New York, by permission of the publishers.)

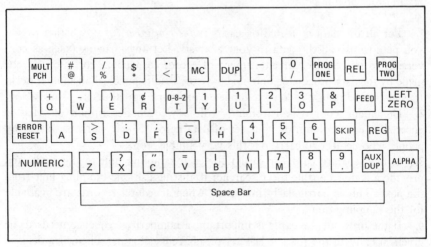

(a) The Keyboard of the 029 Keypunch

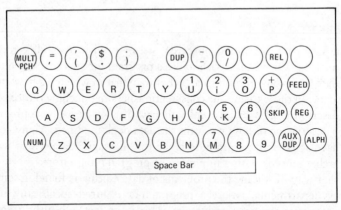

(b) The Keyboard of the 026 Keypunch

commonly used cardpunch (often called "keypunch") equipment and the card that is used with it. One card is used for each line of writing, or line of data. Each column on the card is used for one character or number. Hence, if you were given the information in Figure 4–7, you should interpret this as being 10 cards, the first requiring 30 columns, the second requiring 12 columns, and so on. Several rules for the interpretation of instructions of this kind now need to be given.

FIGURE 4-7
Illustration of a set of punched cards.

```
//bbJØBbbPEARSØNbbb878311,M002
//bEXECbDTPR
bbbb5bbb10
273252
281262
255256
261248
290279
/*
/&
```

1.   Ø stands for the letter O.
0 stands for the number zero.
Ƶ stands for the letter Z.
2 stands for the number 2.
I stands for the letter I.
1 stands for the number 1.

These distinctions are made because the symbols in question frequently are confused when written by most people.

2.   Upper case letters are to be punched literally on the card, in the appropriate column. Lower case letters are *not* to be punched (indeed they cannot be, since there are no lower case letters on the keypunch) but are instructions on how to treat that particular column. For example "b" in a space (corresponding to a column, on the card) means to leave that particular column blank—do not punch anything in it. The meaning of other lower case letters will be discussed later.

Figure 4–8 is a commonly used form to write instructions for filling out data cards. If this is used, the b's need not be written. Such forms are highly recommended; use them whenever they are available.

EXERCISE
4.1   Find a description of the basic systems cards to be used at your computer center for a simple FORTRAN program and punch one set of them.

Field Descriptors for Data

We begin this section by defining what we mean by a *field*. Figure 4–7 shows five cards, each of which has only six digits recorded on it. They are hypothetical STEP math and STEP read scores, each consisting of three digits, so that the scores for the first subjects are 273 and 252. The *field* for the STEP math score comprises columns 1 to 3, while that for the STEP read scores consists of columns 4 to 6. We express this notion formally in

IBM

FORTRAN Coding Form

GX28-7327-6 U/M 050**
Printed in U.S.A.

PROGRAM

PROGRAMMER | DATE

PUNCHING INSTRUCTIONS | GRAPHIC | | PUNCH

PAGE | OF

CARD ELECTRO NUMBER*

C STATEMENT NUMBER	CONT.	FORTRAN STATEMENT	IDENTIFICATION SEQUENCE

COMM.

*A standard card form, IBM electro 888157, is available for punching statements from this form

**Number of forms per pad may vary slightly

DEFINITION 4.1
In data processing terminology, a "data field" is a set of adjacent columns of a data card into which certain information is punched.

One procedure commonly followed is to use a separate card for each individual, or sampling unit, in the study, and then to record all measurements for that person on the card, with each measurement in a different data field. For example, in Figure 4–7, two data fields are specified for one person, one for the STEP math score and the other for the STEP read score.

Another commonly used procedure is followed if only one measurement is needed for each person in a group, but several groups of people are involved in the study. Now, put the first person in each group on the first card (so that if there are five groups, there will be five entries on the card), the second person of each group on the second card, and so on. The two arrangements are diagrammed in Figure 4–9.

When punching data to be used by a specific program, you will need to know how to describe, in programming terms, the fields you chose for each item; that is, the columns in which the data appear need to be specified before the program can be executed. Rules for giving these *field descriptors* follow:

1. The set of field descriptors corresponding to the data on one card is enclosed with parentheses.
2. Each piece of data (score or other number) on a card has a corresponding field descriptor, which describes the data field.
3. Each card in a deck is punched in the same way, so that the same set of field descriptors applies to each card in the deck.

FIGURE 4-9
Two ways to fill out data cards for an educational study. In (b) person 1 in GRP1 is not the same as person 1 in GRP2 or GRP3.

(a) SEVERAL MEASUREMENTS ON EACH PERSON IN ONE GROUP				(b) ONE MEASUREMENT ON EACH PERSON IN EACH OF SEVERAL GROUPS			
Card (person)	STEP MATH	STEP READ	T1 CH	Card (person)	GRP1	GRP2	GRP3
1	XXX	XXX	XX	1	XXX	XXX	XXX
2	XXX	XXX	XX	2	XXX	XXX	XXX
.							
.							
.							
n	XXX	XXX	XX	*n*	XXX	XXX	XXX

FIGURE 4-8
Commonly used form giving instructions for punching data cards. (Courtesy of IBM Corporation)

4. The descriptor for each data field is of the form Fw.d., where

    F   means that a decimal point appears somewhere in the number (it may or may not be punched in the card, since it can be automatically inserted when the number is stored in the computer).

    w   gives the number of adjacent columns used (the "width") for the data field.

    d   is the number of digits which are to the right of the decimal point.

5. The descriptor for each field *not* containing data (it may, in fact, contain data, but you wish to skip it) is wX, where w is the number of adjacent columns in the field (its "width").

6. The beginning column for each data field is not given. Instead, the field descriptors used are punched successively from left to right, and separated by commas, in the same order *in which the fields appear on the card*. The left-hand-most field descriptor refers to the field beginning in column 1; each later field descriptor takes up where the one before it leaves off.

We next consider some examples. Suppose each data card is of the form

```
1  2  3  4  5  6  7  8  9  10 11 12 13 14 15 16 17 18
      2  3  0  6              5  7  2
```

where the digits change from one card to the next. If the first number is 230.6 and the second is 572. and we omitted the decimals to save space and key-punching time, the set of field descriptors will be as follows:

$$(3X, F4.1, 3X, F3.0)$$

that is, "skip the first three columns; the next four are the first datum on the card, with one digit to the right of the decimal; skip the next three columns, the next three are the second datum, with no digits to the right of the decimal." If we had wished to punch the decimals, the data card would have been something like the following:

```
1  2  3  4  5  6  7  8  9  10 11 12 13 14 15
      2  3  0  .  6           5  7  2  .
```

and the set of field descriptors would be

$$(3X, F5.1, 2X, F4.0)$$

If we wish to ignore the first piece of data in the preceding card and store only the second, we would have, for our field descriptors,

$$(10X, F4.0)$$

EXERCISE

4.2   For each of the following data cards, write the appropriate set of field descriptors.

    a.   Two numbers, each of three-digit length, no digits to the right of either decimal.

```
1  2  3  4  5  6  7  8  9  10 11 12 13 14 15
2  6  9  2  5  3
```

b. Three numbers as given, one digit to the right of the decimal for the first, two to the right for the second, and none to the right for the third.

```
1  2  3  4  5  6  7  8  9  10 11 12 13 14 15
   1  5     2  3  6           1  8
```

c. Same as (b) above; ignore the middle number.
d. Same as (b) above; ignore the last number.

An additional rule is useful for simplifying field descriptors. Suppose we wish to enter the data for all four STEP examinations of each person on a single card, and further suppose that we wish to enter the data (three digits for each) in the first 12 columns of the card. Then a sample card would appear as follows:

```
1  2  3  4  5  6  7  8  9 10 11 12
2  7  3  2  5  9  2  6  5  2  8  1
```

and the set of field descriptors, as you have learned them, would be as follows:

(F3.0, F3.0, F3.0, F3.0)

A simpler way of writing this set of field descriptors is (4F3.0).

Suppose the card had been punched with one space between each number, as in the following example:

```
1  2  3  4  5  6  7 8 9 10 11 12 13 14 15 16
2  7  3     2  5  9  2  6  5     2  8  1
```

The set of field descriptors for this, as you have learned them, is

(F3.0, 1X, F3.0, 1X, F3.0, 1X, F3.0, 1X)

This can be written (4(F3.0, 1X)).

In general, suppose you have a pattern for recording part of your data which is repeated several times. Then enclose the part that is repeated in parentheses—call these internal parentheses, to distinguish them from the external parentheses—and precede the internal parentheses with a digit indicating how many times you want the pattern repeated.

EXERCISE

4.3 a. Rewrite the set of field descriptors for Exercise 4.2(a) in simpler form.
     b. Suppose a set of data is as follows:

```
1  2  3  4  5  6  7  8  9  10 11 12 13 14 15 16
   2  3  6        2  6  1        1  3
```

where there are no digits to the right of the decimal in any of the numbers. Write the field descriptors as first learned.
     c. Write the set of field descriptors in a simpler form for the card in (b) above.

Some More Field Descriptors

There are two more kinds of field descriptors that the student will use. We shall consider them in the following order:

1. The I-code, which is used when a decimal point is not part of the data.
2. The E-code, used primarily for output.

The form of the I-code is Iw, where the I means that there is no decimal point—that is, the number is an integer—and w gives the width of the data field, as usual. This form generally is not used to describe observations when computation is required. We will use the I-code when we need a code on a card to identify the person whose records are on the card; for example, we might want to know what population the person was selected from. Its use will be demonstrated later.

The motivation for the E-code is related to one limitation of the F-code. In Fw.d., the width of the data field and the number of places to the right of the decimal are given. For example, F4.2 must be of the form x.xx. Now suppose that we want a field descriptor for the output of a problem when we do not know how large the answer will be. Suppose we have used the descriptor F4.2; consider what to do if the number to be printed turns out to be 35.23 (that is, it is too large to be used with the F4.2 descriptor). There is no way of printing the correct number if it is too large for an F descriptor, but an E descriptor never has this difficulty. The form of the output is ±0.xxxx E xx, where the two digits to the right of the letter E indicate the number of places to the *right* the decimal should be moved to determine the correct number; alternatively, the output may be ±0.xxxx E-xx, where the two digits to the right of the letter E indicate the number of places to the *left* the decimal should be moved to determine the correct number. The sign to the left of the number is the sign of the number itself; the sign to the right of the letter E indicates whether the decimal should be moved to the right or left.

This type of descriptor is very seldom used for input. However since we never know what the answers will be, it is very common to use this form for output; it will be so used for the programs provided with this text.

EXAMPLES

E-TYPE DESCRIPTOR (EXPONENTIAL)	CONVENTIONAL NOTATION
.653271 E 02	65.3271
−.300200 E 01	−3.002
−.456032 E-03	−.000456032
.890346 E-02	.00890346

The E-code requires some additional discussion. The descriptor itself is of the form Ew.d, where w is the field width, as usual, and includes all the output, so that —.456032 E-02 has a field width of 13, for instance. Here d is the number of digits between the decimal place and the letter E. Since all but one place is to the right of the decimal, d represents the number of digits in the answer; this value can be varied at will.

EXERCISE
4.4 Convert the following data in exponential form to conventional notation:
   a. .6032 E 03   b. —.3021 E-01   c. —.9902 E 02
   d. .7891 E-01   e. .992367 E 04   f. .332098 E-01

The Card Sorter

Many statistical programs require that data cards be arranged in a certain order. Although such ordering is not required in this text, the data cards for later programs can be ordered on a sorter to illustrate the procedure. Here we will simply introduce the sorter and provide some very simple problems to demonstrate its capabilities.

A sorter presently in use is pictured in Figure 4–10; it has two functions:

1. All cards placed in the hopper are deposited into one of 11 pockets, according to whether the numeric entry in a specified column (controls on the machine enable you to specify the column) is 0, 1, 2, . . . , 9, or is blank. This enables the user to divide any deck of cards into subdivisions for which the entries in the specified column are all the same.
2. The sorter acts as a counter, giving the number of all cards placed in the hopper.

An exercise using the sorter will be given after the student has completed some preliminary exercises.

TWO USEFUL STATISTICAL PROGRAMS

The programs described in this section are reproduced in Tables K and L of the Appendix, so that they can be made operational if a similar program is not available at the facility on your campus. To make a program "operational," we mean that the proper systems cards for your equipment need to be punched, and someone must try the program to make sure it works. Nine times out of ten, it will not work the first time. Minor changes will need to be made; the best person to do this is one of the resident programmers who is hired by the computer center. The following programs are designed to do more than is described in this section; their other uses will be discussed later. Those using another program need not read further in this chapter.

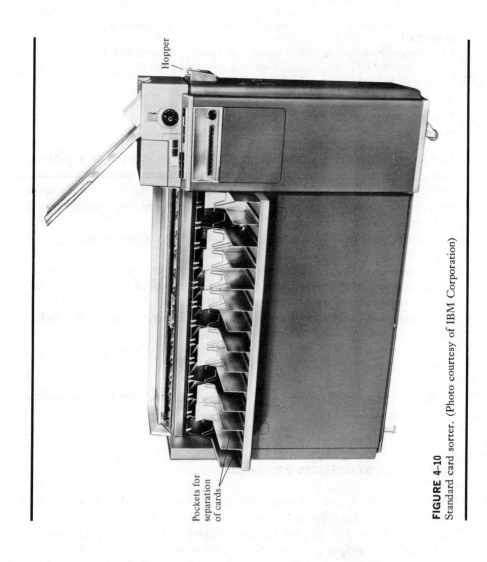

FIGURE 4-10
Standard card sorter. (Photo courtesy of IBM Corporation)

PRGM1: A Program to Calculate Means, Variances, Standard Deviations, Correlation Coefficients.

We will refer to this program as PRGM1. The cards that must be submitted to the computer center for this program are as follows:

1. Systems cards required by your computer center.
2. Source deck, which is the computer program for processing the data. (Appendix K presents a source deck.)
3. Systems cards between the source deck and the rest of the cards.
4. Control cards, which give information on how you want the program used.
5. Data cards.
6. Systems cards that terminate the execution of the program.

Cards for 1, 3, and 6 cannot be specified here—they will be in a fixed format, as given by your computer center.

The cards for 2 above need to be punched up exactly as in Appendix K as a starter; if they do not work, a local programmer can modify them.

The control cards for 4 above will be given next. In Figure 4–9, two kinds of data were shown. Part a indicated several measurements on each person, with *n* people involved. In part b one measurement was made on each person of several different groups of people, and *n* people were in each group. Either type of data is acceptable for this program. For type (a) data, correlation coefficients are appropriate; for type (b) data, they are not, since correlations are obtained between measurement made on the same people. Decide the information you need—based in part on the type of data you have—and fill out your control cards accordingly.

CONTROL CARD 1

Punch a verbal description of the job on this card. If your job is one of several student jobs, your own name may be sufficient; if you are submitting several jobs of your own, you may wish to describe each job with more detail than your name. You may use the entire card for this description, and any characters on a standard keypunch are acceptable. If you do not describe the job, you must still provide this control card; simply leave it blank.

CONTROL CARD 2

COLUMNS	DESCRIPTION OF ENTRY
1–5	The number of measurements on each person if type (a) data is used; the number of groups if type (b) data is used. Right-hand digit in column 5. This number is the same as the number of data fields across each card, and must be no more than 6.
6–9	Leave blank.
10	1 if the correlation coefficient between each of the groups is desired. Otherwise leave blank.
11–80	Leave blank.

CONTROL CARD 3

COLUMN	*DESCRIPTION OF ENTRY*
1	Left-hand parenthesis.
2–11	T78, A3, T1,
12–m, where m is as large as needed	The descriptors for the data fields running across each card. Use the rules provided in the section on Field Descriptors for Data. Remember that the number of fields you referred to as containing data on Control Card 3 must be the same as the first number on Control Card 2. No data should be planned for columns 78–80 in each card.
m + 1	Right-hand parenthesis.

Data Cards

Each card must be punched in a manner consistent with the set of field descriptors given on Control Card 2, with one card for each person if type a data is used, or one card for the data of k people if there are k groups. The last card must be blank, except for the word FIN in columns 78–80. This indicates that the end of the data has been reached.

Description of Computer Output

The first line of output is the contents of control card 1, giving your verbal description of the project. The next lines in the output give Control Cards 2 and 3 and the information on the data cards, so that you can check for possible errors. The next line gives the number of data cards (number of people) used in your deck, to enable you to verify your card count. Then for each group or measurement, output is given in the following form:

	GROUP OR MEASUREMENT NO.			
	1	*2*	...	$K \leq 6$
AVERAGE	XXXX	XXXX	...	XXXX
VARIANCE	XXXX	XXXX	...	XXXX
SORT	XXXX	XXXX	...	XXXX

for the means, variances, and standard deviations. Next are the correlation coefficients, if desired, in the following form:

MEASUREMENT NO.		*MEASUREMENT NO.*			
	1	*2*	*3*	*K-1*	*K*
1	1				
2	r_{21}	1			
3	r_{31}	r_{32}	1		
K − 1	$r_{K-1,1}$	$r_{K-1,2}$	.	1	
K	$r_{K,1}$	$r_{K,2}$	.	$r_{K,K-1}$	1

Where the value 1 appears in the correlation of any measurement with itself, and the value in row i and column j is the correlation between measurements i and j.

EXERCISES

4.5 Using the raw data of Table 3–3 (the first two columns), punch out the set of cards necessary to obtain the correlation coefficient between the science and math scores.

†4.6 Obtain a random sample of size 10 from each of the ability grouped and randomly grouped districts (use your data from Exercises 1.1 and 1.2, if you worked them) and use the computer to obtain the mean, variance, and standard deviation of the STEP science scores for each group. Do not obtain a correlation coefficient.

PRGM2: A Program to Obtain a Scatter Diagram

This program duplicates part of the computations of the preceding program. Although both are acceptable, PRGM2 takes longer both to punch and to execute, and some computer centers may look with disfavor on student use of programs this long. The objective is to avoid the tedium of plotting scatter diagrams by replacing the hand plot with a plot done on the printer. Another way out of this dilemma is to use a printer-plot routine provided in your own computer center or, finally, to have the printer-plot part of this program added to your computer center's library. You will notice that this program (Appendix K) is in two parts, the main program and a subroutine. This last part (which does the plotting) can be lifted out and used separately. Many computer centers have libraries of such subroutines, and if this one, or one like it, is in your library, the main program is all that is needed to carry out the procedure successfully. Unless the subroutine is *exactly* like this one, you will need to have your main program modified to use the subroutine. However, a program of this kind is usually popular, and it may prove to be worth all the effort needed to make it operational.

This program has the following arrangement:

1. Initial systems cards
2. Main program
3. Subroutine (plotter program)
4. Systems cards
5. Control cards
6. Data cards
7. Terminal systems cards

As for PRGM1, parts 1, 4, and 7 are predetermined by the computer center. Parts 2 and 3, in Appendix L, are to be punched exactly as they appear there. We consider parts 5 and 6 next.

CONTROL CARDS

Control Card 1 is the verbal description of the project, as discussed earlier; the entire card is available for it, and any character standard on the keypunch is acceptable.

Control Card 2 is left blank (but must be inserted). This program will do more than we are using it for here, and this card will be employed to use these other options.

Control Card 3 is for the two field specifications used for a single correlation coefficient, and it is used exactly as in PRGM1. It should be noticed that we do not have the option of relating more than two measures in the same run; we must specify the location of two measures only.

COLUMNS	DESCRIPTION OF ENTRY
1–11	(T78,A3,T1,
12–m, where m is as large as needed	Provide the field descriptors for x and y on the card
m + 1	Right-hand parenthesis

For example, if x is in columns 4–6, with y in columns 11, 12 (no digits to the right of the decimal in either number) then control card 3 would be (T78,A3,T1,3X,F3.0,4X,F2.0).

DATA CARDS

These must be punched consistent with Control Card 3 and with the last card being blank, except for FIN in columns 78–80.

Description of Computer Output

This simply consists of the plot of the data, with the correlation coefficient, R = .xxx, below the plot itself, and should be easy to interpret. An example appears in Appendix L.

EXERCISES

4.7 Obtain a computer plot for the scatter diagram of the data in Table 3–3.

4.8 With the data of Table 3–3, use the card sorter to arrange the cards so that the *x* variables (left-hand number) are in increasing order as one goes down through the deck. This can be done by ordering the cards on the basis of the column for the right-hand digit first; then the column for the next-to-right hand digit; and so on. In each case, after the cards are sorted, stack them with the 0 digits on top, the 1 digit next, and so on.

In Chapter 5, we will return to problems of statistical inference, armed with our new computing tools. In each of the remaining chapters, we will add to our collection of useful programs.

SOLUTIONS TO EXERCISES

4.2

a. F3.0,F3.0

b. 2X,F2.1,1X,F3.2,2X,F2.0

c. 2X,F2.1,6X,F2.0

d. 2X,F2.1,1X,F3.2

4.3

a. 2F3.0

b. 2X,F2.0,2X,F3.0,1X,F2.0

c. 2(2X,F3.0),1X,F2.0

4.4

a. 603.2

b. −.03021

c. −99.02

d. .07891

e. 9923.67

f. .0332098

4.5

Assume that the left-handmost character on the following lines is punched in column 1 of the data processing card. One line corresponds to one card.

```
R FOR DATA IN TABLE 3-3
     2      1
(T78,A3,T1,2F3.0)
269254
273253
258238

  .   (to end of data)
  .
259249
(final card is blank, until column 78)
```

Col. 78
↓
FIN

4.6

Random sample obtained as follows:

RANDOMLY GROUPED		ABILITY GROUPED	
266	267	274	244
269	269	287	302
269	272	266	279
279	259	254	253
273	261	271	269

Assume that the left-handmost character on the following lines is punched in column 1.

```
STEP SCIENCE SCORES FOR RG AND AG STUDENTS
     2
(T78,A3,T1,2F3.0)
266274
269287
269266
279254
273271
267244
269304
272279
259253
261269
(final card is blank, until column 78)
```

Column 78
↓
FIN

4.7

For parts 5 and 6, assume that the left-handmost character in the following lines is punched in column 1.

SCATTER DIAGRAM FOR DATA OF TABLE 3.3.
(T78,A3,T1,2F3.0)
269254
271253
273253

.
. (to end of data)

.   Col. 78

259249   ↓
(final card is blank, until column 78)   FIN

REVIEW FOR CHAPTER 4

1. **Layout of cards** for a data processing job.
2. **Field descriptors**
   a. Basic rules:
      Enclose field descriptors in parentheses.
      Same format for all cards in a deck.
      One field descriptor per number to be read (on each of the data cards).
   b. Fw.d is form of descriptor for numbers with decimals.
      w is width of data field.
      d is number of digits to right of the decimal.
   c. wX means "ignore the next w spaces."
   d. Field descriptors are given in order from left to right, beginning in column 1.
   e. Repeated field descriptors; use *n* (list of descriptors).
3. **More field descriptors.**
   a. Iw is form of descriptor for numbers without decimals.
      w is width of data field.
   b. Ew.d is form of descriptor whose dimensions cannot be exceeded in the output.
      Form of number is

$$\underbrace{\pm 0.\overbrace{XXX\ldots X}^{d}E \pm XX}_{w}$$

      w is width of entire data field.
      d is number of digits between the decimal place and the letter E.

CHAPTER 5
INFERENCE FOR
COMPARING
TWO GROUPS

INTRODUCTION

Chapter 3 was the first chapter in which we attempted to draw conclusions about a large group on the basis of a random sample selected from that group. We will expand our efforts in this chapter to include situations involving comparisons.

Comparisons may be drawn between two distinct groups of people, such as rural and urban populations or fast children and average children—or they may be between two halves of the same group which have been treated differently, as with experimental and control groups. In either case, we express the problem in terms of two populations, with a random sample drawn from each of them. We then must use the two random samples to compare the two populations. How we compare them depends on the objective we had in collecting the data; we now turn to an analysis of these goals.

Examples Involving Two Populations

We start by examining the types of questions that can be posed in comparing two populations. To make the problems concrete, suppose

1. A state introduces an adult training program for people wishing updated technical training for local industries. From among all applicants for training, half are selected at random and trained, and the average income of both the trained and untrained groups is obtained five years after completion of the training.

2. A district school superintendent wishes to try out a new math textbook and uses three classes selected at random to evaluate it in terms of end-of-year achievement scores. To control for "Hawthorne effect" (the tendency of a population to do better simply because it is part of an experiment), three more classes are selected to be part of the experiment with their achievement scores to be used for comparison purposes.

There are at least three kinds of questions we can ask for problems of this type:

1. Is there any difference between the population means for the two groups? In terms of the examples given above, we ask:

Does the training program modify the average income of those desiring training after a five-year period?

Does the new textbook change the average achievement scores of district students when compared with the scores of those who used the old textbook?

2. *How close* is the estimate of the difference between the population means to the actual difference? Again, let us consider the following examples:

Suppose the difference in income between sample means for trained versus nontrained personnel was $513 per year. We ask, How close is this difference to the gain we would have if everyone desiring it were trained?

Suppose the gain for the new textbook is 25 points in the four classes used for the project. The superintendent may ask, How close is this estimate to the average gain for the entire district if the book were to be adopted?

3. What action should we take, based on these results? In terms of the examples, this question is

Should the adult training program be adopted on a statewide basis?

Should the math textbook be used in the entire district?

Usually we do not address all three of these questions to the same data; the question to ask depends on the goals of the research project. These are not the only questions we can ask, but they are useful and will serve as an introduction to the topics of this chapter.

The problems described above will be discussed further after we consider some new information on statistical models and populations.

Review of the Situation for One Population

In Chapter 3, we considered the notations

$$(5.1) \qquad\qquad y \sim (\mu, \sigma^2)$$
$$(5.2) \qquad\qquad y \sim N(\mu, \sigma^2)$$

By (5.1) we mean that the random variable y comes from a population with mean equal to μ and variance equal to σ^2. By (5.2) we mean, in addition, that the population is normal. We now reconsider this notation and introduce some additional material that will be useful in comparing two populations.

Suppose we reconsider the population

(5.3)   2, 4, 6, 8, 10, 12

In this case,

(5.4) $$\mu = \frac{2 + 4 + 6 + 8 + 10 + 12}{6} = 7$$

Next let each observation be expressed in terms of the mean plus the deviation of the observation from the mean. For example,

(5.5)
$$
\begin{aligned}
y_1 &= 2 = 7 + (-5) = \mu + \epsilon_1 \\
y_2 &= 4 = 7 + (-3) = \mu + \epsilon_2 \\
y_3 &= 6 = 7 + (-1) = \mu + \epsilon_3 \\
y_4 &= 8 = 7 + (1) = \mu + \epsilon_4 \\
y_5 &= 10 = 7 + (3) = \mu + \epsilon_5 \\
y_6 &= 12 = 7 + (5) = \mu + \epsilon_6
\end{aligned}
$$

Note that ϵ_j represents the amount by which y_j differs from the population mean, μ. (ϵ is the Greek letter epsilon; ϵ_j is pronounced "epsilon sub j.") In terms of a formula, $\epsilon_j = y_j - \mu$ for all values of j. We can say that if the y_j are a population of observations, then the ϵ_j are also a population, where each ϵ_j is obtained by subtracting μ from y_j. Now

(5.6) $$y \sim (\mu, \sigma^2)$$

$$\mu = \frac{1}{N} \sum_{j=1}^{N} y_j$$

$$\sigma^2 = \frac{1}{N-1} \sum_{j=1}^{N} (y_j - \mu)^2$$

We recall Theorem 3.1 which states:

If the mean is subtracted from each observation in a population, a new population is generated which has a mean of zero and the same variance. In symbols,

(5.7)   if $y_j \sim (\mu, \sigma^2)$,   then $y_j - \mu \sim (0, \sigma^2)$

This is precisely the situation we now encounter; the set of ϵ_j are each obtained by subtracting μ from y_j. Thus the ϵ_j are a new population with zero mean and with variance unchanged, and we describe the situation as

(5.8)
$$y_j = \mu + \epsilon_j$$
$$\epsilon_j \sim (0, \sigma^2)$$
$$j = 1, 2, \ldots, n$$

The terms μ and ϵ_j are called the *components* of the observation y_j.

Equation 5.8 is a very simple case of what is sometimes called a statistical model. The word *model* refers to some set of symbols that is intended to reflect what is happening in the real world.

EXERCISES

5.1 Using the data of (5.5), verify that the population mean of the ϵ_j is zero and that the variances for the y_j and the ϵ_j are the same.

5.2 Given the population 1.2, .7, 9.8, 11.2, 21.1, 14.9, 5.8, decompose the observations y_j into components, as in (5.5).

5.3 Calculate the variance of the y_j's in Exercise 5.2. Calculate the mean and variance of the ϵ_j's.

A Statistical Model for Two Populations

Since in this chapter we are comparing two distinct groups, we will next expand the model just introduced to the case of two populations. There are at least two different kinds of situations involved here:

1. We can select a random sample from one population and divide it in half. Then we use some "treatment" such as a new teaching method, with one-half of the sample (often called the "experimental group") and leave the other half untreated (call this the "control group").

2. There may exist two distinct populations which we wish to compare with respect to some measurement, such as the people living in rural counties versus those in urban counties. Here we select a random sample from each group; which group a subject belongs to is not decided by the researcher, as in case 1 above.

The basic distinction between the two situations can be illustrated by a diagram, as in Figure 5–1.

Essentially, the distinction is that in case 1 above the difference between the two groups is imposed after the sample is selected, whereas in case 2, the sample is selected from each of two groups which are already different in some way.

Although the sampling procedures are different, both situations are considered as involving two populations: we sample from two distinct populations in case 2, and we consider the treatment and control groups as samples from two different populations for case 1.

FIGURE 5-1

Two situations for comparison of groups. (a) Experimental and control groups sampled from the same population; (b) sampling from two distinct populations.

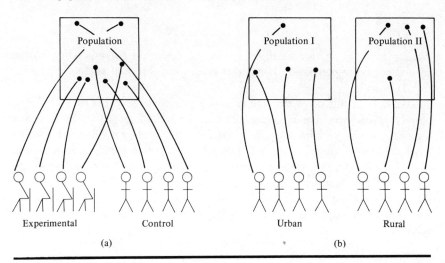

(a)   (b)

A warning is needed at this point. When treatments are imposed after selection of a sample we have reason to believe that there is a cause and effect relationship between the treatments and the resulting observations. If, however, sampling is carried out after the populations have been defined, we can come to no such conclusions. As an example, suppose that a test of social adjustment is administered to two areas, one rural and the other urban. We might be tempted to attribute differences to environmental differences. The danger is that the environmental differences were not imposed—in fact, the differences might well be racial, for example. Two distinct populations usually differ with respect to more than one characteristic, whereas if distinct treatments are imposed on split halves of a sample *from the same population*, the observations can differ only with respect to the treatments.

The model given at the beginning of this chapter must be extended to show two populations. We do this by using an additional subscript to distinguish between the two populations. We have

(5.9) $$y_{1j} = \mu_1 + \epsilon_{1j} \quad \text{for population I}$$
$$y_{2j} = \mu_2 + \epsilon_{2j} \quad \text{for population II}$$
$$\epsilon_{1j} \sim (0, \sigma_1^2)$$
$$\epsilon_{2j} \sim (0, \sigma_2^2)$$

Usually, the population sizes will be different (certainly the number of people in urban counties exceeds that for the rural counties, for instance) and we let

(5.10) $$j = 1, 2, \ldots, N_1 \quad \text{for population I}$$
$$j = 1, 2, \ldots, N_2 \quad \text{for population II}$$

The expression in (5.9) can be written more concisely as

(5.11)
$$y_{ij} = \mu_i + \epsilon_{ij}$$
$$\epsilon_{ij} \sim (0, \sigma_i^2)$$
$$i = 1, 2$$
$$j = 1, 2, \ldots, N_i$$

Note that $\epsilon_{12} \neq \epsilon_{22}$, for example; ϵ_{12} is the deviation corresponding to the second person in population I, whereas ϵ_{22} is for the second person in population II.

We note at this point that the sampling procedure used for case 2 is very closely related to what is commonly called *stratified sampling*. In stratified sampling, we begin with a single population; this is then divided into two or more subgroups, each of which is treated as a separate population. In case 2, we did not consider the two populations as comprising the larger one, although we could have. Both the sampling procedure and the analysis are the same, whether or not the two populations go together to make up one larger population. We will consider stratified sampling in greater detail later.

EXERCISES

5.4　Consider the following populations:

$y_{11} =$	6.5	$y_{21} =$	3.2
$y_{12} =$	2.3	$y_{22} =$	10.6
$y_{13} =$	9.8	$y_{23} =$	7.3
$y_{14} =$	6.7	$y_{24} =$	8.5
$y_{15} =$	4.9	$y_{25} =$	4.6
$y_{16} =$	11.2	$y_{26} =$	3.8

Decompose the y_{ij} into components and label each component as in Exercises 5.2 and 5.3, using the notation of (5.9).

5.5　Calculate μ_1, μ_2, σ_1^2, σ_2^2 for the data of Exercise 5.4.

The sampling model for the comparison of two groups is

(5.12)
$$x_{ij} = \mu_i + e_{ij}$$

where the x_{ij} are sampled from the population of y_{ij}, and the e_{ij} are the ϵ_{ij} corresponding to the y_{ij} that were selected. For example, suppose we select two observations from each of the populations in Exercise 5.4 at random, and further suppose that these observations are as follows:

FROM POPULATION I	FROM POPULATION II
(5.13)　　y_{13}, y_{12}	y_{25}, y_{23}

Then

(5.14)
$$x_{11} = y_{13} \qquad\qquad x_{21} = y_{25}$$
$$x_{12} = y_{12} \qquad\qquad x_{22} = y_{23}$$

In Exercise 5.4

$$\epsilon_{13} = 3.76 \qquad\qquad \epsilon_{12} = -3.64$$
$$\epsilon_{25} = -1.73 \qquad \text{and} \qquad \epsilon_{23} = .97$$

Hence

$$e_{11} = \epsilon_{13} = 3.76 \qquad\qquad e_{21} = \epsilon_{25} = -1.73$$
$$e_{12} = \epsilon_{12} = -3.64 \qquad\qquad e_{22} = \epsilon_{23} = .97$$

Note that the sample sizes frequently will be the same for the two populations, even though the population sizes are different.

EXERCISE

5.6 From each of the two populations of Exercise 5.4, select a random sample of size 2, and write the expressions for each observation in the form of (5.14).

Double Subscripts

We digress, for a moment, to introduce some new notation and to ensure that double subscript notation is familiar to all readers. In the preceding section, we used the notation y_{1j} to indicate observations that came from population I; in general, y_{ij} indicates the jth observation coming from population i. If we set these out in an array, we can indicate some new summation conventions, as in Table 5–1. This is an array corresponding to the data of Exercise 5.4. A term in the table margin represents the sum of all terms in the row or column in line with that term. Note that we may consider a summation over only one of the two subscripts i and j.

A shorthand notation for summed terms is given by capitalizing the summed quantity and replacing the subscript over which the term was summed with a

---

TABLE 5–1

Array of Subscripted Variables to Illustrate Summation Notation

ROW	COLUMN 1	2	3	4	5	6	SUM OF ith ROW
1	y_{11}	y_{12}	y_{13}	y_{14}	y_{15}	y_{16}	$\sum_{j=1}^{6} y_{1j} = Y_{1.}$
2	y_{21}	y_{22}	y_{23}	y_{24}	y_{25}	y_{26}	$\sum_{j=1}^{6} y_{2j} = Y_{2.}$
Sum of ith column:	$\sum_{i=1}^{2} y_{i1}$	$\sum_{i=1}^{2} y_{i2}$	$\sum_{i=1}^{2} y_{i3}$	$\sum_{i=1}^{2} y_{i4}$	$\sum_{i=1}^{2} y_{i5}$	$\sum_{i=1}^{2} y_{i6}$	$\sum_{i=1}^{2}\sum_{j=1}^{6} y_{ij}$
Dot notation:	$Y_{.1}$	$Y_{.2}$	$Y_{.3}$	$Y_{.4}$	$Y_{.5}$	$Y_{.6}$	$= Y_{..}$

dot. This notation is redundant; that is, it is not strictly necessary to both replace the subscript with a dot and capitalize the summed term. Past convention has used this procedure, however.

An additional shortening of subscript notation is

$$(5.15) \qquad \sum_{i=1}^{2} \sum_{j=1}^{6} y_{ij} = \sum_{ij} y_{ij}$$

that is, omit the subscript ranges, and put both subscripts under the same summation sign, if it is to be understood that we are summing over all values of both subscripts.

Since this notation will be used throughout the text, we generalize it. We consider the array

$$(5.16) \qquad \begin{aligned} & x_{ij} \\ & i = 1, 2, \ldots, k \\ & j = 1, 2, \ldots, n \end{aligned}$$

as outlined in Table 5–2.

TABLE 5–2
Generalized Array of Subscripted Variables Illustrating Summation Notation

ROW	COLUMN 1	2	...	j	...	n	ROW TOTALS
1	x_{11}	x_{12}	$\cdots$	x_{1j}	$\cdots$	x_{1n}	$\sum_{j=1}^{n} x_{1j} = X_{1.}$
2	x_{21}	x_{22}	$\cdots$	x_{2j}	$\cdots$	x_{2n}	$\sum_{j=1}^{n} x_{2j} = X_{2.}$
.							
i	x_{i1}	x_{i2}	$\cdots$	x_{ij}	$\cdots$	x_{in}	$\sum_{j=1}^{n} x_{ij} = X_{i.}$
.							
k	x_{k1}	x_{k2}	$\cdots$	x_{kj}	$\cdots$	x_{kn}	$\sum_{j=1}^{n} x_{kj} = X_{k.}$
	$\sum_{i=1}^{k} x_{i1}$	$\sum_{i=1}^{k} x_{i2}$	$\cdots$	$\sum_{i=1}^{k} x_{ij}$	$\cdots$	$\sum_{i=1}^{k} x_{in}$	$\sum_{i=1}^{k} \sum_{j=1}^{n} x_{ij} = X_{..}$
Column Totals	$X_{.1}$	$X_{.2}$		$X_{.j}$		$X_{.n}$	

EXERCISE

5.7 Let

$$z_{11} = 2.9 \quad z_{12} = 13.2 \quad z_{13} = 14.5 \quad z_{14} = 7.8$$
$$z_{21} = 12.3 \quad z_{22} = 4.5 \quad z_{23} = 7.1 \quad z_{24} = 8.7$$
$$z_{31} = 5.2 \quad z_{32} = 6.8 \quad z_{33} = 10.7 \quad z_{34} = 6.2$$

Calculate $Z_{.3}$, $Z_{2.}$, $\displaystyle\sum_{i=1}^{3} z_{i2}$, $Z_{..}$, $\displaystyle\sum_{i} z_{i1}$, and $\displaystyle\sum_{j} z_{3j}$

We next define $\bar{x}_{1.} = \dfrac{1}{n} \displaystyle\sum_{j=1}^{n} x_{1j}$, and, in general,

$$(5.17) \qquad\qquad \bar{x}_{i.} = \frac{1}{n} \sum_{j=1}^{n} x_{ij}$$

with

$$\bar{x}_{.j} = \frac{1}{k} \sum_{i=1}^{n} x_{ij} \quad \text{and} \quad \bar{x}_{..} = \frac{1}{kn} \sum_{ij} x_{ij}$$

These are the means for the observations in the ith row for $\bar{x}_{i.}$, and the jth column for $\bar{x}_{.j}$. The overall or "grand" mean is $\bar{x}_{..}$.

EXERCISE

5.8 Using the data of Exercise 5.7, obtain $\bar{z}_{.3}$, $\bar{z}_{2.}$, $\bar{z}_{..}$, and $\bar{z}_{.4}$.

The Population for the Difference of Two Sample Means

In this section, we will find some results that are useful for the problems of this chapter.

One basic objective of comparing two groups is to look at the difference between the means of the population from which they come. It seems reasonable that we should look at the difference between the sample means in order to learn about differences between the population means. It turns out that just as a sample mean has a population different from that of the original observations, so does the statistic obtained by selecting one sample mean from one population and a second sample mean from another population. Still a third population is generated, consisting of all possible mean differences, and its properties are given in

THEOREM 5.1

Let a random sample of size n_1 be selected from a population with mean μ_1 and variance σ_1^2, and let another random sample of size n_2 be selected from a second

population with mean μ_2 and variance $\sigma_2{}^2$. Then the population of such sample mean differences has mean $\mu_1 - \mu_2$ and variance equal to the sum of the variances of the sample means. In symbols,

$$(5.18) \qquad \text{If} \qquad x_{1j} \sim (\mu_1, \sigma_1{}^2) \qquad \text{and} \qquad x_{2j} \sim (\mu_2, \sigma_2{}^2)$$

$$\text{then} \qquad \bar{x}_1. - \bar{x}_2. \sim \left(\mu_1 - \mu_2, \frac{\sigma_1{}^2}{n_1} + \frac{\sigma_2{}^2}{n_2} \right)$$

EXERCISES

†5.9   The population of STEP science scores has mean 262.6 and variance 149.2 for the randomly grouped fifth grade children. For the corresponding ability grouped children the population mean and variance are 258.8 and 191.0, respectively. Select a random sample of size 3 from each of the randomly grouped and ability grouped districts, and subtract one mean from the other to obtain a single score. Repeat this process 10 times. Calculate your means on a high-speed computer. *Note:* By using END instead of FIN for the last card in each set of data cards, you can process them all with one run of the program.

‡5.10   Compile your 10 scores with those of the other class members, and calculate the following:

    a.   The mean of all such scores in the class (each the difference of two means).

    b.   The variance of all such scores.

In complex situations, we can no longer obtain entire populations for statistics—but the large number you obtain with the preceding instructions should be "close to" the population values. Let $M_{\bar{x}_1.-\bar{x}_2.}$ be the answer for (a) above, with $s^2_{\bar{x}_1.-\bar{x}_2.}$ the answer for (b). Compare $M_{\bar{x}_1.-\bar{x}_2.}$ with $\mu_1 - \mu_2$ and $s^2_{\bar{x}_1.-\bar{x}_2.}$ with $\sigma_1{}^2/n_1 + \sigma_2{}^2/n^2$. *Note:* $n_1 = n_2 = 3$.

STATISTICAL INFERENCE

We next concern ourselves with the three types of questions outlined at the beginning of the chapter. The following section deals with the first of these.

A Hypothesis Test for the Equality of Two Population Means

This section deals with the questions, Is there a difference between the means of two populations? If so, how large is it, and which of the two means is the larger?

A standard way of handling this type of problem is to assume that there is no difference between the population means, and *under this assumption* see whether the difference between the sample means is a plausible value. If not (that is, if the difference between the sample means is very large), reject the assumption and conclude that there is a difference.

This procedure is commonly called a *hypothesis test*. Hypothesis testing is a common approach to statistical inference in the comparison of two populations, and we will consider the topic now.

There is a specific order for reasoning used with this type of inference:

1. Specify the hypothesis H: $\mu_1 = \mu_2$ or $\mu_1 - \mu_2 = 0$.
2. Establish a rule for deciding when $\bar{x}_1. - \bar{x}_2.$ is so large that its coming from a population with mean $\mu_1 - \mu_2 = 0$ is not likely.
3. Observe $\bar{x}_1. - \bar{x}_2.$ and accept or reject H according to the rule.

The material of the preceding sections will be used to carry out these steps.

Step 1. If there is no difference between μ_1 and μ_2, then $\mu_1 - \mu_2 = 0$. Further,

$$(5.19) \qquad \bar{x}_1. - \bar{x}_2. \sim \left(\mu_1 - \mu_2, \frac{\sigma_1^2}{n_1} + \frac{\sigma_2^2}{n_2}\right)$$

so that

$$(5.20) \qquad \frac{\bar{x}_1. - \bar{x}_2. - (\mu_1 - \mu_2)}{\sqrt{\sigma_1^2/n_1 + \sigma_2^2/n_2}} \sim (0, 1)$$

by Theorem 2.2. Note that we have converted the difference between the sample means to standard form, in the manner of Chapter 2. Moreover, $\bar{x}_1. - \bar{x}_2.$ is approximately normal. This comes from a generalization of the central limit theorem (Theorem 2.5). Now assume $n = n_1 = n_2$, and substitute s_1^2 for σ_2^2 and s_2^2 for σ_2^2. By reasoning similar to that which resulted in Theorem 3.4, we find that Expression 5.20 with s_1^2 and s_2^2 substituted has Student's t-distribution. The degrees of freedom associated with it are the sum of the degrees of freedom for s_1^2 and s_2^2, which results in $n_1 + n_2 - 2 = 2n - 2$. Since $\mu_1 - \mu_2 = 0$, we conclude

$$(5.21) \qquad P\left[-t \leq \frac{x_1. - x_2.}{\sqrt{(s_1^2 + s_2^2)/n}} \leq t\right] = .95$$

where $t = t_{(2n-2).975}$.

Step 2. We now establish a rule. Since it is unlikely that the statistic

$$(5.22) \qquad \frac{\bar{x}_1. - \bar{x}_2.}{\sqrt{(s_1^2 + s_2^2)/n}}$$

will lie outside the limits $-t$ and t if $\mu_1 - \mu_2 = 0$, conclude that $\mu_1 - \mu_2 \neq 0$ if this event happens. We can put this in another way: If $\bar{x}_1. - \bar{x}_2.$ is a large value, we can either (1) conclude that an unlikely event has occurred, or (2) reject the assumption that makes the event unlikely. It is customary to do the latter, and we say that we *reject* the hypothesis H: $\mu_1 = \mu_2$ if expression 5.22 lies outside the limits $-t$, t. The fact that an error can be made needs to be emphasized. If there is no difference between the means, it is perfectly possible, on occasion, to have the statistic fall outside the prescribed limits. In fact, this will happen .05 percent of the time, on the average, with the limits we have used.

FIGURE 5–2
Idealized relative frequency histogram for a statistic having a *t*-distribution.

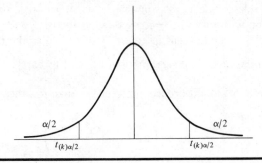

To illustrate, we consider a picture of the relative frequency histogram (Figure 5–2) for

$$(5.23) \qquad \frac{\bar{x}_1. - \bar{x}_2.}{\sqrt{s_1^2/n + s_2^2/n}}$$

If $\mu_1 = \mu_2$, then the mean of the distribution is at 0 as shown in the diagram, and $100 \cdot \alpha/2$ percent of the observations will be in each tail, *even if the difference is really equal to zero.* Your hope, as a researcher, is that this will not happen; therefore you make α small, so that this will be an unlikely event. To get a probability $= \alpha$ that the statistic lies in one of the tails, we put a probability of $\alpha/2$ in each tail. This gives the result of Theorem 5.2. This type of error—the rejection of a hypothesis when it is true—is called a *type I error.* Another type of error will be described later.

We now generalize and formalize this material in

THEOREM 5.2
Let $-t$ and t be values that contain $100 \cdot (1 - \alpha)$ percent of the observations which come from Student's t-distribution with k degrees of freedom. Further, let samples of the same size, n, be selected, either from two distinct populations or from the same population and treated differently, and let μ_1, μ_2 be the population means for the two groups. Then a rule for testing the hypothesis H: $\mu_1 = \mu_2$ is: accept H if

$$(5.24) \qquad -t \le \frac{\bar{x}_1. - \bar{x}_2.}{\sqrt{(s_1^2 + s_2^2)/n}} \le t$$

Reject H otherwise, where

$$s_i^2 = \frac{1}{n-1} \sum_{j=1}^{n} (x_{ij} - \bar{x}_{i.})^2$$

$$t = t_{(2n-2)\,1-\alpha/2}$$

This test has a probability $= \alpha$ of being rejected, if the means are, in fact, equal.

Step 3 is carried out by doing the exercises.

As an example, suppose we wish to determine whether the population mean for the "Me and School" (social adjustment) score of the slow ability grouped children differs from that of the slow randomly grouped children. We set out, therefore, to test the hypothesis $H: \mu_1 - \mu_2 = 0$, where μ is the "Me and School" population mean for the ability grouped children (slow level) and μ_2 is the same population mean for the randomly grouped students.

We begin by selecting a random sample of size 4 from each population, and obtain the following scores:

ABILITY GROUPED STUDENTS		RANDOMLY GROUPED STUDENTS	
ID	SCORE	ID	SCORE
78	22	92	65
21	18	14	40
51	44	77	61
6	57	73	31
$\bar{x}_1. = 35.25$		$\bar{x}_2. = 49.25$	
$s_1^2 = 340.92$		$s_2^2 = 268.25$	

To accomplish this, the ID numbers for slow children only were used (the ID3 column); there were 87 ability grouped and 97 randomly grouped students.

We next calculate the limits within which the expression

$$(5.25) \qquad \frac{\bar{x}_1. - \bar{x}_2.}{\sqrt{(s_1^2 + s_2^2)/n}}$$

ought to lie, if the population means are equal. To decide on α, we note that α is the probability of concluding that the means are different when in fact they are equal. If we let $\alpha = .05$, (with $n = 4$), then

$$(5.26) \qquad t = t_{(2n-2)1-\alpha/2} = t_{(6).975} = 2.447$$

where this value is obtained from Appendix Table F. But

$$(5.27) \qquad \frac{\bar{x}_1. - \bar{x}_2.}{\sqrt{(s_1^2 + s_2^2)/n}} = \frac{35.25 - 49.25}{\sqrt{(340.92 + 268.25)/4}} = -\frac{14.00}{12.34} = -1.13$$

Since 1.13 is within the limits -2.447 and 2.447, we accept $H: \mu_1 = \mu_2$ in; words, we say that we have no evidence for a difference in school adjustment between slow children who are grouped according to ability and those who are grouped in the conventional fashion.

EXERCISES

5.11 Obtain the values $t = t_{(2n-2)1-\alpha/2}$ if
    a. $\alpha = .10, n = 50$ b. $\alpha = .05, n = 20$
    c. $\alpha = .01, n = 35$ d. $\alpha = .50, n = 100$

5.12 Suppose a random sample of size 20 was selected from each of (1) the slow randomly grouped students and (2) the slow ability grouped students with the following results, using the STEP math scores:

SLOW RANDOMLY GROUPED STUDENTS	SLOW ABILITY GROUPED STUDENTS
243	231
245	244
250	239
244	231
258	238
241	235
231	252
258	230
254	243
250	245
239	236
231	235
230	249
241	243
249	245
245	233
233	233
245	230
247	241
243	249

Test the hypothesis that the difference between the population means for the two groups is zero. Let the probability of rejecting the hypothesis when it is true be .10.

†5.13 The students in the ability grouped district were divided on the basis of achievement. From this district, select a random sample of size 10 from the fast students, and another of size 10 from the slow students. List each number obtained from Appendix Table B for each group whether a student could be selected for it or not. Note that using the column headed ID would be very tedious; if you used this column, you would have to select a student, then examine his ability level, and continue to sample until five students are obtained for each level. A quicker way is to use the column headed ID1 (fast students) and that headed ID3 (slow students). For example, the identity numbers in column ID1 correspond only to fast students, so that when a student is selected using the numbers of this column, we are sure that he will be a fast student. From Appendix pages AA15 and AA12, we note that there are 136 fast students and 87 slow ones in the ability grouped district. We need this information to use Table B correctly. By using a statistical test with type I error of .05, answer the question, Do the two groups of students differ with respect to their attitudes about home? Use high-speed data processing equipment.

‡5.14 a. By compiling your results with those of the other class members, calculate the percentage of times the hypothesis was *rejected* in Exercise 5.13.

  b. Calculate the percentage of times the hypothesis was accepted. If $\mu_1 - \mu_2 = 0$, which is the error, part (a) or (b)? If H is false, which is the error, (a) or (b)?

A Confidence Interval for the Difference Between Two Population Means

Assuming that we have established the existence of a difference between two population means, we may now wish to set a confidence interval about the difference between these means. This is designed to answer one of the three basic questions: *How close* is the difference between the sample means to the difference between the population means?

We use the results of (5.20) to arrive at

$$(5.28) \qquad \frac{\bar{x}_1. - \bar{x}_2. - (\mu_1. - \mu_2)}{\sqrt{\sigma_1^2/n_1 + \sigma_2^2/n_2}} \sim N(0, 1)$$

approximately. At this point, we *do not* assume that $\mu_1 - \mu_2 = 0$; hence this expression does not vanish in (5.28). We substitute s_1^2 and s_2^2 for the corresponding values of σ_1^2 and σ_2^2 and, as before, we have

$$(5.29) \qquad \frac{\bar{x}_1. - \bar{x}_2. - (\mu_1 - \mu_2)}{\sqrt{(s_1^2 + s_2^2)/n}}$$

which follows Student's t-distribution with $2n - 2$ degrees of freedom. Thus

$$(5.30) \qquad P\left[-t \le \frac{\bar{x}_1. - \bar{x}_2. - (\mu_1 - \mu_2)}{\sqrt{(s_1^2 + s_2^2)/n}} \le t \right] = 1 - \alpha$$

or

$$(5.31) \quad P\left(\bar{x}_1. - \bar{x}_2. - \sqrt{\frac{s_1^2 + s_2^2}{n}} \cdot t \le \mu_1 - \mu_2 \right.$$

$$\left. \le \bar{x}_1. - \bar{x}_2. + \sqrt{\frac{s_1^2 + s_2^2}{n}} \cdot t \right) = \alpha$$

where

$$t = t_{(2n-2)\,1-\alpha/2}$$

using the inequality rules of Chapter 1. This results in

THEOREM 5.3
Let samples of the same size be selected, either from two distinct populations, or from the same population and treated differently, and let μ_1, μ_2 be the population means for the two groups. Then Expression 5.31 is a $(1 - \alpha) \cdot 100$ percent confidence interval for $\mu_1 - \mu_2$.

As an example, we use the same set of data previously used. Then, if we wish a 90 percent confidence interval, we have $\alpha = .10$, so that $\alpha/2 = .05$, $1 - \alpha/2 = .95$, and

$$(5.32) \qquad t = t_{(2n-2)\,1-\alpha/2} = t_{(6).95} = 1.943$$

From the previous example,

$$\bar{x}_1. - \bar{x}_2. = 14.00$$

$$\sqrt{\frac{s_1^2 + s_2^2}{n}} = 12.34$$

so that our confidence interval is

(5.33) $-(12.34)(1.943) + 14.00 \leq \mu_1 - \mu_2 \leq 14.00 + (12.34)(1.943)$
   $-9.98 = -23.98 + 14.00 \leq \mu_1 - \mu_2 \leq 14.00 + 23.98 = 37.98$

EXERCISES

5.15   From the data obtained earlier, construct:
  a.   A 90 percent confidence interval for $\mu_1 - \mu_2$, using the data of Exercise 5.12.
  †b.   A 90 percent confidence interval for $\mu_1 - \mu_2$, using the data of Exercise 5.13.

‡5.16   Compile the results of Exercise 5.15(b) with those of the class members and calculate the percentage of times that the confidence interval failed to include the correct value for $\mu_1 - \mu_2$.

---

*A Ranking Procedure for Population Means

This section gives procedures for answering the third question asked at the beginning of the chapter. The methods discussed here are designed to help us in making meaningful decisions. We return to the second example at the beginning of the chapter, and we modify it for our first example here. Suppose the textbook currently being used is old and out of print, and the superintendent wishes to choose one of two textbooks for the coming year. Note that now he is not interested in a conclusion to the effect that they are or are not different. In a hypothesis test, we have three alternative results:

1.   They are different and number 1 is better (when the t-test is significant and $\bar{x}_1. > \bar{x}_2.$).
2.   They are different and number 2 is better (when the t-test is significant and $\bar{x}_2. > \bar{x}_1.$).
3.   There is no evidence that they are different (when the t-test is not significant).

A diagram can show these alternatives:

Number 2 is better	No difference	Number 1 is better
$\bar{x}_1. - \bar{x}_2. < -l$	$-l \leq \bar{x}_1. - \bar{x}_2. = 0 \leq l$	$l < \bar{x}_1. - \bar{x}_2.$

In this case, however, the superintendent must choose one of the two books, and he is not permitted the luxury of the middle section of the diagram; he cannot stay on the fence.

There is a reasonable way of minimizing the risk when making such a decision. Consider the average district achievement scores for both textbooks. If either textbook is as much as two months ahead of the other, we want to be sure that we pick the best one; if their difference is less than two months, the decision is less crucial, and we can pick either one without being too far in error. Now any educator may quarrel with our choise of what is a meaningful difference, but he is at liberty to pick any other value which seems more appropriate to him. The point is that for each researcher, there is a difference (l months, say) small enough so that he will not quibble over which textbook to choose if the means differ by less than l.

Next notice that we have been referring to the difference between the population means, not the difference between the *sample* means. Let the sample means for populations 1 and 2 be $\bar{x}_1.$ and $\bar{x}_2.$.

We may find out $\mu_1 - \mu_2$ is greater than l but that $\bar{x}_1. - \bar{x}_2.$ does not reflect this, due to sampling error, and our decision must be based on $\bar{x}_1. - \bar{x}_2.$, since we do not know $\mu_1 - \mu_2$. The rule that we use is, Pick the population whose sample mean is greatest. In Table 5–3 we set up a chart showing what can happen. Notice that since we must make a choice, there is no middle column corresponding to the middle row for the actual situation. So far, we have said nothing about probability statements; now we restate our problem with this in mind:

If the difference between the population means is less than l units, the choice of either population is acceptable; otherwise, we wish to have a probability $\geq p$ of picking the best population.

Referring to Table 5–3, this means that if $\mu_1 - \mu_2 \geq l$, we want $P(\bar{x}_1. - \bar{x}_2. \geq 0) \geq p$, whereas if $\mu_1 - \mu_2 \leq -l$, then we want $P(\bar{x}_1. - \bar{x}_2. < 0) \geq p$. There will be no protection for the situation $-l \leq \mu_1 - \mu_2 \leq l$; this is the case for which we have said we do not need protection.

TABLE 5–3

Decision-Making Scheme for the Choice Between Two Populations

	RESULT OF EXPERIMENT	
ACTUAL SITUATION	$\bar{x}_1. - \bar{x}_2. > 0$ CHOOSE NO. 1	$\bar{x}_1. - \bar{x}_2. < 0$ CHOOSE NO. 2
$\mu_1 - \mu_2 \geq l$	Correct decision probability $\geq p$	Incorrect decision Probability $\leq 1 - p$
$-l < \mu_1 - \mu_2 < l$	Either decision is acceptable	Either decision is acceptable
$\mu_1 - \mu_2 \leq -l$	Incorrect decision Probability $\leq 1 - p$	Correct decision Probability $\geq p$

5.17   An educator wishes to make a decision about whether to switch to ability grouping on the basis of the data in Appendix Table A. He is interested in the social adjustment of the students, and he uses the "Me and School" scores and the following reasoning to evaluate the two districts. If the average of the two districts on the "Me and
School" test differs by more than 10 units, we wish to be sure with probability = .95
of picking the method of grouping which yields the best adjustment. Make up a chart
like Table 5–3, comparing alternative situations with experimental results, substituting
numerical values for p and l. Let population 1 correspond to random grouping; 2 to
ability grouping.

Statistical analysis for problems like Exercise 5.17 is deceptively simple,
but it must not be underrated. This analysis makes one additional assumption:
the variances for the two populations are equal or approximately equal. We
need two items of information to use the procedure: (1) the size, l, of the
difference within which the choice of either population is acceptable, and (2)
the required probability of making a correct decision. Given these two items,
the procedure gives us the sample size, n, to use. We next obtain a total of
$2n$ items (n from each population), and calculate $\bar{x}_1.$ and $\bar{x}_2..$ Then we pick
the population with the most favorable mean—that's all there is to it.

The only thing left to do is to decide on the sample size, n. This is done
in two stages. We first take a preliminary sample of size n_0 from each of the
two populations and obtain

(5.34)
$$s_1^2 = \frac{1}{n_0 - 1} \sum_i (x_{1i} - \bar{x}_1.)^2$$

$$s_2^2 = \frac{1}{n_0 - 1} \sum_i (x_{2i} - \bar{x}_2.)^2$$

$$s^2 = \frac{s_1^2 + s_2^2}{2}$$

Now s^2 is used to obtain the final sample size needed. Suppose l in Figure 5–3
is the size of the difference we want to be sure to detect. If the population
variance is small, as in (a), there is very little overlap between the populations,
and we can be almost sure of identifying the best population by selecting a
single observation from each. Not so with (b); where there is a lot of overlap, we need a larger number of observations to be sure that the ordering of the
sample means is not reversed from that of the population means.

Next we obtain $t_{[2(n_0-1)]p}$, the value from Table F that exceeds $p \cdot 100$ percent of the observations from a population with Student's t-distribution having
$2(n_0 - 1)$ degrees of freedom. Now take a second sample of $n - n_0$ observations from each population where n is the largest of n_0 and

(5.35)
$$\frac{2s^2 t_{[2(n_0-1)]p}^2}{l^2}$$

Note that n is the total number of observations selected in both preliminary

FIGURE 5–3

Two sets of populations, illustrating the importance of the variance in making decisions.

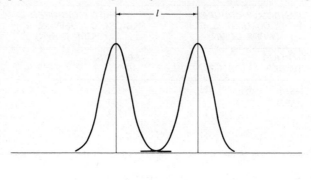

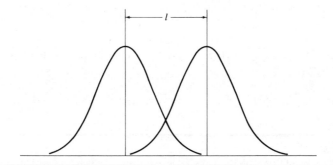

and final samples; in the final sample, take $n - n_0$ more observations. As stated earlier, all that is left to do is to calculate the two sample means, using all n observations in each mean; then choose the population with the most favorable mean. The method is due to Bechhofer et al.*

For example, suppose we wish to decide which of the two grouping methods yields the most favorable home adjustment. We use the "Me and Home" scores, and we decide that if a difference of five units exists between the means for the two districts, we want to be sure to pick the best one, with a probability of .95; this gives $l = 5$ and $p = .95$. We take a preliminary sample of size 5 from each population to get the set of random samples in Table 5–4. In Table 5–4, the location of the series of random numbers is given so that the use of random samples can be verified. Numbers that are inappropriate are omitted from the table.

From these data, we obtain

$$(5.36) \qquad s_1^2 = 130.30, \qquad s_2^2 = 11.70, \qquad n_0 = 5$$
$$s^2 = 71.0, \qquad \text{and} \qquad t_{[2(n_0-1)].95} = t_{(8).95} = 1.86$$

* F. E. Bechhofer, C. W. Dunnett, and M. Sobel, "A Two-Sample Multiple Decision Procedure for Ranking Means of Normal Populations with a Common Unknown Variance." *Biometrica*, **41,** 170–176 (1954).

TABLE 5-4
Random Samples from Two Districts for Comparison of Home Adjustment

| RANDOMLY GROUPED—PAGE B7, COLUMN 15, ROW 16 (WORK DOWN) | | ABILITY GROUPED—PAGE B4, COLUMN 32, ROW 21 (WORK DOWN) | |
SAMPLING NUMBER	OBSERVATION	SAMPLING NUMBER	OBSERVATION
176	17	221	3
195	32	147	5
72	6	246	12
121	4	92	8
337	9	133	8

Hence n is the largest of 5 and $2(71.0)(1.86)^2/25 = 19.7 \cong 20$. This tells us that we must take a random sample of 15 additional observations from each district. We list these in Table 5-5 and then take the sample means for the two populations:

$$\frac{1}{20} \sum_{j=1}^{20} x_{1j} = \bar{x}_{1.} = 10.7 \qquad \text{for the randomly grouped students}$$

$$\frac{1}{20} \sum_{j=1}^{20} x_{2j} = \bar{x}_{2.} = 12.6 \qquad \text{for the ability grouped students}$$

TABLE 5-5
Continuation of Sampling Begun in Table 5-4 (Sampling numbers used are resumed where those of Table 5-4 leave off.)

| RANDOMLY GROUPED | | ABILITY GROUPED | |
SAMPLING NUMBER	OBSERVATION	SAMPLING NUMBER	OBSERVATION
507	26	100	2
385	10	272	2
213	10	205	22
101	17	217	7
438	8	77	39
97	15	373	6
160	1	249	7
200	2	295	4
251	3	96	14
464	8	293	20
489	4	342	7
217	15	397	14
345	6	199	18
26	12	437	39
304	9	333	15
Total from both tables	214	Total from both tables	252
$\bar{x}_{1.}$	10.7	$\bar{x}_{1.}$	12.6

TABLE 5-6

Decision-Making Scheme for Choice of the School District
with Best Home Adjustment Scores

	RESULT OF EXPERIMENT	
ACTUAL SITUATION	$\bar{x}_1. - \bar{x}_2. > 0$ CHOOSE NO. 2	$\bar{x}_1. - \bar{x}_2. < 0$ CHOOSE NO. 1
$\mu_1 - \mu_2 \geq 5$		Error $P(\bar{x}_1. - \bar{x}_2. < 0) < .10$
$-5 < \mu_1 - \mu_2 < 5$		No protection
$\mu_1 - \mu_2 \leq -5$		Correct decision $P(\bar{x}_1. - \bar{x}_2. < 0) \geq .90$

We thus conclude that the randomly grouped students have fewer problems at home on the average than do the ability grouped students.

The procedure does not tell us whether the difference between the two population means is less than 5; it only protects us against the wrong decision if that difference is greater than 5. To reemphasize the point, we construct Table 5–6, similar to Table 5–3. The area for $\bar{x}_1. - \bar{x}_2. > 0$ is shaded since the result of the experiment was that $\bar{x}_1. - \bar{x}_2. < 0$. The point is that we do not know which of the alternative "actual situations" holds. What we do know is the probability of getting the results we did get under each of the alternative situations.

EXERCISE

5.18.   Suppose the data were collected for Problem 5.17, using $n_0 = 5$, and obtaining random samples as follows, for the two districts:

RANDOMLY GROUPED DISTRICT "ME AND SCHOOL"	ABILITY GROUPED DISTRICT "ME AND SCHOOL"
7	14
30	49
49	5
27	30
23	22

Determine the additional number of observations that must be selected from each district in order to achieve the objectives of Exercise 5.17.

Note that in Exercise 5.18 there is little to indicate how to choose n_0, the preliminary sample size. At least five observations seems to be a good rule; if we select a large number of observations for n_0, we may find that

$$(5.37) \qquad n_0 > \frac{2s^2 t_{(2n_0-2)p}^2}{l^2}$$

This means that the preliminary sample is larger than the total number needed to draw a valid conclusion; that is, the preliminary sample was too large and we have wasted our resources.

*Making a Decision Between Two Populations

Next we turn to another kind of problem commonly encountered in education. At the beginning of the chapter, we considered decisions regarding an adult training program and a new textbook on modern math.

An administrator is less interested in determining whether a training program does any good than he is in answering the question, Should we adopt this program? He requires that the program be *very* good before he even considers it; changes involve considerable time and effort in addition to money, and an administrator will want to ensure that he does not exhaust his resources on a mediocre program. In a similar way, a school superintendent will try to be sure that any major changes in curriculum (such as the adoption of an innovative textbook) produce enough improvement to counteract both the cost and possible criticism from a public who may want evidence that the change is in the best interests of their children.

In the first example, the reasoning of the administrator will be somewhat as follows: If the average yearly income five years later of those using the new adult training program is at least $1000 more than that for a control group, we will want to adopt it. If income is between $500 and $1000 more, either decision is acceptable, and if the gain is less than $500, we will definitely not want to use the new program.

Suppose the district using the new math textbook decides on an achievement test for all math students in his district. Then the superintendent can

---

FIGURE 5–4

Decision-making schemes for selection of alternative populations. (a) Choosing the best of two populations; (b) population 1 must be better than population 2 by a wide margin before being chosen.

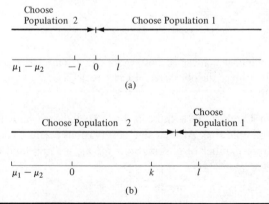

formulate the problem in the following manner: If the average achievement score for the classes using the new text is at least 30 points better than that for a control group, we will want to use the new text. If it is between 15 and 30 points better, either decision is acceptable. An advantage of not more than 15 points should result in a decision to stay with the old text. We want the probability of making the right decision to be at least .95.

These problems are very similar to the type described at the beginning of this section. There is only one difference. Earlier the region in which either decision was acceptable was from $-l$ to l. Now the region is not centered about zero but runs from k to l, as in Figure 5–4. Notice in situation (b) of Figure 5–4 that the dividing line for the decision based on $\bar{x}_1. - \bar{x}_2.$ is halfway between k and l, just as it was previously halfway between $-l$ and l. We choose population 1 if $\bar{x}_1. - \bar{x}_2.$ is closer to l; we choose population 2 if it is closer to k. We note that if $\bar{x}_1. - \bar{x}_2.$ is closer to l, then $\bar{x}_1. - \bar{x}_2. > (k + l)/2$; $\bar{x}_1. - \bar{x}_2.$ is closer to k if $\bar{x}_1. - \bar{x}_2. < (k + l)/2$ since $(k + l)/2$ is the midpoint between k and l. Again we set up a decision-making chart in Table 5–7.

As before, we can make a wrong decision (represented by areas labeled Error) and we want the probability of making a correct decision to be $\geq p$ if the actual situation is either $\mu_1 - \mu_2 \geq l$ or $\mu_1 - \mu_2 \leq k$.

To conduct the experiment, we obtain n_0 observations from each population as before, and calculate $s^2 = (s_1^2 + s_2^2)/2$. Then the total sample size to be obtained from each population is the maximum of n_0 and

$$(5.38) \qquad \frac{8s^2 t^2_{[2(n_0-1)]p}}{(l - k)^2}$$

As before, we augment our random sample from each population with $n - n_0$ additional observations, and we calculate $\bar{x}_1. - \bar{x}_2..$ If

$$\bar{x}_1. - \bar{x}_2. > (k + l)/2 \qquad \text{we choose the new population}$$
$$\bar{x}_1. - \bar{x}_2. < (k + l)/2 \qquad \text{we stay with the old one}$$

TABLE 5–7

Decision-Making Scheme for the Choice Between Two Populations Where One Must Be Better Than the Other by a Specified Margin Before Being Chosen

	RESULT OF EXPERIMENT	
ACTUAL SITUATION	$\bar{x}_1. - \bar{x}_2. > (k + l)/2$ (CLOSER TO l) CHOOSE NO. 1	$\bar{x}_1. - \bar{x}_2. < (k + l)/2$ (CLOSER TO k) CHOOSE NO. 2
$\mu_1 - \mu_2 \geq l$	Correct decision Probability $\geq p$	Error Probability $\leq 1 - p$
$k < \mu_1 - \mu_2 < l$	Either decision is acceptable	Either decision is acceptable
$\mu_1 - \mu_2 \leq k$	Error Probability $\leq 1 - p$	Correct decision Probability $\geq p$

TABLE 5-8

Decision-Making Scheme for Accepting or Rejecting a New Textbook When it Must Be Better Than the Old Textbook by a Specified Margin

	RESULT OF EXPERIMENT	
ACTUAL SITUATION	$\bar{x}_1. - \bar{x}_2. > 22.5$ (CLOSER TO 30) CHOOSE NEW TEXT	$\bar{x}_1. - \bar{x}_2. < 22.5$ (CLOSER TO 15) STAY WITH OLD TEXT
$\mu_1 - \mu_2 \geq 30$	Correct decision $P(\bar{x}_1. - \bar{x}_2. > 22.5) \geq .95$	Error $P(\bar{x}_1. - \bar{x}_2. < 22.5) \leq .05$
$15 < \mu_1 - \mu_2 < 30$	Either decision is acceptable	Either decision is acceptable
$\mu_1 - \mu_2 \leq 15$	Error $P(\bar{x}_1. - \bar{x}_2. > 22.5) \leq .05$	Correct decision $P(\bar{x}_1. - \bar{x}_2. < 22.5) \geq .95$

We continue our example, assuming that teachers 1–10 use the new book and 11–19 are a control group. Now we set up our decision chart in Table 5–8. Here $k = 15$ and $l = 30$, with $p = .95$, as required. Let population 1 correspond to the new text.

Next conduct the experiment, letting $n_0 = 5$; we obtain the sets of data in Table 5–9. There are 293 students in the classes of teachers 1–10, and 251 in those of teachers 11–19. Hence we use sampling numbers less than 294 for the new and less than 252 for the old text. To get the ID number for the old text, simply add 293 to the sampling number obtained from Table B. These data give $s_1^2 = 198.3$, $s_2^2 = 231.8$, and $s^2 = (s_1^2 + s_2^2)/2 = 215.1$. Further,

$$(5.39) \qquad t_{(8).95} = 1.86 \qquad \text{and} \qquad (l - k)^2 = 225$$

so that the total sample size needed will be the maximum of $n_0 = 5$, and

$$(5.40) \qquad \frac{8s^2 t_{(8),95}^2}{(l - k)^2} = \frac{8(215.1)(1.86)^2}{225} = 26.5 \cong 27$$

Hence we need to select $27 - 5 = 22$ more observations from each population. From the data in Table 5–10, we find $\bar{x}_1. - \bar{x}_2. = 2.9$. Our rule is to

TABLE 5-9

Preliminary Sample from Two Halves of Randomly Grouped District

SAMPLING NUMBER	OLD TEXT	SAMPLING NUMBER	NEW TEXT
245	287	93	274
208	289	11	280
69	260	90	271
133	271	68	242
101	260	190	276

TABLE 5–10
Completion of Sample from Two Halves of Randomly Grouped District

SAMPLING NUMBER (ADD 293 FOR ID NO.)	OLD TEXT	SAMPLING NUMBER	NEW TEXT
3	286	78	247
105	276	34	265
99	265	32	257
57	255	101	286
23	274	81	269
167	246	2	276
203	260	56	280
26	247	54	260
69	260	113	251
236	271	239	271
249	274	47	253
155	257	7	247
75	261	291	267
92	274	108	278
122	274	220	278
237	265	182	269
119	276	282	298
174	271	271	276
179	252	154	271
117	259	164	274
225	253	196	248
208	265	237	265
	5821		5886
	$\bar{x}_2. = 264.6$		$\bar{x}_1. = 267.5$

pick the new text if $\bar{x}_1. - \bar{x}_2.$ is closer to 30 than to 15; since this is clearly not the case, we stay with the old text.

We summarize this process in

THEOREM 5.3
Suppose two population means are to be compared under the following conditions:

a. *If $\mu_1 - \mu_2 \geq l$, population 1 is to be chosen.*
b. *If $k < \mu_1 - \mu_2 < l$, either choice is acceptable.*
c. *If $\mu_1 - \mu_2 \leq k$, population 2 is to be chosen.*

Then the following procedure has a probability $\geq p$ of choosing the correct population, if condition a *or* c *holds:*

1. *Choose a preliminary random sample of size n_0 from each population with observations $x_{i1}, x_{i2}, \ldots, x_{in_0}$ where $i = 1, 2$.*
2. *Calculate*

$$s_i^2 = \frac{1}{n_0 - 1} \sum_{j=1}^{n_0} (x_{ij} - \bar{x}_i.)^2$$

$$i = 1, 2$$

where

$$\bar{x}_{i\cdot} = \frac{1}{n_0} \sum_{j=1}^{n_0} x_{ij}$$

$$s^2 = \frac{(s_1^2 + s_2^2)}{2}$$

3. *Obtain n, the maximum of*

$$n_0 \quad and \quad \frac{8s^2 t^2_{[2(n_0-1)]p}}{(l-k)^2}$$

4. *Select a random sample of $n - n_0$ additional observations from each population, and calculate*

$$\bar{x}_{1\cdot} = \frac{1}{n} \sum_{j=1}^{n} \bar{x}_{1j} \quad and \quad \bar{x}_{2\cdot} = \frac{1}{n} \sum_{j=1}^{n} x_{2j}$$

using the observations from both the preliminary and final random samples.
5. *Choose population no. 1 if*

$$\bar{x}_{1\cdot} - \bar{x}_{2\cdot} > \frac{(k+l)}{2}$$

Choose population no. 2 if

$$\bar{x}_{1\cdot} - \bar{x}_{2\cdot} < \frac{(k+l)}{2}$$

No probability statement can be made about the decision if condition b *holds.*

Note that the theorem stated in this fashion includes the case for which we simply want the best of two populations; in that case, $k = -l$.

EXERCISES

5.19   Suppose a school superintendent decides that he will base his decision to change to an ability grouping system on a comparison of the districts in Appendix Table A. He reasons that if average achievement for the district on the STEP reading score is up 35 points, he wants to be sure to change to ability grouping. If the gain is between 15 and 35 points, either decision is acceptable; and he wishes to stay with the old grouping plan if the gain is less than 15 points. The complete data are not available to him, and he must sample from each district in order to make his decision. He selects a random sample of size 8 from each, with the following results:

RANDOMLY GROUPED DISTRICT STEP READING SCORE	ABILITY GROUPED DISTRICT STEP READING SCORE
280	259
307	259
248	251
234	226
239	263
276	251
256	251
267	295

What sample size should he use if he wants a probability = .90 of making a correct decision when the gain is not between 15 and 30 points?

†5.20 Consider only the bright children from the ability grouped and randomly grouped populations. We want to know whether the ability grouping procedure is justified for bright students. We decide that if the advantage of the ability grouped students is 30 or more points in reading achievement, we will conclude that ability grouping is justified for the bright students; if the advantage is less than 20 points, we will reject the ability grouping system. Determine the sample size needed to help decide the matter, with a protection of .90 against making the wrong decision. Use a preliminary sample size of 8 from each population.

†5.21 Carry out the decision-making procedure set up in Exercise 5.20, and draw your own conclusion.

‡5.22 Compile your answer with those of the other members of your class. Calculate the percentage of decisions of each kind.

DATA PROCESSING

Relatively little about programming need be added to this chapter. By using PRGM1, or one like it, we can obtain the means and standard deviations for both samples. Here the correlation coefficient will be zero except for sampling error since there is no reason to believe that subject no. 1 in the first sample is in any way related to subject no. 1 in the second sample, and so on. Accordingly, we use the option to depress the output for the value of r. All that is left is to combine the sample variances for the two populations and to calculate

$$\frac{\bar{x}_1. - \bar{x}_2.}{\sqrt{(s_1^2 + s_2^2)/n}}$$

which is not difficult.

Experiences with Data

As before, the questions in this section are left unstructured, and to answer them, the student is required to carry out the following steps:

1. Decide what measure or measures should be used to help answer the question.
2. Make a sampling plan for collection of data.
3. Execute the sampling plan.
4. Analyze the data, using computer facilities if you wish. Make your own decision with respect to your method of analysis.
5. Draw conclusions on the basis of your findings.

It should be pointed out here that these questions are not limited to problems whose solution is dealt with in this chapter alone. At each stage we will feel free to ask questions that involve any method which has been previously discussed; on occasion, more sophisticated questions will be asked. If the "best" ways to solve the problem have not been treated, you will need to devise your own way of solving it; a simple way will suffice). By taking advantage of data processing facilities, you will be able to try more approaches to a problem in a given length of time.

PROBLEMS

5.1 Is there a real advantage to ability grouping for children, on the average?

5.2 What are the effects of ability grouping on social adjustment?

5.3 Does each of the *non*-"academic achievement" scores really measure a different facet of adjustment, or are they essentially measuring the same thing?

5.4 Is the advantage (or disadvantage) of ability grouping the same for all subject matter areas, or does the effect of ability grouping depend on the academic subject being considered?

5.5 Is the advantage (or disadvantage) of ability grouping the same for all ability levels, or does the effect of ability grouping depend on the ability level of the child?

5.6 Is home adjustment related to achievement at school?

5.7 Within the randomly grouped district, is there any genuine difference in achievement between schools 10 and 11? Interpret your results.

SOLUTIONS TO EXERCISES

5.1

$$y_1 = 2 = 7 + (-5) = \mu + \epsilon_1$$
$$y_2 = 4 = 7 + (-3) = \mu + \epsilon_2$$
$$y_3 = 6 = 7 + (-1) = \mu + \epsilon_3$$
$$y_4 = 8 = 7 + (1) = \mu + \epsilon_4$$
$$y_5 = 10 = 7 + (3) = \mu + \epsilon_5$$
$$y_6 = 12 = 7 + (5) = \mu + \epsilon_6$$
$$\mu_\epsilon = -5 + -3 + -1 + 1 + 3 + 5 = 0/6 = 0$$
$$\sigma_y{}^2 = \tfrac{1}{6}[(2-7)^2 + (4-7)^2 + (6-7)^2 + (8-7)^2 + (10-7)^2$$
$$+ (12-7)^2]$$

$$= \tfrac{1}{5}(25 + 9 + 1 + 1 + 9 + 25)$$
$$= \tfrac{1}{5}(70)$$
$$\sigma_y{}^2 = 14$$
$$\sigma_\epsilon{}^2 = \tfrac{1}{5}[(-5 - 0)^2 + (-3 - 0)^2 + (-1 - 0)^2 + (1 - 0)^2 + (3 - 0)^2$$
$$+ (5 - 0)^2]$$
$$= \tfrac{1}{5}(25 + 9 + 1 + 1 + 9 + 25)$$
$$= \tfrac{1}{5}(70)$$
$$\sigma_\epsilon{}^2 = 14$$

5.2

$$y_1 = 1.2 = 9.24 + (-8.04) = \mu + \epsilon_1$$
$$y_2 = .7 = 9.24 + (-8.54) = \mu + \epsilon_2$$
$$y_3 = 9.8 = 9.24 + (.56) = \mu + \epsilon_3$$
$$y_4 = 11.2 = 9.24 + (1.96) = \mu + \epsilon_4$$
$$y_5 = 21.1 = 9.24 + (11.86) = \mu + \epsilon_5$$
$$y_6 = 14.9 = 9.24 + (5.66) = \mu + \epsilon_6$$
$$y_7 = 5.8 = 9.24 + (-3.44) = \mu + \epsilon_7$$

5.3

$$\sigma_y{}^2 = \tfrac{1}{6}[(1.2 - 9.25)^2 + (.7 - 9.24)^2 + (9.8 - 9.24)^2 + (11.2 - 9.24)^2$$
$$+ (21.1 - 9.24)^2 + (14.9 - 9.24)^2 + (5.8 - 9.24)^2]$$
$$\sigma_y{}^2 = 54.38$$
$$\mu_\epsilon = 0$$
$$\sigma_\epsilon{}^2 = \tfrac{1}{6}[(-8.04 - 0)^2 + (-8.54 - 0)^2 + (.56 - 0)^2 + (1.96 - 0)^2$$
$$+ (11.86 - 0)^2 + (5.66 - 0)^2 + (-3.44 - 0)^2]$$
$$= 54.38$$

5.4

$$y_{11} = 6.5 = 6.90 + (-.40) = \mu_1 + \epsilon_{11}$$
$$y_{12} = 2.3 = 6.90 + (-4.60) = \mu_1 + \epsilon_{12}$$
$$y_{13} = 9.8 = 6.90 + (2.90) = \mu_1 + \epsilon_{13}$$
$$y_{14} = 6.7 = 6.90 + (-.20) = \mu_1 + \epsilon_{14}$$
$$y_{15} = 4.9 = 6.90 + (-2.00) = \mu_1 + \epsilon_{15}$$
$$y_{16} = 11.2 = 6.90 + (4.30) = \mu + \epsilon_{16}$$
$$y_{21} = 3.2 = 6.33 + (-3.13) = \mu_2 + \epsilon_{21}$$
$$y_{22} = 10.6 = 6.33 + (4.27) = \mu_2 + \epsilon_{22}$$
$$y_{23} = 7.3 = 6.33 + (.97) = \mu_2 + \epsilon_{23}$$
$$y_{24} = 8.5 = 6.33 + (2.17) = \mu_2 + \epsilon_{24}$$
$$y_{25} = 4.6 = 6.33 + (-1.73) = \mu_2 + \epsilon_{25}$$
$$y_{26} = 3.8 = 6.33 + (-2.53) = \mu_2 + \epsilon_{26}$$

5.5

$$\mu_1 = 6.90; \qquad \mu_2 = 6.33; \qquad \sigma_1{}^2 = 10.45; \qquad \sigma_2{}^2 = 8.61$$

5.6

If the random samples happen to be 3, 6 for population 1; 5, 1 for population 2:
$$y_{13} = x_{11} = 9.8 \qquad y_{25} = x_{21} = 4.6$$
$$y_{16} = x_{12} = 11.2 \qquad y_{21} = x_{22} = 3.2$$

Then

$$y_{13} = 9.8 = 6.9 + (2.9) = \mu_1 + \epsilon_{13}$$
$$y_{16} = 11.2 = 6.9 + (4.3) = \mu_1 + \epsilon_{16}$$
$$y_{25} = 4.6 = 6.3 + (-1.7) = \mu_2 + \epsilon_{25}$$
$$y_{21} = 3.2 = 6.3 + (-3.1) = \mu_2 + \epsilon_{21}$$
$$x_{11} = 9.8 = 6.9 + (2.9) = \mu_1 + e_{11}$$
$$x_{12} = 11.2 = 6.9 + (4.3) = \mu_1 + e_{12}$$
$$x_{21} = 4.6 = 6.3 + (-1.7) = \mu_2 + e_{21}$$
$$x_{22} = 3.2 = 6.3 + (-3.1) = \mu_2 + e_{22}$$

5.7

$$Z_{.3} = 32.3 \qquad \sum_j z_{3j} = 28.9 \qquad Z_{..} = 99.9$$

$$Z_{2.} = 32.6 \qquad \sum_{i=1}^{3} z_{i2} = 24.5 \qquad \sum_i z_{i1} = 20.4$$

5.8

$$\bar{z}_{.3} \cong 10.8; \qquad \bar{z}_{..} = 8.325; \qquad \bar{z}_{2.} = 8.15; \qquad \bar{z}_{.4} \cong 7.6$$

5.9

The following set of control and data cards used with PRGM1 will result in two means for each set of data; subtract one from the other to obtain the ten single scores referred to in the problem. Assume that the left-handmost character in the following lines is punched in Col. 1.

SAMPLE DATA FOR EX. 3.9
```
            2
(T78,A3,T1,2F3.0)
262256⎫
249282⎬ 1st set of data                              Col. 78
260264⎭                                                  ↓
                                                        END
261269⎫
283269⎬ 2nd set of data
267246⎭
          .
          .
264269⎫
263254⎬ 10th set of data
252259⎭
                                                        FIN
```

5.11

a. 1.663 b. 2.024 c. 2.654 d. .674

[*Note:* When $2(n-1)$ is considerably above 120, use $df = \infty$.]

5.12

$$\bar{x}_1 = 243.85 \qquad \alpha = .10 \qquad s_1^2 = 68.45$$
$$\bar{x}_2 = 239.10 \qquad \alpha/2 = .05 \qquad s_2^2 = 47.67$$
$$df = 38 \qquad 1 - \alpha/2 = .95 \qquad t_{[2(n-1)]1-\alpha/2} = t_{(38).95} = 1.687$$

Calculate

$$\frac{\bar{x}_1 - \bar{x}_2}{\sqrt{(s_1^2 + s_2^2)/n}} = \frac{4.75}{2.41} = 1.97$$

This value should lie between -1.687 and 1.687 if the hypothesis is true. Since it does not, we reject the hypothesis and conclude that $\mu_1 - \mu_2 \neq 0$; that is, the average achievement level for the slow randomly grouped children is not the same as that for the slow ability grouped children. On the basis of the evidence collected here, which method of grouping would you recommend for slow children?

5.13

Random samples obtained were:

Fast students: 3, 4, 18, 0, 0, 39, 9, 1, 10, 22; $\bar{x}_1 = 10.6$
Slow students: 4, 27, 11, 22, 3, 11, 11, 19, 18, 11; $\bar{x}_2 = 13.7$

Assume that the left-handmost characters in the following lines are in column 1.

HOM SCORES FROM AG DISTRICT, FAST AND SLOW
  2
(T78,A3,T1,2F2.0)
0304
0327
1811
0022
0003
3911
0911
0119   Col. 78
1018   ↓
2211
                                                            FIN

$$\frac{\bar{x}_1 - \bar{x}_2}{\sqrt{(s_1^2 + s_2^2)/n}} = \frac{10.5 - 13.7}{\sqrt{(158.5 + 58.9)/10}} = \frac{-3.2}{4.66} = -.69$$

$t_{[2(n-1)]1-\alpha/2} = t_{(18).975} = 2.101 = t$. Since the above quantity lies between t and $-t$, we accept the hypothesis $\mu_1 - \mu_2 = 0$.

5.15

a. $\sqrt{\dfrac{s_1^2 + s_2^2}{n}} = 2.41$

$\bar{x}_1 - \bar{x}_2 = 4.75$
$t = t_{[2(n-1)]1-\alpha/2} = t_{(38).95} = 1.687$
$2.41(-1.687) + 4.75 \leq \mu_1 - \mu_2 \leq 4.75 + 1.687(2.41)$
$-4.07 + 4.75 \leq \mu_1 - \mu_2 \leq 4.75 + 4.07$
$P[.68 \leq \mu_1 - \mu_2 \leq 8.82] = .90$

5.17

ACTUAL SITUATION	$\bar{x}_1 - \bar{x}_2 > 0$ CHOOSE RANDOM GROUPING	$\bar{x}_1 - \bar{x}_2 < 0$ CHOOSE ABILITY GROUPING
$\mu_1 - \mu_2 \geq 10$	Correct decision Probability $\geq .95$	Incorrect decision Probability $\leq .05$
$-10 < \mu_1 - \mu_2 < 10$	Either decision is acceptable	Either decision is acceptable
$\mu_1 - \mu_2 \leq -10$	Incorrect decision Probability $\leq .05$	Correct decision Probability $\geq .95$

5.18

$s_1^2 = 227.2;$ $s_2^2 = 281.5;$ $s^2 = 254.35;$ $p = .95;$ $l = 10;$
$n_0 = 5;$ $t_{(8).95} = 1.86;$
$n = 2(254.35)(1.86)^2/100 = (508.7)(3.46)/100 = 17.6 \cong 18$
Thirteen additional observations needed from each district.

5.19

$n_0 = 8;$ $s_1^2 = 585.7;$ $s_2^2 = 365.3;$ $s^2 = 475.5;$ $l = 35;$ $k = 15$
$t_{(14).90} = 1.345, 8(475.5)(1.345)^2/400 = 6881.53/400 = 17.20 = 18$
He would need ten additional observations from each population.

5.20

$n_0 = 8;$ $l = 30;$ $k = 20;$ $p = .90;$ $t_{(14).90} = 1.345$
Select a random sample of size 8 and make your own decision.

REVIEW FOR CHAPTER 5

1. Double subscript notation

$$x_{ij}$$
$$i = 1, 2, \ldots, k$$
$$j = 1, 2, \ldots, n$$
$$X_{i.} = \sum_{j=1}^{n} x_{ij} \qquad X_{.j} = \sum_{i=1}^{k} x_{ij}$$
$$X_{..} = \sum_{i=1}^{k} \sum_{j=1}^{k} x_{ij} \qquad \bar{x}_{i.} = \frac{1}{n} \sum_{j=1}^{n} x_{ij}$$

2. The statistical model for two populations:

$$X_{ij} = \mu_i + \epsilon_{ij}$$
$$i = 1, 2$$
$$j = 1, 2, \ldots, n$$
$$\epsilon_{ij} \sim (0, \sigma_i^2)$$

3. Hypothesis test for the equality of two population means, with Type I error equal to α:

$$x_{ij} \sim (\mu_i, \ \sigma_i^2)$$
$$i = 1, 2$$
$$j = 1, 2, \ldots, n$$

Note that a sample of size n is selected from each population.

The hypothesis, $H: \mu_1 - \mu_2 = 0$

Rule: Accept H if

$$-t \le \frac{\bar{x}_1. - \bar{x}_2.}{\sqrt{(s_1^2 + s_2^2)/2}} \le t$$

Reject otherwise, where

$$s_i^2 = \frac{1}{n-1} \sum_{j=1}^{n} (x_{ij} - \bar{x}_i.)^2$$

This hypothesis will be rejected $\alpha \cdot 100$ percent of the time when it is true.

4. $(1 - \alpha) \cdot 100$ percent confidence interval for the difference between two population means:

$$\bar{x}_1. - \bar{x}_2. - \sqrt{(s_1^2 + s_2^2)/n} \cdot t \le \mu_1 - \mu_2 \le \bar{x}_1. - \bar{x}_2. + \sqrt{(s_1^2 + s_2^2)/n} \cdot t$$

This interval will include the true difference $(1 - \alpha) \cdot 100$ percent of the time.

5. To determine the sample size needed to properly rank (with probability equal to p) two population means whose difference is at least l units: Select a preliminary sample of n_0 observations from each population and calculate:

$$s^2 = \frac{(s_1^2 + s_2^2)}{2}$$

Then the total sample size is

$$n = \frac{2s^2 t_{(2n_0-2)p}^2}{l^2}$$

unless $n < n_0$. Select $n - n_0$ additional observations from each population.

CHAPTER 6
CATEGORICAL DATA

This chapter is concerned with statistical treatment of data for which numerical measures are not appropriate. These kinds of data are constantly encountered in the social sciences, and an increasing amount of attention is being paid to them by both research workers and mathematicians. Specifically we are interested in ways in which people can be classified rather than measured. For instance, an interviewee either is or is not married; is male or female; belongs to one of several alternative racial groups; and so on. In none of these cases can we order the classifications to say that one classification is "greater than" another. Even when ordering is possible, the measure that would be used for ordering frequently is so rough that a classification scheme is better.

DESCRIPTION OF THE PROBLEM

To clarify these points we will consider an example from the data provided in the text. Suppose we are interested in the relationship between sex and sociometric classification for the fifth grade randomly grouped students. Sex cannot be associated with a numerical value; and although the sociometric classification was obtained from the number of times a student was chosen by others, we can consider it a nonnumerical value for the moment. We ask the question, In this population, does the sex of the individual affect the chance of being an isolate or a star? (Those who are never chosen on the sociometric score are considered "isolates," whereas those chosen often are "stars.")

To investigate this problem, we will select a random sample of students and classify each one after selection. The random sample selected is given in Table 6–1 with classifications. Using these results we set up Table 6–2, which gives a count of the number of people found in each combination of sex and sociometric classification.

TABLE 6–1

Relationship According to Sociometric Classification and Sex of a Random Sample of Fifth Grade Students

ID NUMBER	SEX	SOCIOMETRIC CLASSIFICATION
270	B	3
192	B	2
362	G	2
492	B	4
324	G	4
165	B	3
57	B	3
151	B	3
177	G	3
458	G	2
478	G	3
7	B	3
415	G	2
259	B	2
442	B	4
353	G	3
1	B	3
49	G	3
93	B	4
307	B	2
196	B	3
112	G	2
532	G	2
309	B	3
500	B	1

TABLE 6–2

Contingency Table for a Random Sample of Randomly Grouped Fifth Grade Students, Giving Number of People in Each Combination of Sex and Sociometric Level

SEX	SOCIOMETRIC CLASSIFICATION			
	1 (ISOLATE)	2	3	4 (STAR)
Boy	1	3	8	3
Girl	0	5	4	1

Our question was, Is sex related to sociometric classification? In more concrete terms, we may ask whether a boy or a girl has a better chance of being a star or an isolate. From brief examination of Table 6–2 we surmise that a boy has a better chance than a girl of being either a star or an isolate. The next question to ask is, Do these results reflect the characteristics of the population from which the sample was taken, or are they the result of random fluctuation?

The remainder of this chapter is devoted to the problem of inferring characteristics of a large population on the basis of a random sample when the data are categorical in nature. Before considering this question, however, we need to introduce some basic notions of probability, which will help you understand the methods of this chapter.

INTRODUCTORY PROBABILITY

To introduce the concepts of probability, we will consider the population of randomly grouped fifth grade students classified on the basis of

1. Sociometric category
2. Ability group in which they were placed (1 = bright, 2 = average, 3 = slow)

Since some students had one or the other measure missing, a total of only 527 (instead of 544) can be classified in this way; we will consider this group as our population. The number in each classification appears in Table 6–3.

Our first definition is very specific; we plan to make it more general later.

DEFINITION 6.1
If a student is selected randomly from the population of randomly grouped fifth grade students, the probability that he or she is an isolate is defined as 8/527. The probability that a student is a star is defined as 97/527.

This definition for the probability that a student will be in a certain category is presented as a "reasonable" definition. One feels intuitively that if there is no way of knowing beforehand which student will be selected, then the *proportion* of times a star will be selected should be close to 97/527 if the selection process is repeated many times. Some people feel more at home with the term *percentage;* a probability is a percentage divided by 100.

Note that the number in each classification is in the bottom row of Table 6–3. This is because the numbers in the body of the table correspond to people who are in two categories simultaneously; in other words, there are five slow students who are also stars. The number who are stars *without regard to their*

TABLE 6–3
Contingency Table for the Population of Randomly Grouped Fifth Grade Students Classified According to Ability Level and Sociometric Level

ABILITY LEVEL	SOCIOMETRIC CLASSIFICATION				
	1 (ISOLATE)	2	3	4 (STAR)	TOTAL
1	3	59	143	66	271
2	3	70	65	26	164
3	2	48	37	5	92
Total	8	177	245	97	527

ability level is the total of stars in all three ability levels. This number—97—thus corresponds to the total.

DEFINITION 6.2
The fact that a student selected is a star, an isolate, or in any other classification is termed an "event."

Using as our example the sociometric classifications of Table 6–3, there are four possible events. That is, a student selected at random will be in one of four categories—sociometric classification 1, 2, 3, or 4. We let symbols stand for events; in this case let B_i represent the event, "The student is in sociometric classification i."

DEFINITION 6.3
The event U is considered as the aggregate of all possible events.

In our case, U is equal to the collection B_1, B_2, B_3, B_4; U stands for the "universe" of all possible events.

DEFINITION 6.4
If E represents a type of event, then $N(E)$ is the possible number of events of that type. Frequently, E is described as a set or collection of events of a specified type.

As an example, using the data of Table 6–3 (with SC = sociometric classification):

$$(6.1)$$

B_1 is the set of isolates	$N(B_1) = 8$
B_2 is the set with SC = 2	$N(B_2) = 177$
B_3 is the set with SC = 3	$N(B_3) = 245$
B_4 is the set of stars	$N(B_4) = 97$
	$N(U) = 527$

DEFINITION 6.5
The probability of an arbitrary event type, E, is defined as

$$(6.2) \qquad \frac{N(E)}{N(U)} = P(E)$$

This last definition is the generalization of Definition 6.1 and is consistent with it. That is,

$$(6.3) \qquad P(B_4) = \frac{N(B_4)}{N(U)} = \frac{97}{527}$$

EXERCISES

6.1 Calculate the probability that a student selected randomly from the population of randomly grouped fifth grade students is

    a. A slow student.

    b. An average student.

    c. A fast student.

†6.2 Select a random sample of size 20 from the population of Exercise 6.1. Count the number of students in each ability level and compare the *proportions* with the corresponding probabilities.

We will next consider situations involving more than one type of event. We begin with

DEFINITION 6.6

If X and Y are sets of events, then $X \cap Y$ is read "intersection of X and Y," and is interpreted to mean that event types X and Y have occurred together.

As an example, suppose we let A_1 represent the fast students, A_2 the average students, and A_3 the slower ones. Then

$$A_2 \cap B_1$$

represents the set of students who are of average ability and are also isolates. Referring to Table 6–3, we note that in our case

(6.4) $$N(A_2 \cap B_1) = 3$$

EXERCISES

6.3 Using the notation provided in this section, give the symbolism and the possible number of events for

    a. Fast students who are stars.

    b. Fast students who are isolates.

    c. Average students who are in SC 3.

    d. Average students.

    e. Fast students.

6.4 Select a random sample of size 50 from the population of Table 6–3. Count the number of students in each combination of ability level and sociometric level, and compare the *proportions* with the corresponding probabilities.

6.5 Fill in all probabilities for the entire Table 6–3.

Next we need a symbol for a set with no elements in it.

DEFINITION 6.7

The set having no elements in it is denoted as ϕ (the Greek letter phi).

An example of this set is the set of students of average ability who are also of superior ability in the population of randomly grouped fifth grade students; that is,

(6.5) $$A_2 \cap A_1 = \phi$$

Thus ϕ is the element in set notation that corresponds to zero. That is, if

(6.6) $$A_2 \cap A_1 = \phi, \quad \text{then} \quad N(A_2 \cap A_1) = 0$$

and if

$$N(A_2 \cap A_1) = 0, \quad \text{then} \quad A_2 \cap A_1 = \phi$$

In the same vein, we note that a student will only be in one sociometric classification at a time; that is, a student cannot be both a star and an isolate, or a star and also in sociometric classification 3. Hence

(6.7) $$\begin{aligned} B_1 \cap B_2 = \phi \quad & B_2 \cap B_3 = \phi \\ B_1 \cap B_3 = \phi \quad & B_2 \cap B_4 = \phi \\ B_1 \cap B_4 = \phi \quad & B_3 \cap B_4 = \phi \end{aligned}$$

or, in a briefer notation,

(6.8) $$B_i \cap B_j = \phi \quad \text{if} \quad i \neq j$$

Next consider another symbolism.

DEFINITION 6.8
If X and Y are sets of events, then $X \cup Y$ is read "union of X and Y" and is interpreted to mean that either event type X or event type Y, or both, has occurred.

For examples, we return to Table 6–3. The set of students who are not isolates is denoted

(6.9) $$B_2 \cup B_3 \cup B_4$$

The students who are either fast or stars are $A_1 \cup B_4$, as diagrammed in Table 6–4. The shaded portion represents $A_1 \cup B_4$, so that

(6.10) $$N(A_1 \cup B_4) = 3 + 59 + 143 + 66 + 26 + 5 = 302$$

and

(6.11) $$N(A_1 \cap B_4) = 66$$

EXERCISE
6.6 Again using the notation of this section, give the symbolism and possible number of events for
   a. Students who are of average ability or of either one of the two "middle" sociometric classes
   b. Students who are either isolates or of low ability

TABLE 6–4
Contingency Table to Show the Union of High Ability-Level Students with Stars

ABILITY LEVEL	SOCIOMETRIC LEVEL				TOTAL
	1	2	3	4	
1	3	59	143	66	271
2	3	70	65	26	164
3	2	48	37	5	92
Total	8	177	245	97	527

Now note that from the results of Exercise 6.1,

$$(6.12) \qquad \sum_{i=1}^{4} P(B_i) = 1$$

This reflects a general property of probabilities which is expressed in

THEOREM 6.1
If (1) *the B_i exhaust all possible events $(i = 1, 2, \ldots, n)$, and (2) $B_i \cap B_j = \phi$,
then*

$$(6.13) \qquad \sum_{i=1}^{n} P(B_i) = 1$$

By $P(E) = 1$ we mean that the event E is sure to happen; we interpret $P(E) = 0$ to mean that E is sure *not* to happen. Probabilities are best thought of by the beginning student as proportions, or percentages; and by convention, we will not permit proportions greater than 1 or percentages greater than 100.

Conditional Probabilities

It is now essential that we consider a form of probability in which the sets are restricted in a certain sense. Suppose, returning to Table 6–3, we want to find the probability that a student is a star, when we already know that he is of average ability. We have restricted the set of students being considered to those of average ability only. In this situation the set of possible events is A_2 instead of U. Furthermore, the set of events for which we wish the probability is $B_4 \cap A_2$. The point is illustrated in Table 6–5.

All possible events are indicated by shading; these consist of all the average students. Our particular concern at the moment is to obtain the propor-

TABLE 6-5

Contingency Table for Illustration of Conditional Probability

ABILITY LEVEL	SOCIOMETRIC LEVEL				TOTAL
	1	2	3	4	
1	3	59	143	66	271
2	3	70	65	26	164
3	2	48	37	5	92
Total	8	177	245	97	527

tion of all the average students who are also stars. The *number* of average students who are also stars is $N(A_2 \cap B_4)$. The number of possible events is $N(A_2)$. We define the conditional probability that a student is a star *given that he is of average ability* as

$$(6.14) \qquad P(B_4|A_2) = \frac{N(B_4 \cap A_2)}{N(A_2)}$$

This is the number of the events under consideration, divided by the number of possible events. The preceding expression (6.14) is to be compared with

$$(6.15) \qquad P(B_4) = \frac{N(B_4)}{N(U)}$$

which is the unconditional probability that a student is a star.

We calculate the numerical values for (6.14) and (6.15) as an example:

$$P(B_4) = \frac{97}{257} \cong .184$$

$$P(B_4|A_2) = \frac{26}{164} \cong .159$$

These results tell us that the probability a student will be a star is lower if he is selected from the students of average ability than if he is selected from the entire population, without restriction.

EXERCISES

6.7 Calculate the probability that a student is of average ability if he is a star. Calculate the unconditional probability that a student is of average ability. State your interpretation of the meaning of the difference between the two values.

6.8   Calculate the probability that a student is in sociometric class 2 given that:
   a.   He is of low ability.
   b.   He is of average ability.
   c.   He is of high ability.
Does your knowledge of a student's ability tell you anything about the degree to which he is accepted by his classmates? Interpret your results.

Statistical Independence

The concept of conditional probability will be used here to define the notion of statistical independence. The concept of "independence" is important in virtually all branches of statistics; it was first encountered in this text in the definition of a random sample.

We begin with an intuitive definition; we say that sociometric classification is *independent* of ability level if the ability level of the student tells us nothing about which sociometric class the student is likely to be in. This is just the opposite of what we observed in Tables 6–3 to 6–5; that is, the likelihood of a student being popular increases with greater ability. Hence the ability level of the student is definitely helpful in telling us something about his or her sociometric class.

Next we seek a way of expressing independence algebraically. Our reasoning is as follows: If ability level tells us nothing about the sociometric class, then the conditional probability that a student is a star given that he is of high ability should be the same as the unconditional probability that he is a star. That is, the additional knowledge that the student belongs in class B_4 has not modified the probability. In symbols, we can say

(6.16) $$P(B_4|A_1) = P(B_4)$$

Now we do some algebra:

(6.17) $$P(B_4|A_1) = \frac{N(B_4 \cap A_1)}{N(A_1)} = \frac{N(B_4)}{N(U)} = P(B_4)$$

Multiplying both sides of this equality by $N(A_1)$, and then dividing by $N(U)$

(6.18) $$N(B_4 \cap A_1) = \frac{N(B_4)N(A_1)}{N(U)}$$

(6.19) $$\frac{N(B_4 \cap A_1)}{N(U)} = \frac{N(B_4)}{N(U)} \cdot \frac{N(A_1)}{N(U)}$$

or

$$P(B_4 \cap A_1) = P(B_4)P(A_1)$$

We have thus said that if the event B_4 is independent of A_1, the probability that the two events occur together is the product of their unconditional probabilities. Therefore (using Table 6–5) if B_4 is independent of A_1, we should have

$$(6.20) \qquad P(B_4 \cap A_1) = P(B_4)P(A_1)$$
$$\frac{66}{527} = \frac{97}{527} \cdot \frac{271}{527}$$

The left-hand side of this expression is .125; the right-hand side is .095, approximately. Thus, using our definition, the two events are not independent, and

$$(6.21) \qquad P(B_4 \cap A_1) \neq P(B_4)P(A_1)$$

We now extend this definition to include sets of events.

DEFINITION 6.9
The sets A_i $(i = 1, 2, \ldots, r)$ and B_j $(j = 1, 2, \ldots, c)$ are said to be statistically independent if

$$(6.22) \qquad P(A_i \cap B_j) = P(A_i)P(B_j)$$

for all i and j. Here r stands for the number of rows and c for the number of columns.

We consider a simple example. Table 6–6 gives a hypothetical contingency table contrasting ability level with sex. From the table,

$$(6.23) \qquad P(A_1 \cap B_1) = \frac{N(A_1 \cap B_1)}{N(U)} = \frac{12}{100} = .12$$

and

$$(6.24) \qquad P(A_1) = \frac{N(A_1)}{N(U)} = \frac{30}{100} = .30$$
$$P(B_1) = \frac{N(B_1)}{N(U)} = \frac{40}{100} = .40$$
$$P(A_1)P(B_1) = .12$$

TABLE 6–6
Hypothetical Contingency Table for Ability Level and Sex of Students

ABILITY LEVEL	SEX		TOTAL
	MALE	FEMALE	
1	12	18	30
2	20	30	50
3	8	12	20
Total	40	60	100

In the same way, it can be verified that all probabilities in the body of the table are equal to the product of the corresponding marginal probabilities.

EXERCISES

6.9 Obtain the remaining probabilities in each cell of Table 6–6.

6.10 For each cell with $P(A_i \cap B_j)$ calculated in the previous exercise, calculate $P(A_i) \, P(B_j)$ and compare.

STATISTICAL INFERENCE

We turn next to the problem of drawing conclusions about a population for which a contingency table (such as Table 6–3) is not available. If we have a contingency table we need only examine the properties of the values in the table, since it is a summary of the population. Without such a table, we will select a random sample from the population and construct a new contingency table similar to the one we would like to have for the population. This was done in the introduction, and Exercises 6.2 and 6.4 are similar. When we do this, the counts in each cell are random variables, and they change from one sample to the next.

To construct such a table, let

(6.25) n_{ij} = the observed number of people in the sample who are categorized in the cell corresponding to row i and column j.

To illustrate, we have obtained a random sample of 100 people from the first school district and categorized each person with respect to ability level and sociometric standing. The people in each combination of ability and sociometric levels were then counted; the results are presented in Table 6–7. Then the numbers for (6.25) are:

(6.26)

$n_{11} = 1$	$n_{12} = 9$	$n_{13} = 18$	$n_{14} = 12$
$n_{21} = 0$	$n_{22} = 11$	$n_{23} = 26$	$n_{24} = 4$
$n_{31} = 1$	$n_{32} = 6$	$n_{33} = 10$	$n_{34} = 2$

Note that the *first* subscript tells us which row the number falls in; the *second* subscript gives the column for the number. Thus, n_{23} represents the number of people who are of average ability and are also in sociometric level 3. Next, define

(6.27)
$$\sum_j n_{ij} = n_i.$$

That is, if one sums the elements in a row, replace the j subscript with a dot. The value for i tells us which row was summed. For example, $n_1. = 40$ and is the sum of the elements in the first row.

(6.28)
$$\sum_i n_{ij} = n_{\cdot j}$$

TABLE 6-7

Contingency Table for a Random Sample from the Population of Randomly Grouped
Fifth Grade Students Classified According to Ability Level and Sociometric Level

ABILITY LEVEL	SOCIOMETRIC LEVEL				TOTAL
	1	2	3	4	
1	1	9	18	12	40
2	0	11	26	4	41
3	1	6	10	2	19
Total	2	26	54	18	100

That is, if one sums the elements in a column, replace the i subscript with a dot.
The value for j tells us which column was summed. For example, $n_{.2} = 26$
and is the sum of the elements in the second column.

$$(6.29) \qquad \sum_i \sum_j n_{ij} = n_{..}$$

That is, if one sums both rows and columns, replace both subscripts with dots.

EXERCISE

6.11   Using the data given in Table 6–7, calculate the following values:

a. n_{13}, n_{32}, n_{24} b. $n_{2.}, n_{.3}, n_{.1}$ c. $n_{..}$

A Hypothesis for Independence

Suppose that independence holds in the contingency table; then

$$(6.30) \qquad p_{ij} = P(A_i \cap B_j) = P(A_i)P(B_j)$$

Note that we have introduced the notation p_{ij} to simplify the term $P(A_i \cap B_j)$.
We have to use the contingency table from the sample (Table 6–7) to determine whether equation 6.22 holds for the population from which the sample
was drawn. To do this, we use the approximations which follow:

$$(6.31) \qquad p_{ij} \cong n_{ij}/n_{..}$$
$$P(A_i) \cong n_{i.}/n_{..}$$
$$P(B_j) \cong n_{.j}/n_{..}$$

Our reasoning is as follows: If ability level is independent of sociometric
level, then

$$(6.32) \qquad p_{ij} = P(A_i)P(B_j)$$

and therefore from the above approximations,

$$(6.33) \qquad n_{ij}/n_{..} \cong (n_{i.}/n_{..})(n_{.j}/n_{..})$$

It turns out that our computational problems will be simpler if we multiply both sides of equation 6.33 by $n..$ to get:

(6.34) $$n_{ij} \cong n_i.n_j/n..$$

The left-hand side, n_{ij}, is often referred to as the *observed* cell count; an alternative notation is O_{ij}. The right-hand side is then called the *expected* cell count (that is, expected if independence holds) and is referred to as E_{ij}. We can test statistically to determine whether independence holds by taking the squares of the differences between observed and expected values, dividing each square by the expected value, and then adding them all up. The formula is

(6.35) $$\frac{(n_{11} - n_1.n._1/n..)^2}{n_1.n._1/n..} + \frac{(n_{12} - n_1.n._2/n..)^2}{n_1.n._2/n..} + \cdots$$
$$+ \frac{(n_{34} - n_3.n._4/n..)^2}{n_3.n._4/n..}$$

A more concise notation is

(6.36) $$\sum_i \sum_j \frac{(n_{ij} - n_i.n._j/n..)^2}{n_i.n._j/n..}$$

or, in terms of observed and expected values,

(6.37) $$\sum_i \sum_j \frac{(O_{ij} - E_{ij})^2}{E_{ij}}$$

For different random samples the preceding quantity will vary, and we would like to know how it will behave when independence holds. It turns out that the frequency histogram is like that of Figure 2–7 and is called a *chi-squared* distribution. There are degrees of freedom associated with it. If a table has r rows and c columns, then the above quantity comes from a chi-squared distribution with $(r - 1)(c - 1)$ degrees of freedom. If independence does *not* hold, then the n_{ij} will not be close to $n_i.n._j/n..$ and expression 6.36 becomes very large. It can be seen by looking at Figure 2–8 that very large values are in the right-hand tail of the distribution, and are therefore unlikely if independence does hold. How large the value must be before becoming unlikely depends on the degrees of freedom and is obtained from the chi-squared table (Appendix Table E). Table E gives, at the head of each column, the percentages that are less than the values found in the body of the table. (With the t-distribution we reject the hypothesis with either very large or very small values of the statistic. In this case, however, the hypothesis is rejected only with very large values; hence, we do not divide α into two parts, putting half in each tail. We will not use the lower tail—only the upper one.)

THEOREM 6.2
Let a contingency table be constructed from a random sample as described in (6.26) and Table 6–7. Then, a test of the hypothesis that the two sets of categories are inde-

pendent is given by calculating

$$\sum_i \sum_j \frac{(n_{ij} - n_i.n._j/n..)^2}{n_i.n._j/n..}$$

and rejecting the hypothesis if the foregoing quantity is greater than the point which cuts off the right-hand $\alpha \cdot 100$ percent of a chi-squared distribution with $(r-1)(c-1)$ degrees of freedom. This test has probability α for rejecting the hypothesis when it is true.

Warning: This approach breaks down, if one or more E_{ij}'s whose values are much less than 5 are obtained.

An example will help to establish these ideas more firmly. Consider the data of Table 6–7. For $A_1 \cap B_1$ we have

$$(6.38) \qquad \frac{(n_{11} - n_1.n._1/n..)^2}{n_1.n._1/n..}$$

Now,

$$(6.39) \qquad n_{11} = 1, \quad n_1. = 40, \quad n._1 = 2, \quad n.. = 100$$

Substituting these in (6.38) gives

$$(6.40) \qquad \frac{(1 - .80)^2}{.80} = \frac{(.2)^2}{.8} = .05$$

For $A_1 \cap B_2$,

$$(6.41) \qquad \frac{(n_{12} - n_1.n._2/n..)^2}{n_1.n._2/n..} = \frac{(9 - 10.4)^2}{10.4} = .188$$

This is done for each cell, and all of the terms are added to give

$$(6.42) \qquad \sum_{i=1}^{3} \sum_{j=1}^{4} \frac{(n_{ij} - n_i.n._j/n..)^2}{n_i.n._j/n..} = 9.028$$

If, in fact, we do have independence, we want our chances of concluding that we do not to be .05. So we find in Appendix Table E the value that has an .05 chance of being exceeded by a chi-square variate with $(3-1)(4-1) = 6$ degrees of freedom, which is 12.59. Since the value we obtained is less than 12.59, we accept the hypothesis that independence holds.

We have previously established (see expression 6.21) that sociometric classification is not independent of ability level in the population; now we conclude that in fact independence holds when we use a random sample from the same population. In practice, we will *never* have true independence; what we really have concluded is that sociometric classification is not sufficiently dependent on ability level to enable us to detect dependence with a sample of size 100. Referring back to (6.21), we note that $P(B_4 \cap A_1) \neq P(B_4)P(A_1)$, or

$$\frac{P(B_4 \cap A_1)}{P(A_1)} = P(B_4|A_1) \neq P(B_4)$$

since numerical evaluation gives $66/271 = .244 \neq 97/527 = .184$. Although the probabilities are not exactly alike, they are not sufficiently different to enable us to pick up this difference without a larger sample size. We have made an error, although the seriousness of failing to detect this dependence may not be great.

EXERCISE
6.12   Using the data from Table 6–7, test the hypothesis that ability level is not related to sociometric classification; that is, verify the result obtained in (6.42).

Estimation of the Strength of Relationship

Suppose a researcher has constructed a contingency table as in the preceding section and has rejected the hypothesis that the sets of categories in his study are independent. A reasonable further question is, Since a relationship exists between the two types of events, can we obtain a measure of how strong this relationship is? This question is analogous to asking, in the case of numerical measures, Now that we know that the population correlation coefficient is not zero, just what value *does* it have?

One measure of the strength of relationship when categorical data are used is a modification of a measure proposed by Kullback.* It is similar to the correlation coefficient in that its absolute value is never greater than unity. Since it also never has negative values, it is actually more like the value that would be obtained by squaring the correlation coefficient.

The remainder of this section is a detailed description of how to calculate this measure. Since it is also calculated as part of PRGM3 in Table M of the Appendix, the reader who is willing to forego the computational experience can skip to the material following Exercise 6.15. Then, after digesting the material on the use of PRGM3, he can return to Exercises 6.13–6.15.

We define the terms in the formula first. Let

(6.43) $\qquad\qquad r$ = number of rows in a contingency table
$\qquad\qquad\qquad\qquad c$ = number of columns
$\hat{P}(A_i \cap B_j) = n_{ij}/n..$ = the estimate for the probability in the cell corresponding to row i, column j
$\qquad\hat{P}(A_i) = n_i./n..$ = the estimate for the probability that an element selected at random will be in row i
$\qquad\hat{P}(B_j) = n_{.j}/n..$ = the estimate for the probability that an element will be in column j

---

* Solomon Kullback, *Information Theory and Statistics.* (New York: Dover, 1968), p. 156.

Then our measure of the strength of relationship is the number, H, whose logarithm is

(6.44) $$\sum_{i=1}^{r} \sum_{j=1}^{c} \hat{P}(A_i \cap B_j) \log \hat{P}(A_i \cap B_j) - \tfrac{1}{2} \sum_{i=1}^{r} \hat{P}(A_i) \log \hat{P}(A_i)$$

$$- \tfrac{1}{2} \sum_{j=1}^{c} \hat{P}(B_j) \log \hat{P}(B_j)$$

Our procedure will be to calculate this quantity (some details to be given below), and then to assume that the result is the logarithm of the number that we want. Hence we find the entry in Table C that equals (6.46); H is then the corresponding number in the margin of the table. To calculate (6.46) we obtain three quantities:

Step 1. *For each cell* of the table, calculate the estimated probability times the logarithm of the same probability. For example, in Table 6–7, row 1, column 3, the estimated probability is

$$\hat{P}(A_1 \cap B_3) = \frac{n_{13}}{n_{..}} = \frac{18}{100} = .18$$

We calculate

$$\hat{P}(A_1 \cap B_3) \log \hat{P}(A_1 \cap B_3) = (.18) \log .18 = (.18)(9.2553 - 10)$$
$$= (.18)(9.2553) - (.18)10$$

Add and subtract 90 so that the negative part is a whole number:

$$(.18)(99.2553) - (.18)100 = 17.8660 - 18$$

Subtract and add 8, to make the negative part 10:

$$9.8660 - 10$$

which is the desired result for row 1, column 3.

We repeat this for two more cases, to illustrate some points. For row 1, column 1,

$$\hat{P}(A_1 \cap B_1) \log \hat{P}(A_1 \cap B_1) = (.01) \log .01$$
$$= (.01)(8.0000 - 10) = (.01)(98.0000 - 100)$$
$$= 0.9800 - 1$$
$$= 9.9800 - 10$$

For row 2, column 1, where the estimated probability is zero, the calculated value is also zero:

$$\hat{P}(A_2 \cap B_1) \log \hat{P}(A_2 \cap B_1) = 0 \log 0 = 0$$

Adding all these results, we get

(6.45) $$\sum_{i=1}^{r} \sum_{j=1}^{c} \hat{P}(A_i \cap B_j) \log \hat{P}(A_i \cap B_j) = 119.1007 - 120$$

$$= 9.1007 - 10$$

Step 2. For each row of the table, calculate the estimated probabilities in the margin and use them to obtain

$$\hat{P}(A_1) \log \hat{P}(A_1) + \hat{P}(A_2) \log \hat{P}(A_2) + \hat{P}(A_3) \log \hat{P}(A_3)$$

$$(6.46) \quad .40 \log .40 + .41 \log .41 + .19 \log .19 = 29.5450 - 30$$
$$= 9.5450 - 10$$

Divide this result by 2:

$$4.7725 - 5 = 9.7725 - 10$$

Step 3. *For each column*, repeat step 2. We get

$$(6.47) \quad \hat{P}(B_1) \log \hat{P}(B_1) + \ldots + \hat{P}(B_4) \log \hat{P}(B_4) = 9.7677 - 10$$

(Don't forget to divide by 2.)

Step 4. Subtract the results of steps 2 and 3 from the quantity calculated in Step 1. This is the logarithm of H; that is,

$$\log H = 9.1007 - 10 - (9.7725 - 10) - (9.7677 - 10)$$
$$= 29.1007 - 30 - 9.7725 + 10 - 9.7677 + 10$$
$$= 9.5605 - 10$$

Step 5. Obtain H from the log table (Appendix Table C):

$$(6.48) \qquad\qquad H = .3635 = .36$$

EXERCISES

6.13 Verify (6.48) by completing the computations for Table 6–7.

6.14 For Table 6–6, we have already learned that no relationship exists; obtain H.

6.15 Consider the following hypothetical set of data:

| | ABILITY LEVEL | | | |
SEX	1	2	3	TOTAL
M	0	10	14	24
F	23	0	0	23
Total	23	10	14	47

Clearly, we can now tell the sex of a student simply by knowing the ability level, since all smart students are girls. However, knowing the sex of a student does not tell us everything about the ability level, since a boy can be either average or slow. Obtain H for these data.

Some discussion may aid in interpretation of H. We find that

$$\frac{1}{\sqrt{rc}} \leq H \leq 1$$

The property that H will never reach zero is due to the fact that even if no true relationship exists, the cell counts will still be related to some degree. For example, consider the table of Exercise 6.15 again, keeping the total sample size at 47, but changing the cell numbers.

Suppose we knew all cells but one:

SEX	ABILITY LEVEL			TOTAL
	1	2	3	
M	24	0	0	24
F	0	1	?	
Total	24	1		47

We know that all but one of the girls are of less than average ability, so that 22 is the count going in the cell with the question mark. Even if the relationship is nonexistent, the final cell is always determined once the others are known. That is, the measure of relationship—obtained from the cell counts—can never be zero.

EXERCISES

6.16 Make a contingency table for the relationship between achievement on the STEP math scores and the "Acceptance of Self" scores by first categorizing the students with respect to the math score, x, as:

    a. $x \leq 244$ b. $244 < x \leq 251$
    c. $251 < x \leq 256$ d. $256 < x$

Second categorize students on the basis of the "Acceptance of Self" scores, y:

    a. $y \leq 45$ b. $45 < y \leq 55$
    c. $55 < y$

Use 100 students in your random sample from the ability grouped district. (It is best to do this in groups of 5, sample size of 20 per person, then combine your results.)

6.17 Using the data of Exercise 6.16, test the hypothesis that no relationship exists between ability and self-acceptance.

6.18 Using the data of Exercise 6.16, obtain H.

6.19 Using the same data, return to the original numerical values and calculate the correlation coefficient with its confidence interval, assuming the parent population is normal. Compare r^2 with H.

DATA PROCESSING

For contingency tables, there are two stages in the data processing routine:

1. Count the number of observations in each category.
2. Compute the values for chi-square and H.

If the raw data originally collected have been punched on cards, then the most inexpensive approach is:

1. Count the cards in each cell on a card sorter.
2. Enter the appropriate counts for each category on data cards for the program.
3. Submit the program for processing.

For example, consider the 110 observations for the students of the first four teachers in the randomly grouped district. Suppose we wish to obtain the contingency table for examining the relationship between pupil-level and sociometric classification. To make the example concrete, suppose 110 data cards have been punched as in Table 6–8. Then to obtain the number of observations in each cell (in each combination of pupil-level and sociometric classification), sort first on pupil-level by loading the entire deck of 110 cards, with the sort indicator at column 1 (the column in which pupil-level is given). The result of this pass will be three decks of cards; all cards in each deck have the same pupil level. The decks will be in pockets 1, 2, and 3 of the sorter. Now set the sort indicator at column 17 (for sociometric classification) and load the deck for pupil-level 1. The result will be four smaller decks— one each for sociometric levels 1, 2, 3, and 4. The number of cards in each of these decks will be the number of students who are in both pupil-level 1 and each of the sociometric levels 1, 2, 3, and 4. This gives the appropriate numbers for row 1 of your contingency table, if you have constructed it as in Table 6–7 (page 173). Decks 2 and 3 of the first sort will yield rows 2 and 3 of the table in the same manner.

TABLE 6–8

Instructions for Punching 110 Data Cards

COLUMNS	DESCRIPTION OF ENTRY
1	Pupil level (PL)
2	Sex (S)
3–5	STEP science score
6–8	STEP reading score
9–11	STEP social science score
12–14	STEP mathematics score
15,16	Sociometric score (TI/CH)
17	Sociometric classification (SC)
18,19	"Concept of Self" (CON/SEL)
20,21	"Ideal Self" (IDL/SEL)
22,23	"Acceptance of Self" (ACC/SEL)
24,25	SRA score, "Me and School" (SCH)
26,27	SRA score, "Me and Home" (HOM)
28,29	SRA score, "About Myself" (ME)
30,31	SRA score, "Getting Along With Others"
32,33	SRA score, "Things in General" (GEN)

EXERCISES

†6.20 Divide the first 110 students in the randomly grouped district among the students of your class, and have each student punch his or her share of cards according to the format of Table 6–8.

‡6.21 Pool all the cards punched by your class into one deck. Using the card sorter, count the number of students in each cell of a contingency table constructed with the same cells as that of Table 6–7. Construct the table, using your data.

PRGM3: A Program for Calculation of the Chi-Square Variate for a Contingency Table and for H

This program is easy to use and saves computational labor. Systems cards and the general order of the decks are as usual:

1. Initial systems cards
2. Program deck
3. Systems cards
4. Two control cards
5. Data deck
6. Blank card, except for FIN in column 78–80
7. Terminal systems cards

Parts 1 and 3 are specified as in your own computer center; the program deck is in Appendix M. The first control card is for the verbal description of your job; the second one is as follows:

COLUMN	
4,5	Number of rows in the contingency table ≤ 99
6,7	Number of columns in the table ≤ 13

Each data card contains the number of elements in each cell for one row of the contingency table. That is, the card for the first row is as follows:

COLUMN	DESCRIPTION OF ENTRY
4,5	Number of observations in row 1, column 1
6,7	Number of observations in row 1, column 2
8,9	Number of observations in row 1, column 3

and so on, using two card columns for each cell in the contingency table. The next card is for row 2, and so on; there should be as many data cards as the entry in columns 4 and 5 of the control card.

The output for the program is as follows. First is the output from Control Card 1 giving the verbal description of the job. Next are printed the number of rows and the number of columns, as read from Control Card 2. The data cards are then listed, except for the FIN card. Following this, the total sample size is given. These values are designed to verify that you have filled out your cards properly. The results are then printed as below.

CONTINGENCY TABLE

| ROW | COLUMN | | | | ROW TOTAL |
	1	2	. .	C	
1	$n_{11}/n_{..}$	$n_{12}/n_{..}$	. .	$n_{1C}/n_{..}$	$n_{1.}/n_{..}$
2	$n_{21}/n_{..}$	$n_{22}/n_{..}$	. .	$n_{2C}/n_{..}$	$n_{2.}/n_{..}$
.					
R	$n_{R1}/n_{..}$	$n_{R2}/n_{..}$	. .	$n_{RC}/n_{..}$	$n_{R.}/n_{..}$
Column Total	$n_{.1}/n_{..}$	$n_{.2}/n_{..}$	. .	$n_{.C}/n_{..}$	

Test for Independence: Chi-square = .xxxx E xx
Degrees of Freedom = xxx H = .xxx

The entry in any cell of the table is the estimate of the probability associated with that cell, as discussed in the section on Statistical Inference. The entries in the margin are the probability estimates for each category taken alone, as in Equations 6.43.

EXERCISE

6.22   Using the data of Exercise 6.21 construct the contingency table and chi-square test for independence using PRGM3 or another program available at your computer center. (The chi-square test assumes the data were a random sample—which, in this instance, was not the case.)

Experiences with Data

Note that procedures to be used in this section are not limited to those taught in this chapter. Earlier methods may be preferable to the contingency table approach.

PROBLEMS

6.1   Is there a relationship between popularity and ability? If so, how strong is it?

6.2   Are scores on popularity and home adjustment actually measuring the same thing?

SOLUTIONS TO EXERCISES

6.1

$$P(A_3) = N(A_3)/N(U) = \tfrac{92}{527} = .17$$
$$P(A_2) = N(A_2)/N(U) = \tfrac{164}{527} = .31$$
$$P(A_1) = N(A_1)/N(U) = \tfrac{271}{527} = .51$$

6.3

a. $N(A_1 \cap B_4) = 66$ b. $N(A_1 \cap B_1) = 3$ c. $N(A_2 \cap B_3) = 65$
d. $N(A_2) = 164$ e. $N(A_1) = 271$

6.5

ABILITY LEVEL	SOCIOMETRIC CLASSIFICATION			
	1	2	3	4
1	.006	.11	.27	.13
2	.006	.13	.12	.05
3	.004	.09	.07	.01

6.6

a. $N(A_2 \cup B_2 \cup B_3) = 451$ b. $N(B_1 \cup A_3) = 98$

6.7

$P(A_2|B_4) = .27; P(A_2) = .31$
Being a star decreases the probability that a student will be of average ability.

6.8

a. $P(B_2|A_3) = N(B_2 \cap A_3)/N(A_3) = \frac{48}{92} = .52$
b. $P(B_2|A_2) = N(B_2 \cap A_2)/N(A_2) = \frac{70}{164} = .43$
c. $P(B_2|A_1) = N(B_2 \cap A_1)/N(A_1) = \frac{59}{271} = .22$
The probability that a student is less popular increases as his ability decreases.

6.9

ABILITY LEVEL	SEX		
	MALE	FEMALE	TOTAL
1	.12	.18	.30
2	.20	.30	.50
3	.8	.12	.20
Total	.40	.60	1.00

6.10

$P(A_1 \cap B_1) = P(A_1)P(B_1) = .12$ $P(A_2 \cap B_2) = P(A_2)P(B_2) = .30$
$P(A_1 \cap B_2) = P(A_1)P(B_2) = .18$ $P(A_3 \cap B_1) = P(A_3)P(B_1) = .08$
$P(A_2 \cap B_1) = P(A_2)P(B_1) = .20$ $P(A_3 \cap B_2) = P(A_3)P(B_2) = .12$

6.11

a. $n_{13} = 18; n_{32} = 6; n_{24} = 4$
b. $n_{2.} = 41; n_{.3} = 54; n_{.1} = 2$
c. $n_{..} = 100$
d. $E_{13} = .006(100) = .6; E_{32} = .09(100) = 9; E_{24} = .05(100) = 5$

6.12

$A_1 \cap B_1$: .05; $A_1 \cap B_2$: .188

$A_1 \cap B_3$: $\dfrac{(18 - 21.6)^2}{21.6} = \dfrac{12.96}{21.6} = .6$

$A_1 \cap B_4$: $\dfrac{(12 - 7.2)^2}{7.2} = \dfrac{23.04}{7.2} = 3.2$

$A_2 \cap B_1:$ $\dfrac{(0 - .82)^2}{.82} = \dfrac{.67}{.82} = .82$

$A_2 \cap B_2:$ $\dfrac{(11 - 10.66)^2}{10.66} = \dfrac{14.9}{22.14} = .67$

$A_2 \cap B_3:$ $\dfrac{(26 - 22.14)^2}{22.14} = \dfrac{14.9}{22.14} = .67$

$A_2 \cap B_4:$ $\dfrac{(4 - 7.38)^2}{7.38} = \dfrac{11.42}{7.38} = 1.55$

$A_3 \cap B_1:$ $\dfrac{(1 - .38)^2}{.38} = \dfrac{.38}{.38} = 1.00$

$A_3 \cap B_2:$ $\dfrac{(6 - 4.94)^2}{4.94} = \dfrac{1.12}{4.94} = .23$

$A_3 \cap B_3:$ $\dfrac{(10 - 10.26)^2}{10.26} = \dfrac{.07}{10.26} = .01$

$A_3 \cap B_4:$ $\dfrac{(2 - 3.42)^2}{2.88} = \dfrac{2.02}{2.88} = .7$

Total $= 9.028$

6.14

$H = .43$

6.15

$H = .84$

6.16

Random sample scores obtained:

STEP MATH	ACC SEL	
253	56	PLACED IN COLUMN c, ROW c.
257	27	PLACED IN COLUMN d, ROW a.
256	49	PLACED IN COLUMN c, ROW b.
266	41	PLACED IN COLUMN d, ROW a.
250	57	PLACED IN COLUMN b, ROW c.

Continue in same manner until your size 20 sample has been completed, then combine with the other four members of your group and construct a contingency table for 100 observations. Below is the contingency table for the above five observations:

	a. $x \leq 244$	b. $244 < x \leq 251$	c. $251 < x \leq 256$	d. $25 < x$
a. $y \leq 45$	0	0	0	2
b. $45 < y \leq 55$	0	0	1	0
c. $55 < y$	0	1	1	0

REVIEW FOR CHAPTER 6

1. **Definition of probability:**
   a. Let U be the set of all elements in a population.
   b. Let E be the set of elements in a population which have some characteristic.
   c. $N(E)$ is the number of elements with the characteristic; $N(U)$ is the number of elements in the population.
   d. $P(E) = N(E)/N(U)$.
2. $X \cap Y$ = the intersection of the sets X and Y; the set of elements which belong to both X and Y.
3. $X \cup Y$ = the union of the sets X and Y; the set of elements which belong either to X or to Y (not necessarily to both).
4. $P(X|Y) = N(X \cap Y)/N(Y)$. Conditional probability; the probability for the event X, given that Y is known to be true.
5. **Statistical independence.** Events X and Y are independent if $P(X|Y) = P(X)$ or, alternatively, if $P(X \cap Y) = P(X)P(Y)$
6. **Test for independence in a two-way contingency table,** with r rows and c columns:

$$\sum_{i=1}^{r} \sum_{i=1}^{c} \frac{(n_{ij} - n_{i.}n_{.j}/n_{..})^2}{n_{i.}n_{.j}/n_{..}}$$

is tested by comparing with the value in Appendix Table E (chi-square) corresponding to the column marked $1 - \alpha$ and the row for $(r - 1)(c - 1)$ degrees of freedom, where

$$n_{ij} = \text{the number of elements in row } i, \text{ column } j$$

$$n_{i.} = \sum_{j=1}^{c} n_{ij}$$

$$n_{.j} = \sum_{i=1}^{r} n_{ij}$$

$$n_{..} = \sum_{i=1}^{r} \sum_{j=1}^{c} n_{ij}$$

If this quantity is greater than the value in the table, we reject the hypothesis that the events are independent. That is, there then exists some relationship.

7. **The measure H** for strength of relationship in a two-way contingency table is defined by the expression

$$\log H = \sum_{i=1}^{r} \sum_{j=1}^{c} (\hat{P}A_i \cap B_j) \log \hat{P}(A_i \cap B_j) - \tfrac{1}{2} \sum_{i=1}^{r} \hat{P}(A_i) \log \hat{P}(A_i)$$

$$- \tfrac{1}{2} \sum_{j=1}^{c} \hat{P}(B_j) \log \hat{P}(B_j)$$

where r is the number of rows in the table and c is the number of columns.

CHAPTER 7
THE COMPARISON OF
SEVERAL GROUPS—
ANALYSIS OF VARIANCE

DESCRIPTION OF THE PROBLEM

In Chapter 5 two populations were being compared; in this chapter several populations will be examined, with a random sample selected from each. The reasons for conducting the study are again of paramount importance in deciding the type of analysis to use; some frequently asked questions will be explored here.

Examples Involving Several Populations

To help us arrive at generalizations about several populations, we will expand the examples used at the beginning of Chapter 5.

1. The state superintendent wishes to investigate the effectiveness of two alternative training programs for adults and compare each with a control group which is not given training. From among all applicants for training, two-thirds are selected at random for inclusion in one of the two training programs, and this latter group is then divided into half, each half being assigned to one of the training programs, so that three groups of people are available for study. Average incomes are obtained after a five-year period.

2. A principal has three math textbooks to compare, including the book presently in use. End-of-year achievement scores are to be compared; to control for "Hawthorne effect," the classes using the old text are formally included in the study.

As in Chapter 5, we start by formulating questions that can be asked:

1. Research type (hypothesis test).
   a. Do the training options differ in the degree to which they modify income over a five-year period?
   b. Is the average achievement score for district students affected by the textbook used?
2. Evaluation of population means.
   a. If the training methods are effective, how effective are they, and which is the best?
   b. If the textbooks do modify achievement, which gives the highest achievement, and how much better than the others is it?

These questions will be considered after our statistical model has been modified to fit the new situation.

A Statistical Model

In Chapter 5, double subscripts were introduced, although their use was not strictly necessary. Now, however, they become essential, and we briefly review the doubly subscripted array in Table 7–1.

TABLE 7–1

Generalized Array of Subscripted Variables
Illustrating Summation Notation

ROW	COLUMN						ROW TOTALS
	1	2	$\cdots$	j	$\cdots$	n	
1	x_{11}	x_{12}	$\cdots$	x_{1j}	$\cdots$	x_{1n}	$\sum\limits_{j=1}^{n} x_{1j} = X_{1.}$
2	x_{21}	x_{22}	$\cdots$	x_{2j}	$\cdots$	x_{2n}	$\sum\limits_{j=1}^{n} x_{2j} = X_{2.}$
.							
i	x_{i1}	x_{i2}	$\cdots$	x_{ij}	$\cdots$	x_{in}	$\sum\limits_{j=1}^{n} x_{ij} = X_{i.}$
.							
k	x_{k1}	x_{k2}	$\cdots$	x_{kj}	$\cdots$	x_{kn}	$\sum\limits_{j=1}^{n} x_{kj} = X_{k.}$
Column totals	$\sum\limits_{i=1}^{k} x_{i1}$	$\sum\limits_{i=1}^{k} x_{i2}$	$\cdots$	$\sum\limits_{i=1}^{k} x_{ij}$	$\cdots$	$\sum\limits_{i=1}^{k} x_{in}$	$\sum\limits_{i=1}^{k}\sum\limits_{j=1}^{n} x_{ij} = X_{..}$
	$X_{.1}$	$X_{.2}$	$\cdots$	$X_{.j}$	$\cdots$	$X_{.n}$	

In Chapter 5, (Equation 5.11), we were concerned with the model

(7.1)
$$y_{ij} = \mu_i + \epsilon_{ij}$$
$$i = 1, 2$$
$$\epsilon_{ij} \sim (0, \sigma_i^2)$$
$$j = 1, 2, \ldots, N_i$$

We had two different means and different population sizes, and we allowed that the variance for the ϵ_{ij} could differ between the two populations. Now we allow for k different populations, each with a different variance and possibly k different population sizes, so that the model becomes

(7.2)
$$y_{ij} = \mu_i + \epsilon_{ij}$$
$$\epsilon_{ij} \sim (0, \sigma_i^2)$$
$$i = 1, 2, \ldots, k$$
$$j = 1, 2, \ldots, N_i$$

The array in Table 7–1 is for random samples selected from the k populations, each of size n. Comparing the table with the observations of (7.2), we note that each row corresponds to a population. Since the N_i are not necessarily equal, if Table 7–1 were representing the populations instead of random samples from them, these rows would be of different lengths in order to represent (7.2) exactly.

At this point, we need to consider again a distinction that was made in Chapter 5. It was pointed out that two kinds of sampling procedures both give rise to the same statistical model. We could either sample from one population and then apply two distinct "treatments," one to each half of the sample, or we could select a random sample from each of two distinct populations. In the first case, the two samples must be considered as coming from distinct populations, where the populations differ only with respect to the treatment applied. In the second, the populations may differ not only with respect to some characteristic observed by the researcher (such as an environmental difference) but also in other ways. Consequently, differences in observed scores may be due to one of a large number of causes; the correct cause may not even be suspected, since all the ways in which two populations can differ may not be apparent.

The same reasoning must now be extended to the comparison of several populations. We can either impose k distinct ways of treating samples from the same populations, or we can select random samples from each of k different populations. The situation is illustrated in Figure 7–1, with $k = 3$. *In either case*, we speak of k distinct populations in the final analysis.

Recall that in Chapter 5, we pointed out that if a set of populations is in fact composed of subdivisions of a larger population, we speak of dividing the population into *strata*, and of the sampling process as *stratified sampling*. This is apparent in Figure 7–1, where the urban, suburban, and rural populations are considered separately. Certainly, we can consider the total populations for most geographical areas as being made up of these subdivisions.

FIGURE 7-1

Two situations for comparison of groups. (a) Treatments applied to three different samples from the same population; (b) sampling from three distinct populations.

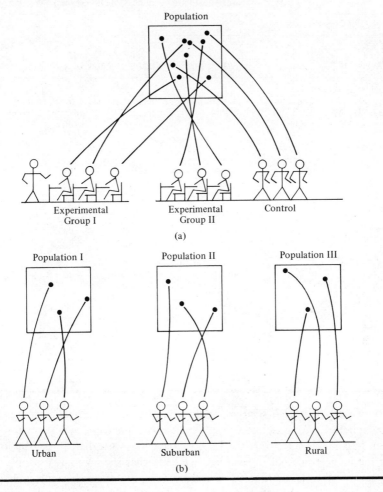

We next formalize these notions in

DEFINITION 7.1

If a population has been defined and subdivided into k smaller populations, and a simple random sample has been selected from each of these, the sampling process is termed "stratified sampling." Each of the subdivisions is termed a "stratum."

Now consider a second example in more detail. In the randomly grouped district, students have been classified into one of three different achievement levels according to their achievement scores for a preceding year. We can consider each pupil-level as a stratum and, if we wish, select a simple random sample of students from each stratum. In practice, we then have to make a

TABLE 7–2

A Stratified Random Sample of Students With Accompanying Observations
Taken from the Randomly Grouped District and Using Ability Levels
as Strata (Measurements are "About Myself" Scores)

BELOW AVERAGE		AVERAGE			
ID NO. ≤ 97	"ABOUT MYSELF" SCORE	ID NO. ≤ 167	"ABOUT MYSELF" SCORE	ID NO. ≤ 279	"ABOUT MYSELF" SCORE
(Use two digits, starting down on row 39, column 19, Page B7, Appendix Table B)		(Use three digits, beginning with row 45, column 19)		(Use three digits, beginning with row 12, column 22)	
01	34	38	64	740	
24	6	843		477	
23	99	352		50	39
21	18	623		491	
99		590		97	11
34	40	587		434	
		277		178	14
		958		536	
		154	27	983	
		592		95	13
		299		192	20
		810			
		815			
		146	5		
		578			
		189			
		756			
		753			
		571			
		83	5		
		676			
		134	25		

list of people in each stratum, with a new set of identification numbers for them, before we can select a simple random sample from each stratum. Notice that in columns ID1, ID2, and ID3, we have done just that, so that by looking at the highest number in each list, we learn that the number of people in the group of slow learners is 97, the number in the average group is 167, and there are 279 in the fast group. To illustrate the selection of a stratified sample, five students were selected from each group, using the sampling numbers (all different) given in Table 7–2. The sampling numbers were obtained consecutively, first for group 3, then for groups 2 and 1, and the SRA "About Myself" (ME) score was recorded. The reader should follow the directions given in the table headings, and verify that the numbers obtained are correct.

STATISTICAL INFERENCE

We now are ready to tackle problems involving several populations with a random sample selected from each. As a first step, recall definition 2.13 which defines unbiased estimates and refers to the mean of all possible values for a statistic. The mean of all possible values is often termed the *expected value* or the *expectation* of the statistic. We can say that s^2 is an unbiased estimate of σ^2 if its expected value is equal to σ^2. We can put this in symbols: If s^2 is an unbiased estimate of σ^2, then

$$(7.3) \qquad\qquad E\{s^2\} = \sigma^2$$

DEFINITION 7.2
The symbolic representation for the expected value of a statistic, z, will be defined to be

$$(7.4) \qquad\qquad E\{z\}$$

As stated earlier, we will be trying to answer two kinds of questions in this chapter; we will consider both in this section. The first question is simply, Are the means of the k populations all equal, or are they different?

Hypothesis Test for Equality of Means

The question posed in this section is essentially preliminary; if the means are different, we may then be interested in determining which is best, or which textbook we should use. Checking the preliminary hypothesis that all means are equal can save us time if we find no evidence for genuine differences between the populations.

Let a random sample of size n be selected from each population, and let x_{ij} be the jth observation from population i. If Table 7–1 is referred to, each row represents the random sample from a distinct population. The hypothesis, in symbolic terms, is

$$H: \mu_1 = \mu_2 = \cdots \mu_k$$

An easy way to translate this into a numerical test is to note that the means are equal if and only if their variance is zero. That is, there is no spread between equal population means; and the two statements

$$(7.5) \qquad\qquad \mu_1 = \mu_2 = \cdots = \mu_k$$

and

$$(7.6) \qquad\qquad \frac{1}{k-1} \sum_{i=1}^{k} (\mu_i - \bar{\mu}.)^2 = 0$$

are equivalent, where

$$(7.7) \qquad\qquad \bar{\mu}. = \frac{1}{k} \sum_{i=1}^{k} \mu_i$$

So we will replace (7.5) with (7.6) and set out to test

$$H: \frac{1}{k-1} \sum_{i=1}^{k} (\mu_i - \bar{\mu}.)^2 = 0$$

since this is equivalent to (7.5). For computational reasons, we will multiply the foregoing equation by n, and use

(7.8)
$$H: \frac{n}{k-1} \sum_{i=1}^{k} (\mu_i - \bar{\mu}.)^2 = 0$$

One logical way to test H is to replace each μ_i in (7.8) with its estimate,

(7.9)
$$\bar{x}_{i\cdot} = \frac{1}{n} \sum_{j=1}^{n} x_{ij}$$

and see how large a value we get. That is, instead of (7.8), calculate

(7.10)
$$ns_{\bar{x}}^2 = \frac{n}{k-1} \sum_{i=1}^{k} (\bar{x}_{i\cdot} - \bar{x}..)^2$$

where

(7.11)
$$\bar{x}.. = \frac{1}{k} \sum_{i=1}^{k} \bar{x}_{i\cdot}$$

and where $s_{\bar{x}}^2$ is the variance between the sample means from the populations; that is,

(7.12)
$$s_{\bar{x}}^2 = \frac{1}{k-1} \sum_{i=1}^{k} (\bar{x}_{i\cdot} - \bar{x}..)^2$$

Since $\bar{x}_{i\cdot}$ is an estimate of μ_i, one might suspect (7.10) to be an estimate of (7.8); and we want to know if the quantity in (7.8) equals zero. Now, it turns out that (7.10) almost estimates (7.8); even though $\mu_1 = \mu_2 = \cdots = \mu_k$, it would be inevitable that the sample means $\bar{x}_1., \bar{x}_2., \ldots, \bar{x}_k.$ would differ somewhat from each other, and so, in general, we should expect

$$\frac{n}{k-1} \sum_{i=1}^{k} (\bar{x}_{i\cdot} - \bar{x}..)^2 > 0 \quad \text{even if} \quad \frac{n}{k-1} \sum_{i=1}^{k} (\mu_i - \bar{\mu}.)^2 = 0$$

We find that the expected value for (7.10) is

(7.13)
$$\frac{n}{k-1} \sum_{i=1}^{k} (\mu_i - \bar{\mu}.)^2 + \frac{1}{k} \sum_{i=1}^{k} \sigma_i^2$$

Put in words, we say that the average value for n times the variance between the sample means is a bit larger than n times the variance between the population means; the discrepancy amounts to

$$(7.14) \qquad \frac{1}{k} \sum_{i=1}^{k} \sigma_i^2$$

EXERCISES

7.1   The randomly grouped fifth grade children have been subdivided on the basis of ability; the means and variances of the STEP science scores for the three ability levels are:

$$\mu_1 = 267.84 \qquad \sigma_1^2 = 136.91$$
$$\mu_2 = 259.38 \qquad \sigma_2^2 = 86.55$$
$$\mu_3 = 252.84 \qquad \sigma_3^2 = 113.73$$

Calculate what the expected value should be for n times the variance between three sample means, each of size 4, and each selected from a different one of the three populations.

7.2   The following random samples were obtained for the three ability levels, using the STEP science scores:

$x_1 = FAST$	$x_2 = AVERAGE$	$x_3 = SLOW$
244	257	233
266	257	247
252	262	255
261	274	251

Calculate $\bar{x}_{1.}$, $\bar{x}_{2.}$, $\bar{x}_{3.}$, and $s_{\bar{x}}^2$, the variance between them. Compare $ns_{\bar{x}}^2$ with the value obtained in Exercise 7.1.

†7.3   Select a random sample of four values from each of the same three populations; calculate $\bar{x}_{1.}$, $\bar{x}_{2.}$, $\bar{x}_{3.}$, and $ns_{\bar{x}}^2$, as in the preceding exercise.

Our procedure is to reject

$$(7.15) \qquad H: \frac{n}{k-1} \sum_{i=1}^{k} (\mu_i - \bar{\mu}.)^2 = 0$$

if the value of

$$ns_{\bar{x}}^2 = \frac{n}{k-1} \sum_{i=1}^{k} (\bar{x}_{i.} - \bar{x}..)^2$$

is highly inflated. The question is, How large must $ns_{\bar{x}}^2$ be before it is "highly" inflated? We note that the average value for $ns_{\bar{x}}^2$ is

$$(7.16) \qquad \frac{n}{k-1} \sum_{i=1}^{k} (\mu_i - \bar{\mu}.)^2 + \frac{1}{k} \sum_{i=1}^{k} \sigma_i^2$$

If

$$\frac{1}{k} \sum_{i=1}^{k} \sigma_i^2$$

is large, then $ns_{\bar{x}}^2$ may be inflated even if

$$(7.17) \qquad \frac{n}{k-1} \sum_{i=1}^{k} (\mu_i - \bar{\mu}.)^2 = 0$$

and we want to guard against this happening. We could use an estimate of

$$\frac{1}{k} \sum_{i=1}^{k} \sigma_i^2$$

alone, and we find this estimate by calculating

$$(7.18) \qquad \frac{1}{n-1} \sum_{j=1}^{n} (x_{1j} - \bar{x}_1.)^2 = s_1^2 \cong \sigma_1^2$$

$$\frac{1}{n-1} \sum_{j=1}^{n} (x_{2j} - \bar{x}_2.)^2 = s_2^2 \cong \sigma_2^2$$

$$\frac{1}{n-1} \sum_{j=1}^{n} (x_{3j} - \bar{x}_3.)^2 = s_3^2 \cong \sigma_3^2$$

and from these, we get

$$(7.19) \qquad \frac{1}{k} \sum_{i=1}^{k} s_i^2 \cong \frac{1}{k} \sum_{i=1}^{k} \sigma_i^2$$

The values s_1^2, s_2^2, and s_3^2 are simply the sample variances for each population taken separately—sometimes called the *within population variances*.

EXERCISE

7.4   Using the data given in Exercise 7.2, obtain the quantities s_1^2, s_2^2, s_3^2. Average the three estimates thus obtained and compare with

$$\frac{1}{k} \sum_{i=1}^{k} \sigma_i^2$$

calculated from the information in Exercise 7.1. Repeat, using the data of Exercise 7.3.

We next combine the results of the last two sections to obtain a test of

$$H: \frac{n}{k-1} \sum_{i=1}^{k} (\mu_i - \bar{\mu}.)^2 = 0$$

Note the following results:

1. The expected value of

$$(7.20) \qquad ns_{\bar{x}}^2 \quad \text{is} \quad \frac{n}{k-1} \sum_{i=1}^{k} (\mu_i - \bar{\mu}.)^2 + \frac{1}{k} \sum_{i=1}^{k} \sigma_i^2$$

2. The expected value of

$$(7.21) \qquad \frac{1}{k} \sum_{i=1}^{k} s_i^2 \quad \text{is} \quad \frac{1}{k} \sum_{i=1}^{k} \sigma_i^2$$

3. If

$$ns_{\bar{x}}^2 \cong \frac{n}{k-1} \sum_{i=1}^{k} (\mu_i - \bar{\mu}.)^2 + \frac{1}{k} \sum_{i=1}^{k} \sigma_i^2$$

and

$$\frac{1}{k} \sum_{i=1}^{k} s_i^2 \cong \frac{1}{k} \sum_{i=1}^{k} \sigma_i^2$$

then *if H is true,*

$$\frac{n}{k-1} \sum_{i=1}^{k} (\mu_i - \bar{\mu}.)^2 = 0$$

and

$$(7.22) \qquad F = ns_{\bar{x}}^2 \Big/ \frac{1}{k} \sum_{i=1}^{k} s_i^2 \cong 1$$

since then the expected values for both quantities are the same.

In (7.17), $ns_{\bar{x}}^2$ is termed the "between-population" or "between-treatment" mean-squares, and

$$s^2 = \frac{1}{k} \sum_{i=1}^{k} s_i^2$$

is called the "within-population" or "within-treatment" mean-squares.

Now recall that $E\{\ \}$ is the symbolism for the expected value of the quantity within the parentheses. Thus we can summarize:

1. For the between-treatment mean-squares:

$$(7.23) \qquad E\{ns_{\bar{x}}^2\} = E\left\{\frac{n}{k-1}\sum_{i=1}^{k}(\bar{x}_{i.} - \bar{x}..)^2\right\}$$

$$= \frac{1}{k}\sum_{i=1}^{k}\sigma_i^2 + \frac{n}{k-1}\sum_{i=1}^{k}(\mu_i - \bar{\mu}.)^2$$

The expected value is affected by both the mean of the population variances and the variance of the population means. If $\mu_1 = \mu_2 = \cdots = \mu_k$, the variance of these means is zero, and then

$$(7.24) \qquad E\{ns_{\bar{x}}^2\} = \frac{1}{k}\sum_{i=1}^{k}\sigma_i^2$$

2. For the within-treatment mean-squares,

$$(7.25) \qquad E\left\{\frac{1}{k}\sum_{i=1}^{k}s_i^2\right\} = \frac{1}{k}\sum_{i=1}^{k}\sigma_i^2$$

If the population means are equal, then the expected values of

$$ns_{\bar{x}}^2 \qquad \text{and} \qquad \frac{1}{k}\sum_{i=1}^{k}s_i^2$$

are the same, and the ratio of the two quantities should be close to unity, within sampling error. This leads us to reason as follows:

Assume that there is no difference between the population means and, *under this assumption*, determine whether the ratio

$$(7.26) \qquad F = ns_{\bar{x}}^2 \Big/ \frac{1}{k}\sum_{i=1}^{k}s_i^2$$

is a plausible value; it should be close to 1. If it is very large (if there is a lot of variability in the sample means), reject the assumption and conclude that there are genuine differences between the population means. As with the t-test in Chapter 5, we can state our reasoning in the following way: If F is a large value we can either (1) conclude that the means are equal and that an unlikely event has happened, or (2) reject the assumption, which makes the event unlikely. It is customary to do the latter, and we say that we reject the hypothesis:

$$H: \mu_1 = \mu_2 = \cdots = \mu_k$$

if F as calculated in (7.26) is unlikely when the hypothesis is true.

The only remaining question is to determine how large F needs to be before we conclude that the means are different. Appendix Table J enables the researcher to determine this.

The term "degrees of freedom" is used again here; now we must consider both the numerator and denominator. The degrees of freedom for the numerator are $k - 1$; those for the denominator are $k(n - 1)$ (obtained by adding the within-treatment degrees of freedom). Table J has two parts, one for the values exceeded by the upper 5 percent and one for the upper 1 percent of the sample F's *when the population means are the same.* In both parts, one cell corresponds to each combination of l and m degrees of freedom, where the column l corresponds to the degrees of freedom for the numerator, and the row m specifies the degrees of freedom for the denominator. We consider

---

DEFINITION 7.3

$$(7.27) \qquad\qquad F_{(l,m)\,p}$$

is defined as the numerical value which exceeds $(100)p$ *percent of statistics which are the between-treatment mean-squares divided by within-treatment mean squares under the following conditions:*

1. *The degrees of freedom for the numerator (between treatments) is l,*
2. *The degrees of freedom for the denominator (within treatments) is m.*
3. *The population means are all equal.*

Using this definition, we can formalize a test of the hypothesis $H: \mu_1 = \mu_2 = \cdots \mu_k$ as follows:

THEOREM 7.1
Let a random sample of size n be selected from each of k populations, where x_{ij} is the jth observation selected from population i; that is,

$$(7.28) \qquad\qquad x_{ij} \sim (\mu_i, \sigma_i^2)$$
$$i = 1, 2, \ldots, k$$
$$j = 1, 2, \ldots, n$$

We may now test the hypothesis $H: \mu_1 = \mu_2 = \cdots = \mu_k$ as follows. Let $F_{(l,m)\,1-\alpha}$ be defined as in Definition 7.3, and

$$(7.29) \qquad s_{\bar{x}}^2 = \frac{1}{k-1} \sum_{i=1}^{k} (\bar{x}_{i.} - \bar{x}..)^2$$

$$s^2 = \frac{1}{k} \sum_{i=1}^{k} s_i^2 = \frac{1}{k} \sum_{i=1}^{k} \frac{1}{n-1} \sum_{j=1}^{n} (x_{ij} - \bar{x}_{i.})^2$$

Then, use the rule:

Reject H if $F = ns_{\bar{x}}^2/s^2 \geq F_{[k-1,k(n-1)]1-\alpha}$; *accept H otherwise.*
The hypothesis then has probability $= \alpha$ *of being rejected if it is true.*

EXERCISES

7.5 Obtain the values $F_{(3,16).99}$, $F_{(2,12).95}$, and $F_{(4,15).95}$ from Table J.

7.6 Suppose four math textbooks were being tested, one in each of four schools. Further, suppose that ten students were selected randomly from each school, and given the STEP math test, resulting in the following scores:

TEXTBOOK NO. 1	TEXTBOOK NO. 2	TEXTBOOK NO. 3	TEXTBOOK NO. 4
238	244	267	248
230	246	250	259
242	248	264	263
220	248	284	255
234	259	260	257
218	248	255	258
225	249	268	252
224	242	248	254
248	254	256	250
229	233	273	265

Test the hypothesis that there is no difference between the average achievement scores made using the four different textbooks. Use a desk calculator. Let $\alpha = .05$.

†7.7 Using the results of Exercises 7.2 to 7.4, calculate two F scores, one for each of the two sets of data used previously. Repeat the hypothesis test $H: \mu_1 = \mu_2 = \mu_3$ for each set of data, recording in each case whether the hypothesis was accepted or rejected. Let $\alpha = .05$.

‡7.8 Compile the results of your hypothesis testing with those of the other members of your class. Calculate the percentage of times the hypothesis was (a) accepted, and (b) rejected, for the data of 7.3

A Modification of the Statistical Model

In this section, a change will be introduced for the model

$$(7.30) \qquad y_{ij} \sim (\mu_i, \sigma_i^2)$$
$$i = 1, 2, \ldots, k$$
$$j = 1, 2, \ldots, n$$

The reason for the change will not be apparent until more complicated models are encountered in later chapters. It is used here to present the ideas in a setting familiar to the reader.

Suppose we let $k = 3$, $n = 5$, and y_{ij} be the numbers appearing in (7.31) below, *for three populations:*

(7.31)
$$
\begin{aligned}
y_{11} &= 7 & y_{21} &= 8 & y_{31} &= 13 \\
y_{12} &= 11 & y_{22} &= 7 & y_{32} &= 4 \\
y_{13} &= 2 & y_{23} &= 1 & y_{33} &= 8 \\
y_{14} &= 21 & y_{24} &= 6 & y_{34} &= 16 \\
y_{15} &= 19 & y_{25} &= 3 & y_{35} &= 9
\end{aligned}
$$

For this case, $\mu_1 = 12$, $\mu_2 = 5$, $\mu_3 = 10$. The model we have been using is

(7.32) $$ y_{ij} \sim (\mu_i, \sigma_i{}^2) \quad \text{or} \quad y_{ij} = \mu_i + \epsilon_{ij} $$

where $$ \epsilon_{ij} \sim (0, \sigma_i{}^2) $$

Next we can write each μ_i as the sum of the average of all μ_i plus the deviation from that average. For instance,

(7.33)
$$
\begin{aligned}
\bar{\mu}. &= \tfrac{1}{3}(\mu_1 + \mu_2 + \mu_3) = 9 \\
\mu_1 &= 9 + 3 = \bar{\mu}. + 3 \\
\mu_2 &= 9 - 4 = \bar{\mu}. - 4 \\
\mu_3 &= 9 + 1 = \bar{\mu}. + 1
\end{aligned}
$$

We use the symbols τ_1, τ_2, τ_3 (the Greek letter tau, standing for "treatments") to represent the deviations of μ_1, μ_2, μ_3 from the average of the treatment means. Letting $\mu = \bar{\mu}.$,

(7.34)
$$
\begin{aligned}
\mu_1 &= \mu + \tau_1 \\
\mu_2 &= \mu + \tau_2 \\
\mu_3 &= \mu + \tau_3
\end{aligned}
$$

Now we can substitute the quantities in (7.34) into (7.32); for example, if

$$ y_{2j} = \mu_2 + \epsilon_{2j} $$

then

$$ y_{2.} = \mu + \tau_2 + \epsilon_{2j} $$

and, in general

$$
\begin{aligned}
y_{ij} &= \mu = \tau_i + \epsilon_{ij} \\
i &= 1, 2, \ldots, k \\
j &= 1, 2, \ldots, n
\end{aligned}
$$

EXERCISES

7.9 Consider the terms

$$
\begin{aligned}
y_{11} &= 4.5 & y_{21} &= 17.1 & y_{31} &= 9.1 & y_{41} &= 8.3 \\
y_{12} &= 2.7 & y_{22} &= 16.0 & y_{32} &= 13.3 & y_{42} &= 2.9 \\
y_{13} &= 6.3 & y_{23} &= 13.8 & y_{33} &= 6.7 & y_{43} &= 11.6
\end{aligned}
$$

as consisting of four distinct populations, each of size 3. Calculate the following quantities: $\mu, \tau_1, \tau_2, \tau_3, \tau_4, \epsilon_{ij}$ ($i = 1, \ldots, 4; j = 1, 2, 3$).

7.10 Express the quantities μ_1, μ_2, μ_3 of Exercise 7.1 in terms of the components μ, τ_1, τ_2, τ_3, giving the numerical values for each of the terms.

The Analysis of Variance Table

One method of laying out the computations for the hypothesis test has become popular primarily because it generalizes easily to more complex situations, just as does the model of the preceding section. The quantities to be computed are almost those already given. The formulas and the constants to be used for division are found in Table 7–3. The expected values after division by the constants are also given.

The "total" sum-of-squares is obtained by summing the squares of the deviations of each observation from the mean of all observations in the experiment (the "grand" mean). The degrees of freedom are the total number of observations in the experiment less one. Then

1. The sum of the degrees of freedom for between-treatment and within-treatment sums-of-squares equals the degrees of freedom for the total sum-of-squares.

2. Adding the between-treatment and within-treatment sums-of-squares gives the total sum-of-squares.

EXERCISE

7.11 Construct an analysis of variance table for the set of data in Exercise 7.2. Test the hypothesis $H: \mu_1 = \mu_2 = \mu_3$.

---

*The Ranking Problem

In this section we will interpret the results of an experiment. We will not just conclude that the means are (or are not) different from each other; we will now ask, How are the training programs related with respect to income over a five-year period? Or we will ask, How should the three textbooks be ranked with respect to scores on a test for motivation in mathematics?

To come to conclusions in this section, we must make the additional assumptions that the population variances are all approximately equal, and that the parent populations are normal. The second assumption is not essential with a sample size of about 20 or more, since the sample means will be approximately normal [see the central limit theorem (2.5) in Chapter 2] and the procedure will then be valid.

Next suppose that we order the population means from smallest to largest, with "adjacent" means being next to each other. We agree that if any two adjacent means have a difference less than *l*, either may be chosen as the most favorable. Furthermore, we want the probability of properly ranking all pairs of adjacent means whose difference $> l$ to be at least *p*. Note that *l* now refers to *any* adjacent pair among the *k* population means.

The general approach is very similar to that in Chapter 5; we select a preliminary random sample of n_0 observations from each of the *k* populations. From this we calculate *n*, the final sample size that must be selected, and then we draw an additional sample of size $n - n_0$ from each population. We finally

TABLE 7-3

One-Way Analysis of Variance Table

SOURCE	df	SUM-OF-SQUARES	MEAN-SQUARES	EXPECTED MEAN-SQUARES
Between populations	$k-1$	$\sum_{i=1}^{k} n(\bar{x}_{i\cdot} - \bar{x}_{\cdot\cdot})^2$	$\dfrac{1}{k-1}\sum_{i=1}^{k} n(\bar{x}_{i\cdot} - \bar{x}_{\cdot\cdot})^2$	$\dfrac{1}{k}\sum_{i=1}^{k}\sigma_i^2 + \dfrac{n}{k-1}\sum_{i=1}^{k}(\mu_i - \bar{\mu}_\cdot)$
Within populations	$k(n-1)$	$\sum_{i=1}^{k}\sum_{j=1}^{n}(x_{ij} - \bar{x}_{i\cdot})^2$	$\dfrac{1}{k(n-1)}\sum_{i=1}^{k}\sum_{j=1}^{n}(x_{ij} - \bar{x}_{i\cdot})^2$	$\dfrac{1}{k}\sum_{i=1}^{k}\sigma_i^2$
Total	$kn-1$	$\sum_{i=1}^{k}\sum_{j=1}^{n}(x_{ij} - \bar{x}_{\cdot\cdot})^2$		

compute the sample means for each of the k populations and rank the populations on the basis of the sample means.

We calculate n, the final sample size needed from each population, as follows. Let x_{ij} be the jth observation from population i, where $j = 1, 2, \ldots, n_0$ and $i = 1, 2, \ldots, k$. Then let

$$(7.35) \qquad s_i^2 = \frac{1}{n_0 - 1} \sum_{j=1}^{n_0} (x_{ij} - \bar{x}_{i\cdot})^2$$

$$s^2 = \frac{1}{k} \sum_{i=1}^{k} s_i^2$$

$$i = 1, 2, \ldots, k$$

We calculate n as the maximum of the two values

$$n_0 \qquad \text{and} \qquad \frac{2s^2 h^2}{l^2}$$

where h is a value obtained from Appendix Table I when $k = 3$, under the appropriate value for p and the degrees of freedom, $k(n_0 - 1)$, of s^2.

If $k > 3$, use the approximation

$$(7.36) \qquad h = t_{[k(n_0-1)]p^{1/(k-1)}}$$

which will be explained in a later section.

As an example, we ask the question, Which student ability level has the most popular students in the randomly grouped district? We use the times-chosen score (TI/CH), a sociometric measure, to determine this. We obtain an initial random sample of size 5 from each of the three ability levels. Next we specify $l = 5$; that is, we won't be fussy about which of a pair of means is ranked higher if their difference is less than 5, but we want to rank them correctly if their difference exceeds 5.

Now specify $p = .90$, so that our probability of properly ranking adjacent means whose difference exceeds 5 will be $\geq .90$. Our random samples are

FAST	AVERAGE	SLOW
16	20	16
13	11	8
8	5	8
12	32	15
23	7	8
$\bar{x}_1 = 14.4$	$\bar{x}_2 = 15.0$	$\bar{x}_3 = 11.0$
$s_1^2 = 31.3$	$s_2^2 = 123.5$	$s_3^2 = 92.0$

This gives

$$(7.37) \qquad s^2 = \frac{s_1^2 + s_2^2 + s_3^2}{3} = \frac{31.3 + 123.5 + 92.0}{3} = 82.27$$

The degrees of freedom are $k(n_0 - 1) = 3 \cdot 4 = 12$ and using Table I (since $k = 3$), we have $h = 1.781$. This gives n as the maximum of 5, and

$$(7.38) \qquad 2s^2 \left(\frac{h}{l}\right)^2 = 2(82.27) \left(\frac{1.781}{5}\right)^2 = 20.88 \cong 21$$

Thus in this case $n = 21$, and we must pick 16 additional observations from each population:

FAST	AVERAGE	SLOW
23	10	11
31	15	11
5	17	13
15	4	35
14	29	9
4	17	25
35	19	5
14	0	5
14	26	5
32	20	1
37	7	11
30	6	40
18	9	10
25	10	4
41	22	2
14	4	12

Means calculated from all observations are

$$\bar{x}_{1.} = 20.19, \qquad \bar{x}_{2.} = 13.81, \qquad \text{and} \qquad \bar{x}_{3.} = 12.10$$

and we thus rank the ability levels with fast students chosen most frequently, average students next, and slow students least. The probability of correctly ranking all pairs of means differing by more than 5 units is at least .90. Let us summarize this:

THEOREM 7.2

Suppose k population means are to be ranked under the following conditions:

a. *If any two adjacent means differ by at least l units, we want to rank them properly.*

b. *If a pair of means differs by less than l units, the order of ranking is not crucial.*

Then the following procedure has a probability $\geq p$ of properly ranking all pairs of means whose differences exceed l units:

1. *Choose a preliminary sample of n_0 units from each of the k populations, with observations*

$$x_{i1}, x_{i2}, \ldots, x_{in_0}$$
$$i = 1, 2, \ldots, k$$

2. *Calculate*

$$s_i{}^2 = \frac{1}{n_0 - 1} \sum_{j=1}^{n_0} (x_{ij} - \bar{x}_i.)^2$$

$$i = 1, 2, \ldots, k$$

$$\bar{x}_i. = \frac{1}{n_0} \sum_{j=1}^{n_0} x_{ij}$$

$$s^2 = \frac{1}{k} \sum_{i=1}^{k} s_i{}^2$$

(s^2 *is the same as the error mean square in an analysis of variance table for k populations, n_0 observations per population.*)

3. *Obtain n, the maximum of n_0, and $2s^2(h/l)^2$ where if $k = 3$, h is obtained rrom Table I, using the appropriate column corresponding to p and the row corresponding to $k(n_0 - 1)$ degrees of freedom. (If $k > 3$, use the approximation $h = t_{[k(n_0-1)]p^{1/(k-1)}}$).*

4. *Select a random sample of $n - n_0$ additional observations from each population, and calculate*

$$\bar{x}_i. = \frac{1}{n} \sum_{j=1}^{n} x_{ij}$$

$$i = 1, 2, \ldots, k$$

5. *Rank the populations on the basis of the order of magnitude of the sample means.*

EXERCISES

7.12 Suppose we wish to compare the three ability levels with respect to "Concept of Self" (CON/SEL) score in the ability grouped district and wish to make sure (with a probability of .90) of properly ranking adjacent populations whose average scores differ by more than five units. Further, suppose that we have selected three random samples as follows:

ABILITY LEVEL 1 (FAST)	ABILITY LEVEL 2 (AVERAGE)	ABILITY LEVEL 3 (SLOW)
38	45	30
41	50	45
51	49	38
46	46	43
50	32	49

State the additional number of observations that must be selected from each level to meet the required objectives.

†7.13 Carry out the experiment as given in Exercise 7.12, and rank the ability levels with respect to their "Concept of Self" score. (A high score is good.)

Using the Approximation for More than Three Populations

At this point, we will see how to obtain the approximation given in (7.36). This section is provided for reference if you encounter a situation involving more than three populations; thus it may be omitted at first reading.

Note that $t_{(m)p}$ is the value in Appendix Table F corresponding to m degrees of freedom and probability p. Further, $p \cdot 100$ percent of all observations from a population having Student's t-distribution are less than this value.

To obtain h, we carry out the steps illustrated in the following example. Suppose a superintendent wishes to rank four schools with respect to average achievement on the STEP reading score. He wants to be sure with a probability $= .95$ of properly ranking all pairs of schools whose average reading achievement scores differ by more than 5 units. Suppose he samples 10 students from each school and obtains

$$s^2 = \frac{s_1{}^2 + s_2{}^2 + s_3{}^2 + s_4{}^2}{4} = 133.5$$

We need to know how many more observations must be selected from each of the four populations in order to ensure the desired protection. To find this, we evaluate

$$\frac{2s^2h^2}{l^2} = \frac{2(133.5)h^2}{5^2}$$
$$= 10.68h^2$$

and the only unknown quantity is h. Now $k = 4$, $n_0 = 10$, $p = .95$, and

$$h = t_{[k(n_0-1)]\,p^{1/(1-k)}}$$

Step 1. Find $k(n_0 - 1) = 4(10 - 1) = 36$.
Step 2. Find $p^{1/(k-1)} = .95^{1/3}$, the cube root of .95, by using logarithms (see expression 1.48). The log of the cube root of .95 is $\frac{1}{3}$ log .95.

$$\log \ .95 = \ 9.9777 - 10$$
$$= 29.9777 - 30$$

(add and subtract 20 to make the negative value divisible by 3)

$$\tfrac{1}{3} \log .95 = \log .95^{1/3} = 9.9926 - 10$$
$$.95^{1/3} = \ .9830$$

Step 3. Find $t_{(36).983}$ by interpolation in Table F. Interpolate first with respect to probabilities at both 30 and 40 degrees of freedom:

$t_{(30).975}$	$t_{(30).983}$	$t_{(30).990}$
2.042	2.262	2.457

$t_{(40).975}$	$t_{(40).983}$	$t_{(40).990}$
2.021	2.234	2.423

Next interpolate with respect to the degrees of freedom:

$t_{(30).983}$	$t_{(36).983}$	$t_{(40).983}$
2.262	2.245	2.234

Hence $h = 2.245$.

Step 4. Evaluate

$$10.68h^2 = 10.68(2.245)^2$$
$$= 53.83 \cong 54$$

Thus 54 is the total number of observations to be selected from each population, so select 44 additional ones from each of the four schools, then rank the schools on the basis of the sample means.

The value for n obtained in this fashion will be somewhat larger than necessary, but this method must be used until tables are available for $k > 3$.

EXERCISES

7.14　Suppose a sociologist is interested in the home adjustment of children in the various ability levels from both districts. There are six populations to select from; the sociologist wishes to rank all six levels with respect to the average home adjustment as measured by the "Me and Home" score. He would like a probability = .90 of properly ranking adjacent means whose difference exceeds 10 units. Five students are selected at random from each population and their scores are recorded:

RANDOMLY GROUPED DISTRICT			ABILITY GROUPED DISTRICT		
FAST STUDENTS	AVERAGE STUDENTS	SLOW STUDENTS	FAST STUDENTS	AVERAGE STUDENTS	SLOW STUDENTS
2	11	9	15	36	18
10	12	10	9	0	0
3	0	8	24	27	3
10	6	3	4	8	15
0	10	3	16	14	32

How many additional observations should the sociologist sample from each population to assure the required protection when the populations are ranked?

†7.15　Obtain the additional observations required and rank the populations.

DATA PROCESSING FOR THE ANALYSIS OF VARIANCE

The computations for an analysis of variance table are time consuming, and the ranking procedure for population means involves calculation of the within-population mean-squares for an analysis of variance with n_0 observations from each population. A program to compute the entries in an analysis of variance table is therefore useful; such a program is presented next.

Use of PRGM1 for Analysis of Variance

In Figure 4–9, we noted that there are two types of data that can be entered on a deck of cards. Example (a) is an illustration of several measurements made on a single group of people, or sampling units. Example (b), which we shall consider here, consists of several groups with the same measurement made on the people from each group. The observation for the ith person from each of the groups is punched in the ith data card, so that if there are k groups, there will be k observations punched in each card, consistent with the set of field descriptors given on your control card. The outline of the deck is:

1. Systems cards (as usual, see instructions from your own computer facility)
2. The program, as listed in Appendix Table K
3. Systems cards
4. Three control cards
5. Data cards
6. FIN card, for end of data
7. Final systems cards

As before, 1, 3, and 7 cannot be described here.

CONTROL CARD 1
Give the description of the job that you wish to have printed on the output. The entire card is available for this message, and any characters that are on a standard keypunch can be used.

CONTROL CARD 2

COLUMN	DESCRIPTION OF ENTRY
1–5	Number of groups of data; right-hand digit of number must be in column 5.
10	Blank; this is = 1 if correlation coefficients are desired; in this case, they are not appropriate.
15	1, to indicate that analysis of variance table is desired.

CONTROL CARD 3
COLUMN

1–11	(T78, A3, T1,
12–m, where m is as large as needed.	The set of field descriptors for your set of data; this should be consistent with the number k of groups you specified on the first control card. The rules for accomplishing this are given in Chapter 4.
m + 1	Right-hand parenthesis.

DATA CARDS
Data cards are filled out consistently with Control Card 2, with the restriction that no data should be entered in columns 78–80, which are reserved for the card just following the data, where FIN, for "finish" is punched.

FIN CARD

1–77	blank
78–80	FIN

The output for this program consists of the listing of the data cards and the sample means for each population, exactly as in Chapter 4. Next comes the analysis of variance table as follows:

ANALYSIS OF VARIANCE

Source	DF	SS	MS	F
Populations	$(k - 1)$	.xxxx E xx	.xxxx E xx	xxxx E xx
Error	$k(n - 1)$	.xxxx E xx	.xxxx E xx	
Total	$kn - 1$	.xxxx E xx		

The lower case letters will be replaced by numbers. The capital letters will appear exactly as they are. Numbers in the SS column are sums-of-squares; those in the MS column are the sums-of-squares divided by their degrees of freedom, and the number in the F column is MS_{POP}/MS_{ERROR}.

Batch Processing

In this section, we will exploit a property of PRGM1, and of all the other programs provided with this text, which should cut down on computer costs and on programming time for student use. When the FIN on the card following the data is replaced by END, the control cards and deck for another set of data follow immediately, beginning with the next card. Thus an arbitrary number, m, can be processed on the same "pass" of the program, by using the following arrangement:

1. Systems cards
2. The program from the appendix
3. Systems cards
4. Sets of data, as follows:
   Control cards for deck 1
   Data deck 1
   END card
   Control cards for deck 2
   Data deck 2
   END card
   .
   .
   .
   Control cards for deck $m - 1$
   Data deck $m - 1$
   END card
   Control cards for deck m
   Data deck m
   FIN card
5. Final systems cards.

Note that no systems cards go between any two data decks. The reason for the "heading" card should be more evident now: it permits the output for different students or for different jobs of the same student to be identified when the decks are placed together and run as just described. Each job can differ from every other job since the control cards are part of each data deck. We will call this procedure "batch processing." One simple term, used previously, needs to be defined formally:

DEFINITION 7.4
One submission of a program to the computer, involving compilation (translation to assembler language) and execution, using the data provided, is termed a "pass" or a "run" of the program.

For the remaining computer-oriented exercises, students may form groups and batch-process the data so that you will need to fill out only one set of systems cards.

Using Decks of Data Cards Not Punched According to the Specifications of This Text

The programs in this book have been designed for flexibility, so they may be used for decks that were not punched specifically for these programs. Suppose someone has a deck of cards already punched and brings them to you for analysis of the data. If the arrangement in Figure 4–9 (either (a) or (b)) has been used, you will be able to take the deck as it is, and after filling out of the control cards properly, you may do the processing without repunching the deck. First, however, we will consider the rules for two more codes.

The "T" and "An" Codes

If we encounter Tn in a set of field descriptors, we start reading in column n of the data card being read. A field descriptor needs to accompany this symbol, which enables us to skip around on a card. For example, Control Card 2 of PRGM1 begins (T78,A3,T1,; thus we begin reading in column 78, 79, 80. Next we move to column 1. The An format allows us to punch letters as well as numbers in the next n columns. The result is then stored in the computer and used for printing alphabetic output where needed; information stored in this way cannot be used for computing.

Now we review the use of this information with PRGM1. In the program, the first item read on each data card is the space reserved for either END or FIN. This space does not need to be columns 78–80; it can be any place on a card where data is not being read from (that is, the space may contain data, but you are not using it on this run of the program). The program is written to continue to read more cards as long as either END or FIN is not encountered in the first three columns specified in Control Card 2. These must always be given in A format—(Tn, A3,—where the three columns can be anywhere on the card that is appropriate. Then you can indicate with the following Tn where to begin reading next.

For example, suppose we have the following situations, assuming three groups or measures: with a three-digit integer for measure 1; two digits, one place to the right of the decimal, for measure 2; and four digits, two to the right of the decimal, for measure 3:

COLUMN FOR FIN OR END	COLUMN FOR DATUM 1	COLUMN FOR DATUM 2	COLUMN FOR DATUM 3	CONTROL CARD 2
36–38	1–3	15,16	64–67	(T36,A3,T1,F3.0,11X,F2.1,47X,F4.2)
1–3	24–26	27,28	51–54	(A3,20X,F3.0,F2.1,22X,F4.2)
78–80	1–3	4,5	6–9	(T78,A3,T1,F3.0,F2.1,F4.2)
21–23	11–13	29,30	41–44	(T21,A3,T11,F3.0,15X,F2.1,10X,F4.2)

EXERCISES

In Exercises 6.19 and 6.20 you punched a set of 110 data cards, with all measurements made for a single student on the same card. There are no data entered on the cards from column 34 on, so use columns 78–80 for entering END or FIN on the final card.

7.16   Write out the control cards for obtaining the correlations between the STEP reading and social science scores.

7.17   Obtain the correlation coefficients between the following six scores in one pass:

1.	STEP reading	(Cols. 6–8)
2.	STEP mathematics	(Cols. 12–14)
3.	Sociometric score (TI/CH)	(Cols. 15,16)
4.	SRA "Me and School"	(Cols. 24,25)
5.	SRA "Me and Home"	(Cols. 26,27)
6.	SRA "About Myself"	(Cols. 28,29)

If you have a deck of cards where there is no set of three adjacent columns without data in them, you will have to use a "roving" position for the END or FIN card. Since we can have no more than six measurements in a run, simply use three adjacent columns which are not part of the data fields for the six measurements on the run. The next run, using other measurements, may have data overlapping the position used the last time; and you may have to change the location used for END and FIN for different runs. To illustrate the point, in Exercise 7.17, columns 9–11 are not being used for the run, so that END or FIN could be punched in columns 9–11 on the final card and the program would work properly if Control Card 2 began with (T9,A3,.

Two Kinds of Error

In Theorem 7.1 the probability for rejecting $H: \mu_1 = \mu_2 = .. = \mu_k$ when it is true was given. In Exercise 7.8, we considered a case for which the hypothesis

TABLE 7–4

Chart Giving Two Kinds of Error for Hypothesis Testing

WE CONCLUDE	ACTUAL SITUATION	
	H TRUE	*H FALSE*
H true	Correct conclusion	Type II error $= \beta$
H false	Type I error $= \alpha$	Correct conclusion

is false and calculated the percentage of times when we accepted it. Both events are errors; which is more important to avoid depends on the situation. We summarize the problem in Table 7–4.

Suppose we were comparing several textbooks with respect to math achievement; the alternatives can be expressed in terms of the risk of adopting one book when it is no better than the others (type I $= \alpha$), compared with the risk of considering the books to be equal when one is considerably better (type II $= \beta$). Which risk is least desirable may depend on the school district. We bring out the point here to warn the research worker that he can make more than one kind of error, and to encourage him to consider both kinds when in designing experiments.

EXERCISES

†7.18 Repeat Exercises, 7.3 and 7.4, and 7.7, using a sample size of 10 for your random sample. Use PRGM1 for the calculations.

†7.19 Record the results of testing the hypothesis H: $\mu_1 = \mu_2 = \mu_3$, using the data of Exercise 7.18. Let $\alpha = .05$ as in Exercises 7.7.

†7.20 Compile your results with those of the other class members and calculate the percentage of times the hypothesis was (a) rejected, and (b) accepted. Compare with the percentages obtained in Exercise 7.11. Suggest reasons for differences between the results if there are any.

Experiences with Data

Design and execute experiments to answer the following questions. Use any technique or techniques from earlier chapters. These questions do not involve only procedures taught in Chapter 7.

PROBLEMS

7.1 How are home adjustment and ability level related?

7.2 How is the gap between "Concept of Self" and "Ideal Self" related to "Acceptance of Self"?

7.3 Does the assignment of children to slow classes affect their popularity? How?

7.4   Does the assignment of children to slow classes affect their achievement? How?

7.5   Can teachers affect the social adjustment of children?

7.6   Are there differences between schools in the social adjustment of the students? In the home adjustment of the students?

7.7   Does the assignment of children to fast classes affect their social adjustment? Their achievement? How?

7.8   Is ability grouping equally beneficial (or detrimental) to both fast and slow students? If so, in what way? If not, explain what happens.

SOLUTIONS TO EXERCISES

7.1

$$\frac{n}{k-1} \sum_{i=1}^{k} (\mu_i - \bar{\mu}.)^2 + \frac{1}{k} \sum_{i=1}^{k} \sigma_i^2 = 225.64 + 112.4 = 338.04$$

7.2

$$\bar{x}_{1.} = 255.8; \ \bar{x}_{2.} = 262.5; \ \bar{x}_{3.} = 246.5; \ s_{\bar{x}}^2 = 64.57; \ n s_{\bar{x}}^2 = 4 s_{\bar{x}}^2 = 258.28$$

7.4

$$s_1^2 = 94.92; \ s_2^2 = 64.33; \ s_3^2 = 91.67$$

$$\text{Average} = \tfrac{1}{3} \sum_{i=1}^{3} s_i^2 = 83.64$$

$$\tfrac{1}{3} \sum_{i=1}^{3} \sigma_i^2 = 112.4$$

7.5

$$F_{(3,16).99} = 5.29; \ F_{(2,12).95} = 3.89; \ F_{(4,15).95} = 3.06$$

7.6

$$n s_{\bar{x}}^2 = 1891.5; \ s^2 = 73.32; \ F = 1891.5/73.32 = 25.8$$

$$F_{[k-1,k(n-1)].05} = F_{[3,18].05} = 3.16. \ \text{Reject } H.$$

7.9

$\mu = 9.35;$	$\tau_1 = -4.85;$	$\tau_2 = 6.28;$	$\tau_3 = .35;$	$\tau_4 = -1.75;$
$\mu_1 = 4.5;$	$\mu_2 = 15.63;$	$\mu_3 = 9.70;$	$\mu_4 = 7.60$

$\epsilon_{11} = 0$	$\epsilon_{21} = 1.47$	$\epsilon_{31} = -.6$	$\epsilon_{41} = .7$
$\epsilon_{12} = -1.8$	$\epsilon_{22} = .37$	$\epsilon_{32} = 3.6$	$\epsilon_{42} = -4.7$
$\epsilon_{13} = 1.8$	$\epsilon_{23} = -1.83$	$\epsilon_{33} = -3.0$	$\epsilon_{43} = 4.0$

7.10

$$\mu = 260.02; \ \tau_1 = 7.82; \ \tau_2 = -.64; \ \tau_3 = -7.18$$

7.11

SOURCE	df	SUM-OF-SQUARES	MEAN SQUARES	EXPECTED MEAN SQUARES
Between populations	2	516.4	258.2	338.64
Within populations	9	752.75	83.63	112.4
Total	11	1268.92		

7.12

$2s^2(h/l)^2$; $s_1^2 = 31.7$; $s_2^2 = 52.3$; $s_3^2 = 53.5$; $s^2 = 45.8$; $h = 1.781$; $l = 5$
$91.6(1.781/5)^2 = 91.6(.071)$; $n = 6.5 \cong 7$; $n - n_0 = 2$
Obtain two additional observations from each population.

7.14

$s_1^2 = 42$; $s_2^2 = 24.2$; $s_3^2 = 11.3$; $s_4^2 = 57.3$; $s_5^2 = 210$; $s_6^2 = 164.3$; $l = 10$;
$s^2 = 84.85$; $.90^{1/5} \cong .979$; $h = t_{(24).979} = 2.179$; $n = 2(84.85)(2.179)^2/100 = 8$;
$n - n_0 = 3$
You will need three additional observations.

7.16

Assume that the left-handmost character in the following lines is punched in column 1.

CORRELATION COEFFICIENT BETWEEN STEP READ AND STEP SCI SCORES
    2   1
(T78,A3,T1,5X,2F3.0)

7.17

Assume that the left-handmost character in the following lines is punched in column 1.

R BETWEEN STEP READ,STEP MATH,TI/CH,SCH,HOM,ME
    6   1
(T78,A3,T6,2F3.0,F2.0,7X,3F2.0)

{ Data Cards

Col. 78
↓

END

REVIEW FOR CHAPTER 7

1. The statistical model for several populations

$$y_{ij} = \mu_i + \epsilon_{ij}$$
$$i = 1, 2, \ldots, k$$
$$j = 1, 2, \ldots, N_i$$

2. Stratified sampling

3. Hypothesis test for equality of means. Let

$$x_{ij} = (\mu_i, \sigma_i^2)$$
$$i = 1, 2, \ldots, k$$
$$j = 1, 2, \ldots, n$$

A test of H: $\mu_1 = \mu_2 \cdots = \mu_k$ is carried out as follows:

1. Calculate

$$ns_{\bar{x}}^2 = \frac{n}{k-1} \sum_{i=1}^{k} (\bar{x}_{i.} - \bar{x}_{..})^2$$

This is n times the variance of the sample means.

2. Calculate

$$\frac{1}{k} \sum_{i=1}^{k} s_i^2$$

where

$$s_i^2 = \frac{1}{n-1} \sum_{j=1}^{n} (x_{ij} - \bar{x}_{i.})^2$$

This is the mean of the sample variances.

3. $ns_{\bar{x}}^2 \Big/ \dfrac{1}{k} \displaystyle\sum_{i=1}^{k} s_i^2$ should be approximately equal to 1, if the population means are equal.

Test H: $\mu_1 = \mu_2 = \cdots = \mu_k$ with the rule:

$$\text{Accept } H \text{ if } ns_{\bar{x}}^2 \Big/ \frac{1}{k} \sum_{i=1}^{k} s_i^2 = F < F_{[k-1, k(n-1)]\,1-\alpha}$$

$$\text{Reject } H \text{ if } \quad F \geq F_{[k-1, k(n-1)]\,1-\alpha}$$

where $F_{[k-1, k(n-1)]\,1-\alpha}$ is obtained from Appendix Table L, using the row corresponding to $k - 1$, and the part of the table corresponding to $1 - \alpha$.

4. A statistical model for several populations

$$y_{ij} = \mu + \tau_i + \epsilon_{ij}$$
$$i = 1, 2, \ldots, k$$
$$j = 1, 2, \ldots, n$$
$$\epsilon_{ij} \sim (0, \sigma_i^2)$$

5. The analysis of variance table

SOURCE	df	SUM-OF-SQUARES	MEAN-SQUARES
Between populations	$k - 1$	$\sum_{i=1}^{k} n(\bar{x}_{i.} - \bar{x}..)^2$	$\dfrac{1}{k-1} \sum_{i=1}^{k} n(\bar{x}_{i.} - \bar{x}..)^2$
Within populations	$k(n - 1)$	$\sum_{i=1}^{k} \sum_{j=1}^{n} (x_{ij} - \bar{x}_{i.})^2$	$\dfrac{1}{k(n-1)} \sum_{i=1}^{k} \sum_{j=1}^{n} (x_{ij} - \bar{x}_{i.})^2$
Total	$kn - 1$	$\sum_{i=1}^{k} \sum_{j=1}^{n} (x_{ij} - \bar{x}..)^2$	

6. Ranking of k populations. Sample size needed to ensure (with probability $= p$) that all pairs of means whose difference exceeds l units are properly ranked:

Select n_0 preliminary observations from each population, and obtain

$$s^2 = \frac{1}{k} \sum_{i=1}^{k} s_i^2$$

n is then the maximum of n_0 and $2s^2h^2/l^2$, where h is obtained from Appendix Table I when $k = 3$. If $k > 3$,

$$h = t_{[k(n_0-1)]\, p^{1/(k-1)}}$$

CHAPTER 8
REGRESSION ANALYSIS

This chapter will deal extensively with a problem introduced in Chapter 3, when the correlation coefficient was presented with the goal of establishing a connection or strength of relationship between any two measures. Now we wish to change our objective and employ one of the variables to estimate what the other will be. Previously, there was no distinction in the way we regarded the two variables; now one becomes the predictor, and the other is the predicted variable.

DESCRIPTION OF THE PROBLEM

We introduce this topic by describing two situations in which prediction is useful:

1. One of the variables occurs later in time than the other, and we want to use the earlier variable to predict what the later one will be like. A classic example of this uses college grade-point average (GPA) as the later variable and high school GPA the earlier one.

2. One of the observations is much more expensive to obtain than the other. For example, to obtain the Stanford-Binet intelligence quotient (IQ) requires considerable time spent by a professional test administrator with a single student. A school district cannot afford to have every child tested in this fashion and will replace such a measure with a class administered IQ-type test that can be given by the regular teacher after brief instruction on how to administer it. We may well be interested in knowing how close the class version comes to the results of the more expensive test, when both types are available for some sample of students. The intention is to use this result with students for whom the Stanford-Binet test is not available.

The problems outlined are among the ones for which regression methods are useful. Before describing how to handle them, however, we must introduce some necessary geometry.

Graphing Equations

In Chapter 3, scatter diagrams were constructed using the pairs of random variates (x_i, y_i), where i ranged over all people in the sample. This method of plotting points on a graph can be used to describe equations, as we will now see. If we drop the subscript i, we can consider pairs of members (x, y), where x gives the coordinate on the horizontal axis (called the abscissa) and y gives that for the vertical axis (called the ordinate). For example, Figure 8–1 provides the point corresponding to $(3, 7)$. This is *not* equal to the point $(7, 3)$; the order in which the numbers appear is important.

Next consider the equation

$$(8.1) \qquad y = \frac{5 - 2x}{3} = \frac{5}{3} - \left(\frac{2}{3}\right) x$$

For each value of x in this equation, we will obtain a value for y. If $x = 3$,

$$(8.2) \qquad y = \frac{5}{3} - \left(\frac{2}{3}\right) 3 = \frac{5}{3} - 2 = \frac{5}{3} - \frac{6}{3} = \frac{-1}{3}$$

If $x = 12$,

$$(8.3) \qquad y = \frac{5}{3} - \left(\frac{2}{3}\right) 12 = \frac{-19}{3}$$

and finally if $x = 18$,

$$(8.4) \qquad y = \frac{5}{3} - \left(\frac{2}{3}\right) 18 = \frac{5}{3} - \frac{36}{3} = \frac{-31}{3}$$

Next we plot these points in Figure 8–2. Notice that all three points lie on a straight line. Furthermore, if we substitute *any* value x into the equation

---

FIGURE 8-1
Simple diagram for the points $(3, 7)$ and $(7, 3)$.

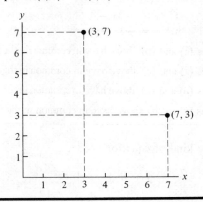

FIGURE 8-2

Graph for plotting the points $(3, -\frac{1}{3})$, $(12, -\frac{19}{3})$, and $(18, -\frac{31}{3})$.

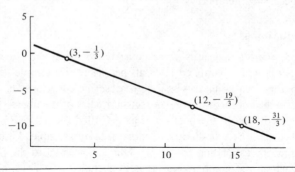

TABLE 8-1

Pairs x, y for a Linear Equation

x	y
3	$-1/3$
12	$-19/3$
18	$-31/3$

$y = \frac{5}{3} - (\frac{2}{3})x$, we obtain a value, y, which will be on the same straight line. The pairs x, y can also be put into a simple table, as in Table 8-1.

We will find that any equation of the form

$$(8.5) \qquad y = a + bx$$

can be plotted in the same way, and each plot will be a straight line. For this reason, (8.5) is often termed a *linear equation*.

EXERCISES

8.1 Plot graphs of the following equations:

 a. $y = 3x - 5$ b. $y = 3x + 1$
 c. $y = x - 5$ d. $y = x + 1$
 e. $y = 2x + 3$ f. $y = -3x - 1$
 g. $y = -2x - 1$ h. $y = -3x + 3$

8.2 What do equations (a) and (b) above have in common in the formula? In the graph?

8.3 What do equations (a) and (c) above have in common in the formula? In the graph?

8.4 What do equations (b) and (d) above have in common in the formula? In the graph?

8.5 What do equations (f) to (h) above have in common in the formula? In the graph?

We turn to a new kind of equation:

$$(8.6) \qquad y = a + bx + cx^2$$

TABLE 8-2

Pairs of Numbers for a Quadratic Function

x	$3 - x + 2x^2 = y$
-3	$3 - (-3) + 2 \cdot (-3)^2 = 24$
-2	$3 - (-2) + 2 \cdot (-2)^2 = 13$
-1	$3 - (-1) + 2 \cdot (-1)^2 = 6$
0	$3 - (0) + 2 \cdot 0^2 = 3$
1	$3 - 1 + 2 \cdot 1^2 = 4$
2	$3 - 2 + 2 \cdot 2^2 = 9$
3	$3 - 3 + 2 \cdot 3^2 = 18$

FIGURE 8-3
Graph for plotting points which satisfy the equation $y = 3 - x + 2x^2$.

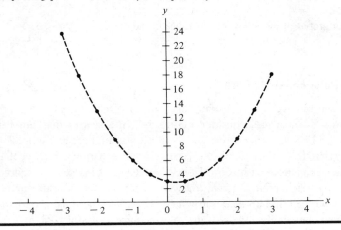

where now a term involving x^2 is also included. Consider

$$(8.7) \qquad\qquad y = 3 - x + 2x^2$$

To be systematic, we calculate value of y corresponding to $x = -3, -2, -1,$ 0, 1, 2, and 3, in Table 8–2. Figure 8–3 is a graph corresponding to this set of points, with a point corresponds to each pair of numbers.

Now the points no longer lie on a straight line; the rate of increase or decrease in y is not constant but changes as the values of x change. Plotting a polynomial *of degree 2* is as easy as plotting a linear equation. We include two definitions at this point;

DEFINITION 8.1
A "*polynomial*" in x is defined as a function of the form

$$a + bx$$
$$a + bx + cx^2$$
$$a + bx + cx^2 + dx^2$$

or in general,

$$a + a_1x + a_2x^2 + \cdots + a_nx^n$$

where x is a variable which can take on an arbitrary value.

DEFINITION 8.2
The "degree" of a polynomial is defined as the highest value of the exponents appearing in that polynomial.

For example, degrees of the polynomials in Definition 8.1 are 1, 2, 3, and *n*, respectively.

EXERCISE
8.6 Plot graphs of the following equations in the range $-5 \leq x \leq 5$:
   a. $y = 1 - 2x + 3x^2$ b. $y = -4 + 5x - x^2$ c. $y = 1 + 2x + 3x^2$

Fitting Polynomials to Data

In this section we will consider how formulas can be used for prediction purposes. To illustrate, consider Figure 3–7, the scatter diagram for STEP math and STEP science scores, which appears again here as Figure 8–4. Now suppose that from these data, we can write an equation which enables us to estimate a student's math score from knowledge of his science score. In this case (using teacher No. 1), we know both sets of scores. But our reasoning is that if we can find an equation which works for these data, perhaps it will work for other data, and we thus may acquire a useful tool for predictive

FIGURE 8–4
Scatter diagram for STEP math and STEP science scores for the first class (teacher No. 1), randomly grouped fifth-grade students.

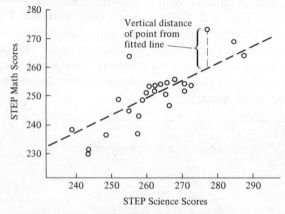

FIGURE 8-5

Hypothetical scatter diagram showing a "perfect" relationship between math and science achievement scores.

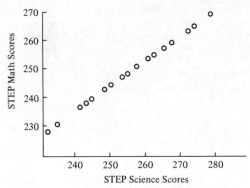

purposes. A more practical use would be the prediction of college GPA from knowledge of high school GPA. Now if all the points of Figure 8-4 lay on a straight line, all we would have to do would be to find its equation, and then if we knew the science score for a student we could tell exactly what his math score would be, as in Figure 8-5.

The equation for Figure 8-5 is

$$(8.8) \qquad y = 39.0 + .825x$$

Suppose now that a student's science score is 260. Then this equation is used to obtain his math score; that is, if y is his math score, we have

$$y = 39.0 + .825(260) = 253.5$$

If his science score is 240, then his math score is

$$y = 39.0 + .825(240) = 237.0$$

Similarly, a science score of 280 corresponds to a math score of

$$y = 39.0 + .825(280) = 270.0.$$

The correspondence is so good that we would not need to administer the math test—the science score tells us all we need to know.

In practice, however, the correspondence is never that good. We have the data of Figure 8-4, not those of Figure 8-5. The question is whether we can do anything with data that are less precise. We will find that we can, by using a straight line that passes through the points and reveals their general trend. This is the dotted line in Figure 8-4, and its equation is

$$y = 62.24 + .72x$$

The general form of this equation is

(8.9) $y = a + bx$
$a = \bar{y}. - b\bar{x}.$

$$b = r_{xy} \frac{s_y}{s_x} = \sum_{i=1}^{n} (x_i - \bar{x}.)(y_i - \bar{y}.) \bigg/ \sum_{i=1}^{n} (x_i - \bar{x}.)^2$$

$$s_y = \frac{1}{n-1} \sum_{i=1}^{n} (y_i - \bar{y}.)^2$$

$$s_x = \frac{1}{n-1} \sum_{i=1}^{n} (x_i - \bar{x}.)^2$$

$$r_{xy} = \frac{1}{n-1} \sum_{i=1}^{n} \frac{(x_i - \bar{x}.)(y_i - \bar{y}.)}{s_x s_y}$$

These formulas are obtained by making the sample variance of the points from the line as small as possible. To find the sample variance, we take the squared vertical deviation of each point from the line; we then make the average of all these as small as possible. One such vertical deviation is diagrammed in Figure 8–4. Now although we cannot predict *exactly* what the math score will be on the basis of the science score, we can do better than if we did not know the science score at all. We consider

---

DEFINITION 8.3
Construction of a line through a series of data points as described in the preceding paragraph is termed "fitting" a regression line to the observations.

The word *regression* came from the observation that those who tend to test highest on the x variable are lower on the y value relative to the others in the group. Galton, a British scientist, first observed that children of the tallest fathers tend to be less tall than their fathers; they "regress" and are less prominent with respect to that characteristic.

EXERCISE
8.7 Fit a line through the data for Figure 3–9, obtaining the data from page AR1, teacher No. 1. Make a scatter diagram for the figure and draw the fitted line on the diagram.

What we have learned thus far gives rise to some questions:

Does the regression equation help us to predict some variable more accurately than we otherwise could?

We obtained our equation from the sample data; how do we know that the results we obtained are genuine and can be depended on if we use new data selected from the same population?

How much improvement in accuracy is possible by using a regression equation for a given set of data?

Solutions to questions like these will be proposed after a statistical model is developed to describe the situation. The questions then need to be translated into terms that make use of the model in order to obtain a solution.

A Statistical Model for Linear Regression

To illustrate, we return to the first classroom among the randomly grouped students and consider it as a *population*, rather than as a random sample from a larger population. We have 31 pairs of observations as in Figure 8–4. Let the one whose vertical distance from the fitted line is diagrammed be y_{24}, and let the corresponding x value be x_{24}. The point for x_{24} on the fitted line is the intersection of the two dotted lines. This is

$$(8.10) \qquad (x_{24},\ 62.24 + .72x_{24})$$

The right-hand value is our equation $a + bx$. It gets us close to y_{24}, but it is not exactly equal to it. The vertical distance diagrammed in Figure 8–4 we will lablel ϵ_{24}; this value may be either positive or negative, and it represents the amount by which the equation fails to give exactly y_{24}. If we wish, we can write

$$(8.11) \qquad y_{24} - 62.24 - .72x_{24} = \epsilon_{24} \qquad \text{or} \qquad y_{24} = 62.24 + .72x_{24} + \epsilon_{24}$$

For each pair of observations (x_i, y_i), we can calculate ϵ_i so that

$$(8.12) \qquad \begin{aligned} y_i &= 62.24 + .72x_i + \epsilon_i \\ i &= 1, 2, \ldots, 25 \end{aligned}$$

We find that

$$\sum_{i=1}^{25} \epsilon_i = 0 \qquad \text{and we define} \qquad \frac{1}{23} \sum_{i=1}^{25} \epsilon_i^2 = \sigma^2$$

as in the past, except that now we divide by $N - 2$. This is our statistical model for a population for which a regression analysis is needed. The pair (x_{24}, y_{24}) which is diagrammed is $(276, 272)$; the predicted y score is

$$62.24 + .72(276) = 260.96$$

Hence

$$(8.13) \qquad 272 - 260.96 = 11.04 = \epsilon_{24}$$

Now that we are considering the (x_i, y_i) where $i = 1, 2, \ldots, 25$ as a population, we use different symbols for the equation. Earlier we had

(8.14) $y = a + bx$

for the fitted line. Now we use

(8.15) $y = \alpha + \beta x$

(β is the Greek letter "beta") and the general form of the model is

(8.16) $y_i = \alpha + \beta x_i + \epsilon_i$
                                       $i = 1, 2, \ldots, N$

We continue the convention of using Greek symbols for the population constants. Often, instead of using Roman letters for the sample values of the constants, a caret over the Greek letter is employed (as $\hat{\alpha}$ or $\hat{\beta}$).

At this point, the reason for using

$$\frac{1}{N-2} \sum_{i=1}^{N} \epsilon_i^2 \quad \text{instead of} \quad \frac{1}{N-1} \sum_{i=1}^{N} \epsilon_i^2$$

will be explained. To illustrate, we return to a single population with a single observation:

(8.17) $\sigma^2 = \dfrac{1}{N-1} \displaystyle\sum_{i=1}^{N} (x_i - \mu)^2$

$$\mu = \frac{1}{N} \sum_{i=1}^{N} x_i$$

One parameter (μ) of the population had to be calculated, and we subtracted one from the total population size before dividing. Here,

(8.18) $\sigma^2 = \dfrac{1}{N-2} \displaystyle\sum_{i=1}^{N} (y_i - \alpha - \beta x_i)^2$

$$\beta = \frac{\Sigma (x_i - \bar{x}.)(y_i - \bar{y}.)}{\Sigma (x_i - \bar{x}.)^2}$$

$$\alpha = \bar{y}. - \beta \bar{x}.$$

Now two parameters have to be calculated, and we subtract 2 from N before dividing. The rule is general and will be used frequently.

EXERCISE

8.8 The following observations were taken from the second class, randomly grouped students, and are to be considered as a population:

i	"ACCEPTANCE OF SELF" = y_i	"ME AND HOME" = x_i
1	43	6
2	42	3
3	49	14
4	37	6
5	51	1
6	36	24
7	57	1
8	31	12
9	56	5
10	51	21
11	45	1

Calculate α, β, and ϵ_i where $i = 1, 2, \ldots, 11$, and $\sigma^2 = \dfrac{1}{9} \displaystyle\sum_{i=1}^{n} \epsilon_i^2$. Make a scatter diagram, and plot the regression line.

STATISTICAL INFERENCE FOR LINEAR REGRESSION

Two basic questions are usually asked when a regression model is being used. The first is, Are we doing any good by using a regression model? The second is, How much good are we doing with this model? These questions will now be considered in detail, starting with the second question.

A Measure of the Effectiveness of the Regression Equation

At the end of Chapter 3, we considered a measure, r, of the strength of the relationship between two variables. We wish now to obtain a similar measure for the regression model. We assume that a simple random sample has been selected from the population, and we then perform some calculations analogous to those used in an analysis of variance table.

One additional assumption is made for regression analysis. This is that that ϵ_i are *normal*. Although there is reason to believe that these procedures work if the ϵ_i are reasonably bell shaped, even if they are not normal, the evidence is not yet complete on this point. With this note of caution, we next outline our reasoning for this measure.

To illustrate the explanation, consider again Figure 3–8, which is a scatter diagram for the relationship between academic achievement in science and home adjustment scores. As can be observed, there is more scatter than in Figure 3–8, and it seems that a less strong relationship exists here. The constants for the regression line are

(8.19)
$$a = \bar{y} - b\bar{x}. = 41.53$$

$$b = \frac{\displaystyle\sum_{i=1}^{n} (x_i - \bar{x}.)(y_i - \bar{y}.)}{\displaystyle\sum_{i=1}^{n} (x_i - \bar{x}.)^2} = -.115$$

if we consider these observations as a sample. Figure 8–6 is a reproduction of Figure 3–9 with the regression line fitted through these points.

The strength of the relationship is not a function of how steep the line is; we could change the slope simply by changing the scaling system for one of the axes. We can measure the accuracy of the predictor, however, by noting that the total sum-of-squares for the predicted variable, which is ·

$$\sum_{i=1}^{n} (y_i - \bar{y}.)^2$$

can be partitioned into the part that is not predicted by the equation and the part that is. The portion of the sum-of-squares not predicted by the equation is

$$\sum_{i=1}^{n} e_i^2 = \sum_{i=1}^{n} (y_i - a - bx_i)^2$$

and the rest of the sum-of-squares is

$$\frac{\left[\sum (x_i - \bar{x}.)(y_i - \bar{y}.) \right]^2}{\sum (x_i - \bar{x}.)^2}$$

FIGURE 8–6
Regression of "Me and Home" adjustment scores on science achievement.

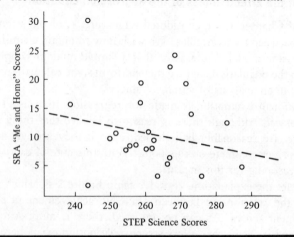

We have

$$(8.20) \quad \sum(y_i - \bar{y})^2 = \sum_{i=1}^{n} (y_i - a - bx_i)^2 + \frac{\left[\sum_{i=1}^{n} (x_i - \bar{x})(y_i - \bar{y}) \right]^2}{\sum_{i=1}^{n} (x_i - \bar{x})^2}$$

Equation 8.20 can be expressed in words as

(8.21)   total variation = unpredicted variation + predicted variation

From (8.21) we see that the proportion of the total variation that can be predicted is

(8.22)   predicted variation ÷ total variation

By referring back to (8.20) we find this proportion is

$$(8.23) \quad \frac{\left[\sum (x_i - \bar{x})(y_i - \bar{y}) \right]^2}{\sum (x_i - \bar{x})^2} \cdot \frac{1}{\sum (y_i - \bar{y})^2}$$

$$= \frac{\left[\sum (x_i - \bar{x})(y_i - \bar{y}) \right]^2}{\sum (x_i - \bar{x})^2 \sum (y_i - \bar{y})^2}$$

However, we have seen (8.23) before; it is the square of the correlation coefficient, or r^2. We repeat this new interpretation for r^2: $100 \cdot r^2$ is the percentage of the variability in y that can be accounted for or eliminated by use of the variable x. A value close to unity thus indicates a strong relationship. To use this measure, we return to Figures 3–8 and 3–9. For the first, $r^2 = .865$; for the second, $r^2 = .034$. We can now verify what we could see in the scattergram—the x value of the first figure is a better predictor. In the second case, the predictor accounts for almost none of the variability in y; that is, academic achievement in science tells us virtually nothing about the number of problems a student says he is having at home.

As might be expected, the population value for r^2 is ρ^2.

EXERCISES

8.9   By using the data from Exercise 8.7, what percentage of the home adjustment score can be accounted for by the school adjustment score?

†8.10   From the population of randomly grouped students, select a random sample of 10 people and obtain a regression equation using STEP reading scores as a predictor, and times-chosen on the sociometric test for the variable to be predicted. Discuss your results.

‡8.11   In the population of randomly grouped students, the population regression equation for the data of Exercise 8.12 is $y = -45.270 + .2264x$.

Calculate the average of all a and b obtained in your class, and compare these results with α and β.

A Hypothesis Test for the Effectiveness of the Regression Equation

Some readers may have realized that if the predictor is useless, then $\rho = 0$. Hence a test for the hypothesis $H: \rho = 0$ is a way of deciding whether the predictor is useful at all, and this is a perfectly valid test to use. A procedure in the format of an analysis of variance table generally will be used, however. This procedure will be easy to generalize to the cases taken up in Chapter 9.

Our computations will follow the format of Table 8–3.

TABLE 8–3

Analysis of Variance for Regression Analysis

SOURCE	df	SUM-OF-SQUARES	EXPECTED MS
Regression	1	$[\Sigma(x_i - \bar{x}.)(y_i - \bar{y}.)]^2/\Sigma(x_i - \bar{x}.)^2 = SS_R$	$\beta^2 \Sigma(x_i - \bar{x}.)^2 + \sigma^2$
Error	$n - 2$	$\Sigma(y_i - \bar{y}.)^2 - SS_R = SS_E$	σ^2
Total	$n - 1$	$\Sigma(y_i - \bar{y}.)^2 = SS_{TO}$	

We reason that if the predictor is useless, then $\beta = 0$. In that case,

$$\frac{MS_R}{MS_E} = \frac{SS_R}{SS_E/(n - 2)}$$

should be close to unity, since their expected values are the same. To see that a useless predictor implies a zero value for β, look at Figures 8–4 and 8–6 again. The line becomes less steep as the predictive value of x decreases and finally it becomes almost flat if the value of x tells us virtually nothing about y. A flat line corresponds to the equation

$$(8.24) \qquad y = \alpha$$

for which $\beta = 0$.

Returning to Table 8–3, if β is, in fact, equal to zero, then MS_R/MS_E comes from a population having an F distribution with 1 and $n - 2$ degrees of freedom, and we use this fact to construct our test.

THEOREM 8.1

Let $F_{(1,m)1-\gamma}$ represent the value that exceeds $(1 - \gamma) \cdot 100$ percent of the observations from a population having an F distribution with 1 and m degrees of freedom in the numerator and denominator, respectively. Then a test of the hypothesis $H: \beta = 0$ in the statistical model

$$(8.25) \qquad \begin{aligned} y_i &= \alpha + \beta x_i + \epsilon_i \\ \epsilon_i &\sim N(0, \sigma^2) \\ i &= 1, 2, \ldots, N \end{aligned}$$

is given by the rule:

Reject H if $SS_R/[SS_E/(n-2)] \geq F_{(1,n-2)1-\gamma}$; *accept* H *otherwise, where* $SS_R = [\Sigma(x_i - \bar{x}.)(y_i - \bar{y}.)]^2/\Sigma(x_i - \bar{x}.)^2$ *and* $SS_E = \Sigma(y_i - \bar{y}.)^2 - SS_R$. *The probability of rejecting* H *if* $\beta = 0$ *is equal to* γ.

EXERCISES

8.12 Using the data from Exercise 8.9, test the hypothesis that home adjustment tells us nothing about school adjustment for a given individual.

8.13 Using your data from Exercise 8.10, test the hypothesis that academic achievement on the STEP reading score tells us nothing about the times a student is chosen on a sociometric score. Use $\gamma = .05$.

8.14 By compiling the result for the entire class, calculate the percentage of times the hypothesis was *accepted*.

8.15 From the population of randomly grouped students select a random sample of 10 students, obtaining the "Me and Home" and STEP math scores for each. Test the hypothesis that the "Me and Home" scores tell us nothing about the math scores, using $\gamma = .10$. Calculate, for the class, the percentage of times the hypothesis was *rejected*.

8.16 What type error was computed in Exercise 8.14? In Exercise 8.15?

DATA PROCESSING FOR LINEAR REGRESSION

This section will provide a description of the use of a program to do the following:

1. Calculate the regression equation for a set of data.
2. Plot a scattergram for the data.
3. Plot the regression equation for the data.

The Use of PRGM2 to Plot the Regression Equation for a Scatter Diagram

We use PRGM2 for regression analysis. As in all programs for the text, the order of the cards in your deck is:

1. Systems cards
2. The program listing from Appendix L, or a systems card which calls up that program from the computer center library
3. Systems cards
4. Control cards
5. The data deck
6. An END or FIN card
7. Final systems cards.

Now 4, 5, and 6 can be repeated as often as desired, simply using the FIN card after the final data deck. We describe these first.

CONTROL CARD 1
This is to write the verbal description of your job, using all 80 columns.

CONTROL CARD 2

COLUMN	DESCRIPTION OF ENTRY
1-8	(T78, A3,
12-m	Two field descriptors, the first for the x, or independent variable, and the second for y. An easy way to do this is to use the Tn notation, giving first the column in which the observation for x begins and second that column for y. For example, if the x observation had three digits in columns 21, 22, 23 (no places to the right of the decimal) and the y variable was in columns 9 and 10 with one place to the right of the decimal, Control Card 2 would be as follows:

(T78,A3,T21,F3.0,T9,F2.1)

	Each card in the data deck must then be punched consistent with the preceding set of field descriptors. Notice that the x observation need not come first on the card, although it may do so. One x and one y observation to a card.
m + 1	Right-hand parenthesis

THE DATA DECK
The data deck may be your own set of punched cards or a deck already punched by someone else; the foregoing rules will enable you to specify the data fields to be used for x and y in the deck. Occasionally observations will be missing for either x or y. This will not be a problem if the data field was left blank. The program is designed to omit the data from any card in which either x or y (or both) is not present, and the sample size will be adjusted accordingly.

The output for this program consists of a scatter-gram accurate to within one printed line. The data points are represented by zeros; the "fitted" regression line is plotted using asterisks. Below the plot is given the equation

$$y = a + bx$$

with numerical values substituted for a and b. An example of output for this program appears in Appendix L.

EXERCISE
8.17 Reanalyze the data of Exercise 8.10, using PRGM2, and compare with the desk calculator version. The results should be very close to each other.

Experiences with Data

PROBLEMS
8.1 Do the schools of the randomly grouped district differ with respect to the degree of importance placed on academic achievement?

8.2 Do boys and girls differ with respect to the degree of importance placed on academic achievement?

8.3 Take any two of the SRA scores and determine the degree to which one can be predicted from the other.

SOLUTIONS TO EXERCISES

8.1

a.

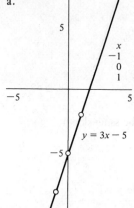

x	$y = 3x - 5$
-1	-8
0	-5
1	-2

b.

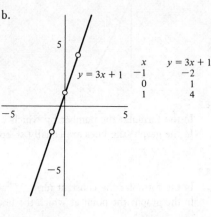

x	$y = 3x + 1$
-1	-2
0	1
1	4

c.

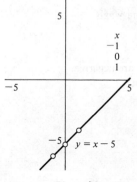

x	$y = x - 5$
-1	-6
0	-5
1	-4

d.

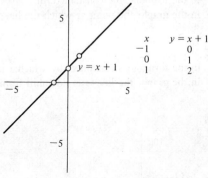

x	$y = x + 1$
-1	0
0	1
1	2

e.

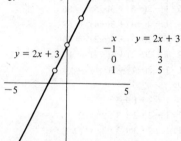

x	$y = 2x + 3$
-1	1
0	3
1	5

f.

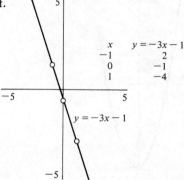

x	$y = -3x - 1$
-1	2
0	-1
1	-4

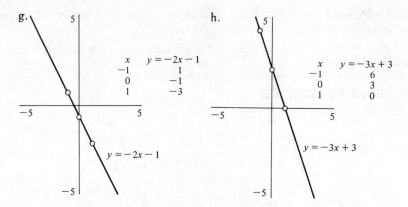

g.

x	y = -2x - 1
-1	1
0	-1
1	-3

y = -2x - 1

h.

x	y = -3x + 3
-1	6
0	3
1	0

y = -3x + 3

8.2

In the formula: the number by which x is multiplied.

In the graph: the lines are equally steep (they have the same slope).

8.3

In the formula: the constant term.

In the graph: the point at which the lines intersect the y axis.

8.4

In the formula: the constant term.

In the graph: the point at which the lines intersect the y axis.

8.5

In the formula: all numbers by which x is multiplied are negative.

In the graph: the lines run downhill from left to right.

8.6

a.

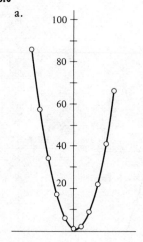

x	$y = 1 - 2x + 3x^2$
-5	$1 - 2(-5) + 3(-5)^2 = 86$
-4	$1 - 2(-4) + 3(-4)^2 = 57$
-3	$1 - 2(-3) + 3(-3)^2 = 34$
-2	$1 - 2(-2) + 3(-2)^2 = 17$
-1	$1 - 2(-1) + 3(-1)^2 = 6$
0	1
1	$1 - 2 \cdot 1 + 3 \cdot 1^2 = 2$
2	$1 - 2 \cdot 2 + 3 \cdot 2^2 = 9$
3	$1 - 2 \cdot 3 + 3 \cdot 3^3 = 22$
4	$1 - 2 \cdot 4 + 3 \cdot 4^2 = 41$
5	$1 - 2 \cdot 5 + 3 \cdot 5^2 = 66$

b.

c.

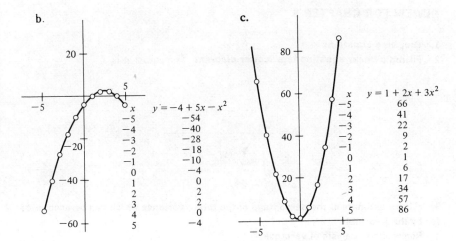

x	$y = -4 + 5x - x^2$
-5	-54
-4	-40
-3	-28
-2	-18
-1	-10
0	-4
1	0
2	2
3	2
4	0
5	-4

x	$y = 1 + 2x + 3x^2$
-5	66
-4	41
-3	22
-2	9
-1	2
0	1
1	6
2	17
3	34
4	57
5	86

8.7

x = "Getting Along with Others"; y = "Me and Home"
$s_x^2 = 174.66$; $s_{xy} = 70.25$; $s_y^2 = 52.25$
$b = s_{xy}/s_x^2 = 70.25/174.66 = .40$
$\bar{x}. = 19.08$; $\bar{y}. = 11.40$; $a = \bar{y}. - b\bar{x}. = 11.40 - .40(19.08)$
The regression equation is $y = 3.77 + .40x$

8.8

$s_x^2 = 66.27$; $s_{xy} = -22.36$; $b = -22.36/66.27 = -.34$;
$a = 45.27 - (-.34)8.55 = 48.18$
The regression equation is $y = 48.18 - .34x$

$\epsilon_1 = -3.14$	$\epsilon_5 = 3.16$	$\epsilon_9 = 9.52$
$\epsilon_2 = 5.58$	$\epsilon_6 = -4.02$	$\epsilon_{10} = 9.96$
$\epsilon_3 = 5.58$	$\epsilon_7 = 9.16$	$\epsilon_{11} = -2.84$
$\epsilon_4 = -9.14$	$\epsilon_8 = -13.10$	

$\sigma^2 = 70.08$

8.12

The quantities needed are:

$\Sigma(y_i - \bar{y}.)^2 = 706.2$; $\Sigma(x_i - \bar{x}.)^2 = 662.7$; $\Sigma(x_i - \bar{x}.)(y_i - \bar{y}.)^2 = -223.6$;
$n = 25$

The regression analysis of variance table is as follows:

SOURCE	df	SUM-OF-SQUARES	MEAN-SQUARES
Regression	1	$(-223.6)^2/662.7 = 75.4$	75.4
Error	23	$706.2 - 75.4 = 630.8$	27.43
Total	24	706.2	

$F = 75.4/27.43 = 2.75$; $F_{(1, 23).05} = 4.28$
Accept $H: \beta = 0$; that is, there is insufficient evidence to show that the degree of
school adjustment is of help in predicting home adjustment.

REVIEW FOR CHAPTER 8

1. **Graphing equations**
2. **Fitting a linear equation to a scatter diagram.** The equation is

$$y = a + bx$$

$$b = \frac{\sum\limits_{i=1}^{n} (x_i - \bar{x}.)(y_i - \bar{y}.)}{\sum\limits_{i=1}^{n} (x_i - \bar{x}.)^2}$$

$$a = \bar{y}. - b\bar{x}.$$

3. **r^2 is an estimate of the percentage of the total y variance which can be accounted for by the x variable**
4. **Regression analysis of variance**

SOURCE	df	SUM-OF-SQUARES	EMS
Regression	1	$\dfrac{[\Sigma(x_i - \bar{x}.)(y_i - \bar{y}.)]^2}{\Sigma(x_i - \bar{x}.)^2} = SS_R$	$\beta^2\Sigma(x_i - \bar{x}.)^2 + \sigma^2$
Error	$n - 2$	$\Sigma(y_i - \bar{y}.)^2 - SS_R = SS_E$	σ^2
Total	$n - 1$	$\Sigma(y_i - \bar{y}.)^2 = SS_{TO}$	

5. **Test of the hypothesis $H: \beta = 0$ in the statistical model**

$$y_i = \alpha + \beta x_i + \epsilon_i$$
$$\epsilon_i \sim N(0, \sigma^2)$$
$$i = 1, 2, \ldots, N$$

Reject H if $SS_R/[SS_E/(n-1)] \geq F_{(1,n-2)1-\gamma}$. Accept H otherwise, where SS_R and SS_E are obtained from the analysis of variance table in 4 above. This hypothesis has probability $= \gamma$ of being rejected if it is true.

CHAPTER 9
CLUSTER SAMPLING

DESCRIPTION OF THE PROBLEM
The Purpose and Definition of a Cluster Sample—Nested Designs

In Chapters 6, 7, and 8, three important kinds of statistical problems with their solutions were introduced. Briefly, these were:

1. Collection of data that can be categorized, but for which numerical values are not appropriate
2. Collection and analysis of numerical data coming from several populations
3. Analysis of relationships between numerical measures made on the same population

Many statistical problems can be solved by using one or more of these approaches.

In Chapter 1, instructions were given for the selection of a simple random sample from a population, and we have used this technique up to the present. Often, however, the selection of a simple random sample is a very expensive process. If we wish to select such a sample from a state, for example, we have to make a list with a number corresponding to every person in the state; then we use a list of random numbers to obtain our sample. Making up that list, which would include several million people, would be a very expensive, if not impossible, task. Moreover, once the random sample is decided on, the actual selection of the sample can be very expensive if personal interviews are involved. Members of the sample may be located far from each other geographically, so that the interviewer's travel time is increased and efficient use of time is decreased.

To overcome these obstacles, sampling units are often grouped into *clusters* of many units each, as in Figure 9–1. This illustration is a simplification of natural divisions into which a geographical area can be divided. Each division is termed a "cluster." Divisions 1, 2, and 3 are rural areas, in the center,

FIGURE 9-1
Grouping sampling units into clusters.

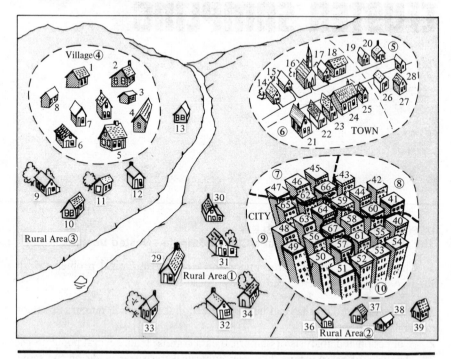

lower right-hand, and upper left-hand areas of the illustration. Division 4 is a rural village, and the remaining divisions (5 to 10) are intended to represent urban areas. Here the number of people in each cluster is approximately equal, although frequently there will be fewer people in the rural districts. Now we select a cluster at random (the list of clusters is much smaller than that for the original sampling units) and then select the original sampling units at random within each of the selected clusters. Consider the advantages to this procedure. First, the size of the sampling lists to be made up is much smaller; we need only make up a list of clusters, and then a list of original sampling units for only those clusters that were selected. In Figure 9-1, each dwelling is to be considered as an original sampling unit, and each has been numbered so that the list for simple random sampling runs from 1 to 67. There are, however, 10 clusters, so that a list of clusters is simply the numbers from 1 to 10. Table 9-1 presents the sampling lists for clusters 2, 3, and 9. The numbers assigned within each cluster are termed the "list numbers," while those originally assigned in Figure 9-1 are the "original numbers."

This procedure yields data that have many of the properties of the data coming from a simple random sample; statistical inference procedures are available, and the cost of making the list goes down, as does travel time for conducting interviews. We should note, however, that we pay for these advantages with decreased accuracy. To see this, consider what would happen

TABLE 9–1

Sampling Lists for a Cluster Sample

CLUSTER 2		CLUSTER 3		CLUSTER 9	
ORIGINAL NUMBERS	LIST NUMBERS	ORIGINAL NUMBERS	LIST NUMBERS	ORIGINAL NUMBERS	LIST NUMBERS
36	1	9	1	48	1
37	2	10	2	49	2
38	3	11	3	50	3
39	4	12	4	51	4
		13	5	56	5
				57	6
				63	7
				64	8
				65	9

if we selected clusters 1, 2, and 3, which are all rural. Our sample would be less representative of the population and this would result in greater variance of the measurements made during the sampling. Hence we sacrifice accuracy of the results in order to decrease the cost of taking the sample.

Sometimes our attention may be focused on the cluster itself, for reasons other than economy in taking the sample. As an example, consider our randomly grouped school district, where we use schools as clusters. We may be interested in learning whether there exist genuine differences between schools with respect to either achievement or social adjustment. We are not interested only in those schools used in the study but in all schools in the district. Hence we select a random sample of schools and then, within each school, a random sample of students to measure.

Cluster sampling thus has two objectives; the first is economy, and the second is a study of the influence of cluster differences on variability of the original sampling units. We summarize this in

---

DEFINITION 9.1

A "cluster sample" is defined to be a sample in which the original sampling units are classified together in groups called "clusters." A simple random sample of clusters is selected in a first stage, after which a simple random sample of the original sampling units is selected from within each cluster obtained in the first stage.

A Statistical Model for Cluster Sampling—Components of Variance

To obtain an adequate statistical model, we first consider y_{ij} to be observation j within cluster i. Then if the average of all values in cluster i is $\bar{y}_i.$, and the deviation of this average from the overall mean is $\bar{y}_i. - \bar{y}..$, we can rewrite y_{ij} in the following manner:

$$(9.1) \qquad y_{ij} = \bar{y}.. + (\bar{y}_i. - \bar{y}..) + (y_{ij} - \bar{y}_i.)$$

That is, any observation is the sum of

1. The overall mean
2. The deviation of the ith cluster mean from the overall mean
3. The deviation of the observation from the ith cluster mean

We can rewrite this as

$$(9.2) \qquad y_{ij} = \mu + c_i + e_{ij}$$

where μ = the overall mean
c_i = the effect due to the ith cluster
e_{ij} = the deviation from the ith cluster
$i = 1, 2, \ldots, k$
$j = 1, 2, \ldots, N_i$

Since the cluster is selected at random and e_{ij} is selected at random within the ith cluster, we have

$$(9.3) \qquad c_i \sim (0, \sigma_c^2) \qquad \text{and} \qquad e_{ij} \sim (0, \sigma_e^2)$$

where $i = 1, 2, \ldots, k < K$, and $j = 1, 2, \ldots, n < N_i$; that is, we have a sample of $k < K$ clusters and $n < N_i$ sampling units within the ith cluster. Note that the within-cluster variability is assumed to be essentially the same from one cluster to the next. If the experiment is repeated, there is a certain probability of using some of the same clusters. Often there will be an entirely new set of clusters; however, some clusters may be used in both samples. The same cluster will not show up twice in one experiment, but it may show up in repetitions of the experiment.

DEFINITION 9.2
The "first stage" of a cluster sample is the sampling procedure used to select the clusters. The "second stage" is the procedure used to select sampling units within each cluster. This procedure is often termed "two-stage cluster sampling."

DEFINITION 9.3
The "primary sampling unit" for two-stage cluster sampling is the cluster itself. The "secondary sampling unit" is the sampling unit within the cluster.

A diagram such as Figure 9–2 may clarify these ideas. The secondary sampling units (ssu's) are nested in the primary sampling units (psu's), according to Definition 9.1. The statistical model

$$(9.4) \qquad \begin{aligned} y_{ij} &= \mu + c_i + e_{ij} \\ i &= 1, 2, \ldots, k \\ j &= 1, 2, \ldots, n \\ c_i &\sim (0, \sigma_c^2) \\ e_{ij} &\sim (0, \sigma_e^2) \end{aligned}$$

is called the *components of variance* model. Eisenhart (1947) wrote a well-known

FIGURE 9-2
Diagrammatic illustration of two-stage cluster sampling.

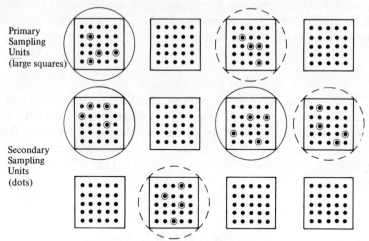

First stage samples – large circles
Second stage samples – small circles
Solid circles–first two–stage sample
Dashed circles–second two–stage sample

paper, distinguishing by analysis of variance between the model of Chapter 7 for several populations and this model for several clusters. The major difference is that in the situation of Chapter 7, the same populations were used in a repetition of the study, whereas in this model, different "populations" are used. Here, the "populations" are clusters, and they are random variables. Eisenhart termed the model of Chapter 7 the "fixed" model (or Model I), and that of this chapter the "random" model (or Model II). The two statistical models placed side by side are:

$$(9.5)$$

	MODEL I	MODEL II
	$y_{ij} = \mu + \tau_i + e_{ij}$	$y_{ij} = \mu + c_i + e_{ij}$
	τ_i fixed	$c_i \sim (0, \sigma_c^2)$
	$e_i \sim (0, \sigma_e^2)$	$e_{ij} \sim (0, \sigma_e^2)$
	$i = 1, 2, \ldots, k$	$i = 1, 2, \ldots, k$
	$j = 1, 2, \ldots, n$	$j = 1, 2, \ldots, n$

EXERCISE

9.1 Using the randomly grouped students, make a list of teachers, and consider these as the primary sampling units (psu's). Conduct a two-stage cluster sample using students as the secondary sampling units (ssu's) with four psu's in the experiment, and five ssu's selected from each psu. Write out all sampling lists used and describe your sampling procedure carefully at each stage, giving the list of random numbers used, the specific random numbers selected, and the decision corresponding to each random number.

Triple Subscripting

We now need to expand our subscript notation again. Since two subscripts are needed to describe a two-stage sample, we are left without a subscript to use for different populations, unless we add one more. Triple subscripting is obtained for an observation, x, as:

(9.6) $$x_{ijl}$$

As an example, suppose we want to compare a set of schools, and we are to obtain a two-stage sample from each, with teachers as the first stage and students as the second stage. If we use two schools, three teachers in each school, and five students for each teacher, then x_{ijl} represents the observation for student l, within teacher j's class, in school i. The ranges for the subscripts are

$$i = 1, 2, \text{ or } k$$
$$j = 1, 2, 3, \text{ or } n$$
$$l = 1, 2, 3, 4, 5, \text{ or } m$$

We can no longer construct a diagram for x_{ijl} as we did in Table 5–2; this would require a three-dimensional table. However, we can extend the notation in analogous fashion. We have

(9.7)
$$X_{ij\cdot} = \sum_{l=1}^{m} x_{ijl} \qquad X_{i\cdot l} = \sum_{j=1}^{n} x_{ijl}$$

$$X_{\cdot jl} = \sum_{i=1}^{k} x_{ijl} \qquad X_{i\cdot\cdot} = \sum_{j=1}^{n} \sum_{l=1}^{m} x_{ijl}$$

$$X_{\cdot j\cdot} = \sum_{i=1}^{k} \sum_{l=1}^{m} x_{ijl} \qquad X_{\cdot\cdot l} = \sum_{i=1}^{k} \sum_{j=1}^{n} x_{ijl}$$

$$X_{\cdot\cdot\cdot} = \sum_{i=1}^{k} \sum_{j=1}^{n} \sum_{l=1}^{m} x_{ijl}$$

Capitalization of the letter and replacement of some or all of the subscripts by a dot indicates a subtotal in which the replaced subscripts have been summed. If the dot notation is used with a lower case letter having a bar over it, such as $\bar{x}_{\cdot jl}$, we mean that the subtotal has been averaged.

EXERCISE

9.2 Following are the "Me and School" scores for two schools, three classes in each school, and five students in each class. The first two schools of the randomly grouped students were used, and two-stage sampling was used in each school.

STUDENT	SCHOOL 1			SCHOOL 2		
	CLASS 1	CLASS 2	CLASS 3	CLASS 1	CLASS 2	CLASS 3
1.	18	29	40	23	4	0
2	30	12	30	66	36	16
3	33	23	72	43	19	53
4	42	30	6	35	20	62
5	66	31	51	15	1	41

y_{ijl} represents student l, in class j, in school i. Obtain $Y_{1..}$, $Y_{12.}$, $Y_{21.}$, and $Y_{1.3}$.

Cluster Sampling with Several Populations

The situation to be described here is relatively simple. As in Chapters 5 and 7, we have several populations to compare. In the past, the populations have been obtained by one of two methods:

1. We obtained a sample from a single population which we divided into k parts, each of size n. We then applied one of the k different treatments to each part.

2. We had k distinct populations and obtained a sample from each.

In the present case, the single population, or the k distinct populations, are so large that a simple random sample is not a feasible proposition. Hence we consider a cluster sample for each of the k treatments for case 1 or a separate cluster sample from each of the k populations for case 2. Note that earlier we took a single random sample of size kn and divided it into k parts for case 1. Now we select a sample of kn psu's, each with a subsample of m units. We divide this into k sets of n psu's each and apply a different one of the k treatments to each set of n psu's. The situation is diagrammed in Figure 9–3.

Such problems arise frequently. Comparison of rural and urban populations on almost any measure would be an example; the populations are too large to make a simple random sample a feasible proposition, and so a cluster sample is conducted within each. If, within a single state, one wishes to compare two methods of administering a welfare program, a simple random sample of households is impractical; cluster sampling must be resorted to, and a different treatment must be applied to each sample.

The statistical model is an extension of the one of the preceding section; we have

$$(9.8) \qquad y_{ijl}$$

as the observation for the lth person, within the jth cluster (or primary sampling unit), in population i. This gives

$$(9.9) \qquad y_{ijl} = \mu + \tau_i + c_{ij} + e_{ijl}$$

FIGURE 9–3

Two ways of obtaining two populations with cluster sampling.

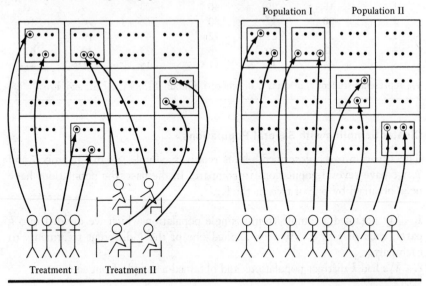

Treatment I   Treatment II

where e_{ijl} = the effect due to person l within cluster j of population i
where $l = 1, 2, \ldots, n$

c_{ij} = the effect of the jth cluster within population i where $j = 1, 2, \ldots, n$

τ_i = effect due to population i where $i = 1, 2, \ldots, k$

μ = the overall mean, as usual

τ_i = constant

$c_{ij} \sim (0, \sigma_c^2)$

$e_{ijl} \sim (0, \sigma_e^2)$

Note that there are certain assumptions here:

1. The between-cluster variability is the same within different populations.

2. The within-cluster variability does not change from one cluster to the next.

The purpose of calling attention to these assumptions is not to insist that they hold exactly, but to warn the reader that some of the following results may not be valid if the assumptions are *seriously* violated. By seriously, we mean, for instance, that the assumption of equality of variances will be seriously violated if the ratio of any two variances is not within $\frac{50}{100}$ of unity.

The observations for any population can be expressed in terms of the components of (9.9). We have

$$(9.10) \qquad y_{ijl} = \bar{y}_{\ldots} + \bar{y}_{i..} - \bar{y}_{\ldots} + \bar{y}_{ij.} - \bar{y}_{i..} + y_{ijl} - \bar{y}_{ij.}$$
$$= \mu + \tau_i + c_{ij} + e_{ijk}$$

where
$$\tau_i = \bar{y}_{i..} - \bar{y}_{...}$$
$$c_{ij} = \bar{y}_{ij.} - \bar{y}_{i..}$$
$$e_{ijl} = y_{ijl} - \bar{y}_{ij.}$$

for all i, j, and l. If this model is a reasonable one, we can decompose our observations in this form, and we let

(9.11)
$$\sigma_c{}^2 = \sum_{i=1}^{k} \sum_{j=1}^{n} \frac{(\bar{y}_{ij.} - \bar{y}_{i..})^2}{k(n-1)}$$

$$\sigma_e{}^2 = \sum_{i=1}^{k} \sum_{j=1}^{n} \sum_{l=1}^{m} \frac{(y_{ijl} - \bar{y}_{ij.})^2}{kn(m-1)}$$

EXERCISES

9.3 Consider the data of Exercise 9.2 as a population and calculate the following values:
  a. μ, τ_i where $i = 1, 2$.
  b. c_{ij} where $j = 1, 2, 3$.
  c. e_{ijl} where $l = 1, 2, \ldots, 5$.

9.4 Using the data of Exercise 9.2, calculate $\sigma_c{}^2$ and $\sigma_e{}^2$.

ANALYSIS OF VARIANCE FOR CLUSTER SAMPLING

In this section, we will find that some of the techniques treated earlier are not yet available for cluster sampling. Specifically, procedures for ranking of means are not covered. Other methods are described, many of considerable practical value.

Unbiased Estimates of Variance Components

We return to a single population in which we have conducted a cluster sample. In (9.4), the model was given as

(9.12)
$$y_{ij} = \mu + c_i + e_{ij}$$
$$i = 1, 2, \ldots, k$$
$$j = 1, 2, \ldots, n$$
$$c_i \sim (0, \sigma_c{}^2)$$
$$e_{ij} \sim (0, \sigma_e{}^2)$$

We indicated previously that cluster samples are sometimes selected to identify causes for variability in some numerical measure. In considering schools as clusters and students within schools as the secondary sampling units, we tried to determine the relative amount of variability in achievement that is attributable to school differences, and compare this with student vari-

TABLE 9-2

Analysis of Variance Table for the Components of Variance Model

SOURCE	df	SUM-OF-SQUARES	EMS
Primary sampling unit	$k - 1$	$\displaystyle\sum_{i=1}^{k} n(\bar{y}_{i\cdot} - \bar{y}_{\cdot\cdot})^2 = SS_C$	$n\sigma_c^2 + \sigma_e^2$
Secondary sampling unit	$k(n - 1)$	$\displaystyle\sum_{ij} (y_{ij} - \bar{y}_{i\cdot})^2 = SS_E$	σ_e^2

ability in achievement. Put in this fashion, we can then use estimates of σ_c^2 and σ_e^2 to compare these relative sources of variability. Hence we now turn to point estimates of what are sometimes called the "components of the variance." An analysis of variance table is a simple way of presenting these results; Table 9.2 presents the results for this model. Note that to obtain an estimate of the ssu error, we obtain the sum-of-squared deviations from the mean *for each psu*. These are then added together. Since we thus obtain no squared deviations *between* psu's, the resulting value is not a function of σ_c^2, which is the between-psu variation. The situation is diagrammed in Figure 9-4.

From Table 9.2, we know that $MS_E = SS_E/k(n - 1)$ is an unbiased estimate of σ_e^2, so that

$$(9.13) \qquad\qquad MS_E = \hat{\sigma}_e^2$$

To obtain an estimate of σ_c^2, we note that

$$(9.14) \qquad\qquad E\{MS_C\} = n\sigma_c^2 + \sigma_e^2$$

Next note that if

$$MS_A \cong n\sigma_c^2 + \sigma_e^2 \qquad \text{and} \qquad MS_E = \sigma_e^2$$

then

$$(9.15) \qquad\qquad \frac{MS_C - MS_E}{n} \cong \sigma_c^2$$

Thus the expression on the left-hand side of (9.15) is an unbiased estimate of

FIGURE 9-4

Rationale for estimate of secondary sampling unit error.

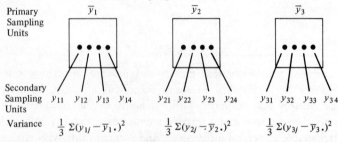

σ_c^2. On occasion, this estimate may have a negative value; when it does, we conclude that σ_c^2 is negligible, and c_i can be omitted from the model (9.12).

EXERCISES

9.5   Use the data of Exercise 9.2 (second school only) and construct the analysis of variance of Table 9–2. Obtain estimates of σ_c^2 and σ_e^2. What do these estimates represent?

9.6   Select a random sample of five classes from the randomly grouped school district, and three students from each class. Record the data for the STEP science and STEP reading scores. Repeat the experiment so that you have two sets of data selected in the same way. Using model (9.12), explain what σ_c^2 and σ_e^2 mean in the present context.

9.7   Obtain point estimates of σ_c^2 and σ_e^2 for both cluster samples obtained in the preceding problem, using the STEP reading score.

9.8   What is the relative class influence on individual achievement?

Comparison of Several Populations with Cluster Sampling

Some additional sampling concepts will be developed in this section; these will be needed for the last part of the chapter.

DEFINITION 9.4
A sampling unit is said to be larger than another if each of the first contains more than one sampling unit of the second. By this definition, primary sampling units are larger than secondary sampling units.

DEFINITION 9.5
An experimental unit is defined with respect to a particular treatment, and it is the largest sampling unit to which one treatment is applied.

As an example, suppose two methods of grouping students are applied to a district where three schools are selected randomly for each grouping method, making six schools in all. To measure the results, two classrooms are selected at random from each of the schools, and the students in each of the selected classes are given a battery of 15 tests. In this case, the treatment is one of two grouping methods, and the experimental units—the largest sampling unit to which a single treatment level is applied—are the schools. Second-stage sampling units are the classrooms; but a larger sampling unit, the school, has a single treatment level applied to it; hence the classrooms are not experimental units. Using model (9.10), we have

(9.16)
$$y_{ijl} = \mu + \tau_i + c_{ij} + e_{ijl}$$
$$i = 1, 2, \ldots, k$$
$$j = 1, 2, \ldots, n$$
$$l = 1, 2, \ldots, m$$

Here c_{ij} is the effect due to the experimental unit.

DEFINITION 9.6

The "experimental error" in an analysis of variance table is the mean-squares term corresponding to the experimental unit.

To determine the analysis for this kind of data, we begin with the analysis of variance in Table 9–3. Note that the treatment mean-square expected value includes the term $m\sigma_c^2 + \sigma_e^2$. If $\tau_1 = \tau_2 = \ldots = \tau_k$, then this expected value equals the expected value for the psu sum-of-squares. This is the sum-of-squares corresponding to the experimental units, and it is the experimental error. The ratio of the treatment mean-squares to the experimental error will be close to unity if the treatment means are equal, and a test of the hypothesis that they are equal is given in

---

THEOREM 9.1

Let cluster samples be selected from k populations, with n primary sampling units and m secondary sampling units. Let the model for the populations be

$$
\begin{aligned}
(9.17) \qquad y_{ijl} &= \mu + \tau_i + c_{ij} + e_{ijl} \\
\tau_i &= \text{constant} \\
i &= 1, 2, \ldots, k \\
c_{ij} &\sim N(0, \sigma_c^2) \\
j &= 1, 2, \ldots, n \\
e_{ijl} &\sim N(0, \sigma_e^2) \\
l &= 1, 2, \ldots, m
\end{aligned}
$$

Then a test of the hypothesis $H: \tau_1 = \tau_2 = \ldots = \tau_k$ is given by the rule:

$$
(9.18) \qquad \text{Reject } H \text{ if } \frac{SS_T/(k-1)}{SS_C/k(n-1)} \geq F_{[k-1,k(n-1)]1-\alpha}
$$

Accept H, otherwise, where

$$
SS_T = mn \sum_{i=1}^{k} (\bar{y}_{i..} - \bar{y}...)^2
$$

$$
SS_C = m \sum_{i=1}^{k} \sum_{j=1}^{n} (\bar{y}_{ij.} - \bar{y}_{i..})^2
$$

Here $F_{[k-1,k(n-1)]1-\alpha}$ is the value that exceeds $1 - \alpha$ percent of the variates from a population with an F distribution with $k - 1$ and $k(n - 1)$ degrees of freedom. H has a probability $= \alpha$ of being rejected, if true.

Note that the experimental error is $SS_C/k(n - 1)$ and that we use this for the denominator of our F test. This is generally true; that is, the denominator for the F test will always be the experimental error, and the researcher ought to identify this term *prior to collecting his data*. Otherwise, he may fail

TABLE 9–3

Analysis of Variance with Cluster Sampling in Several Population

SOURCE	df	SUM-OF-SQUARES	
Treatments	$k - 1$	$mn \sum_{i=1}^{k} (\bar{y}_{i..} - \bar{y}...)^2 = SS_T$	$\dfrac{mn}{t - 1} \sum_{i=1}^{k} \tau_i^2 + m\sigma_c^2 + \sigma_e^2$
Primary sampling units	$k(m - 1)$	$n \sum_{i=1}^{k} \sum_{j=1}^{m} (\bar{y}_{ij.} - y_{i..})^2 = SS_C$	$m\sigma_c^2 + \sigma_e^2$
Secondary sampling units	$kn(m - 1)$	$\sum_{i=1}^{k} \sum_{j=1}^{n} \sum_{l=1}^{m} (y_{ijl} - \bar{y}_{ij.})^2 = SS_E$	σ_e^2

to collect data he can use for the experimental error, and thus he will be unable to construct a valid test of his hypothesis.

We reiterate, the experimental error is defined relative to the treatments used and is a particular size of sampling unit. The researcher needs to identify this sampling unit and to make sure that its variance is estimated.

EXERCISES

9.9   Use the data of Exercise 9.2, considering the schools as two distinct populations, and construct the analysis of variance of Table 9–3. Test the hypothesis that the schools do not differ with respect to the students' adjustment to school. Let $\alpha = .05$.

9.10   Using the fast students, select a cluster sample from each school district, using teachers as psu's and students as ssu's. Test the hypothesis that there is no difference between ability grouping and random grouping for fast students on the STEP reading score. Use two psu's and five ssu's for each population.

Data Processing for Analysis of Variance with Cluster Sampling

The components of variance model of the beginning of the chapter has an analysis of variance table identical to that of Chapter 7, and PRGM1 can be used. For cluster sampling with different populations, we use PRGM4, which has the following layout:

1.   Systems cards
2.   The program listing in Appendix N
3.   Systems cards
4.   Control cards
5.   Data deck
6.   END or FIN card
7.   Final systems cards

At this point, we will cover parts 4, 5, and 6 of the program.

CONTROL CARDS

We will have two control cards for this program: the first is the verbal description of the job, for which all 80 columns of the card are available, as usual; the second gives the field descriptors for the data to be used, enclosed by parentheses. Somewhere on each data card a code must be given, telling from which population and which psu within the population the observation was made.

The field descriptors must be as follows:

1. Specify the three columns from which END or FIN will read on the final card. The corresponding columns in the data deck may contain numbers, but they are not being used for this particular job.

2. Provide two field descriptors in In (integer) format. These are for the card columns in which the codes for the population and psu number from which the observation was taken appear.

3. The field descriptor for the measurement used for your analysis of variance must be specified.

The rules of Chapter 4 will be used again here; reread them if necessary.

As an example of this procedure, suppose the observation is in columns 60–64 (two places to the right of the decimal, five significant digits). Further suppose that the codes for population number and psu within the population are in columns 78 (for population) and 79 and 80 (for psu number). Since columns 1 to 3 are not being used for this job, we decide to use them for our END card. Then Control Card 2 should be

$$(A3, T78, I1, I2, T60, F5.2)$$

Recall that T1 is not needed before the A3, since if nothing is given there, it is assumed that we are beginning in column 1.

DATA DECK

The data deck can be any deck already punched if the population and psu codes are punched in each card of the deck. This is a natural thing to do in any event; you are then protected if you drop the deck, since putting it back in order on the sorter is a simple matter.

The output for this program includes:

1. Verbal description of your job.

2. Listing of Control Card 2.

3. Printout of information on your data cards, so that you can check for possible errors.

4. A table giving the number of primary sampling units in each population. (These will all be equal if you have filled out your data cards correctly.)

5. A table giving the second-stage sample size for each combination of population and primary sampling unit. These values also should be equal.

6. The analysis of variance table, which includes sums-of-squares (SS), mean-squares (MS), and expected mean-squares (EMS) columns. In the output for the EMS column

$$\text{SA corresponds to} \sum_{i=1}^{k} \tau_i^2/(k-1)$$

SB is for σ_c^2

SE is σ_e^2

Thus the numbers in this column ought to be nm, m, and unity for the first row, with n and unity for the second, and unity only for the third.

7. Next follows the F value.

8. A table of the sample means corresponding to the populations is the last entry in the output.

An example of this output appears in Appendix N.

This program is designed to work properly even if the number of observations is unequal from one psu to the next, or if the numbers of psu's changes from one population to the next. The F value will not be valid for a probability statement, however, if the coefficients for SB are not fairly close to each other in the populations and psu rows. Specifically, this means that if you happen to have missing observations (perhaps a teacher or student was sick), you can proceed with the analysis anyway. In this text, the formulas for the "unbalanced" or unequal sample size case are omitted, however.

In filling out Control Card 2, it is important to remember that the program was written so that the first field descriptor refers to the space for END or FIN; the second and third to the places for the population and psu codes; and the fourth descriptor is for the measurement being used for the analysis of variance. *The program distinguishes between descriptors on the basis of their order.*

EXERCISES

9.11 Using the data from Exercise 9.7, obtain the analysis of variance table as given in Table 9–2. Compare point estimates of σ_c^2 and σ_e^2 with the estimates obtained in Exercise 9.7. Use PRGM1 for your calculations.

9.12 Obtain the analysis of variance table for the data of Exercise 9.10, using PRGM4. Compare with the results of Exercise 9.10.

REGRESSION WITH CLUSTER SAMPLING

The problem that gives rise to the need for regression analysis in cluster sampling is the same problem encountered in the preceding section. We are interested in the relationship between two variables under conditions that make the selection of a simple random sample impractical. This situation could arise, for example, if we were interested in the relation between income and number of class hours of formal vocational training, both in and out of high school, for an entire state. Cluster sampling must be resorted to because of the large number of people in the state.

Now the statistical model must account for the clusters. We have

(9.19)
$$y_{ij} = \mu + \beta x_{ij} + c_i + e_{ij}$$
$$c_i \sim (0, \sigma_c^2)$$
$$e_{ij} \sim (0, \sigma_e^2)$$

and β is fixed.

Computation of the population values is now becoming more complicated. They will be given on occasion, but their formulas will be omitted. The point to be made here is that we wish to obtain an estimate of β, the relationship between x and y, when an additional component due to the primary sampling unit is present.

A good procedure for obtaining the regression coefficient is to ignore the sampling procedure used; that is, use PRGM4 without paying attention to the psu and ssu numbers, even though you may wish to punch them on the data cards. If you are performing the calculations by hand, simply use a single subscript for the data, with a different subscript whenever either i or j is different. For example, consider three clusters as follows:

CLUSTER NUMBER	OBSERVATION NUMBER	SINGLE SUBSCRIPT	OBSERVATIONS	
1	1	1	x_1	y_1
1	2	2	x_2	y_2
2	1	3	x_3	y_3
2	2	4	x_4	y_4
2	3	5	x_5	y_5
3	1	6	x_6	y_6
3	2	7	x_7	y_7

Then perform the calculations as in Chapter 8.*

EXERCISES

9.13 Using the cluster sample of Exercise 9.6, obtain the STEP reading scores for the same students and, using PRGM2, calculate the regression coefficient for predicting the science score from the reading score.

9.14 Select a cluster sample of students from the randomly grouped fifth grade students, using classes as psu's and students as ssu's. Obtain the regression equation with times chosen as the predicted variable and the STEP reading score as the predictor.

* For the more experienced statistician, this can be thought of as a weighted average of the within-cluster and between-cluster values for β.

Use six classes as psu's and seven students in each class. Compare with your results for Exercise 8.12.

9.15 Test the hypothesis $H: \beta = 0$ for the data of Exercise 9.14.

CLUSTER SAMPLING WITH CATEGORICAL DATA

This section is a brief discussion of what needs to be done when the data are categorical in nature. The answer is simple. Do exactly what you did for simple random sampling. The procedures discussed in Chapter 6 are still valid; however, if you want to know whether a relationship changes between clusters, this does not hold. In this case we are considering clusters as different populations; we will not consider the use of contingency tables with different populations in this text.

Experiences with Data

PROBLEMS

9.1 Are the teachers a meaningful influence on the achievement of students?

9.2 Do teachers have more influence on achievement or on social adjustment?

9.3 Among average students, is the importance of achievement to students the same among randomly grouped students as among ability grouped students?

SOLUTIONS TO EXERCISES

9.1

Begin sampling on page B8, upper left-hand corner, and sample teachers first. Teacher numbers run from 1 to 19, so use two-digit numbers from 1 to 19. We have (ignoring two-digit numbers greater than 19) 14, 17, 10, 7 for our random sample; these will correspond to teachers 1, 2, 3, and 4.

Next select five students from each class, using two-digit numbers beginning with line 23, the line after the number for teacher 7 was selected. (*Note:* For each teacher, we must know how many students there are to know the number above which we ignore the random numbers.)

For teacher 14, there are 29 students; we number them from the top of the page. Using page B8, line 23, and working down, select the students 24, 7, 17, 11, 13.

For teacher 17, there are 31 students; we are now in columns 3 and 4, line 4. Continuing from there, we get students 14, 2, 28, 6, 11, which brings us to line 22, columns 3 and 4.

For teacher 10, there are 30 students; we begin at line 22, columns 3 and 4, and get students 11, 13, 4, 24, 2. Finally, for teacher 7 (23 students) we have students 19, 21, 16, 4, and 11.

We now can construct the following layout (psu's = teachers; ssu's = students), to allow room for the data to be used later:

TEACHER NUMBER

14		17		10		7	
STUDENT NUMBER	OBSER-VATION	STUDENT NUMBER	OBSER-VATION	STUDENT NUMBER	OBSER-VATION	STUDENT NUMBER	OBSER-VATION
24		14		11		19	
7		2		13		21	
17		28		4		16	
11		6		24		4	
13		11		2		11	

9.2

$Y_{1..} = 513$; $Y_{12.} = 125$; $Y_{21.} = 182$; $Y_{1.3} = 128$

9.3

a. $\mu = \frac{643}{18} = 35.72 = \bar{y}...$

$\tau_1 = \bar{y}_{1..} - \bar{y}... = \frac{354}{9} - \mu = 39.33 - 35.72 = 3.61$

$\tau_2 = \bar{y}_{2..} - \bar{y}... = \frac{289}{9} - \mu = 32.11 - 35.72 = -3.61$

$k = 2$; $n = 3$; $m = 3$

b.
$c_{11} = 7.67 \quad c_{21} = -1.11$
$c_{12} = -11.3 \quad c_{22} = -18.78$
$c_{13} = 3.67 \quad c_{23} = 19.89$

c.
$\epsilon_{111} = -14.00 \quad \epsilon_{211} = 12.00$
$\epsilon_{112} = -5.00 \quad \epsilon_{212} = 4.00$
$\epsilon_{113} = 19.00 \quad \epsilon_{213} = -16.00$

$\epsilon_{121} = -5.00 \quad \epsilon_{221} = 5.67$
$\epsilon_{122} = 2.00 \quad \epsilon_{222} = 6.67$
$\epsilon_{123} = 3.00 \quad \epsilon_{223} = -12.33$

$\epsilon_{131} = 29.00 \quad \epsilon_{231} = 1.00$
$\epsilon_{132} = -37.00 \quad \epsilon_{232} = 10.00$
$\epsilon_{133} = 8.00 \quad \epsilon_{233} = -11.00$

9.4

$\sigma_c^2 = 950.20/4 = 237.55$

= sum-of-squares of all c_{ij} divided by $k(n-1) = 4$

$\sigma_e^2 = 3760.67/12 = 313.39$

= sum-of-squares of all ϵ_{ije} divided by $kn(m-1) = 12$

9.5

SOURCE	df	SUM-OF-SQUARES	EMS
Classes	2	3(749.53) = 2248.5	$3\sigma_c^2 + \sigma_e^2$
Students within classes	6	866.7	σ_e^2

$3\sigma_c^2 + \sigma_e^2 \cong 2248.5/2 = 1124.25$

$\sigma_e^2 \cong 866.7/6 = 144.45$

$3\sigma_c^2 \cong 1124.25 - 144.45 = 979.8$

$\sigma_c^2 = 979.8/3 = 326.6$

Hence from these data

σ_e^2 = variance for the students = 144.45
σ_c^2 = variance for the classes = 326.6

Class variability is considerably greater than student variability *in this case.*

9.9

SOURCE	df	SUM-OF-SQUARES	MS
Schools	1	26.0642	26.0642
Classes (psu's)	4	950.1993	237.55
Students (ssu's)	12	3760.67	313.39

$H: \tau_1 = \tau_2$ is tested with $MS_{\text{sch}}/MS_{\text{cl}}$ (classes are the experimental units; sch = schools, cl = classes).
Using $F_{(1,4).05} = 7.71$, we have $MS_{\text{sch}}/MS_{\text{cl}} = 26.06/237.55 = .11 < 7.71$.
Accept $H: \tau_1 = \tau_2$. No evidence that the schools are different with respect to school adjustment.

REVIEW FOR CHAPTER 9

1. Cluster sampling
2. The statistical model for cluster sampling

$$y_{ij} = \mu + c_i + e_{ij}$$
$$i = 1, 2, \ldots, k$$
$$j = 1, 2, \ldots, n$$
$$c_i \sim (0, \sigma_c^2)$$
$$e_{ij} \sim (0, \sigma_e^2)$$

3. Analysis of variance with cluster sampling

SOURCE	df	SUM-OF-SQUARES	EMS
Primary sampling units	$k - 1$	$\sum_{i=1}^{k} n(\bar{y}_{i.} - \bar{y}..)^2 = SS_C$	$n\sigma_c^2 + \sigma_e^2$
Secondary sampling units	$k(n - 1)$	$\sum_{ij} (y_{ij} - \bar{y}_{i.})^2 = SS_E$	σ_e^2

$MS_C = SS_C/(k - 1)$; $MS_E = SS_E/k(n - 1)$
Since $MS_E \cong \sigma_e^2$, $MS_C \cong n\sigma_c^2 + \sigma_e^2$; $(MS_C - MS_E)/n \cong \sigma_c^2$; and we have estimates of σ_e^2 and σ_c^2 for comparison purposes.

4. Comparison of several populations with cluster sampling
   a. The statistical model is

$$y_{ijl} = \mu + \tau_i + c_{ij} + e_{ijl}$$
$$i = 1, 2, \ldots, k$$
$$j = 1, 2, \ldots, n$$
$$l = 1, 2, \ldots, m$$
$$c_{ij} \sim (0, \sigma_c^2)$$
$$e_{ijl} \sim (0, \sigma_e^2)$$

and τ_i is fixed.

b.   Analysis of variance table

SOURCE	df	SUMS-OF-SQUARES	EMS
Between populations	$k - 1$	$\sum_i nm(\bar{y}_{i..} - \bar{y}_{...})^2 = SS_C$	$\dfrac{nm}{k - 1} \displaystyle\sum_{i=1}^{k} \tau_i^2 + m\sigma_c^2 + \sigma_e^2$
Between psu's within populations	$k(n - 1)$	$\sum_{ij} m(\bar{y}_{ij.} - \bar{y}_{i..})^2 = SS_C$	$m\sigma_c^2 + \sigma_e^2$
Between ssu's within psu's	$kn(m - 1)$	$\sum_{ijl} (y_{ijl} - \bar{y}_{ij.})^2 = SS_E$	σ_e^2

c.   A test for H: $\tau_1 = \tau_2 = \ldots = \tau_k$: Use $MS_T/MS_C = F$. Reject H if $F \geq F_{[k-1, k(n-1)]1-\gamma}$; accept H otherwise. This hypothesis has probability $= \gamma$ of being rejected if true.

5. Analysis of categorical data and regression with cluster sampling. Data should be analyzed as though they were selected with a simple random sample in both cases.

APPENDIXES

APPENDIX A
Raw Data from Comparable School Districts

This appendix contains raw data from the fifth grades of two western school districts with comparable characteristics. In one district the students were grouped in classes according to ability, whereas students in the other district were randomly grouped.*

The headings for both sets of data are the same; a description of each item follows:

ID1   Sampling number for students with high ability level. These numbers include only people in this category, and are provided to simplify the sampling process when a random sample is to be selected from the high ability level students only. The numbers are also furnished for the district that did not group their students according to ability, so that comparisons can be made between the two districts.

ID2   Sampling number for students with average ability.

ID3   Sampling number for students with less than average ability.

ID   Sampling number for students in the entire district, without regard to ability level.

PL   Pupil ability level. This was determined on the basis of achievement scores for the preceding year: 1 = high achievers; 2 = average achievers; 3 = low achievers.

S   Sex of student: 1 = male; 2 = female.

STEP   Science achievement score, *Sequential Tests of Educational Progress*
SCI   (STEP), form 4-B.

STEP   Reading achievement score, STEP, form 4-A.
READ

STEP   Social studies achievement score, STEP, form 4-A.
SOC

STEP   Mathematics achievement score, STEP, form 4-B.
MATH

TI   A sociometric measure giving the times each student was chosen
CH   by classmates as one of the five students most desired to (a) sit next to, (b) study with, and (c) move to another classroom with. The times chosen in each of these categories were added together.

* The contents of this table is part of a study reported by W. R. Borg, "Ability Grouping in the Public Schools," *J. Exper. Educ.* (December 1965). The data were reported as part of a project carried out at Utah State University, a public nonprofit institution. The work was supported in part by the Cooperative Research Program, United States Office of Education, Department of Health, Education and Welfare. The opinions expressed in this publication do not necessarily reflect the position or policy of the Office of Education, and no official endorsement by the Office of Education should be inferred.

SC   Sociometric classification. This was derived from preceding score. Those not chosen by anyone were "isolates"; those chosen 2–9 times were in classification 2, 10–21 times in classification 3, and above 21 in classification 4—the "stars."

CON   Concept of Self
SEL

IDL   Ideal Self
SEL

ACC   Acceptance of Self
SEL

The preceding three scores came from the same test, the "Look at Yourself" scale. Personal characteristics such as kind, witty, and selfish, were described, and the student was asked to answer each of the following three questions on a five-place scale:

1. "This is like (unlike) me"—for Concept of Self.
2. "I would like (not like) this to be me"—for Ideal Self.
3. "I like (dislike) being as I am in this respect"—for Acceptance of Self.

High scores represent desirable characteristics; undesirable traits such as selfish were scored high if the student indicated an absence of the trait.

SCH   Science Research Associates (SRA), "Me and School"—designed to measure adjustment to the school environment. The score for a student indicates the number of problems he or she had in this area, so that a high score indicates poor adjustment.

HOM   SRA—"Me and Home"—designed to measure adjustment at home for each student. High indicates poor adjustment.

ME   SRA—"About Myself"—a measure of how the student regards himself. High score is unfavorable.

GET   SRA—"Getting Along with Others"—a measure of the quality
ALO   of relationships with other students. High score indicates unfavorable adjustment.

GEN   SRA—"Things in General"—a measure to summarize the student's feelings with respect to his personal morale. High score is unfavorable.

TABLE A, PART I

AR1

Elementary School Grade Five Randomly Grouped 1959–1960

```
SCHOOL NO.   10        TEACHER NO.    1
ID1ID2ID3  ID  PLS  STEPSTEPSTEPSTEPTI   SCCUNIDLACCSCHHUMME  GETGEN
                    SCI READSOC MATHCH   SELSELSEL            ALU

       1    1 2 1  269 271 262 254 21 3  50 49 57 65 23 53 46 42
 1          2 1 2  271 276 263 253 34 4  41 51 57 22  0  3  0  7
 2          3 1 2  273 271 262 253  0 1  42 51 56 21 15 35 25 37
    2       4 2 1  258 251 248 238  6 2  40 51 23 44 16 42 43 50
 3          5 1 2  287 303 273 263 18 3  46 51 56 29  6 14  8 29
       1    6 3 2  254 251 253 245 12 3  51 51 57 43  8 34 17 37
    3       7 2 1  251 247 255 249 19 0  43 51 57 46 11 34 33 46
 4          8 1 2  239 240 237 238  9 2  42 49 45 62 16 46 10 12
    4       9 2 1  266 267 265 251 19 3  48 51 57 25  7 10  4 21
    5      10 2 1  266 283 273 254  8 2  42 49 57 26 22 18 22 49
 5         11 1 1  283 280 284 269 45 4  44 49 39 18 13 17 17 27
       2   12 3 1  250 234 232 236  8 2   0  0 55 40 10  7  5 32
    6      13 2 2  255 259 252 262 19 3  50 51 57 23  9 28 18 24
       3   14 3 2  267 260 254 247  7 2  43 49 57 30  6 22  8 29
       4   15 3 1  244 235 238 231  1 2  48 49 55 47 30 43 45 41
 6         16 1 2  262 250 266 253 33 4  48 50 52 19 10 11  5 24
 7         17 1 2  260 261 261 251 13 3  46 49 55 51  8 49 20 50
    7      18 2 2  261 274 257 253 18 3  40 49 50 33 12 43 30 39
 8         19 1 1  258 252 250 243  6 2  45 49 57 26  9 11 11 12
    8      20 2 1  263 271 262 253  3 2  48 51 57 39  3  9  8  9
       5   21 3 1  244 238 247 231  8 2  39 43 57 66  2 34 21  9
 9         22 1 1  271 283 268 254  6 2  47 51 57 32 19 27 33 59
    9      23 2 1  262 259 253 251  3 2  45 46 52 53  8 45 19 45
10         24 1 1  276 319 281 272 38 4  51 49 52  7  3 15  7  8
       6   25 3 1  259 274 260 249 11 3  48 53 42 52 19 42 22 47
```

TABLE A, PART I *(Continued)*   **AR2**

Elementary School Grade Five Randomly Grouped 1959–1960

SCHOOL NO. 10   TEACHER NO.   2

ID1	ID2	ID3	ID	PLS		STEP SCI	STEP READ	STEP SOC	STEP MATH	TI	CH	SC SEL	CON SEL	IDL SEL	ACC	SCHH	HOME	GET AL	GEN
10			26	2	2	262	256	251	245	4	2	37	46	41	31	12	40	17	31
11			27	1	2	254	265	251	252	6	2	45	49	45	31	6	32	5	30
12			28	1	1	262	254	261	249	13	3	42	53	41	20	12	19	11	20
	7		29	3	1	254	267	244	239	3	2	44	44	45	63	32	49	48	56
13			30	1	2	263	269	257	244	20	3	49	54	57	8	7	22	2	15
	8		31	3	1	254	267	256	245	16	3	42	50	43	57	6	39	22	41
	9		32	3	2	253	257	250	251	5	2	48	49	42	14	3	14	14	25
14			33	1	1	248	231	244	230	10	3	42	49	49	48	14	10	6	3
	11		34	2	1	263	265	265	256	27	4	46	49	51	16	1	10	1	18
15			35	1	1	271	283	269	257	23	4	45	49	36	33	24	57	51	51
16			36	1	1	276	256	257	263	24	4	45	50	57	19	1	0	4	12
17			37	1	2	261	276	261	256	30	4	42	51	31	23	12	11	7	11
	12		38	2	1	262	261	249	249	19	3	54	48	56	22	5	4	5	14
		10	39	3	2	257	267	256	244	11	3	46	51	51	33	21	38	29	32
18			40	1	2	276	263	273	261	30	4	52	51	45	12	1	15	5	13
	13		41	2	1	247	235	236	244	3	2	37	52	51	62	28	54	21	44
19			42	1	2	283	295	271	257	26	4	52	51	45	6	1	12	6	10
	11		43	3	1	252	257	243	235	4	2	40	51	45	73	25	16	10	13
20			44	1	2	269	274	259	257	17	3	38	49	38	28	29	47	43	38
21			45	1	1	283	292	271	258	10	3	51	53	43	49	15	47	39	56
	14		46	2	2	269	283	262	264	28	4	51	51	45	30	9	9	15	25
		12	47	3	1	248	253	243	239	5	2	45	49	40	48	12	11	13	31
	15		48	2	1	262	263	259	253	19	3	46	53	41	32	9	27	17	40
22			49	1	2	266	251	252	259	13	3	50	51	57	24	12	27	11	25
23			50	1	2	260	263	259	258	12	3	47	50	51	24	9	30	27	43
	16		51	2	2	258	255	259	251	6	2	51	53	51	19	9	33	5	9

TABLE A, PART I (*Continued*)   **AR3**
Elementary School Grade Five Randomly Grouped 1959–1960

SCHOOL NO.   10   TEACHER NO.   3

ID1	ID2	ID3	ID	P	S	STEP SCI	STEP READ	STEP SOC	STEP MATH	TI	CH	SC SEL	CON SEL	IDL SEL	ACC	SCH	HOMME	GET ALD	GEN
	17		52	2	1	267	276	255	257	32	4	47	54	47	28	12	28	19	46
	18		53	2	2	258	267	260	249	9	2	48	49	43	38	9	17	12	18
	19		54	2	2	254	260	250	249	11	3	48	51	57	38	11	22	13	27
24			55	1	1	273	269	266	259	20	3	37	49	45	13	10	18	12	29
	20		56	2	1	267	280	273	260	16	3	43	52	51	26	11	42	17	33
25			57	1	1	273	280	278	259	13	3	43	51	35	40	15	30	28	26
	21		58	2	2	266	265	268	254	25	4	43	48	51	15	5	6	3	11
26			59	1	2	258	292	259	254	13	3	43	48	37	30	10	21	20	27
27			60	1	1	258	244	254	251	6	2	41	51	44	72	29	69	71	48
	22		61	2	2	263	257	260	249	9	2	51	51	49	42	23	33	40	38
	23		62	2	1	248	248	239	233	6	2	41	47	42	53	15	64	45	56
28			63	1	2	269	278	268	263	16	3	41	49	33	58	26	55	27	52
	24		64	2	1	271	269	258	245	10	3	44	51	45	11	2	1	2	7
		13	65	3	1	252	247	247	233	15	3	48	51	51	27	8	37	14	36
	25		66	2	2	264	278	260	243	9	2	40	49	37	39	28	46	17	37
	26		67	2	1	262	274	259	253	13	3	39	42	0	57	26	49	31	43
29			68	1	1	279	283	278	259	31	4	46	51	41	54	26	37	27	45
	27		69	2	1	249	242	239	235	3	2	46	46	43	28	11	15	16	16
30			70	1	1	283	280	271	256	20	3	49	49	53	32	21	26	12	31
31			71	1	1	287	283	284	259	6	2	38	48	43	31	11	29	18	42
32			72	1	2	287	289	271	264	19	3	43	47	47	6	6	10	2	15
	28		73	2	1	269	274	262	241	24	4	40	41	38	52	9	18	7	8
33			74	1	1	267	278	263	254	13	3	44	57	53	22	7	8	1	6
	29		75	2	1	252	248	255	244	16	3	41	52	50	51	7	34	16	37
	30		76	2	2	263	254	262	252	18	3	46	53	53	24	9	19	8	49
		14	77	3	2	255	263	266	239	14	3	43	51	46	40	2	11	2	0

TABLE A, PART I (Continued) AR4
Elementary School Grade Five Randomly Grouped 1959–1960

SCHOOL NO. 11   TEACHER NO. 4

ID1	ID2	ID3	ID	PL	S	STEP SCI	STEP READ	STEP SOC	STEP MATH	TI	CH	SCC SEL	ONIDL SEL	ACC SEL	SCH	HOM	ME	GET ALO	GEN
		15	78	3	2	243	247	236	235	2	2	48	49	57	57	24	92	68	21
34			79	1	2	267	254	246	252	8	2	48	47	49	20	10	13	9	11
35			80	1	2	266	280	251	250	38	4	41	49	33	35	18	10	4	25
36			81	1	1	266	269	256	249	10	3	43	51	57	28	7	16	7	14
37			82	1	2	263	276	269	257	10	3	48	49	57	17	2	23	12	23
	31		83	2	1	263	263	257	254	20	3	45	47	57	15	15	26	27	21
38			84	1	1	258	252	250	244	8	2	49	51	55	6	1	1	0	12
	32		85	2	2	259	274	256	260	21	3	45	49	57	38	9	21	8	13
	33		86	2	2	263	267	269	261	31	4	47	49	51	34	12	26	18	27
		16	87	3	1	244	247	235	236	3	2	47	49	53	43	7	9	6	4
	34		88	2	1	264	263	265	253	22	4	49	51	57	28	7	12	6	27
39			89	1	2	302	274	266	260	11	3	42	48	57	23	12	11	11	16
	35		90	2	2	264	271	258	250	14	3	50	51	57	31	4	17	4	17
40			91	1	2	267	274	259	250	20	3	45	48	45	35	14	15	16	19
41			92	1	1	267	259	252	263	14	3	42	48	53	23	7	13	12	19
42			93	1	1	267	274	262	253	35	4	40	51	57	46	12	51	30	51
		17	94	3	1	237	231	239	238	6	2	49	49	57	70	27	50	26	59
	36		95	2	1	255	259	253	252	8	2	42	49	49	49	17	27	11	21
		18	96	3	1	269	263	258	256	3	2	47	53	57	66	24	57	41	62
43			97	1	1	233	234	253	254	5	2	42	49	53	36	15	33	10	17
44			98	1	1	263	271	266	259	21	3	45	51	55	29	3	10	11	21
45			99	1	1	263	274	256	251	12	3	43	51	57	16	3	0	0	8
46			100	1	2	258	269	259	251	7	2	44	48	54	22	13	43	14	33
47			101	1	2	264	286	266	259	21	3	0	0	51	27	17	36	26	36
48			102	1	1	269	289	268	264	40	4	54	51	55	6	4	8	0	5
49			103	1	2	263	283	252	258	29	4	43	51	31	48	25	25	32	65
		19	104	3	2	233	226	253	233	2	2	47	51	57	10	2	3	3	4
50			105	1	1	267	267	256	257	15	3	46	34	53	33	13	39	15	31
	37		106	2	1	257	243	246	245	26	4	46	49	57	17	18	44	79	39
	38		107	2	1	266	269	266	258	9	2	45	49	55	52	29	64	45	46
51			108	1	1	266	278	266	252	9	2	48	48	39	31	19	30	9	26
		20	109	3	2	256	263	256	250	5	2	43	50	51	39	12	39	12	29
52			110	1	1	276	286	271	260	13	3	45	51	51	17	2	7	2	13

TABLE A, PART I *(Continued)*   AR5

Elementary School Grade Five Randomly Grouped 1959–1960

SCHOOL NO. 11   TEACHER NO. 5

ID1	ID2	ID3	ID	P	L	S	STEP SCI	STEP READ	STEP SOC	STEP MATH	TI	CH	SC SEL	CON SEL	IDL SEL	ACC	SCHH	OMME	GET ALO	GEN
	39		111	2	1		249	247	245	249	12	3	42	48	57	23	11	47	12	30
	40		112	2	2		249	252	248	250	3	2	38	49	27	21	12	67	41	50
53			113	1	1		261	251	251	257	10	3	44	49	55	47	27	66	44	38
		21	114	3	1		247	246	246	230	2	2	49	51	57	40	0	18	12	18
54			115	1	2		253	250	254	251	16	3	0	0	57	50	13	32	17	36
	41		116	2	1		259	250	256	250	19	3	49	51	43	19	4	17	11	27
55			117	1	1		261	257	251	247	27	4	49	49	57	2	1	1	0	0
56			118	1	1		276	263	261	265	17	3	44	53	57	24	13	29	22	16
57			119	1	1		269	265	262	259	13	3	44	51	57	20	7	15	6	17
58			120	1	1		248	239	237	238	4	2	44	49	55	44	7	30	17	24
	42		121	2	1		269	274	268	253	8	2	43	51	51	15	4	9	7	21
59			122	1	2		253	255	250	256	17	3	44	49	57	18	1	8	5	16
60			123	1	2		264	267	252	247	7	2	48	49	57	1	0	0	0	5
	43		124	2	2		256	252	256	244	31	4	46	55	57	37	7	21	9	27
61			125	1	1		263	265	256	253	8	2	43	49	53	15	3	15	5	12
62			126	1	2		271	276	269	258	3	2	44	49	51	34	19	41	23	24
63			127	1	2		276	274	262	266	13	3	48	49	57	33	4	16	6	15
64			128	1	2		256	259	252	244	14	3	49	49	55	0	3	0	3	2
	44		129	2	1		264	271	257	251	12	3	47	51	57	20	4	24	12	17
	45		130	2	1		0	237	232	0	2	2	0	0	0	0	0	0	0	0
65			131	1	2		259	254	265	238	12	3	45	51	57	49	17	37	23	62
	46		132	2	2		252	263	255	249	29	4	57	51	57	41	7	21	13	42
	47		133	2	2		273	280	263	266	14	3	26	51	53	23	11	33	17	29
66			134	1	2		273	280	262	265	18	3	38	48	53	36	19	31	26	40
		22	135	3	1		252	237	243	236	5	2	41	49	45	39	6	13	0	29
		23	136	3	1		267	246	253	254	7	2	46	49	57	57	15	99	26	36
	48		137	2	1		261	274	257	256	7	2	47	47	57	25	15	15	9	16
67			138	1	2		273	286	265	261	13	3	44	51	57	19	3	14	7	12
		24	139	3	1		247	246	242	231	13	3	49	49	57	15	3	6	2	3
	49		140	2	2		269	278	260	240	18	3	48	49	57	21	3	14	13	13
68			141	1	1		267	276	256	254	12	3	43	51	55	23	6	8	4	29
69			142	1	1		261	257	251	256	10	3	53	51	53	4	0	10	11	4
70			143	1	1		261	278	256	266	21	3	45	51	57	38	18	50	40	28
71			144	1	1		283	271	266	260	11	3	43	49	50	39	9	20	13	37

TABLE A, PART I *(Continued)*   **AR6**

Elementary School Grade Five Randomly Grouped 1959–1960

SCHOOL NO.   11   TEACHER NO.   6

ID1	ID2	ID3	ID	PL	S	STEP SCI	STEP READ	STEP SOC	STEP MATH	TI	CH	SCCON SEL	IDL SEL	ACC SEL	SCH	HOM	ME	GET AL	GEN
		25	145	3	2	244	230	236	233	10	3	53	49	55	41	33	80	67	36
72			146	1	2	259	292	271	264	17	3	49	50	46	15	7	16	8	14
73			147	1	1	267	286	268	269	62	4	44	55	49	28	10	31	18	24
74			148	1	1	279	286	260	263	8	2	48	48	56	28	10	35	8	27
	50		149	2	1	263	257	257	249	4	2	42	48	52	23	12	17	14	23
75			150	1	2	254	251	247	250	14	3	46	49	57	40	12	36	18	49
	51		151	2	1	246	241	248	243	15	3	43	55	47	37	17	27	22	20
		26	152	3	1	263	263	254	253	9	2	52	49	57	11	1	6	2	3
	52		153	2	1	237	233	241	230	0	1	45	48	57	56	22	35	22	39
76			154	1	1	287	271	278	276	39	4	44	51	49	22	2	12	5	25
77			155	1	2	264	292	266	256	1	2	39	48	36	40	14	58	48	40
78			156	1	2	253	263	253	247	16	3	53	49	57	0	1	2	1	2
	53		157	2	1	255	253	252	245	3	2	47	52	52	64	32	61	40	46
79			158	1	2	269	265	268	258	32	4	45	49	53	25	6	11	9	18
80			159	1	2	261	276	271	252	17	3	47	49	57	34	10	38	36	43
81			160	1	2	260	269	252	256	12	3	54	51	57	0	1	9	3	5
	54		161	2	2	246	254	243	230	4	2	41	47	55	19	5	10	5	9
	55		162	2	2	260	265	259	249	27	4	47	49	57	24	7	20	5	25
	56		163	2	2	262	265	256	261	20	3	44	49	57	10	3	9	4	5
82			164	1	1	262	274	263	256	22	4	51	53	55	16	3	1	0	3
	57		165	2	1	269	278	259	253	18	3	43	51	47	26	13	26	14	20
83			166	1	1	269	271	271	261	36	4	46	46	55	11	1	2	2	6
	58		167	2	1	253	247	246	240	6	2	50	49	57	24	26	48	29	48
		27	168	3	2	251	251	249	243	8	2	48	49	53	28	11	11	3	25
84			169	1	2	255	263	257	258	12	3	49	53	57	17	6	10	4	17
		28	170	3	1	241	242	243	236	10	3	53	53	57	7	3	6	0	12
		29	171	3	1	254	274	260	250	5	2	49	53	57	4	1	2	2	9
85			172	1	1	264	259	257	253	5	2	46	51	57	26	5	16	5	27
86			173	1	1	279	271	263	263	0	1	49	51	57	10	8	39	13	22
87			174	1	2	261	271	265	239	12	3	46	49	57	53	5	39	24	27
	59		175	2	1	249	241	243	247	8	2	42	49	57	62	5	19	9	15
88			176	1	2	266	259	258	252	14	3	43	49	45	36	17	50	32	52
89			177	1	2	264	260	257	257	12	3	45	49	57	15	5	22	12	26
		30	178	3	1	249	248	239	238	16	3	50	49	57	22	8	10	8	10

TABLE A, PART I (Continued)

Elementary School Grade Five Randomly Grouped 1959–1960

AR7

SCHOOL NO. 12   TEACHER NO. 7

ID1	ID2	ID3	ID	P	L	S	STEP SCI	STEP READ	STEP SOC	STEP MATH	TI	CH	SC SEL	CON SEL	IDL SEL	ACC	SCH	HOM	ME	GET AL	GEN O
	60		179	2	1		252	249	251	240	17	3	46	50	53	27	14	29		22	36
90			180	1	2		264	283	263	239	10	3	50	49	55	36	9	24		17	44
91			181	1	2		261	286	265	243	38	4	45	49	57	31	16	8		9	53
92			182	1	2		257	269	258	258	12	3	48	47	57	6	3	0		0	0
	61		183	2	2		255	260	248	249	22	4	45	49	47	36	16	41		19	44
93			184	1	1		260	257	258	247	27	4	50	50	55	45	19	39		10	13
		31	185	3	2		248	251	253	240	10	3	47	49	55	34	8	16		12	20
	62		186	2	2		256	252	263	247	7	2	45	49	57	36	15	28		26	41
94			187	1	1		249	250	236	254	25	4	46	50	53	16	7	22		20	11
95			188	1	2		231	263	251	235	9	2	50	49	57	6	3	13		2	1
	63		189	2	1		260	239	246	245	11	3	47	51	57	27	4	13		10	14
96			190	1	1		261	276	255	258	12	3	43	46	43	20	6	31		25	23
97			191	1	2		252	263	247	236	17	3	49	49	55	5	0	11		1	3
	64		192	2	1		246	238	236	230	8	2	50	49	57	23	3	9		9	30
98			193	1	1		260	261	257	257	13	3	47	53	49	35	8	36		37	69
99			194	1	2		262	265	248	251	2	2	0	0	53	24	13	27		25	31
	65		195	2	2		227	242	229	235	11	3	52	48	53	46	32	84		55	45
		32	196	3	1		256	248	245	243	12	3	42	50	57	53	16	32		16	22
		33	197	3	1		225	239	0	0	5	2	0	0	0	0	0	0		0	0
		34	198	3	1		248	253	245	236	8	2	46	49	45	40	27	40		44	29
		35	199	3	2		225	0	230	233	5	2	49	51	53	62	37	91		60	43
	66		200	2	2		245	245	250	236	6	2	46	53	57	31	2	35		16	32
	67		201	2	1		245	249	249	230	0	1	50	49	57	29	10	25		17	16

TABLE A, PART I *(Continued)*   AR8

Elementary School Grade Five Randomly Grouped 1959–1960

SCHOOL NO.   12   TEACHER NO.   8

ID1	ID2	ID3	ID	P	L/S	STEP SCI	STEP READ	STEP SOC	STEP MATH	TI	CH	SCC SEL	UNIDL SEL	LACC SEL	SCH	HOMME	GET	GEN	ALU
	68		202	2	2	246	0	240	239	10	3	39	49	43	53	29	65	46	49
	69		203	2	1	0	253	0	0	18	3	49	51	55	40	2	11	3	7
	70		204	2	2	256	263	244	231	12	3	49	51	47	27	3	26	12	24
100			205	1	2	262	280	266	253	48	4	53	49	49	34	4	42	27	44
	71		206	2	2	259	252	245	239	8	2	47	49	57	40	8	19	15	41
101			207	1	1	273	261	260	267	23	4	49	51	55	24	5	19	13	17
		36	208	3	1	225	232	227	230	10	3	46	54	57	46	0	45	53	45
	72		209	2	2	256	249	249	253	3	2	46	51	57	14	7	7	2	6
102			210	1	2	0	C	0	0	18	3	48	49	57	13	9	10	4	21
	73		211	2	2	247	247	241	230	4	2	48	50	51	47	6	43	31	51
	74		212	2	1	248	243	250	243	13	3	52	49	57	18	1	10	15	11
103			213	1	1	291	274	269	261	24	4	50	50	55	17	10	15	5	13
104			214	1	2	266	269	262	254	51	4	50	49	55	2	0	3	0	9
	75		215	2	2	266	265	252	252	15	3	41	51	40	39	3	40	24	46
105			216	1	2	256	253	255	247	7	2	34	41	29	24	21	57	45	49
106			217	1	1	261	271	262	252	4	2	42	49	49	62	15	41	35	40
107			218	1	1	262	257	252	249	12	3	45	49	57	46	12	49	43	60
		37	219	3	1	250	250	248	239	35	4	44	49	57	41	5	14	17	29
108			220	1	1	273	278	263	256	5	2	49	49	55	25	9	13	9	39
	76		221	2	1	258	260	252	235	5	2	49	52	43	68	18	42	33	42
	77		222	2	1	253	251	243	236	4	2	46	53	57	49	20	15	17	46
109			223	1	1	267	265	255	259	31	4	43	50	55	22	14	29	21	24
	78		224	2	2	246	242	236	283	1	2	38	49	57	48	17	30	25	32
110			225	1	2	267	286	266	257	20	3	44	51	51	25	13	29	3	31
	79		226	2	1	254	250	260	257	3	2	44	53	47	39	24	37	24	48
111			227	1	1	266	257	257	259	4	2	45	49	47	42	13	38	22	38
		38	228	3	2	257	233	246	247	4	2	42	48	47	35	9	59	23	55
		39	229	3	1	0	232	0	0	4	2	48	49	51	39	5	11	4	5
		40	230	3	2	250	245	237	235	4	2	42	48	51	30	7	10	7	17

TABLE A, PART I *(Continued)*   **AR9**

Elementary School Grade Five Randomly Grouped 1959–1960

SCHOOL NO.   13   TEACHER NO.   9

ID1	ID2	ID3	ID	PLS		STEP SCI	STEP READ	STEP SOC	STEP MATH	TI	CH	SCC	UN	IDL	ACC SEL	SCH SEL	HOM SEL	GET ALG	GEN
112			231	1	2	310	283	271	263	3	2	42	46	56	14	7	9	13	25
	80		232	2	2	260	249	255	259	15	3	44	53	57	33	0	6	3	15
113			233	1	2	269	276	261	254	24	4	46	52	42	27	10	21	13	18
	81		234	2	1	269	283	263	253	17	3	38	49	37	31	33	44	12	26
		41	235	3	1	244	253	242	238	8	2	44	49	53	31	10	26	21	7
114			236	1	1	252	250	257	253	6	2	52	51	57	43	19	62	45	32
115			237	1	2	259	265	260	251	14	3	42	50	29	53	26	63	45	51
		42	238	3	2	266	257	260	252	9	2	44	49	56	34	22	45	32	41
	82		239	2	1	269	271	265	247	29	4	49	51	57	14	0	1	0	0
116			240	1	1	266	269	259	256	18	3	47	55	56	64	16	23	16	40
	83		241	2	2	261	267	266	245	18	3	49	51	55	7	4	5	1	5
	84		242	2	1	264	265	247	245	19	3	41	50	56	15	0	9	3	15
117			243	1	1	259	263	253	247	18	3	46	51	56	42	4	17	4	32
118			244	1	2	259	260	252	249	18	3	47	49	57	23	8	25	7	25
	85		245	2	2	269	289	262	259	13	3	45	50	44	43	35	54	35	37
		43	246	3	1	257	249	243	247	8	0	44	49	56	58	12	12	13	33
	86		247	2	1	279	280	259	259	5	2	54	50	57	29	4	9	5	11
	87		248	2	1	261	254	260	236	3	2	44	49	0	5	22	16	10	13
119			249	1	2	271	269	261	265	7	2	46	49	57	2	3	7	0	9
	88		250	2	1	252	259	246	241	6	2	49	53	53	34	10	19	6	21
		44	251	3	2	256	244	248	240	3	2	44	49	56	17	2	8	3	10
120			252	1	1	269	260	251	249	17	3	50	49	57	18	6	6	0	6
		45	253	3	1	0	0	0	0	1	2	52	51	48	45	6	15	18	30
121			254	1	2	0	0	0	0	12	3	46	53	52	26	22	11	7	59
	89		255	2	2	276	263	265	254	2	2	42	51	56	49	44	57	51	62
122			256	1	2	262	276	259	249	26	4	48	50	57	16	8	9	3	10
123			257	1	1	287	269	284	265	28	4	46	50	55	39	12	39	17	40
	90		258	2	2	266	246	260	244	4	2	43	47	49	77	16	65	44	45
124			259	1	1	261	269	266	257	4	2	43	50	49	25	1	21	14	19
125			260	1	1	276	295	284	256	33	4	47	52	50	22	1	8	6	5
	91		261	2	2	269	298	263	257	4	2	46	51	46	25	13	19	7	16
		46	262	3	1	251	259	249	247	1	2	51	54	57	53	28	63	37	67
126			263	1	1	266	260	259	244	33	4	44	48	55	32	10	33	12	22

TABLE A, PART I (Continued)   **AR10**

Elementary School Grade Five Randomly Grouped 1959–1960

SCHOOL NO.   13   TEACHER NO.   10

ID1	ID2	ID3	ID	PL	S	STEP SCI	STEP READ	STEP SOC	STEP MATH	TI	CH	SC SEL	CON SEL	IDL SEL	ACC	SCHH	OMME	GET ALO	GEN
		47	264	3	1	269	257	263	244	2	2	47	48	53	35	13	9	12	21
127			265	1	2	279	269	260	264	22	4	47	48	49	12	15	11	11	33
		48	266	3	1	258	260	255	253	2	2	49	52	49	46	22	39	0	28
128			267	1	1	263	263	259	247	10	3	42	46	45	27	20	30	23	26
	92		268	2	2	262	274	248	256	9	2	42	48	37	66	30	39	53	54
129			269	1	1	251	248	241	245	17	3	47	48	46	31	3	13	9	28
130			270	1	1	287	276	266	263	18	3	43	53	38	45	15	44	30	52
	93		271	2	1	271	276	261	247	22	4	49	49	45	48	4	10	11	19
	94		272	2	1	267	274	258	256	10	3	51	53	57	12	0	1	0	0
	95		273	2	2	250	276	243	244	10	3	49	49	50	19	9	15	4	18
131			274	1	2	267	292	265	259	6	2	45	49	41	41	4	31	16	29
132			275	1	2	276	274	269	266	13	3	46	50	56	8	16	3	1	9
133			276	1	2	263	260	251	256	16	3	49	51	49	25	4	28	18	12
134			277	1	1	273	265	271	263	16	3	48	51	57	37	3	13	12	15
	96		278	2	2	254	265	248	247	10	3	46	49	55	35	18	29	43	56
135			279	1	1	291	276	273	264	24	4	46	46	49	20	4	4	8	23
136			280	1	1	250	242	242	245	5	2	50	49	56	47	4	12	5	1
		49	281	3	1	258	243	244	243	5	2	25	31	52	60	28	45	32	40
137			282	1	1	287	298	278	263	19	3	44	53	37	21	1	31	4	16
138			283	1	2	276	274	260	264	10	3	50	52	52	8	10	12	1	18
		50	284	3	2	250	252	244	239	8	2	36	54	38	62	21	48	16	32
139			285	1	2	283	289	271	257	14	3	46	50	44	11	9	17	4	14
140			286	1	2	267	260	261	264	19	3	49	53	55	21	0	10	0	3
141			287	1	2	279	289	269	269	33	4	43	49	35	9	7	8	8	20
		51	288	3	1	257	263	257	251	10	3	50	50	52	8	0	5	0	4
142			289	1	2	276	298	278	269	34	4	46	48	49	14	7	12	6	21
		52	290	3	2	257	252	246	239	8	2	46	41	50	33	10	23	6	24
	97		291	2	2	259	267	246	241	6	2	44	49	52	14	2	10	4	5
		53	292	3	2	260	280	262	258	40	4	47	49	37	26	12	19	7	15
	98		293	2	1	263	260	254	253	10	3	39	49	37	52	4	32	13	45

TABLE A, PART I (*Continued*) AR11

Elementary School Grade Five Randomly Grouped 1959–1960

SCHOOL NO. 13   TEACHER NO. 11

ID1	ID2	ID3	ID	PL	S	STEP SCI	STEP READ	STEP SOC	STEP MATH	TI	CH	SC SEL	CON SEL	IDL SEL	ACC	SCH	HOMME	GET ALO	GEN
	99		294	2	1	253	247	245	249	26	4	45	51	51	23	7	12	5	14
143			295	1	2	262	278	265	253	15	3	53	51	53	15	0	3	0	0
144			296	1	1	271	286	261	254	22	4	41	47	37	38	9	31	27	34
145			297	1	1	263	269	256	254	5	2	51	52	51	26	7	20	9	15
146			298	1	2	264	278	249	254	27	4	51	49	0	39	4	8	1	11
147			299	1	1	283	278	273	259	20	3	48	53	57	26	12	23	15	21
148			300	1	2	257	271	255	245	9	2	45	48	40	25	11	30	24	32
	100		301	2	1	261	250	241	0	23	4	35	52	0	53	16	32	31	59
149			302	1	1	271	263	262	254	5	2	49	51	55	49	13	14	3	4
150			303	1	2	267	286	266	254	15	3	43	46	53	36	28	20	9	17
	101		304	2	2	259	265	256	253	18	3	42	51	54	26	9	16	7	0
151			305	1	2	283	283	271	261	16	3	45	49	47	30	5	23	11	22
	102		306	2	1	263	274	288	250	20	3	49	52	44	47	31	51	56	46
152			307	1	1	296	307	288	269	9	2	48	52	57	42	12	36	29	29
153			308	1	1	256	236	243	249	18	3	46	51	55	45	16	12	3	11
	103		309	2	1	253	241	247	259	13	3	54	50	55	38	17	17	13	36
154			310	1	1	253	253	248	256	0	0	46	50	53	41	11	34	14	28
		54	311	3	2	243	251	253	245	6	2	42	53	53	36	8	3	0	15
		55	312	3	1	246	237	229	230	19	3	42	51	51	40	29	18	37	23
	104		313	2	2	261	271	254	250	17	3	44	49	53	18	4	6	2	5
155			314	1	2	263	286	256	252	18	3	46	51	49	50	18	62	27	28
156			315	1	2	291	298	275	272	21	3	49	49	51	24	2	5	7	18
157			316	1	1	273	274	265	256	14	3	43	46	56	35	7	10	7	22
158			317	1	1	266	283	262	265	3	2	41	41	34	32	6	21	25	15
159			318	1	2	251	261	263	254	12	3	40	45	39	22	18	31	23	30
		56	319	3	2	250	247	240	235	17	3	43	48	49	51	25	45	48	42
		57	320	3	1	259	257	249	245	9	2	37	49	51	18	10	12	10	18
	105		321	2	1	276	265	265	269	16	3	45	49	54	47	14	30	9	31
160			322	1	2	261	265	258	254	16	3	45	50	52	20	6	32	5	15
	106		323	2	2	250	252	244	240	5	2	42	41	53	34	34	44	56	20
	107		324	2	2	273	315	275	274	45	4	45	48	46	10	2	4	2	3

TABLE A, PART I (Continued)   **AR12**

Elementary School Grade Five Randomly Grouped 1959–1960

SCHOOL NO.   14   TEACHER NO.   12

ID1	ID2	ID3	ID	P	S	STEP SCI	STEP READ	STEP SOC	STEP MATH	TI CH	SC SEL	CON SEL	IDL SEL	ACC	SCHH	OMME	GET ALO	GEN
		58	325	3	2	271	276	253	251	22	4	44	49	57	21	10	23	23	28
	108		326	2	1	261	269	262	251	4	2	46	53	57	38	11	25	8	19
	109		327	2	2	259	269	254	249	5	2	38	49	23	42	13	27	21	35
161			328	1	1	263	286	263	249	23	4	47	51	41	36	9	16	8	11
162			329	1	1	260	267	247	263	20	3	44	49	57	31	5	11	5	6
163			330	1	2	271	271	257	249	19	3	50	49	57	7	2	10	4	9
	110		331	2	2	254	254	263	256	13	3	44	47	57	40	21	29	20	20
164			332	1	1	261	259	258	247	8	2	53	51	51	15	4	12	10	5
165			333	1	1	253	263	269	251	18	3	47	51	57	30	7	22	14	23
166			334	1	2	276	271	259	259	11	3	49	49	57	16	1	11	4	21
		59	335	3	1	253	257	254	239	25	4	46	49	41	44	19	61	39	54
	111		336	2	2	256	252	258	249	15	3	43	50	41	26	9	13	9	16
167			337	1	1	271	252	265	258	16	3	40	49	53	35	9	19	13	25

TABLE A, PART I *(Continued)*   **AR13**

Elementary School Grade Five Randomly Grouped 1959–1960

```
SCHOOL NO.   14        TEACHER NO.   13
ID1ID2ID3  ID  PLS STEPSTEPSTEPSTEPTI SCCONIDLACCSCHHOMME GETGEN
                   SCI READSOC MATHCH   SELSELSEL            ALU

        60 338 3 1 246 238 246 253  0 1 38 52 57 69 27 69 65 68
        61 339 3 2 257 247 246 235 15 3 49 48 57 15 15 14  6 28
168        340 1 2 267 265 258 261  3 2 48 50 57  9  6  6  4 14
        62 341 3 1 279 267 259 263 12 3 40 45 41 34 13 20 18 19
169        342 1 2 287 295 268 263 14 3 45 49 41 31 20 66 52 42
   112     343 2 1 264 292 265 261 36 4 50 51 57 24  7 13  9 25
170        344 1 2 283 286 266 265 25 4 45 50 57 14  0 37  8 15
        63 345 3 1 269 271 257 245  3 2 47 53 57 17  6 15  7 23
171        346 1 2 287 283 273 265 13 3 44 49 51 26  6 24 21 32
   113     347 2 1 259 245 244 241 28 4 44 49 54 14  5  9  3  5
172        348 1 2 279 276 258 252 13 3 44 49 53 25  7 21 16 24
173        349 1 1 283 295 284 258 32 4 45 49 49 31  3  3  2 20
        64 350 3 2 256 255 260 249  7 2 44 50 54 32 18 17  8 24
   114     351 2 2 283 298 266 264 25 4 47 49 39 12 10 16 13 12
        65 352 3 2 248 244 244 245 15 3 46 49 57 33  5 12  8 13
        66 353 3 2 273 289 266 264 12 3 47 49 57 16  6 29 14 40
174        354 1 1 259 261 262 250  9 2 49 51 55  9  2  0  1  4
        67 355 3 2 250 244 245 236 11 3 46 51 57 36  3  9  4 14
   115     356 2 1 266 269 269 245 16 3 44 52 57 38 19 29 16 33
175        357 1 2   0   C   0   0  4 2 46 49 57 21  9 27 12 35
        68 358 3 1 244 242 243 243  8 2 35 45 33 43 19 37 30 34
176        359 1 1 291 260 253 258 29 4 45 49 44 44 20 31 10 33
        69 360 3 1 271 252 258 250 14 3 47 51 54 30  9 14 12 21
        70 361 3 2 263 248 249 247 15 3 45 51 57 27  5  3  4 10
177        362 1 2 262 260 257 260  5 2 48 51 55 41 14 39 17 11
178        363 1 2 262 274 259 258 17 3 48 51 55 27  8 14  8 19
   116     364 2 1 259 244 251 257 16 3 52 51 55 30  7 28 18 25
   117     365 2 1 273 251 257 261  0 1 46 53 40 27 10 24 24 34
179        366 1 1 302 292 288 263 31 4 46 49 49 16  1  2  0  5
   118     367 2 1 269 259 261 265  8 2 42 49 27 69 33 68 54 52
180        368 1 2 279 261 271 263  8 2 44 49 53 24  5 19 16 26
        71 369 3 2 239 247 237 240 15 3 48 49 55  7  2  0  1  0
```

TABLE A, PART I *(Continued)* AR14

Elementary School Grade Five Randomly Grouped 1959–1960

```
SCHOOL NO.    14        TEACHER NO.    14
ID1ID2ID3  ID   PLS STEPSTEPSTEPSTEPTI  SCCONIDLACCSCHHOMME GETGEN
                    SCI READSOC MATHCH   SELSELSEL          ALU
```

ID1	ID2	ID3	ID	P	L	S	STEP SCI	STEP READ	STEP SOC	STEP MATH	TI CH	SC SEL	CON SEL	IDL SEL	ACC	SCHH	OMME	GET ALU	GEN
181			370	1	2		258	253	252	253	19	3	38	51	55	76	25	86	83	61
	119		371	2	1		269	269	268	250	6	2	44	53	57	43	11	25	17	18
182			372	1	2		279	292	263	269	18	3	47	51	57	39	12	16	13	18
	120		373	2	1		251	233	251	243	10	3	42	50	55	33	3	30	12	23
	121		374	2	1		257	250	252	251	8	2	47	51	45	51	16	28	19	28
183			375	1	1		276	276	262	258	23	4	53	53	57	18	4	12	4	16
	122		376	2	1		273	271	261	260	14	3	46	55	51	30	12	18	19	28
	123		377	2	1		262	269	263	245	2	2	45	49	57	28	8	17	14	47
		72	378	3	1		260	246	255	247	13	3	41	46	50	38	21	28	26	44
184			379	1	2		279	280	262	258	23	4	42	48	57	44	19	49	40	43
185			380	1	1		291	319	275	276	7	2	42	48	40	28	26	41	26	42
	124		381	2	1		261	254	251	251	7	2	43	49	57	42	10	38	16	33
		73	382	3	1		235	246	231	235	3	2	45	51	57	31	9	11	6	25
186			383	1	1		276	286	271	261	25	4	46	49	49	23	5	8	4	11
	125		384	2	2		261	245	257	249	3	2	50	49	57	42	6	12	0	0
187			385	1	1		283	274	265	258	22	4	41	47	55	30	10	37	15	15
	126		386	2	1		283	289	263	257	26	4	42	49	55	18	6	16	8	16
	127		387	2	2		247	255	245	240	16	3	49	50	57	46	13	42	11	25
	128		388	2	2		273	267	259	254	17	3	49	49	57	25	12	6	3	9
188			389	1	2		263	276	278	256	15	3	47	49	57	39	7	10	6	19
189			390	1	1		253	236	243	244	22	4	32	44	57	32	26	28	15	38
190			391	1	2		263	261	263	258	10	3	52	51	53	3	0	1	0	3
	129		392	2	1		258	265	261	256	4	2	51	51	55	42	14	34	19	52
		74	393	3	2		252	257	252	235	13	3	49	51	56	32	4	8	4	29
191			394	1	1		257	260	258	263	11	3	43	50	55	32	10	25	9	17
		75	395	3	2		238	241	240	230	1	2	47	49	57	35	5	11	2	14
	130		396	2	2		269	254	262	252	7	2	40	50	37	27	4	57	16	20
192			397	1	2		269	278	266	252	16	3	44	49	55	18	19	20	25	26
	131		398	2	1		279	276	268	253	36	4	40	50	57	21	9	22	8	22

TABLE A, PART I (*Continued*)   **AR15**

Elementary School Grade Five Randomly Grouped 1959–1960

SCHOOL NO. 15   TEACHER NO. 15

ID1	ID2	ID3	ID	P	L/S	STEP SCI	STEP READ	STEP SOC	STEP MATCH	TI	CH	SC SEL	CONI SEL	DL SEL	ACC	SCHH	OMME	GET ALO	GEN
193			399	1	2	263	298	273	264	37	4	45	49	50	7	10	15	4	12
194			400	1	1	263	286	262	258	3	2	42	50	52	33	7	19	11	21
	132		401	2	2	261	265	253	252	6	2	36	48	22	32	4	64	22	39
195			402	1	2	262	295	266	260	19	3	49	51	57	11	0	5	5	5
196			403	1	1	258	256	242	251	20	3	49	49	51	33	8	27	5	42
	133		404	2	2	238	256	243	230	4	2	0	0	54	55	27	68	65	68
	134		405	2	1	262	271	252	259	33	4	41	51	57	18	8	25	21	29
197			406	1	2	260	274	252	241	3	2	45	51	57	22	5	24	7	29
198			407	1	1	264	249	258	249	17	3	0	0	56	26	18	21	32	37
	135		408	2	2	264	256	266	269	15	3	44	49	51	11	7	7	2	9
199			409	1	1	261	283	257	256	35	4	46	49	53	22	9	26	12	31
200			410	1	2	0	259	259	244	20	3	44	49	47	22	11	24	21	48
201			411	1	2	264	280	261	264	23	4	39	53	57	10	17	32	22	21
202			412	1	2	269	276'	251	257	40	4	42	50	37	16	10	22	9	29
203			413	1	1	267	252	260	265	13	3	43	49	44	18	5	16	6	15
	136		414	2	1	258	267	249	247	11	3	42	51	51	21	10	18	9	24
204			415	1	2	263	274	253	241	7	2	38	46	44	49	32	69	62	43
		76	416	3	2	256	263	260	243	11	3	49	51	57	26	6	14	6	5
205			417	1	1	279	298	281	263	14	3	44	49	46	26	7	19	12	26
206			418	1	1	271	249	246	254	12	3	44	51	57	47	20	37	40	41
207			419	1	2	276	292	278	270	30	4	48	50	48	29	4	7	3	18
208			420	1	1	259	283	261	261	9	2	45	48	50	13	5	28	4	22
		77	421	3	2	248	252	249	226	12	3	41	48	41	61	40	69	40	46
	137		422	2	1	258	240	249	239	4	2	44	51	38	41	25	25	6	22
209			423	1	2	257	254	250	251	15	3	50	51	55	9	1	0	2	9
210			424	1	1	262	255	260	250	18	3	44	49	49	17	8	6	8	12
	138		425	2	1	243	230	243	230	5	2	53	53	49	11	0	10	10	0
211			426	1	2	258	271	261	258	8	2	44	49	47	19	11	26	16	37
212			427	1	2	263	278	262	254	11	3	42	51	33	11	7	7	7	11
213			428	1	2	283	283	268	276	10	3	46	49	43	23	8	8	16	24
		78	429	3	1	261	242	244	238	0	1	42	42	18	34	19	35	30	29
		79	430	3	2	264	276	263	258	10	3	42	48	53	3	9	4	11	30

TABLE A, PART I (*Continued*)   **AR16**
Elementary School Grade Five Randomly Grouped 1959–1960

```
SCHOOL NO.   15        TEACHER NO.   16
ID1ID2ID3 ID  PLS STEPSTEPSTEPSTEPTI  SCCONIDLACCSCHHUMME GETGEN
                  SCI READSOC MATHCH   SELSELSEL        ALO

        80 431 3 1 266 271 266 253 11 3 44 46 57 30  5  5  4  4
    139    432 2 1 239 252 243 245 10 3 39 49 55 62 26 37 15 19
214        433 1 1 257 265 259 241 16 3 45 49 51 15  4  1  2 13
215        434 1 2 267 298 278 257 13 3 41 53 49  6  8 20  6 33
216        435 1 2 264 280 265 252 20 3 44 53 47 19 10 24  6 25
217        436 1 2 296 303 269 263 11 3 46 49 39 10  4 12  2 15
    140    437 2 1 253 265 259 254  7 2 46 49 53 23  5 10  7  5
218        438 1 2 262 265 265 256 11 3 46 50 46 33  8 19 13 34
219        439 1 1 276 252 252 253 16 3  0  0 57  5  3  0  0  2
220        440 1 2 259 269 251 240 15 3 45 51 47 57 25 49 41 44
        81 441 3 1 259 250 254 243 18 3 43 44 52 30  7 23 26 16
    141    442 2 1 266 243 254 245 24 4 39 49 57 27  4  9  4  8
    142    443 2 1 266 265 259   0 22 4 46 49 57 18  7  4  0  5
    143    444 2 1 276 269 260 251  7 2 42 51 57 34  7 11  6 15
221        445 1 1 273 283 268 254 25 4 47 51 44 52 20 58 37 42
222        446 1 1 276 292 269 245 17 3 48 53 44 14  2  8  4 10
223        447 1 1 261 253 259 257 19 3 43 51 55 43 21 33 32 41
224        448 1 1 279 257 273 260 13 3 48 53 52 23 12  8  5  8
225        449 1 2 283 289 261 256  9 2 42 50 49 19 18 26  7 29
```

TABLE A, PART I *(Continued)* **AR17**
Elementary School Grade Five Randomly Grouped 1959–1960

SCHOOL NO.   15   TEACHER NO.   17

ID1	ID2	ID3	ID	P	L	S	STEP SCI	STEP READ	STEP SOC	STEP MATH	TI CH	SC	CON	IDL	ACC	SCH	HOM	ME	GET ALO	GEN
												SEL	SEL	SEL						
226			450	1	2	262	267	257	254	14	3	49	53	46	23	3	10	4	17
227			451	1	2	261	278	251	253	17	3	47	49	55	8	0	0	0	1
228			452	1	2	261	261	252	253	9	2	40	47	31	27	37	39	49	44
	82		453	3	1	257	249	243	240	7	2	53	41	57	27	11	24	20	26
	83		454	3	1	256	265	252	241	10	3	41	52	56	46	12	26	18	39
229			455	1	1	283	255	261	256	52	4	54	51	56	24	8	8	8	37
	144		456	2	1	248	242	242	243	21	3	45	51	52	30	4	18	9	18
230			457	1	1	266	267	261	258	14	3	54	51	55	14	8	7	1	23
231			458	1	2	262	256	261	254	8	2	42	50	55	44	19	30	23	29
	84		459	3	1	229	244	238	245	11	3	45	49	53	38	9	28	12	25
	85		460	3	1	255	246	244	233	11	3	40	49	51	34	18	29	23	50
	145		461	2	1	256	250	254	241	17	3	46	49	53	37	8	21	12	32
	146		462	2	2	266	280	248	254	5	2	50	49	55	15	10	5	13	16
	86		463	3	1	244	242	235	233	8	2	45	54	57	48	11	39	49	43
	147		464	2	2	256	256	254	249	11	3	52	49	57	12	8	9	0	11
232			465	1	1	267	278	278	258	37	4	50	49	54	13	2	6	2	2
233			466	1	2	257	246	247	251	7	2	51	53	55	25	1	5	2	11
234			467	1	1	266	271	246	260	41	4	39	49	35	45	23	42	26	21
	148		468	2	2	245	251	251	238	7	2	0	0	53	29	12	13	12	16
235			469	1	2	269	289	275	276	37	4	42	51	56	42	15	38	22	28
236			470	1	1	248	242	244	247	1	2	47	53	51	24	12	57	37	51
237			471	1	2	244	265	253	238	17	3	42	48	47	70	24	55	33	61
	87		472	3	1	264	252	259	250	11	3	46	53	57	27	2	24	9	21
238			473	1	1	276	257	246	251	12	3	44	47	57	33	13	27	14	15
	88		474	3	1	243	236	228	240	1	2	48	51	51	30	15	2	1	7
	149		475	2	2	244	247	241	238	9	2	55	53	57	42	9	51	8	3
	150		476	2	2	254	253	249	243	6	2	47	49	51	17	3	2	1	19
239			477	1	2	260	265	258	259	9	2	38	59	25	26	7	37	24	30
240			478	1	2	283	269	265	258	11	3	46	47	56	38	19	55	46	31
	151		479	2	2	267	274	258	256	28	4	53	49	57	8	0	15	11	31
241			480	1	1	246	234	241	245	3	2	45	54	47	22	16	57	44	16

TABLE A, PART I (*Continued*)   **AR18**
Elementary School Grade Five Randomly Grouped 1959–1960

SCHOOL NO. 16   TEACHER NO. 18

ID1/ID2/ID3	ID	P	L	STEP SCI	STEP READ	STEP SOC	STEP MATH	TI	CH	SC SEL	CON SEL	IDL SEL	ACC	SCH	HUM	ME	GET GEN ALO
152	431	2	1	258	247	241	247	18	3	35	47	33	67	31	63	53	51
242	432	1	1	273	269	258	258	26	4	0	0	57	25	8	2	7	22
243	483	1	1	263	250	254	247	20	3	40	39	45	56	26	24	22	28
153	484	2	1	262	261	257	244	3	2	36	49	50	65	17	46	33	39
244	485	1	2	279	303	275	264	24	4	42	52	37	33	13	32	19	42
154	486	2	2	253	253	252	235	5	2	38	51	49	39	6	27	24	51
245	487	1	2	267	283	273	257	5	2	45	51	57	20	3	5	0	0
246	488	1	1	269	280	262	264	29	4	44	51	51	29	17	17	19	30
247	489	1	2	287	276	273	259	19	3	49	51	50	8	4	11	5	8
89	490	3	2	249	255	260	235	19	3	46	49	54	31	16	15	11	35
155	491	2	1	246	243	249	240	4	2	0	0	51	48	21	42	36	39
248	492	1	1	259	256	261	263	28	4	45	50	53	16	6	6	4	8
249	493	1	2	264	265	268	258	17	3	37	51	31	52	15	58	36	44
90	494	3	1	257	247	243	240	30	4	46	51	51	59	16	48	26	46
156	495	2	1	239	237	245	233	9	2	47	50	49	55	16	25	20	25
157	496	2	2	247	247	253	250	9	2	47	50	51	32	4	7	5	17
250	497	1	1	264	269	263	257	4	2	48	49	50	43	20	28	27	36
251	498	1	2	263	260	260	261	17	3	44	49	37	25	5	23	4	34
158	499	2	2	262	254	249	249	14	3	48	49	48	35	24	7	8	13
252	500	1	1	273	280	275	260	0	1	42	51	47	69	19	51	38	34
253	501	1	2	266	289	269	260	35	4	48	49	39	36	14	33	19	45
159	502	2	2	256	252	255	236	12	3	47	51	55	22	12	17	29	20
91	503	3	1	261	232	238	243	8	2	42	49	35	48	9	22	4	0
160	504	2	1	269	269	262	253	8	2	45	50	47	39	12	37	20	39
254	505	1	1	264	267	255	251	12	3	47	53	49	54	20	23	12	15
255	506	1	2	252	257	253	256	13	3	46	49	49	36	9	14	5	23
161	507	2	1	259	259	253	245	10	3	39	47	55	46	26	54	65	52
256	508	1	2	273	278	265	265	14	3	46	51	43	44	18	88	44	68
257	509	1	2	258	271	258	251	6	2	40	51	45	40	18	33	26	26
92	510	3	1	252	254	249	256	5	2	47	53	46	65	14	62	20	45
258	511	1	2	257	278	259	254	14	3	45	51	35	44	25	66	57	42

TABLE A, PART I *(Continued)*   **AR19**
Elementary School Grade Five Randomly Grouped 1959–1960

```
SCHOOL NO.   16      TEACHER NO.   19
ID1ID2ID3 ID  PLS STEPSTEPSTEPSTEPTI  SCCONIDLACCSCHHOMME GETGEN
                  SCI READSOC MATHCH    SELSELSEL          ALO

259        512 1 1 296 263 263 259  9 2 43 49 45 21  4  7 12  6
    162    513 2 1 269 260 254 249 17 3 40 45 45 43  9 32 21 35
260        514 1 1 283 269 269 265 25 4 42 53 52 21 13 33 16 17
261        515 1 1 279 254 255 253 20 3 45 53 53  0  0  1  0  3
262        516 1 2 310 280 288 264 15 3 54 51 51 16 12 28 12 13
263        517 1 2 283 274 266 259 10 3 47 49 51 17 12 10  7 13
264        518 1 2 261 253 254 257  8 2 43 49 53 19 12 23 15 36
    163    519 2 2 259 265 261 251  9 2 55 53 53  3  1  4  0 12
265        520 1 2 261 260 259 258 25 4 50 49 51  1  1  1  0  1
266        521 1 1 264 274 258 261 19 3 49 51 52 23  9 19 19 21
267        522 1 2 267 292 275 267 21 3 49 51 51 14  2  4  1 10
268        523 1 2   0   0   0   0 20 3 50 51 48  6  6 12  5  8
    164    524 2 1 267 257 268 254  4 2 38 50 25 45 31 56 41 44
269        525 1 2 279 269 275 261 19 3 44 49 37  4  5 11 12 15
270        526 1 1 264 261 265 261 17 3 49 50 47  8  2  7  2  5
271        527 1 1 256 271 259 254 12 3 48 51 39 11  7 15  5 20
       93  528 3 2 243 247 240 235 10 3 51 52 45 38  6  1  0 29
272        529 1 1 269 271 261 260 15 3 49 52 51 47 15 57 26 61
    165    530 2 2 260 265 252 253 10 3 48 52 55 21 11 31  7 28
           531 9 1   0   0   0   0 12 3 44 49 50 30 15 43 30 33
273        532 1 2 263 265 259 253  6 2 51 51 51  7  2  1  7 16
274        533 1 1 276 267 262 258 16 3 51 51 51  9  3  5  7 13
       94  534 3 2 276 263 269 257  5 2 43 51 39 28 51 11 10 20
    166    535 2 2 251 269 249 251  4 2 47 49 53 13  2 10  5  3
275        536 1 2 266 265 260 253 18 3 52 51 55 33  8 16 10 27
276        537 1 2 261 276 263 250  8 2 50 49 57  2  0  0  0  1
277        538 1 2 287 292 278 256 34 4 50 49 53  5  2  8  2  7
       95  539 3 1 260 253 248 235  4 2 41 48 38 26 14 37 34 28
278        540 1 1 266 278 263 261 24 4 53 52 51  3  1  2  0  1
       96  541 3 2 259 261 254 249 11 3 39 50 56 24  7 31 21 22
279        542 1 2 260 274 260 249 13 3 50 51 51 10  3  9  9 12
    167    543 2 2 271 274 262 259 20 3 50 49 51  1  0  1  0  2
       97  544 3 1 252 246 243 241 20 3 40 51 27 27  3 14 11  9
```

TABLE A, PART II

AA1

Elementary School Grade Five Ability Grouped 1959–1960

SCHOOL NO. 1   TEACHER NO. 8

ID1ID2ID3	ID	PL	S	STEP SCI	STEP READ	STEP SOC	STEP MATH	TI	CH	SC	CON SEL	IDL SEL	ACC SEL	SCH	HOMME	GET ALO	GEN
1	1	2	1	251	245	254	238	7	2	47	53	51	63	31	65	56	63
2	2	2	1	254	245	242	244	15	3	50	54	47	53	8	9	16	64
3	3	2	1	264	255	257	252	9	2	46	49	35	24	4	16	11	15
4	4	2	2	243	247	241	236	13	3	45	49	51	26	6	10	6	14
5	5	2	1	266	274	258	231	12	3	53	41	53	9	3	3	7	0
6	6	2	1	249	238	243	236	10	3	33	50	51	14	8	22	8	15
7	7	2	1	261	257	263	247	11	3	49	54	53	42	4	19	2	35
8	8	2	1	243	252	249	235	11	3	38	50	39	33	15	52	44	44
9	9	2	2	247	260	246	239	0	1	49	40	49	14	6	11	5	2
10	10	2	1	248	239	246	258	27	4	50	53	41	15	5	12	2	18
11	11	2	2	247	248	240	244	13	3	42	48	51	26	7	42	17	23
12	12	2	1	256	259	255	231	11	3	46	51	53	25	12	19	23	17
13	13	2	2	253	245	244	240	17	3	47	55	43	57	20	44	34	52
14	14	2	1	256	245	246	250	3	2	53	52	53	43	17	18	0	9
15	15	2	1	263	267	269	245	16	3	47	50	47	14	8	13	12	17
16	16	2	1	238	233	243	230	26	4	54	54	55	24	2	7	3	5
17	17	2	1	255	252	244	239	15	3	59	46	55	45	6	21	12	24
18	18	2	2	250	245	240	240	44	4	39	48	27	18	18	49	42	65
19	19	2	2	258	252	253	244	4	2	38	49	49	14	1	12	12	11
20	20	2	1	241	233	243	233	2	2	42	44	43	57	19	85	67	63
21	21	2	2	237	241	236	236	17	3	48	51	55	21	13	19	3	18
22	22	2	1	257	244	244	241	14	3	42	50	49	29	0	3	14	13
23	23	2	1	273	265	258	259	10	3	49	55	53	64	30	54	60	61
24	24	2	1	257	260	265	240	29	4	53	51	53	47	6	17	9	16
25	25	2	2	243	243	241	251	24	4	44	49	30	51	29	47	32	44
26	26	2	1	263	253	256	250	13	3	43	51	55	12	10	6	1	7
27	27	2	1	244	246	237	247	9	2	59	46	33	42	0	7	2	20
28	28	2	1	262	259	257	251	15	3	46	49	47	20	6	9	8	17
29	29	2	2	253	263	250	241	20	3	41	46	47	46	8	20	15	22

TABLE A, PART II (*Continued*)   **AA2**

Elementary School Grade Five Ability Grouped 1959–1960

SCHOOL NO.   1   TEACHER NO.   9

ID1ID2ID3	ID	P	L/S	STEP SCI	STEP READ	STEP SOC	STEP MATH	TI/CH	SC SEL	CON SEL	IDL SEL	ACC	SCH	HOM	ME	GET ALO	GEN
30	30	2	2	263	260	256	252	5	2	47	51	45	41	15	36	34	59
31	31	2	1	262	271	266	264	33	4	43	49	55	25	7	17	9	17
32	32	2	2	249	255	247	239	28	4	43	49	55	38	18	48	47	44
33	33	2	1	250	242	242	245	40	4	0	0	0	0	0	0	0	0
34	34	2	1	244	247	243	235	9	2	43	50	47	26	8	32	15	36
35	35	2	1	267	257	266	252	15	3	43	49	45	55	22	43	29	25
36	36	2	1	261	261	253	249	18	3	47	49	49	29	7	24	9	18
37	37	2	2	255	259	249	249	6	2	39	49	55	17	11	30	6	49
38	38	2	1	256	259	252	241	10	3	45	51	52	61	28	31	19	40
39	39	2	2	255	286	249	244	4	2	43	49	25	39	9	42	32	52
40	40	2	1	271	254	256	253	24	4	47	49	57	24	5	6	10	7
41	41	2	2	253	256	256	247	4	2	48	49	40	39	8	44	9	29
42	42	2	2	256	255	255	244	23	4	40	52	41	45	18	41	31	36
43	43	2	2	266	252	254	251	28	4	44	49	49	29	18	43	25	47
44	44	2	2	250	253	251	243	10	3	41	50	43	40	27	40	10	31
45	45	2	2	251	254	249	243	27	4	39	47	47	22	7	17	7	22
46	46	2	2	243	251	249	239	8	2	42	48	47	26	2	26	11	7
47	47	2	1	251	263	250	0	4	2	46	49	51	20	4	20	8	37
48	48	2	1	269	283	269	252	15	3	46	54	53	27	18	29	32	41
49	49	2	1	262	269	258	251	7	2	42	52	37	49	10	51	37	52
50	50	2	1	260	252	251	249	1	2	54	51	51	24	14	8	14	22
51	51	2	1	253	240	250	231	12	3	40	49	25	58	39	80	75	65
52	52	2	2	263	252	247	244	8	2	41	49	39	21	12	26	17	28
53	53	2	1	251	253	250	240	6	2	41	48	46	44	11	15	17	26
54	54	2	2	258	252	253	254	25	4	43	51	41	35	12	18	10	32
55	55	2	2	264	274	262	254	19	3	48	49	53	8	3	7	6	17
56	56	2	1	264	259	262	258	10	3	40	50	29	61	31	65	51	47
57	57	2	1	267	257	247	264	14	3	45	49	43	34	9	31	13	19
58	58	2	2	251	259	253	257	16	3	0	0	0	0	0	0	0	0
59	59	2	1	252	252	254	249	19	3	0	0	51	35	15	39	16	43
60	60	2	1	269	263	263	257	45	4	44	51	53	30	13	12	9	20
61	61	2	2	257	274	249	249	11	3	46	51	43	39	12	27	19	31
62	62	2	1	267	263	269	261	9	2	46	51	32	48	21	63	49	69
63	63	2	1	246	244	244	236	1	2	44	45	50	26	14	21	10	11
64	64	2	2	255	269	254	240	8	2	46	49	51	27	11	24	7	6

TABLE A, PART II *(Continued)*   **AA3**
Elementary School Grade Five Ability Grouped 1959–1960

SCHOOL NO.   1   TEACHER NO.   10
ID1ID2ID3 ID   PLS STEPSTEPSTEPSTEPTI SCCONIDLACCSCHHOMME GETGEN
                       SCI READSOC MATHCH   SELSELSEL   ALO

ID1ID2ID3	ID	P	L	S	STEP SCI	STEP READ	STEP SOC	STEP MATH	TI CH		SC SEL	CON SEL	IDL SEL	ACC	SCH	HOM	ME		GET ALO	GEN
1	65	3	1		237	234	226	235	2	2	40	45	45	90	24	61			54	67
2	66	3	1		246	245	242	233	14	3	44	49	49	34	19	28			17	32
3	67	3	1		229	240	234	240	27	4	44	52	47	41	2	8			5	24
4	68	3	1		231	235	234	235	7	2	45	42	39	59	10	60			37	40
5	69	3	1		225	229	233	241	16	3	44	51	41	24	6	18			26	10
6	70	3	1		245	259	237	231	19	3	47	48	45	57	6	59			41	40
7	71	3	1		227	236	239	230	39	4	46	51	51	31	11	20			13	25
8	72	3	1		231	238	240	231	3	2	41	51	47	69	19	36			9	22
9	73	3	1		229	236	237	230	13	3	44	50	49	41	12	14			5	12
10	74	3	1		238	232	242	238	13	3	49	49	49	41	21	32			25	18
11	75	3	2		225	226	239	230	13	3	43	50	37	64	31	61			56	54
12	76	3	1		242	231	236	233	3	2	54	57	47	34	13	17			11	7
13	77	3	1		233	242	240	230	0	1	39	51	45	62	39	81			65	60
14	78	3	1		227	231	239	230	13	3	50	50	49	40	15	39			27	14
15	79	3	2		251	242	237	252	8	2	51	49	45	40	19	34			21	24
16	80	3	1		249	248	239	230	21	3	45	49	45	15	13	15			7	27
17	81	3	2		253	245	245	243	13	3	41	49	35	32	14	56			42	47
18	82	3	1		237	235	243	235	3	2	48	52	31	73	29	59			36	48
19	83	3	2		233	233	235	230	22	4	41	49	45	28	1	16			8	21

TABLE A, PART II *(Continued)*   **AA4**

Elementary School Grade Five Ability Grouped 1959–1960

SCHOOL NO. 1   TEACHER NO. 11

ID1 ID2 ID3	ID	P	S	STEP SCI	STEP READ	STEP SOC	STEP MATH	TI	CH	SC SEL	CON SEL	IDL SEL	ACC	SCH	HOM	GET	GEN ALO
65	84	2	1	260	257	249	249	26	4	41	49	51	52	17	45	33	50
66	85	2	1	266	259	266	257	8	2	50	48	49	31	20	26	34	38
67	86	2	2	259	257	254	250	6	2	41	51	31	25	5	8	3	11
68	87	2	2	257	254	254	250	14	3	53	49	51	9	4	13	1	6
69	88	2	1	260	261	251	245	3	2	41	51	41	36	16	21	15	35
70	89	2	2	256	260	244	241	6	2	44	51	49	48	21	30	20	37
71	90	2	1	259	255	251	249	31	4	45	49	47	33	11	10	9	9
72	91	2	2	259	252	262	238	16	3	41	49	47	38	14	42	15	21
73	92	2	2	259	252	258	260	16	3	46	49	37	32	8	29	8	31
74	93	2	1	263	252	255	250	3	2	38	49	39	48	38	76	71	68
75	94	2	2	259	263	250	252	12	3	49	49	50	64	23	35	46	52
76	95	2	1	276	259	259	252	6	2	0	0	47	42	15	45	30	45
77	96	2	2	256	278	246	257	11	3	51	49	48	22	14	31	12	19
78	97	2	1	269	276	269	258	12	3	46	49	47	59	36	12	27	37
79	98	2	2	258	252	255	231	10	3	45	49	29	32	8	26	31	35
80	99	2	2	252	255	250	247	15	3	51	49	47	43	8	47	10	30
81	100	2	2	257	259	253	245	15	3	47	49	-51	17	2	26	13	43
82	101	2	1	259	254	251	243	4	2	0	0	0	0	0	0	0	0
83	102	2	1	263	261	260	267	28	4	44	49	35	46	13	30	15	27
84	103	2	2	250	259	246	241	11	3	54	51	37	42	13	37	18	57
85	104	2	2	256	259	255	252	3	2	45	50	47	51	33	78	64	56
86	105	2	1	256	260	256	254	12	3	45	52	49	45	19	30	23	48
87	106	2	2	269	267	255	254	29	4	42	50	49	49	10	50	41	51
88	107	2	2	259	253	254	254	17	3	52	51	51	7	4	10	7	19
89	108	2	1	256	256	265	245	3	2	60	49	43	15	7	15	6	14
90	109	2	1	302	295	278	270	23	4	47	51	47	35	18	39	14	41
91	110	2	1	279	265	263	257	9	2	41	50	53	35	23	27	20	33
92	111	2	1	251	244	244	239	6	2	48	55	53	32	0	24	2	33
93	112	2	2	251	250	249	245	3	2	44	49	51	46	13	46	27	38
94	113	2	1	254	244	249	243	6	2	45	49	53	10	10	7	4	16
95	114	2	1	262	260	253	250	9	2	0	.0	49	26	15	14	15	33
96	115	2	2	259	276	262	254	26	4	42	49	45	22	1	25	11	33
97	116	2	1	262	254	255	245	.26	4	50	49	47	32	12	29	23	48
98	117·	2	1	267	271	275	258	9	2	46	50	43	43	11	35	19	47

TABLE A, PART II (Continued) AA5
Elementary School Grade Five Ability Grouped 1959–1960

SCHOOL NO. 1 TEACHER NO. 12

ID1	ID2	ID3	ID	P	LS	STEP SCI	STEP READ	STEP SOC	STEP MATH	TI	CH	SCC SEL	ONI SEL	DLACC SEL	SCHH	OMME	GET ALO	GEN
1			118	1	2	269	289	273	269	41	4	47	49	55	9	0	1	0 7
2			119	1	1	0	0	0	0	21	3	46	61	53	45	29	43	26 45
3			120	1	2	266	292	269	254	23	4	42	51	29	45	8	15	4 32
4			121	1	2	263	276	266	251	10	3	40	51	29	49	5	39	19 22
5			122	1	1	269	271	269	265	8	2	44	54	51	36	8	20	15 26
6			123	1	2	255	259	261	250	8	2	47	52	53	46	18	22	8 14
7			124	1	2	257	274	263	251	11	3	41	49	39	31	20	21	16 37
8			125	1	2	266	292	259	257	5	2	43	47	35	20	6	13	9 14
9			126	1	2	264	283	259	257	12	3	47	51	46	20	3	6	8 8
10			127	1	1	283	274	266	265	14	3	47	49	40	29	10	37	30 23
11			128	1	1	266	269	266	265	11	3	44	49	53	24	1	3	0 6
12			129	1	2	273	286	269	266	16	3	42	51	55	28	10	44	26 17
13			130	1	2	259	252	266	241	17	3	49	51	43	29	9	11	20 37
14			131	1	2	279	283	271	257	17	3	42	49	53	12	3	15	11 31
15			132	1	1	267	269	268	263	13	3	47	53	41	35	19	39	29 46
16			133	1	1	271	256	260	252	11	3	46	51	50	38	8	15	23 35
17			134	1	2	287	280	268	266	34	4	47	51	55	10	5	7	4 20
18			135	1	2	287	303	268	263	6	2	39	52	45	30	0	32	7 31
19			136	1	2	287	292	259	259	17	3	49	50	43	36	6	21	2 24
20			137	1	2	273	271	266	256	18	3	46	49	43	16	0	7	4 25
21			138	1	1	253	265	253	254	5	2	34	50	50	26	9	18	17 27
22			139	1	1	283	280	268	270	5	2	34	36	42	45	20	38	24 21
23			140	1	1	267	280	266	263	24	4	47	46	48	31	8	25	14 20
24			141	1	2	258	259	243	251	9	2	39	49	33	47	9	34	13 26
25			142	1	1	261	271	254	244	13	3	51	51	55	34	10	8	7 12
26			143	1	2	263	283	259	251	28	4	43	51	45	16	1	24	4 10
27			144	1	1	267	274	265	260	13	3	46	49	49	15	1	3	1 11
28			145	1	2	261	289	266	257	22	4	39	51	27	37	15	56	31 49
29			146	1	1	279	267	259	259	20	3	43	51	27	28	15	24	12 10
30			147	1	2	260	254	253	240	12	3	44	49	41	22	5	10	11 41
31			148	1	2	276	280	278	259	12	3	46	60	46	43	14	25	15 30
32			149	1	2	273	295	275	274	5	2	42	48	45	11	2	12	8 12
	99		150	2	2	273	295	262	261	27	4	41	49	53	34	9	39	20 52
33			151	1	2	258	254	248	249	5	2	49	51	49	32	13	18	7 35
34			152	1	2	260	283	257	250	3	2	40	51	44	56	24	46	38 38

TABLE A, PART II *(Continued)* **AA6**

Elementary School Grade Five Ability Grouped 1959–1960

```
SCHOOL NO.   2      TEACHER NO.   13
ID1ID2ID3 ID  PLS STEPSTEPSTEPSTEPTI SCCONIDLACCSCHHOMME GETGEN
                   SCI READSOC MATHCH    SELSELSEL         ALO

         20 153 3 1 244 242 251 245 20 3 40 48 49 50 11 18 10 18
         21 154 3 2 261 257 252 251  5 2 27 53 39 18 11 23 22 50
         22 155 3 2 256 250 252 243 17 3 38 51 31 38  7 54 38 46
         23 156 3 2 243 252 244 238 13 3 41 49 49 52 22 62 59 49
         24 157 3 1 225 240 238 230 14 3 53 51 57 15  5  9  0 16
         25 158 3 2 242 250 241 239 28 4 45 50 37 51 14 44 20 42
         26 159 3 1 253 246 249 247 10 3 44 49 51 31  3  5  1 19
         27 160 3 1 227 229 232 235 15 3 41 43 42 37 12 30 32 25
         28 161 3 1 241 226 228 230  4 2 39 51 49 47 27 64 54 52
         29 162· 3 2 243 247 248 241 16 3 42 47 47 52 23 18 18 15
         30 163 3 1 256 234 242 247 16 3 48 49 51 46 21 45 37 42
         31 164 3 2 249 249 237 238  3 2 49 54 57 41  5 12  3 18
         32 165 3 2 243 242 243 231 12 3 38 49 23 38 24 76 81 57
         33 166 3 1 247 242 237 230 20 3 46 49 45 23 11 20 17 15
         34 167 3 2 239 242 244 241 25 4 44 49 49 31  9 18 14 24
         35 168 3 1 266 252 251 250 12 3 43 50 47 46 15 19 24 20
         36 169 3 2 252 252 238 244 15 3 43 50 35 33 18 79 35 59
         37 170 3 1 262 256 261 253 18 3 48 51 47 48 22 38 17 29
         38 171 3 2 246 247 242 233 18 3 48 47 35 73 13 19  8 37
         39 172 3 2 242 242 249 230  9 2 45 53 43 53 10 20 24 26
         40 173 3 1 239 230 236 235  7 2 44 51 50 66 32 63 44 52
         41 174 3 1 231 243 236 239  9 2 46 49 51  0  0  0  0  1
```

TABLE A, PART II (*Continued*)   **AA7**

Elementary School Grade Five Ability Grouped 1959–1960

SCHOOL NO.   2   TEACHER NO.   14

ID1ID2ID3	ID	PL	S	STEP SCI	STEP READ	STEP SOC	STEP MATH	TI CH	SC	CONID	LACC	SCH	HUMME		GET GEN ALO	
100	175	2	2	250	251	247	240	3	2	52	53	53	41	27	52	48 68
101	176	2	1	253	257	255	244	4	2	42	51	41	45	9	43	39 54
102	177	2	2	264	269	256	258	16	3	41	49	20	32	20	40	33 39
103	178	2	1	259	254	251	249	30	4	45	48	53	52	9	24	20 19
104	179	2	2	249	261	260	250	14	3	48	49	43	45	14	34	22 32
105	180	2	2	254	251	253	244	4	2	0	0	42	37	2	32	14 26
106	181	2	1	266	269	265	256	10	3	46	50	48	44	24	41	20 43
107	182	2	2	259	265	254	245	50	4	44	47	44	69	33	70	53 51
108	183	2	2	251	254	246	250	6	2	34	50	39	53	22	59	30 35
109	184	2	1	262	252	257	251	13	3	33	45	21	52	24	53	56 66
110	185	2	1	283	254	263	260	3	2	41	68	45	15	9	9	8 19
111	186	2	2	262	286	266	254	34	4	39	53	51	40	17	45	25 28
112	187	2	1	263	271	260	260	10	3	51	50	55	42	5	13	1 8
113	188	2	2	253	256	255	0	13	3	39	51	33	65	21	35	16 19
114	189	2	1	271	261	261	258	12	3	48	51	57	34	1	11	1 26
115	190	2	1	283	274	278	258	2	2	44	51	53	33	9	30	22 27
116	191	2	2	250	252	245	247	10	3	46	50	45	90	36	75	70 75
117	192	2	1	253	253	257	252	9	2	36	51	34	53	22	40	31 44
118	193	2	2	258	261	251	250	13	3	39	51	53	45	8	19	25 37
119	194	2	2	260	256	263	250	11	3	45	51	49	43	12	28	21 42
120	195	2	1	276	263	268	256	46	4	43	51	57	36	5	27	7 13
121	196	2	2	259	257	255	247	8	2	39	53	57	38	7	14	11 25
122	197	2	1	244	251	249	251	14	3	39	51	49	56	35	87	67 64
123	198	2	2	254	255	256	247	29	4	45	52	44	15	11	15	19 17
124	199	2	1	271	269	266	254	4	2	46	49	35	50	18	34	29 39
125	200	2	1	254	251	250	249	13	3	47	49	53	31	6	7	1 12
126	201	2	2	241	252	252	236	5	2	42	46	45	5	3	8	0 1
127	202	2	2	271	269	259	250	11	3	43	49	41	20	8	44	33 13
128	203	2	1	264	269	269	254	19	3	32	47	52	38	10	14	19 19
129	204	2	2	251	260	250	235	19	3	42	53	57	53	19	11	9 30
130	205	2	1	271	269	268	257	9	2	42	53	50	56	22	37	21 49
131	206	2	2	263	253	249	243	3	2	44	51	55	35	9	20	16 34
132	207	2	1	264	276	269	253	5	2	38	50	45	39	8	22	5 16
133	208	2	2	253	259	250	236	41	4	43	50	53	9	0	1	1 8

TABLE A, PART II (*Continued*)   AA8

Elementary School Grade Five Ability Grouped 1959–1960

SCHOOL NO.   2   TEACHER NO.   15

ID1ID2ID3	ID	PL	S	STEP SCI	STEP READ	STEP SOC	STEP MATH	TI	CH	SC SEL	CON SEL	IDL SEL	ACC	SCH	HOM	ME	GET ALO	GEN
35	209	1	2	252	259	256	253	20	3	47	51	49	34	14	14		13	17
36	210	1	1	273	271	271	266	3	2	47	49	53	24	3	11		8	5
37	211	1	1	273	280	257	261	8	2	44	47	40	17	5	10		7	23
38	212	1	2	262	271	254	260	11	3	51	49	57	6	3	7		1	7
39	213	1	1	271	280	263	259	7	2	45	53	57	20	4	14		18	13
40	214	1	1	287	298	273	279	28	4	39	52	47	22	5	10		4	20
41	215	1	2	266	280	263	249	11	3	50	52	54	9	0	4		0	4
42	216	1	2	263	267	261	263	39	0	45	52	0	17	8	14		15	14
43	217	1	2	257	276	252	250	20	3	47	53	55	20	7	19		16	20
44	218	1	1	260	260	249	254	23	4	46	49	49	36	13	11		6	27
45	219	1	1	263	274	266	264	5	2	36	47	34	32	18	23		6	12
46	220	1	1	267	265	259	265	6	2	43	49	40	29	7	14		19	34
47	221	1	2	264	261	265	254	7	2	51	51	57	26	3	27		6	21
48	222	1	1	269	269	259	257	30	4	38	51	57	29	6	25		7	32
49	223	1	1	259	261	263	256	31	4	44	52	51	12	4	3		7	37
50	224	1	1	279	292	273	266	14	3	40	51	46	59	18	32		22	51
51	225	1	2	260	269	257	259	15	3	39	54	57	23	9	12		11	11
52	226	1	2	263	269	259	257	29	4	48	49	57	23	9	17		7	19
53	227	1	1	271	263	260	252	10	3	44	48	50	8	5	7		4	19
54	228	1	1	310	298	266	272	3	2	43	51	35	32	22	15		11	26
55	229	1	2	259	278	257	256	5	2	42	51	53	50	26	57		41	52
56	230	1	2	259	263	260	256	21	3	48	49	57	26	8	24		8	18
57	231	1	2	271	283	266	236	15	3	46	50	49	23	18	41		23	36
58	232	1	2	273	283	262	267	9	2	43	49	37	4	3	9		7	11
59	233	1	2	249	276	257	256	12	3	41	51	45	11	4	12		10	17
60	234	1	2	269	286	269	259	4	2	46	51	51	20	11	16		9	16
61	235	1	2	276	267	258	257	13	3	49	41	49	55	39	44		24	43
62	236	1	2	276	280	268	265	7	2	45	49	50	9	3	4		2	16
63	237	1	1	291	278	284	272	4	2	45	51	57	54	18	23		18	63
64	238	1	2	258	251	251	252	9	2	44	51	49	34	12	23		6	18
65	239	1	2	260	269	261	256	12	3	47	51	57	36	7	13		8	24
66	240	1	1	269	283	261	266	24	4	41	44	53	25	4	14		1	10
67	241	1	2	259	269	259	247	10	3	45	52	23	27	9	27		20	19
68	242	1	1	271	274	268	260	23	4	44	49	43	23	5	20		5	28
69	243	1	2	269	271	262	261	19	3	44	53	53	25	9	13		8	18

TABLE A, PART II *(Continued)*   **AA9**

Elementary School Grade Five Ability Grouped 1959–1960

SCHOOL NO.   3   TEACHER NO.   5
ID1ID2ID3 ID   PLS STEPSTEPSTEPSTEPTI SCCONIDLACCSCHHOMME GETGEN
                     SCI READSOC MATHCH   SELSELSEL   ALO

42	244	3	1	257	249	243	233	26	4	49	51	55	37	12	31	16	24
43	245	3	2	249	226	238	236	22	4	36	39	21	36	23	83	54	75
44	246	3	2	248	251	252	241	11	3	46	50	55	27	12	19	29	21
45	247	3	1	225	230	230	233	0	1	51	36	24	24	9	39	27	9
46	248	3	1	259	248	246	249	6	2	44	49	55	14	0	4	0	1
47	249	3	2	242	239	241	240	12	3	48	49	57	18	7	6	13	5
48	250	3	1	239	231	236	233	7	2	49	52	57	22	0	1	0	0
49	251	3	1	235	226	226	231	16	3	51	49	57	24	0	8	2	0
50	252	3	2	0	241	236	0	15	3	0	0	0	0	0	0	0	0
51	253	3	1	249	234	231	244	30	4	38	49	57	44	14	21	20	24
52	254	3	1	247	235	233	240	10	3	44	48	43	47	26	47	70	61
53	255	3	1	241	237	233	236	28	4	45	49	57	60	18	34	24	38
54	256	3	2	238	241	236	235	2	2	54	49	55	30	2	17	7	21
55	257	3	1	248	230	235	230	3	2	40	53	46	49	34	54	44	46
56	258	3	1	273	265	260	247	27	4	41	51	43	31	12	25	23	30
57	259	3	1	256	248	240	233	21	3	48	51	55	11	4	14	5	7
58	260	3	2	262	253	248	245	7	2	43	51	57	39	5	22	12	14
59	261	3	2	244	226	234	230	5	2	0	0	50	64	31	69	54	40
60	262	3	1	283	267	271	261	2	2	41	49	21	15	7	15	5	6
61	263	3	2	286	257	244	239	28	4	45	49	57	25	1	12	4	24

TABLE A, PART II *(Continued)*   **AA10**
Elementary School Grade Five Ability Grouped 1959–1960

SCHOOL NO.   3   TEACHER NO.   6

ID1ID2ID3	ID	P	L	S	STEP SCI	STEP READ	STEP SOC	STEP MATH	TI	CH	SC SEL	CON SEL	IDL SEL	ACC	SCHH	OMME	GET ALO	GEN
134	264	2	2		253	255	252	241	14	3	41	47	48	58	24	38	45	55
135	265	2	1		262	248	254	245	23	4	49	49	53	16	1	16	14	27
136	266	2	1		276	256	263	259	24	4	43	47	57	20	3	6	0	17
137	267	2	1		250	247	242	239	22	4	37	49	52	39	16	40	19	18
138	268	2	2		252	254	251	241	19	3	45	49	49	4	0	5	4	11
139	269	2	1		259	248	258	249	3	2	41	50	54	53	12	34	6	18
140	270	2	2		247	253	243	233	12	3	51	47	51	45	16	38	42	55
141	271	2	1		263	247	257	240	13	3	49	55	57	19	2	14	1	19
142	272	2	1		276	254	261	261	25	4	47	49	57	22	2	10	8	28
143	273	2	1		260	265	259	258	3	2	44	51	55	45	6	28	21	51
144	274	2	2		254	253	250	238	12	3	44	49	47	35	8	15	8	17
145	275	2	1		261	265	257	249	26	4	42	52	56	40	18	35	35	23
146	276	2	1		266	263	258	257	10	3	43	49	56	13	11	29	15	16
147	277	2	1		271	257	260	252	5	2	50	51	57	35	5	9	4	20
148	278	2	1		254	245	244	230	21	3	42	46	27	60	33	58	67	78
149	279	2	1		259	260	256	256	16	3	38	51	28	53	35	66	58	49
150	280	2	2		256	257	255	244	12	3	44	49	57	43	6	30	13	40
151	281	2	1		267	260	256	247	16	3	50	49	52	31	7	16	10	40
152	282	2	2		251	249	239	238	8	2	0	0	44	61	33	52	46	45
153	283	2	1		253	252	256	251	19	3	47	49	54	14	6	11	13	14
154	284	2	2		254	257	254	254	6	2	41	46	54	10	14	28	38	30
155	285	2	1		264	260	258	250	26	4	44	49	54	28	5	13	8	18
156	286	2	2		250	247	248	245	2	2	41	52	41	65	44	69	71	66
157	287	2	2		250	274	259	235	9	2	48	55	57	43	3	11	6	29
158	288	2	1		262	252	256	243	5	2	38	48	57	34	11	46	29	27
159	289	2	1		287	261	251	256	8	2	42	51	57	15	2	19	3	8
160	290	2	1		0	255	252	251	6	2	0	0	0	0	0	0	0	0
161	291	2	1		274	263	265	260	12	3	0	0	57	26	8	31	22	33

TABLE A, PART II (*Continued*)   **AA11**

Elementary School Grade Five Ability Grouped 1959–1960

SCHOOL NO.   3   TEACHER NO.   7

ID1ID2ID3	ID	P	S	STEP SCI	STEP READ	STEP SOC	STEP MATH	TI	TCH	SCCON SEL	IDLA SEL	CCSCH SEL	HOM	ME	GET ALO	GEN
70	292	1	2	276	289	263	258	21	3	45	49	46	12	10	16	2 31
71	293	1	2	267	282	257	252	17	3	47	47	48	43	20	31	24 43
72	294	1	2	263	256	246	259	6	2	41	47	35	21	18	44	35 20
73	295	1	1	261	263	265	252	39	4	47	51	48	34	4	16	6 14
74	296	1	2	271	283	257	253	21	3	43	51	50	19	16	34	26 27
75	297	1	2	264	267	253	258	6	2	46	51	51	33	11	41	16 27
76	298	1	2	244	259	247	245	12	3	45	50	56	18	2	4	1 7
77	299	1	1	283	267	265	256	14	3	44	51	48	14	16	60	20 28
78	300	1	2	256	269	253	251	10	3	47	48	43	38	12	37	12 20
79	301	1	2	267	286	273	263	16	3	40	49	41	31	13	43	21 24
80	302	1	1	263	257	252	252	17	3	49	51	51	19	9	25	20 30
81	303	1	1	266	252	251	251	4	2	44	51	55	36	13	33	24 21
82	304	1	2	264	256	258	259	28	4	42	49	25	19	4	17	13 34
83	305	1	1	258	248	257	252	4	2	49	51	51	12	5	5	1 5
84	306	1	2	262	269	261	247	6	2	47	51	41	16	3	11	1 6
85	307	1	1	271	274	266	253	18	3	46	43	49	41	9	25	11 21
86	308	1	1	287	278	269	263	23	4	46	53	45	63	15	39	22 24
87	309	1	2	276	283	268	261	21	3	52	51	50	5	3	4	1 14
88	310	1	1	269	261	266	258	2	2	43	44	45	42	30	56	38 50
89	311	1	2	261	252	257	256	6	2	49	49	49	9	4	7	4 11
90	312	1	2	279	271	261	254	12	3	44	51	49	36	14	30	22 21
91	313	1	1	269	286	265	266	23	4	51	49	51	21	4	17	14 24
92	314	1	1	276	263	262	251	14	3	47	49	45	23	3	19	25 21
93	315	1	1	283	292	273	266	9	2	41	52	52	26	24	23	17 9
94	316	1	2	256	265	258	253	11	3	46	49	47	4	3	5	3 11
95	317	1	1	317	292	278	270	34	4	43	52	44	19	7	13	14 19
96	318	1	1	310	265	269	269	23	4	50	51	51	6	0	7	1 7
97	319	1	2	269	267	259	252	27	4	44	44	38	7	3	10	13 10
98	320	1	2	264	263	260	256	29	4	36	51	37	32	9	42	15 19
99	321	1	1	261	256	249	251	2	2	43	49	49	57	34	39	35 38
100	322	1	2	257	249	250	239	3	2	0	0	48	5	0	29	9 13
101	323	1	1	263	247	256	250	7	2	42	48	37	25	2	25	2 8
102	324	1	1	266	271	268	254	24	4	46	54	57	23	3	14	9 16
103	325	1	2	267	255	258	245	9	2	41	49	51	26	6	27	15 24

TABLE A, PART II (*Continued*)   **AA12**
Elementary School Grade Five Ability Grouped 1959–1960

SCHOOL NO.   4   TEACHER NO.   1

ID1	ID2	ID3	ID	PLS	STEP SCI	STEP READ	STEP SOC	STEP MATH	TI CH	SC	CON SEL	IDL SEL	ACC SEL	SCHH OM	OMF	GET ALO	GEN
62	326	3	2	250	236	240	243	14	3	50	53	56	58	15	30	37	55
63	327	3	1	253	241	251	230	26	4	42	53	51	32	36	87	54	57
64	328	3	1	235	226	229	235	16	3	0	0	0	31	19	30	15	21
65	329	3	1	241	242	253	239	8	2	0	0	54	29	15	27	22	26
66	330	3	1	247	234	236	243	26	4	43	50	55	55	17	38	42	41
67	331	3	1	247	238	234	239	28	4	48	49	57	21	19	20	23	15
68	332	3	1	227	226	227	230	17	3	0	0	46	55	24	45	41	43
69	333	3	1	237	233	236	231	15	3	39	50	57	63	15	18	12	21
70	334	3	1	233	226	238	238	19	3	46	48	56	47	3	0	1	0
71	335	3	1	246	238	238	236	30	4	45	47	55	19	3	20	6	6
72	336	3	2	257	240	248	249	7	2	38	51	57	13	4	4	1	1
73	337	3	1	244	236	238	238	7	2	42	51	56	52	16	42	38	46
74	338	3	2	243	243	240	240	28	4	47	51	57	14	2	7	5	11
75	339	3	1	243	242	245	243	10	3	47	51	57	43	18	18	3	3
76	340	3	1	233	227	242	241	9	2	30	43	20	55	28	61	23	1
77	341	3	1	237	234	236	235	13	3	43	43	25	28	17	41	15	5
78	342	3	2	258	241	251	253	21	3	52	50	56	22	7	1	5	7
79	343	3	1	233	236	240	233	12	3	46	51	56	64	37	60	56	56
80	344	3	1	251	246	249	230	13	3	51	51	57	2	1	1	0	2
81	345	3	1	249	233	237	238	10	3	50	51	29	63	32	54	13	0
82	346	3	2	247	246	245	244	7	2	55	51	57	25	3	14	25	37
83	347	3	2	247	252	247	233	13	3	0	0	56	16	3	16	14	41
84	348	3	1	238	226	228	230	11	3	42	39	57	28	4	3	71	0
85	349	3	1	252	239	246	241	7	2	33	43	50	52	18	52	41	64
86	350	3	2	246	247	243	244	12	3	45	49	57	26	11	26	23	25
87	351	3	1	255	246	252	249	9	2	0	0	57	13	11	40	42	33

TABLE A, PART II *(Continued)*   **AA13**
Elementary School Grade Five Ability Grouped 1959–1960

```
SCHOOL NO.    4        TEACHER NO.     2
ID1ID2ID3 ID  PLS STEPSTEPSTEPSTEPTI  SCCONIDLACCSCHHOMME  GETGEN
                   SCI READSOC MATHCH     SELSELSEL            ALO
```

ID1ID2ID3	ID	P	L	S	STEP SCI	STEP READ	STEP SOC	STEP MAT	TI HCH	SC	CON	IDL	ACC	SCH	HO	MME	GET AL	GEN O
162	352	2	2		250	283	273	254	9	2	42	49	48	24	8	36	25	40
163	353	2	2		251	238	234	233	3	2	44	49	48	46	16	34	31	37
164	354	2	1		267	263	266	244	4	2	44	49	47	60	27	41	36	59
165	355	2	1		258	257	256	253	15	3	48	49	53	61	6	76	30	63
166	356	2	2		264	252	245	247	2	2	0	0	55	45	14	24	18	22
167	357	2	1		250	236	248	244	28	4	50	48	31	46	19	59	39	50
168	358	2	1		266	260	258	259	26	4	39	49	21	39	18	33	30	36
169	359	2	2		269	259	258	251	13	3	41	49	49	24	6	12	16	38
170	360	2	2		248	252	248	238	3	2	41	49	39	64	23	78	60	54
171	361	2	2		262	265	249	250	1	2	39	48	38	49	21	48	30	61
172	362	2	1		266	267	261	245	11	3	46	51	43	38	10	31	34	33
173	363	2	2		239	247	235	238	6	2	0	0	55	46	26	43	46	65
174	364	2	1		251	234	244	240	4	2	42	49	35	54	11	22	10	9
175	365	2	1		263	265	261	253	22	4	47	49	49	21	3	10	4	5
176	366	2	1		237	237	243	241	8	2	40	49	41	68	32	82	54	50
177	367	2	1		255	236	251	249	16	3	44	51	52	54	14	37	5	0
178	368	2	2		243	265	261	253	26	4	41	49	38	61	17	45	33	35
179	369	2	1		256	253	251	243	9	2	40	49	47	29	10	29	13	6
180	370	2	2		252	247	251	247	17	3	41	49	46	49	27	53	43	57
181	371	2	2		262	265	258	252	22	4	0	0	55	32	27	23	25	45
182	372	2	2		251	252	247	249	21	3	46	49	40	27	17	33	16	24
183	373	2	1		263	251	255	253	13	3	46	49	34	36	6	21	12	24
184	374	2	1		267	261	268	257	22	4	45	51	55	4	1	3	3	27
185	375	2	1		256	242	244	254	10	3	39	51	31	28	6	25	23	51
186	376	2	1		251	260	251	241	27	4	39	49	36	62	30	71	61	59
187	377	2	2		283	283	263	257	17	3	0	0	57	32	4	17	9	31
188	378	2	1		252	247	256	243	2	2	51	49	51	32	8	49	58	18
189	379	2	1		261	245	250	250	10	3	46	49	48	16	2	3	3	22
190	380	2	2		258	271	263	253	12	3	53	53	53	25	12	31	11	31
191	381	2	1		242	252	239	233	4	2	28	34	34	72	30	82	63	72
192	382	2	2		244	242	240	231	5	2	0	0	47	83	40	66	59	58
193	383	2	1		248	248	251	240	4	2	44	49	53	27	9	25	8	17
194	384	2	2		256	257	256	247	36	4	44	49	51	20	6	12	2	21

TABLE A, PART II (*Continued*)   AA14

Elementary School Grade Five Ability Grouped 1959–1960

SCHOOL NO.   4   TEACHER NO.   3

ID1ID2ID3	ID	PLS	STEP SCI	STEP READ	STEP SOC	STEP MATH	TI CH	SC	CON	ID	LAC	CSC	HHO	MME	GET ALD	GEN
195	385	2 2	253	255	253	258	10	3	53	49	44	49	27	63	55	61
196	386	2 2	254	247	249	230	9	2	43	49	57	24	0	5	2	6
197	387	2 1	261	283	268	250	5	2	43	50	57	58	17	48	36	38
198	388	2 1	266	267	258	251	27	4	43	49	44	28	5	32	13	37
199	389	2 1	287	286	271	247	21	3	40	50	51	26	11	18	8	36
200	390	2 2	254	253	254	250	10	3	50	51	57	20	0	3	3	4
201	391	2 1	234	238	236	230	14	3	38	52	53	52	30	54	47	38
202	392	2 1	246	265	242	250	20	3	43	48	53	23	15	35	19	35
203	393	2 1	266	269	253	250	18	3	41	51	57	38	15	19	21	55
204	394	2 2	255	250	246	251	19	3	40	49	57	36	6	18	3	20
205	395	2 2	250	252	246	226	9	2	43	51	57	37	15	32	30	44
206	396	2 1	246	231	241	249	6	2	45	44	54	80	24	53	29	87
207	397	2 2	271	260	256	247	11	3	0	0	53	24	14	40	31	34
208	398	2 1	262	263	252	250	22	4	47	51	57	26	18	13	6	33
209	399	2 1	246	242	249	254	8	2	42	49	46	54	27	63	57	52
210	400	2 1	242	237	232	245	17	3	33	49	21	25	24	18	2	16
211	401	2 2	249	252	245	230	20	3	48	49	57	28	15	39	8	17
212	402	2 1	242	238	246	228	15	3	50	51	57	21	3	15	5	19
213	403	2 1	259	259	255	244	7	2	42	52	55	38	25	36	22	30
214	404	2 2	260	274	258	253	11	3	40	49	31	30	8	40	20	40
215	405	2 2	256	261	248	244	10	3	44	51	55	27	13	37	17	44
216	406	2 1	266	265	265	249	6	2	50	49	57	21	11	32	26	25
217	407	2 2	259	260	260	249	19	3	48	49	47	13	7	29	12	60
218	408	2 2	256	248	246	241	21	3	48	51	57	33	6	19	18	30
219	409	2 1	271	252	258	244	14	3	0	57	28	23	18	12	42	
220	410	2 1	253	252	245	230	19	3	49	51	57	15	7	6	0	35
221	411	2 1	269	267	252	250	7	2	49	49	57	21	5	14	3	19
222	412	2 2	255	267	249	229	22	4	45	51	57	33	9	24	10	44
223	413	2 2	259	263	251	254	37	4	0	0	55	28	5	30	7	23
224	414	2 2	260	274	258	253	4	2	40	49	56	33	18	34	20	29

TABLE A, PART II (Continued)   **AA15**

Elementary School Grade Five Ability Grouped 1959–1960

SCHOOL NO.   4   TEACHER NO.   4

ID1ID2ID3	ID	P	L	STEP SCI	STEP READ	STEP SOC	STEP MATH	TI	CH	SC SEL	CON SEL	IDL SEL	ACC	SCH	HOMME	GET ALO	GEN
104	415	1	2	261	269	256	250	30	4	44	51	57	22	10	13	8	6
105	416	1	2	296	295	269	259	17	3	44	53	55	44	22	26	18	44
106	417	1	2	262	263	259	249	11	3	41	53	23	72	24	55	53	63
107	418	1	1	276	260	265	261	14	3	38	51	23	32	13	44	23	48
108	419	1	1	279	286	269	270	4	2	47	51	57	12	1	2	1	4
109	420	1	1	276	295	278	265	21	3	44	46	40	40	11	22	17	52
110	421	1	1	282	280	285	261	11	3	39	53	20	32	9	24	27	32
111	422	1	1	267	278	269	253	24	4	45	51	19	55	42	34	22	41
112	423	1	1	263	274	275	266	18	3	0	0	55	17	6	14	5	9
113	424	1	1	261	252	258	265	11	3	0	0	51	31	16	57	21	46
114	425	1	2	283	0	0	266	9	2	0	0	0	0	0	0	0	0
115	426	1	1	273	253	268	258	3	2	40	52	55	19	13	29	12	25
116	427	1	2	260	267	263	261	14	3	45	51	23	23	5	15	10	28
117	428	1	1	266	251	256	258	13	3	44	51	57	29	4	8	12	17
118	429	1	2	264	267	269	257	7	2	48	53	50	14	3	21	7	24
119	430	1	2	262	283	271	266	10	3	46	53	51	44	6	14	17	14
120	431	1	1	269	271	261	266	9	2	41	53	55	66	11	49	40	54
121	432	1	1	273	276	269	260	8	2	38	55	39	44	12	24	17	19
122	433	1	1	302	283	271	266	13	3	44	52	41	35	17	27	22	38
123	434	1	2	261	269	263	263	5	2	44	53	57	54	18	44	19	57
124	435	1	2	266	286	259	264	4	2	39	53	47	35	25	77	38	40
125	436	1	1	279	267	269	259	7	2	0	0	45	61	12	30	6	57
126	437	1	2	266	286	262	253	7	2	43	53	19	80	39	84	58	63
127	438	1	1	273	276	278	261	17	3	51	53	51	10	6	8	2	35
128	439	1	2	269	276	269	250	9	2	46	52	45	20	3	32	8	28
129	440	1	2	262	278	257	250	39	4	43	49	55	38	15	38	22	44
130	441	1	2	266	269	268	266	16	3	37	53	35	50	19	55	35	35
131	442	1	1	279	278	268	260	26	4	48	51	55	47	26	42	25	40
132	443	1	2	302	295	275	272	1	2	46	53	57	42	16	39	27	67
133	444	1	2	279	274	266	274	26	4	47	51	53	58	20	53	31	45
134	445	1	2	266	278	261	257	28	4	0	0	0	0	0	0	0	0
135	446	1	1	264	278	266	247	11	3	36	45	0	0	0	0	0	0
136	447	1	1	259	274	263	252	17	3	35	35	54	40	22	37	21	33

TABLE B

Random Numbers

0417	3242	5704	5045	8933	8192	8752	8784	3934	4546	1872	0816
5047	7441	9223	8369	7209	7936	2735	4986	5299	6918	3817	0637
9474	1108	1380	8314	7459	9932	2458	5362	0043	2004	1639	1796
6021	9962	5585	3851	2846	2414	8873	1515	9231	1751	7425	8797
5956	6559	5752	5483	1124	7400	4287	9117	6125	4694	3038	5982
8551	7465	7830	9798	8313	1696	5364	6914	3212	7045	3357	6738
0217	0662	2016	6139	8688	6879	3084	6594	1808	1497	2716	2819
2468	9441	4432	1624	9855	4515	8401	9766	2987	0030	3300	9527
7462	9027	7005	0782	1651	2869	2352	8295	8598	6937	4240	3005
9873	2191	4295	6047	7626	1335	9878	4250	1099	8343	0161	5881
3836	0093	6033	5357	7847	8869	2588	5712	0977	4456	7939	7529
3729	4612	4104	3120	1787	2636	9734	4682	0491	0803	0403	5192
7522	8407	2741	0784	0035	3158	8631	3363	2494	4699	5749	2200
1462	8970	0666	3264	3595	2191	0793	5038	3090	3201	1395	9565
4832	2904	3937	7489	9497	9579	2005	5817	6858	8796	1056	7175
3544	6691	8252	9295	1501	5354	8613	3488	3410	9075	3753	0846
1301	0192	9444	4937	4625	3314	8260	9728	4033	6639	3541	1493
7096	9135	9045	3458	2243	2336	3826	1929	7142	5493	8681	2652
7783	2830	6940	6163	4524	1673	9320	0869	1332	0168	9020	2610
4478	3380	9980	9460	6937	6487	6482	0514	4743	3835	0320	7404
1541	2612	1801	7302	7597	9867	0826	6158	9511	1649	4294	0921
6882	3004	6089	9496	2174	7577	5897	7185	0040	5576	3090	8359
2346	8844	1952	2119	5144	1796	4476	0690	3862	6957	6986	9300
2927	3865	6846	6287	6111	0081	5489	2203	3815	3060	4030	6639
3564	1629	7702	1545	9955	5828	5372	9775	0306	3857	0390	7627
2254	4882	9007	0105	9567	6456	2630	7679	2400	5292	0148	3265
8256	0149	6591	8204	9902	5580	4364	5960	6488	5283	3311	2320
4115	3816	5859	0809	2117	5422	3484	2106	1277	8709	0760	6185
0268	5942	3237	5944	6533	5698	5392	1066	7870	7624	4913	0866
0974	8055	9561	4871	3181	5248	2853	9890	3663	2967	4836	2308
0327	1186	4175	4374	8668	2641	7831	3218	8827	4000	5458	1353
7094	0833	8485	7415	8127	2027	9021	5883	4111	1724	3342	4534
7132	1982	7704	8388	0991	0459	3834	8874	8736	2546	6652	7001
2134	9794	9565	9240	9353	2962	3595	4909	7100	8414	6585	3786
3450	6629	8727	2698	7643	1578	0677	9862	3075	9694	0490	5692
9742	7219	5638	8856	2392	4647	6355	6303	0628	7034	6558	6038
7210	8915	8600	1370	0818	2578	8101	5403	9514	8454	5098	4505
1151	6357	7788	9516	6998	6345	5090	3436	4808	7926	4281	4353
7594	6387	9972	2351	4355	4976	0655	9150	9007	1690	9076	9241
3768	9433	2690	1242	3242	8270	0447	8247	5463	8552	2146	5908
6136	3642	6629	6999	2332	1006	5044	1215	1892	0411	5444	8961
4772	7984	4953	7863	2607	4873	5773	0779	2715	9283	1262	4027
2808	0601	8338	4618	2660	4402	2470	5201	8976	7044	1485	5512
9707	8638	4463	9042	4083	3117	1959	3703	4583	4174	3796	5214
7121	5797	0694	1987	5678	6179	5974	0233	7636	3718	3587	8060
6073	3898	8732	7307	5254	5761	7284	1855	5575	6749	0320	1183
4216	4650	9958	7894	7743	5411	2781	7990	2910	5547	7091	2624
1924	7924	0234	0084	8400	9642	2258	6767	0281	0780	2152	5887
5956	2752	2904	2661	9828	5017	1648	4738	3591	8908	1129	6603
9457	7311	8754	6729	1585	8956	9466	6194	1970	6072	8701	7555
7023	4145	1665	2683	1115	2539	5201	8355	3320	4725	8472	8310
3610	6870	8731	0556	4756	3536	8413	8649	6180	9238	9810	5716
6009	4608	3571	9954	7585	5925	7282	0370	6680	6748	0372	1501
5654	0414	1600	5871	0830	2139	5364	2932	9312	9486	3101	3237
1510	9932	5998	6600	5617	4308	5294	2990	0291	4837	6408	4909

TABLE B (Continued)   **B2**

Random Numbers

0213	1276	5743	2973	6147	0130	5454	1552	0230	7413	2404	7712
4634	8393	8651	6370	0359	4820	5689	0760	3358	3304	9604	7889
0902	4408	8332	0319	6926	8686	9782	0525	5108	5923	9565	4088
8437	3836	7080	7956	4013	2472	8716	0045	1827	0559	6905	6406
6285	0061	3796	2229	9208	5191	8273	2921	3069	2119	5098	1517
3215	5639	4902	8657	7826	9037	3790	1410	4350	3409	1306	7156
1182	2691	5505	8812	3324	0634	3888	7628	0772	5981	8941	9812
8402	2109	7036	3234	6078	7358	9448	0463	7748	2324	4215	4368
8278	0354	7626	2567	6765	7490	4058	6934	5088	8118	2920	4453
0442	2573	1465	5632	0605	2943	2208	6761	0696	3327	3696	2236
0154	0798	3401	3221	8718	3320	1460	8878	0127	0862	4033	6434
2314	5973	5013	6325	2829	0052	4855	8657	8249	1583	5252	7265
6323	2556	8431	7579	9595	9360	9805	4586	9272	4364	2730	7106
8068	4457	4128	4657	0785	2797	9718	3140	1377	9999	7600	5610
5255	1042	8958	4364	5566	4117	4613	0621	2212	7683	6194	8017
2356	1978	0665	6190	1157	1228	6956	0682	1492	2815	3460	5426
1413	9644	5143	4062	8086	1962	8997	6324	6966	4887	6625	5763
4958	7881	2663	5046	6308	2435	7832	5078	9983	4197	5330	4209
7282	5815	9350	3764	8433	6724	4446	6157	6925	6140	4514	1825
0322	5504	0131	1249	6312	6635	3002	8294	2746	1831	6269	1137
0401	2172	9427	7013	7234	0285	6602	7049	2873	3799	6935	7416
2085	5765	5826	3069	5982	8272	5792	0307	9714	5518	5680	4419
5392	2586	6987	8646	8997	6170	6045	0738	0025	3507	0815	3325
2614	5760	1035	4369	6904	2103	0481	3953	9390	0767	0089	3634
0996	3275	0686	4636	1645	8146	4071	1116	0056	0288	1225	4759
7530	2355	6356	6946	4470	4301	5579	4764	8378	7389	8930	7078
2100	8902	4510	6938	1043	3810	3478	6571	8130	9637	4653	1187
5244	0780	7483	7875	9903	8539	2113	5821	5913	3090	5319	4107
6771	3665	1053	3334	0533	3190	4340	7333	4936	3619	7293	1188
1486	8225	5980	1853	7295	7093	6904	7589	3394	2064	1843	2478
8283	7390	9797	2273	5465	2330	4797	7815	3715	1960	8320	2286
8835	2430	5069	8542	5635	6928	0853	2765	8913	8592	1338	0699
2153	6630	0398	2717	2724	1890	6829	3959	2295	8135	8175	5804
1253	5280	0406	4916	5841	0797	2216	6123	6788	5627	2669	5365
8173	0753	0960	8985	5267	0740	7040	5580	0118	0484	1842	6699
3615	1401	5868	2600	2790	3333	4892	9353	2096	8396	1512	3507
7434	3039	1324	0595	1650	4549	2442	3709	0274	8267	7136	8411
6242	1750	4328	0218	2350	2141	1697	0912	0199	2989	6139	9936
4366	6773	1344	7111	0563	9383	1230	2934	6533	2796	7978	2705
4426	2213	3442	0732	3413	3895	2652	0859	1280	9952	8192	9582
3762	6338	4171	7982	0356	0296	8568	8748	5374	3507	2680	4515
2972	7195	6424	3790	4924	5430	8262	0705	9872	2887	8471	4842
2815	3310	4531	7392	3576	4926	7371	9893	3016	9061	7223	1788
5717	8215	7835	3071	7912	9834	7794	8256	9391	2038	7711	7924
8144	7551	2010	4097	6494	2088	4082	5698	7453	3437	3543	0326
0073	7502	4356	8622	2524	7547	2563	7455	1664	2890	2366	8187
7832	3303	9334	6274	3638	5367	9455	8429	5481	7022	2806	3633
6547	6584	0577	4208	0053	2448	4209	3225	1463	9760	5388	4490
8449	0281	5648	1360	7326	1712	4339	0631	4731	2713	3695	7757
3283	9886	9772	9653	9971	2954	7984	1315	6038	4392	2010	2530
7090	9768	4802	0902	2191	5030	0456	7468	0702	7000	5689	1131
5584	3323	9682	8184	1961	8112	1025	3145	9643	9552	0526	7189
8402	5708	8627	0395	4722	4781	6183	4072	8787	6071	7343	9423
0450	7892	3301	8775	2945	8691	5644	5645	3070	7618	8073	9880
6619	0799	5220	4128	7786	9568	7334	7886	1311	6895	9571	5374

TABLE B (*Continued*)   **B3**

Random Numbers

6106	8267	4649	3493	9120	3280	7604	6102	8183	4177	1412	0884
2591	7590	2223	5028	0165	5737	2940	6002	9557	3324	3926	3644
6532	6391	9559	9837	2984	9376	9399	2005	7444	6618	2710	6701
5812	4569	5105	9504	1083	0964	6031	7514	0801	7182	5883	0657
0999	0074	1459	8084	5374	9484	8540	5885	8448	7725	0319	2388
1460	7264	0444	7290	9743	2852	9420	0853	0340	4363	3118	9443
8595	6583	2148	3636	2488	2205	0834	5160	3453	4272	4560	8909
2418	4329	4208	6288	9853	2525	6477	6136	8524	5919	8791	9480
7760	1236	7580	4358	7927	8334	8665	6983	3910	0615	8502	5471
6315	8645	5036	2414	9157	3222	6919	2510	2791	4158	9827	1543
0814	0997	8649	2927	9715	1952	4274	8078	9998	7288	3745	6875
7547	3407	2518	4439	3973	3890	7583	0490	4692	3737	0197	7544
3494	3068	6964	4170	2341	6519	8044	9591	5152	4595	1201	5855
4319	3225	0477	3835	8716	7776	8216	9312	1927	7756	9197	5375
9477	8487	5633	7414	3782	5969	1775	6929	5593	1202	6874	0422
0668	0211	5254	9619	0433	6024	2247	9266	5374	8850	4734	8754
9917	0717	5046	3826	7539	0805	6974	4606	4865	7738	2642	6212
3498	5077	8981	8194	8336	6267	2575	9050	1122	5284	1604	2069
7976	9240	3653	8757	9666	9187	8129	6086	3359	5378	2038	3826
4609	3226	7872	8196	8331	6221	2349	8106	7501	2047	4773	0218
8353	8155	3746	9087	0802	3035	0991	8628	2850	9448	1033	1172
7733	5849	5495	0334	2547	2278	0745	3970	7112	6945	7660	3460
1817	9767	2244	5567	3203	9115	5860	3128	6026	8008	3815	0815
0558	6014	1061	2237	3873	3102	3754	4608	3861	1695	5417	7249
4737	3183	6469	0166	2771	5134	5861	8962	1018	5456	3569	2315
1767	9767	2701	8299	5485	8220	9958	5769	4990	8020	3211	7086
3613	7908	4930	8411	6089	0838	0229	3833	0934	1112	8264	9573
3062	2218	5747	4516	5377	1618	1313	3321	8105	8741	9505	8359
4610	2433	3104	6731	2447	4101	2587	8612	8389	2821	1427	3175
6202	8639	6015	8338	5896	0332	8931	0599	3210	3871	4338	1188
8087	7833	4217	4805	0878	2022	4231	7185	5034	5539	7931	7735
5028	0557	8086	3507	8268	8046	3860	0747	9739	1709	2608	0267
8127	6361	5024	2901	2188	7016	2406	1290	6091	4931	4770	4239
2499	6847	8587	9904	2136	3682	2866	4063	8584	4935	2354	9709
7071	5038	6594	4222	5985	7910	3593	0370	9883	5965	6846	7389
2721	9827	4473	8389	0083	4993	9214	0342	9130	1701	8034	2893
5048	4253	0087	2250	2714	6035	1788	6409	2363	6502	7745	7947
7979	6352	6304	0651	7170	7163	8448	6220	1285	1729	8810	7299
4506	1349	7537	3087	0684	6322	1780	3778	6650	5895	5522	0077
0767	3906	6533	4044	5465	6394	9177	7516	2507	7398	1824	4361
9745	9223	7635	2803	8103	3394	7438	4083	7554	8577	3481	3692
0821	1696	2784	1438	3573	8501	8848	6579	9844	9847	0488	4305
1444	9917	6505	9776	0107	2659	4988	6001	1112	2661	5958	1795
7150	6747	6130	6056	1169	2510	4536	4630	6955	0059	7754	5998
6199	3214	3494	2039	0793	6406	1297	0132	9119	3528	9096	2822
5066	4995	4380	1325	8528	9246	8720	9105	6151	4961	4406	1783
1046	0226	1942	9621	0248	4896	7151	8835	8657	2425	6636	7990
8215	7382	0358	5713	1059	4932	0064	6000	5420	8519	2334	7334
2999	1995	4974	1892	6581	2461	5538	1079	6627	0055	0689	3635
5610	0946	5182	2578	8830	9778	9203	7214	0458	7824	2817	6489
3580	3083	6275	9906	2957	8591	4933	2279	9281	5175	7523	8562
3664	4920	6548	5007	1106	1579	9517	2894	1706	4193	9807	1102
8347	0165	5872	3746	9624	4031	7570	9148	6753	8186	8344	6384
3214	1823	2011	5663	5879	4305	2920	8776	6374	9262	8207	5882
1427	5626	0917	4867	0946	1875	2735	9534	2589	9729	5072	2868

TABLE B (Continued)   **B4**

Random Numbers

1560	3551	7265	1630	4395	1698	0635	8532	5478	6076	7153	8238
5049	6151	1467	3440	7437	3661	5036	7268	8282	4278	1129	8276
9493	2477	9425	4252	0688	5862	8979	1113	5868	5184	8297	3125
4074	6322	1265	0695	2786	0461	7693	2006	2797	8732	7217	4713
3326	7541	5308	3981	6115	0863	0143	3091	7259	5737	9085	2882
5525	7208	3522	6266	5895	8979	0813	4071	7109	6013	2098	8468
1926	5341	4714	0218	8879	1315	7972	6003	4267	1575	1043	2084
3120	9962	1699	0533	7907	2639	4676	4302	3729	3657	8379	7358
8743	6233	8710	6159	8569	5978	8750	8697	3434	2326	3051	7377
6802	4417	5287	1969	4234	7687	8012	8892	1239	7406	3288	3073
8847	5421	2905	8638	5683	6354	6976	4674	5261	9497	9633	2328
7271	2671	0586	9478	1597	4277	1287	9234	3819	9806	4462	8518
0952	9051	5739	2969	6166	0274	6150	4432	1243	7569	4232	7268
5516	7690	6492	9746	0048	2568	4980	6768	5784	3797	0721	0157
4453	5306	1757	2792	0939	0500	4551	2809	5895	0092	7493	4130
7345	6896	5275	9579	0006	3820	2866	2817	1110	1308	7855	5358
1453	0496	9897	4917	0427	8310	6020	1329	3789	0774	0545	6303
2915	0766	8357	3250	4289	6482	0297	3440	7968	6853	9403	4737
3799	0159	6765	9164	4096	2101	5742	5543	1578	9580	3280	3465
1267	6418	7100	4839	5141	7293	7483	9268	8255	6121	2432	9499
5106	5146	4921	3212	4980	0974	1024	7375	5033	3822	7639	1435
9854	6212	8581	5583	6270	7367	7777	0352	2124	9573	8323	3785
7798	2723	6158	2439	9214	3335	7079	2465	1073	4258	5888	7011
9074	1340	6379	6214	9871	3297	0947	6007	7516	1032	8550	2013
5130	2658	9782	4767	0565	0482	7808	2511	4795	6177	3901	7819
1798	0423	6352	4305	8664	3240	1469	9652	4692	1281	5459	1225
8225	8320	5898	0507	9961	5205	1576	2616	1507	5501	9444	7150
7908	3099	7417	6612	2921	8015	1799	8658	5763	6653	8051	8427
8103	2768	3685	7199	0028	5376	2002	3629	3757	9876	5450	3812
3822	8623	7338	6424	2501	7195	0657	9190	9223	2630	2767	2936
2712	9849	4683	9461	4615	2544	3732	9491	3364	4765	8308	6967
7026	9456	3500	5896	3878	0203	6313	6049	9479	2428	9262	3721
8962	0288	1070	3826	3328	5529	3223	9577	8455	4540	1139	5977
5609	9863	8695	3404	2174	2404	4860	7519	1379	0601	1193	1748
9753	2786	8945	8595	1062	9014	4527	6039	5489	8580	2078	5249
2790	9502	1900	5881	8188	6199	3500	5209	9752	1626	1994	7325
6006	0110	6611	8671	2531	7141	0070	6154	6291	2363	7557	4077
6453	2023	4061	6164	0432	7119	8828	8897	3929	3504	5663	2444
3698	0189	7851	5410	1799	2103	6431	9661	0084	3557	0583	1487
3674	8656	8873	5335	2156	4918	0105	6372	7282	6346	2541	8126
5890	2204	0216	1459	6812	7739	5128	1112	0521	3119	4025	6080
0256	6810	8560	0071	3384	9668	7549	8282	1752	5976	0091	6763
9759	7689	8301	0606	8931	8128	8394	7210	7713	1384	8889	0876
5258	3664	4659	4980	7945	2852	5607	7973	7379	2515	8683	9463
8630	6617	2028	2619	7458	1181	9965	9157	5263	9161	7602	3157
0530	4761	3800	9949	5500	3458	1243	6337	6836	3983	2373	8394
9007	8498	9929	3089	9173	7236	0852	9995	2297	3828	2293	9313
5236	7602	8484	2489	8580	9072	7217	1652	4959	4886	4684	4127
2602	8474	7425	8281	2863	2650	0133	6949	0494	0420	8077	4682
5396	0239	2871	5075	4609	1974	0366	4429	3280	9818	9390	7980
3371	8408	0106	4968	8851	8398	0726	8775	6118	7732	1331	8398
8408	4872	3557	7492	2943	0228	4885	7252	9552	2044	6293	9363
9540	2980	2017	5281	3531	3659	0172	8099	7050	9404	2978	3231
2586	6437	5352	4178	6897	3780	0608	9626	2290	7103	2007	8118
0641	0784	8935	6552	8898	4417	6419	8764	4817	0020	6769	0434

TABLE B (*Continued*)   **B5**

Random Numbers

1685	6206	2070	6568	0777	5547	6291	7818	0294	1398	5741	1868
9539	0417	6652	6157	7077	7048	8601	8173	1626	6199	2563	9584
4439	0375	2303	0439	1912	7517	7892	9702	7184	5788	0076	8358
9466	1574	4254	1358	9857	6922	2821	4630	2394	2692	4609	3428
9086	3663	0203	8252	7684	1835	1852	4600	0931	4187	6747	2796
6051	1144	2408	4149	3221	1987	2928	9688	1778	3471	4827	7725
2904	7901	1268	6495	7560	6904	3377	8130	8387	7152	7429	0202
4353	4302	6636	1101	6880	1371	6304	5491	6208	7827	1089	6090
6741	5631	3118	8031	0125	8474	9719	2048	4819	0480	9511	2748
0889	0601	5602	8202	8798	8971	4643	7117	0919	1462	0500	9840
4542	8692	1278	9435	5108	5739	8456	9090	8435	8800	6885	2105
0670	5069	4388	0703	4730	2049	9728	9922	1979	2582	7679	2833
7887	1824	9960	3344	0420	2427	0776	2818	9923	4170	5720	6784
9226	4303	2781	7963	2749	4826	4220	1884	3324	2993	8043	1318
5519	1253	7846	5799	4181	2897	9756	2463	6973	9667	5247	4478
9644	7557	8550	3288	2778	7072	7433	0947	8786	4193	6085	8773
7874	8288	8862	8585	1750	3233	3644	2769	3817	7982	3542	9412
4593	2844	5730	8782	1124	7705	6119	7366	9126	8464	8655	5752
6614	7915	7970	6582	7762	7333	4139	8835	5754	5015	8304	4682
3360	8024	7899	5183	0004	3381	0246	1046	4065	4972	3246	4728
9157	2393	1939	0102	3154	8010	9675	5961	8686	8468	2634	9598
3880	6898	6466	6713	2084	2089	3783	3894	9316	0852	1268	9937
8213	9841	5134	2234	7197	3079	3701	4491	3643	1435	5825	2032
9765	0306	3945	0917	****	1746	0478	7153	8614	7310	6336	2221
6305	7839	0291	1192	4530	6455	7959	9658	6322	1005	9134	5758
2339	2215	2241	3512	0899	3788	4641	3752	0747	0712	7547	8873
5312	2019	4304	7654	7188	4245	0771	6425	1612	1846	6568	2796
7664	0818	5931	8224	5963	1766	6924	5651	1590	8678	7764	8478
0993	9656	9002	7109	1637	5841	0317	9330	3128	4803	0665	0760
8578	4624	0543	1638	4948	4939	5104	6178	1130	1178	6894	0760
2518	8266	6932	7197	0799	0018	2915	7329	7743	0494	3273	5197
1721	3554	5837	3040	5704	6867	9864	7380	5507	6623	0172	1426
7005	9198	2140	0058	1091	6021	6306	3645	5117	7898	1335	6930
9567	5032	4091	9256	8719	9007	5570	2362	4036	2961	1443	2005
9046	6227	5953	9671	4451	9665	7931	0602	2229	7954	7665	4407
7458	5084	3376	4504	6640	9304	6061	2632	1243	3770	1439	4698
5238	9150	7759	4200	5370	4425	8218	9478	2909	2152	6735	1042
5634	4424	5842	5231	8811	5786	5420	0446	3894	9352	1064	2215
3719	2377	0788	3336	2926	7531	8854	5343	2369	6129	5453	7556
6261	9557	0995	9959	0799	5159	3764	6151	3030	2824	9674	2627
8695	8525	2895	0645	7811	1062	6078	6905	6735	8259	8943	9326
5466	8864	3984	4131	8930	6398	8019	0527	0994	1218	8360	9202
9972	7016	2341	0905	4365	8039	8951	1355	7575	3251	1331	8724
0370	3701	8877	9951	9818	9344	7705	2135	3464	1567	8225	5253
7490	7663	8571	2458	7607	3519	2646	4208	1435	0739	1519	2465
1112	4492	6943	1230	4894	8294	5717	9656	6484	2005	3670	3980
0849	9273	8001	4546	5267	0688	6724	4147	4366	8879	3976	3945
7888	1821	9937	3229	9942	0597	4102	9236	8497	7857	0672	3315
3845	3233	4793	9659	4815	1959	8417	2868	1459	2940	4509	0593
2977	2528	8376	7502	9628	0250	4847	6833	7373	2737	0066	5766
4001	2108	6642	0878	5494	5059	0909	9926	1372	8900	1051	6206
7776	0801	4826	1743	7029	6486	5656	5558	2442	4635	5829	3259
7094	3232	5551	4219	5349	4127	6619	2573	5866	2038	9441	8299
4827	4270	2176	4626	8168	7374	0730	8016	1527	7017	8356	6982
6690	7305	3620	5974	3263	5807	5478	0606	4331	0530	4203	0447

TABLE B (Continued)

Random Numbers

4854	5102	6929	5650	1543	8406	6552	3657	2972	4916	2745	2230
8676	1985	3821	5061	5982	0343	8216	6211	3323	4039	4330	9626
8788	6094	7471	9984	2659	6099	2667	1114	2675	6025	2079	8250
0789	0479	5779	0361	0153	7668	4637	8803	1090	7313	4063	8561
4803	1765	7365	8307	3558	6581	7462	5546	6118	6794	5704	3081
7145	5144	6560	3065	9348	8506	6905	4875	7108	8775	8674	3068
0344	4453	3622	1659	7354	9188	8947	0987	5401	3520	2513	3399
7777	6072	6444	4017	6101	0456	7823	2837	6608	4120	5246	4396
9161	5406	9989	1277	7758	5061	0539	7686	1270	8442	9224	9363
3159	4691	9713	6060	8938	9094	4117	2861	0109	4907	8455	6573
3339	0879	5225	3441	3617	0732	1840	4452	0151	0838	3666	4457
3744	2354	0427	1375	4406	4061	4713	1728	7951	2151	1352	8749
0328	3223	6388	9322	8437	6726	4422	5996	6179	3112	3057	0333
4489	3936	3208	3830	4105	0162	4020	2668	9822	4923	1141	2542
4976	6983	7111	9820	4921	1149	2603	5277	8231	1894	7284	6658
4391	6424	9022	6320	6723	3453	0214	0203	9294	3935	9966	4375
6561	9989	0885	5411	4497	8285	9235	0845	1955	4131	7189	5953
1015	2515	5958	3113	5061	2343	8514	9997	3352	0142	0684	2829
0819	9452	9343	0990	1849	2187	6477	9183	6805	8181	7845	3439
0026	9207	5009	7192	8068	3680	9469	3690	6924	8328	7655	0979
6978	3057	5537	5714	4450	5273	1585	2055	8067	9907	6841	1883
9723	1394	0858	2599	7874	3850	2234	8753	2414	5707	2518	3742
9789	5054	2222	7848	7092	1919	7686	8845	3896	3771	7562	1438
0567	0459	7652	1781	1817	4868	2855	3321	4234	5514	4974	0220
6556	7356	5135	4606	1417	7054	9564	3903	7342	8925	7470	4490
9713	7868	9790	7931	9476	5472	7549	6045	8333	5594	8565	1042
9168	5632	1280	6995	0451	9750	4439	8890	3387	0311	1383	5499
0542	3763	7700	2333	4703	7219	0984	0931	6730	2005	1459	0710
1130	0396	2205	9662	8130	1820	7749	0119	0970	4748	9763	5843
7191	0557	8620	6706	2655	5577	9562	7184	7043	7603	2228	4941
9596	3109	2285	5734	3836	1409	3931	0900	0021	2030	1990	3666
4088	1529	2384	0546	1822	6017	9701	4065	7024	5642	0631	3013
2397	7264	2006	6664	1927	1591	2201	8884	3496	1018	4646	8715
0475	4412	2197	3473	1061	5111	1113	0684	4087	8363	3396	5107
0075	4486	6241	7072	6268	3958	7338	8408	4400	0734	4799	2190
9950	9996	0422	2571	1626	6621	5088	0939	9840	0593	4998	4650
2912	5623	7533	4593	9760	7217	5464	7834	7827	6454	8277	1581
4990	5711	9356	4734	4201	2598	7774	3264	9618	8334	3444	5660
2963	6841	4382	4718	8875	0783	4824	1901	7985	0804	2960	0520
6486	4231	7016	4012	0929	9470	8458	5523	7010	2357	1050	5090
1088	0717	4516	0638	3185	3373	1569	9058	0230	9853	7049	3619
8272	7060	7915	3947	2443	9140	2851	4842	3397	6799	0228	0172
8980	2333	3180	8086	9896	6599	0535	3819	8096	4204	2358	6314
6659	3131	8850	4926	9902	5079	1362	2455	2475	2757	4261	0758
6199	0368	6416	5186	3373	3564	1029	4098	5329	5091	2589	9711
4965	2394	9677	6518	2014	3419	2386	3544	9795	6875	3090	6669
2203	3195	9341	7291	9678	2451	7603	3557	2914	5473	6614	0428
3045	4417	9096	4824	7076	9045	0581	2086	7287	4946	4091	0033
3379	9973	9431	6830	6099	5123	5842	8948	1109	6123	6758	5441
1824	1974	5430	4812	****	6692	0154	0696	2795	0502	7858	2632
5071	6741	4804	8152	5680	0710	3142	2459	6477	6728	2080	1925
2827	9642	2408	7669	4343	7038	3135	5470	4606	8406	8983	8245
8619	7511	7494	7367	6752	4210	4491	9056	3914	1980	6653	2098
2712	7392	9945	3142	9346	7796	2665	5829	0985	3450	1841	9992
3382	0363	1743	7192	7467	0077	3253	8826	3684	2667	2845	3067

TABLE B *(Continued)*

Random Numbers

2799	9185	9925	6879	1954	9810	1275	9362	4701	3946	1366	2677
3772	8537	7271	6795	5328	0815	6944	4324	3448	1772	9603	1672
3602	6566	6978	2777	3857	8146	4165	1674	2565	0320	8835	0134
1290	6529	7566	6636	1717	0578	8019	2911	5294	5563	5731	4324
4362	7255	4269	0323	3516	8189	7488	1244	9953	8704	2651	7568
1549	1184	3162	8315	1431	3756	9651	4105	7772	9687	8174	1857
7576	8743	4271	6939	3198	6735	1630	9170	0344	9536	4120	8898
6312	7788	9918	9412	7213	8571	6510	1919	2923	0268	5296	9366
8530	6886	4550	5324	1001	8083	9494	4216	9848	1145	8235	9106
0520	1164	2302	3333	9279	5676	0548	2208	8310	9993	5165	1051
9827	9498	8547	5802	7892	5134	9776	2454	6740	8353	9459	1576
4324	1765	1673	4152	9851	1740	1779	5009	4050	9213	8830	0066
0922	4943	1358	3659	9735	5477	5250	2206	5986	6063	2500	0437
0116	6768	9561	6457	2693	8050	4056	1892	4843	2033	8608	3354
2654	5733	0515	1494	4322	2491	6049	3870	8781	7855	8100	7911
4560	6165	5945	0191	7636	4097	5862	8294	7009	7406	1359	1501
6771	7118	1770	6556	3407	1434	7945	4763	7074	9579	3811	6654
5625	3862	2542	0498	0110	6178	6079	0871	0512	5229	6772	3570
0468	0681	9871	3095	9731	0536	5631	8963	3103	7951	9777	7102
4614	3768	1080	2566	5680	0983	4781	9838	5996	7435	0644	6952
5916	2932	4347	9698	9063	7095	1002	2158	3927	4144	9518	9810
3197	0892	6584	1471	9572	4192	9006	6312	6816	4084	3160	2205
4790	8901	0291	1640	7221	8572	6438	1482	0954	2382	5707	2800
5440	7436	5656	7019	1206	4067	3543	4660	6067	4463	2178	2901
7806	0732	4135	8221	2111	8680	3081	0367	4473	3536	0955	3905
4839	3884	9759	3593	3731	0048	6711	9835	8616	3175	1507	0468
9248	1279	4437	5115	0753	8483	4121	8380	3189	3714	3590	8110
6349	5105	3490	4993	8548	6345	1139	9731	8135	1234	4190	4035
6501	2695	7662	1712	1316	2486	3074	6069	8747	7860	8440	9897
3418	1439	7873	4285	4849	0532	9550	2513	9130	2159	0784	5273
4581	0032	8958	3461	0147	9731	7065	4810	5272	8343	2613	0588
0015	4794	8631	8637	4145	7142	5542	8975	3974	3068	2643	8243
5669	9827	7943	9214	3803	9890	5109	1645	3893	8552	6277	0693
7662	9738	9469	9170	9798	6258	9366	9872	4937	0772	0197	4236
3637	3703	9483	3571	6083	4356	1390	9131	2278	1492	8445	7246
7468	9596	0360	5799	1551	7111	8712	8271	1218	2866	6236	1618
3586	6959	9475	4222	0058	2344	3546	0180	9165	3374	7753	6156
7157	7539	0822	7076	5059	6669	4486	6891	0975	3827	4186	0675
6373	2164	5628	4292	5101	1976	5948	7905	3892	2212	8242	9547
3100	2684	8198	5034	6424	3234	1593	0450	8358	6104	1399	3455
8141	7752	3242	9684	8923	6381	7982	0461	0928	1415	0140	8101
7348	1180	0942	5032	1721	5035	4720	3003	5541	6215	7425	8613
4855	1615	5993	1423	4599	4787	7329	0895	9406	8383	5642	8407
9661	2308	6895	0598	1534	3820	9113	0294	9748	5838	7299	1253
1830	9696	1711	3000	2603	8612	8248	1981	7654	8096	9693	5297
4541	9573	6572	3273	0484	3454	6363	7093	5290	7906	9821	7775
8260	9584	3163	2717	7835	2562	4855	6070	2723	1713	5769	9196
3261	6798	1439	7452	1762	3507	5184	9542	0596	7701	0837	5715
6757	9108	3833	1026	1659	0724	9407	9932	4924	0162	6654	8464
0899	9214	7193	0233	6658	7852	7195	2499	0240	8947	1519	8590
7874	9928	8705	2879	8927	7655	5582	4599	7355	2737	0229	6739
8368	9560	2049	6257	9095	8259	7703	1883	1967	4905	1648	5745
9639	6133	0043	5068	0015	4483	6760	0211	0432	0689	0247	5278
9446	9172	0017	7552	5159	2985	1480	2014	8766	4464	7894	7190
2090	7830	8173	8569	7852	9995	9302	5858	1423	5821	2116	0309

Random Numbers

2811	4080	9183	8379	7631	0371	3550	7961	5815	3239	7100	3451
6800	9743	7263	5886	9952	6734	0838	4421	8978	4080	3681	5366
9066	6097	4992	5073	5516	7435	4966	2883	2601	9661	4560	0408
1413	4803	6105	3398	5445	2092	3541	2422	2658	4155	1006	8638
2777	8920	8528	0889	8577	3465	3592	0372	9904	6072	7299	9144
9173	2742	3896	8696	7110	4401	2412	4863	7472	1066	9151	5309
9500	9217	9799	5842	6866	8613	9886	1802	1840	4820	2360	0783
3456	3688	1021	2932	8403	4031	8559	5071	3400	4760	7959	4907
7814	2723	6010	1557	5251	7489	7678	8666	2891	9350	0082	6339
7302	6758	4831	8162	5490	9483	7481	9544	9934	3706	2833	3641
6351	5336	4855	1107	2954	7757	9957	9924	9936	0301	2377	1556
7944	3653	0428	9689	4280	8478	2349	7790	5599	3485	0520	1751
5828	9207	2787	3860	8078	3724	9643	4345	9284	6597	6021	6754
6340	7250	6443	3406	2452	4059	2284	7175	2493	0388	9890	5849
6079	3838	8310	5321	7137	4936	5379	7853	8703	1542	0925	1671
1706	5196	5817	8141	6490	5676	5641	2764	5813	0006	7720	6260
8086	2170	0251	1976	9593	9774	2305	5866	4451	3914	3423	5309
1048	8503	1587	3000	3714	5286	8290	2167	8388	0827	9470	9373
1006	1684	1049	1138	7380	4044	7840	0646	3312	4059	4552	0775
3687	5140	7662	9711	9308	8445	6898	5382	0211	2828	5071	4975
4211	0489	5031	5786	9442	4574	2467	3637	9619	4984	3330	5128
0797	8630	4607	9970	8355	0400	7206	9637	2967	1068	9703	8606
4311	8416	1693	4416	1258	7805	5509	2813	7294	8448	5042	4219
9935	1640	0423	7779	2866	7185	7317	9237	9569	4283	9573	8891
7190	3116	3986	5876	9378	3386	5916	5020	6873	6063	4518	2538
4569	4575	6329	6796	3812	1714	5971	0404	8687	8481	2704	9895
5034	1150	1594	9217	0953	2770	8041	3318	7541	5381	4413	8055
8613	9176	7543	2674	8156	4873	5830	1125	4276	5533	4708	8456
8365	4084	9214	8532	8265	2802	2424	9330	4160	0989	8495	2068
5954	7108	9063	0409	0883	1618	1759	5991	0114	6767	9574	6539
3073	9582	9841	2804	8260	4319	1574	0579	9303	0607	9918	4041
4989	3558	6450	6680	2031	2065	4104	6044	9328	1565	5443	8572
2441	7502	3045	0747	7076	5739	0748	2836	0284	6177	4507	1453
8150	5826	1606	7196	8725	7583	6978	3622	8925	0954	5396	3792
4185	0987	8256	0647	9580	1659	3733	7464	1189	9957	9042	4637
6442	6923	3557	9036	2202	1893	1539	2197	9329	6198	3230	3591
2480	2560	3043	5213	3894	6445	3628	3759	9909	5619	4533	6628
8968	4157	4235	7995	9852	7156	4272	1226	8905	2398	4240	3858
4990	5218	6396	1415	0927	2827	8624	6297	0169	4337	4507	8004
7462	2737	9260	0929	2239	5071	0271	5989	3496	7077	1003	2322
4904	8524	7007	5329	8909	5494	2787	7274	8559	5887	8285	6732
5824	4355	3716	3098	5140	2963	1518	2435	0949	3783	4158	0897
7963	9703	6552	1982	2920	9687	1839	3854	6570	4733	9268	3009
4646	0793	2940	0505	6572	4886	0167	7026	0652	0676	8184	3026
4495	9737	7971	0194	9423	4790	3937	0509	7618	1129	8212	9109
0747	2503	8297	7249	8825	7708	6826	1583	8061	4123	2187	6021
6441	4453	8751	2424	5792	2930	5456	6364	9081	7207	1514	4222
1702	2213	7963	7860	5491	2209	3833	3122	4232	7294	5677	8415
9393	0623	9203	9613	4846	2564	1770	7543	9327	8073	4494	4303
5374	3512	2709	4647	3499	9173	3544	8708	0354	3756	9350	2296
9619	7054	5751	1023	4381	7078	3035	4510	9749	7901	9671	6914
4445	4448	6679	0042	0144	0483	1607	5290	7279	6063	0871	0657
6099	0682	9205	9091	1699	8375	4965	4412	1789	1025	0049	1064
5950	6120	3171	3943	5117	5217	5250	4551	0052	9353	5653	9738
7552	7669	8048	9261	3138	5477	4620	8427	8979	8035	7395	2060

TABLE B *(Continued)*

Random Numbers

5803	6275	5421	6055	7539	0735	6560	2748	7445	9941	2639	6371
4472	9494	6713	4838	8609	8111	1183	4102	3965	6868	5526	1344
8332	7896	2384	3240	7990	8779	0761	5556	6486	8910	5085	0321
6155	4044	8870	6825	1121	5306	1742	2703	0539	8905	8581	1340
0810	2800	9510	1855	5543	6565	9500	7916	1992	0712	6339	1631
2732	1714	5699	8768	1316	8986	2072	1554	0674	0063	4311	5298
2985	0233	4532	5097	9792	2876	9125	8871	1099	6752	0623	2967
2200	6497	9180	6603	6999	2568	2415	1381	6553	6888	2355	2135
1612	0459	8246	5350	7884	9155	3968	1418	2792	3991	8813	6962
2456	2079	0367	3496	7668	4546	8262	8660	7598	7651	7524	6283
9983	3356	0288	1524	6553	5601	4626	7346	2441	8532	9224	8556
8322	2930	2676	9688	4049	7096	6136	2955	2506	8438	8079	2529
2462	2012	9919	1403	9148	2262	1240	7082	1326	4220	3387	2344
3583	0401	0158	7341	2622	9661	4370	9267	6275	4249	9017	5861
4010	1316	1805	8985	7665	5128	1781	4534	1173	6231	6833	4918
8013	3818	0789	0377	5158	7551	8889	5373	2241	5087	0348	6310
4723	1552	6799	6828	9780	7224	5326	6936	3683	9669	4872	2210
9410	6572	4746	9326	3244	5532	3994	4175	9105	7054	0380	8796
9359	6993	7722	3396	0878	4707	0343	9692	5064	3158	3377	1836
0624	7217	7687	1168	7822	6423	8140	1037	2963	8444	3994	7969
1870	9496	0143	5395	1085	7956	7970	6215	5562	7437	4563	0444
1592	5561	9038	4176	3711	4687	4719	6136	4344	0839	5934	8056
4934	7094	8162	5126	7301	7667	0298	2779	3994	8952	7770	6049
6367	3762	5269	7762	9147	5027	7841	1801	0234	5198	9081	7701
4484	7591	5191	2824	0228	5950	3650	8355	7274	8451	5240	5385
5147	2417	8178	7319	0308	5981	3114	4857	1111	2956	7737	9812
9244	7155	9733	4000	6403	2416	6867	9459	4951	4577	2907	6245
1311	1662	8171	4064	0848	8511	3428	3971	2976	2115	5907	6403
5257	3913	6168	1790	5231	5277	4581	9994	8735	2464	6167	4825
3449	7264	2543	9886	6430	9600	9732	1996	4383	8337	0579	8438
5413	6541	0528	4293	1013	7437	5505	6097	7033	7328	0669	8069
2388	1709	8762	7184	4251	0846	6821	3309	8471	1040	0006	0674
3989	7864	1283	6921	9979	7587	5709	5976	4474	3060	8092	1010
3232	0306	2745	3714	7580	2055	4110	6164	9995	4490	6987	1509
6171	3444	5121	9735	2319	6295	6903	4762	6447	5825	6924	9117
2387	2271	2145	2432	5287	9835	1424	0028	7359	3896	7147	7819
2592	5176	7730	9797	9213	7106	9717	4346	8628	2650	8247	5636
9592	6826	4629	6339	6373	1188	9770	7929	9643	6502	2221	4807
8858	9883	9575	8508	4867	2631	1984	8227	1511	5020	6519	3938
4955	4293	1159	8323	9502	2107	7126	3796	8640	7683	8331	0844
0084	2908	6687	3953	3536	5641	2020	1354	9942	7472	5350	4856
0981	2184	4276	6002	7531	1166	9217	4807	5883	2036	9274	7315
0423	6707	6435	8247	1564	5163	6906	4968	7650	1189	8290	9035
9602	6299	1377	1573	7046	8119	5301	8703	4676	9479	4795	3459
7596	4447	8316	9875	4408	7574	5769	6450	6773	2594	4603	4272
4211	6817	3000	6648	2887	7488	8943	6270	7128	6337	3876	6218
2425	8593	9730	1040	8676	2691	8063	4161	2399	6940	0054	7864
6694	9392	6105	2104	7683	7159	3806	8406	6183	1443	3010	5076
3365	4509	6764	0004	9151	4868	6850	7289	2086	6910	2690	3944
9456	1243	2351	2924	6382	1977	4423	8743	2652	7225	9489	1906
6033	9045	9973	8431	0828	9089	7082	0690	0403	6207	3616	5833
2458	2252	1384	8040	5783	2339	1983	0849	7241	5808	9681	5812
7740	4137	5162	3733	5943	2062	8882	4731	8455	8146	2782	3380
5246	1055	9112	5180	9068	7787	5114	0603	7588	0100	2312	2972
7024	5397	9164	6413	6005	8312	5824	0139	8416	9251	9761	5306

TABLE B (Continued)

Random Numbers

3982	6137	0991	0707	5328	5602	5660	3537	0287	9889	6748	1485
8178	5705	0625	2409	8825	1274	8217	7837	3063	7851	9534	6546
3473	1926	0301	4469	4104	4399	9462	7181	7928	2938	6276	1211
0785	3808	5784	0435	0551	9391	1385	3795	0303	7665	3263	0596
4209	9886	1434	9636	4907	2719	2145	8404	1120	1077	6385	8618
4245	7910	9254	4330	2695	7201	8946	8870	2705	6405	4084	6857
4386	4608	8170	7549	1760	2622	9894	5762	5525	1296	8047	6623
7312	4268	9802	0398	4169	1436	1096	3649	2035	9366	7877	2973
6945	4911	6960	7560	2720	8286	5236	6836	3894	1840	6000	9436
2618	0783	1132	9750	8311	2115	7889	8298	8783	8017	9056	2183
1596	9929	5206	1878	4416	9595	7822	0581	3090	3306	2026	2408
6211	5594	7668	5655	4922	8636	7521	7397	6695	3600	1344	5658
1855	0206	4545	5414	1576	0732	0210	4670	6126	4728	3236	6868
2082	0678	5329	5875	7291	0871	9605	9792	2308	5722	3557	9848
7071	3795	9129	0620	1560	3781	8643	7830	9192	4680	5349	9972
1697	0432	7317	0015	4232	5258	3459	3434	9476	5945	0388	8825
9462	7343	8904	7338	3893	7311	8833	7198	3691	7365	0971	9545
8531	5280	4897	1863	7111	5897	1384	5226	8903	6384	8180	1627
6140	2192	7895	7641	4791	9976	6739	0652	3263	3708	2883	3924
7595	0255	3172	6738	1880	0645	6944	5862	2676	3301	5718	4602
6148	5470	7484	5676	6698	9105	4352	4165	5824	7455	2316	6802
9970	8601	1873	3827	6108	2203	8251	9676	3797	5695	0002	8751
2490	6184	4694	2509	2814	4300	0474	4143	0591	6259	2234	7074
2338	0363	1135	3537	1008	4220	6243	9483	0708	8901	7029	2070
9158	6314	5467	5972	6628	6026	6500	4770	0118	7780	5617	3677
1513	5983	2279	9831	8476	2376	7968	6423	6831	3176	7581	6900
3168	6911	2949	5498	6448	9205	7199	0353	7325	0778	8739	5437
3970	4888	3595	7579	3116	0484	4860	4805	5091	7303	7998	2263
1591	9182	0769	1975	4931	1812	6494	2663	7528	1201	9454	5911
0382	9093	1122	4895	9272	1579	6027	1950	7454	7175	5965	1211
3582	0593	1319	2582	3617	8467	8248	3283	5473	3288	0471	3231
5144	1786	4427	0484	3063	4016	6529	3037	9454	9396	1288	3168
7411	5956	9040	0637	2460	9030	2036	0949	7366	5656	7642	4947
0909	0929	7391	5989	9409	2557	0659	0943	9726	9869	1682	1272
2496	3527	8698	0439	4358	2193	3938	3892	7903	2394	3237	7875
8120	7844	3988	3326	4068	4472	0223	1091	4536	7394	3545	4724
6436	6098	8666	7113	4683	4076	2312	7185	2304	9160	4230	2934
9537	0815	9063	7037	0661	0629	7826	1291	7314	2261	7746	6126
7037	7090	9211	1452	5815	1818	8575	5086	3341	4274	5577	4994
9771	3676	4119	1630	2709	1589	5147	6584	3184	9842	0401	3826
9347	1649	5767	9762	6672	2173	2990	8381	3373	4809	8501	7721
9815	9406	8095	3919	0661	8696	6225	9087	8495	9186	8656	9266
7688	2736	7221	8705	7242	5104	5444	6728	1373	7688	3768	3415
6577	8723	3147	0375	3925	0178	5740	2836	5355	6612	1471	9320
2684	2225	9195	5145	8113	2373	1227	6001	4964	5776	9974	7862
7406	3680	5431	9464	7902	2234	2290	3627	1158	4303	5395	3641
3294	6995	2324	0987	5003	1141	1817	0634	7446	8972	6820	0168
9628	6256	0883	8994	6013	5132	6676	3867	3118	3902	5354	7005
3845	0023	5539	3025	8297	2556	0661	0962	9829	0310	3400	7613
5077	1950	6001	8457	6735	4300	5184	2410	7798	5102	0428	6652
6058	6479	4350	7786	7571	5349	3951	5571	7864	7042	1477	5486
9624	8374	3623	6372	5629	6420	7864	9404	5646	9242	4635	4634
6087	4818	4122	1371	1128	4428	6415	8634	4075	6740	3766	1934
7710	8850	3714	2634	2371	0525	1811	6136	0521	7900	2709	5154
6543	2876	8363	4299	0528	4473	2087	2262	4791	8389	7217	7805

TABLE B (Continued)

Random Numbers

1874	1002	9145	5849	2788	4090	9447	9875	4227	6487	0883	6913
3529	8961	2000	1354	0118	8527	0096	3840	2173	8475	1293	1489
7291	0348	6470	5685	5882	4123	1804	3712	6042	2842	2672	0453
8671	7951	9663	6423	1566	1590	5448	8380	1250	2085	1255	8764
1296	8896	1713	0215	5866	3266	6801	1411	7254	0823	9651	0501
6148	2383	8965	2346	3388	9215	4798	5856	1950	8998	6437	7642
7919	8737	1148	8255	9196	0883	2532	7246	0686	8902	7238	3310
4724	8550	8784	5756	5485	1101	7244	3553	6126	4779	3536	8207
7417	0639	7077	6715	6599	9154	5539	0848	5232	3760	5475	9009
4779	7592	2542	6925	8668	9685	0096	3410	9595	6873	4887	7464
0802	7639	8614	2939	0104	4173	4100	7048	5386	8880	4811	8939
0342	1594	6492	4604	9196	3739	9669	4363	9161	5698	1744	9179
9375	3640	7468	2048	5078	2035	6507	0723	5774	8141	6878	8004
6118	4676	2992	5871	8300	6958	7052	9687	4654	0741	2566	8725
9255	7003	8719	9287	7254	9938	4346	6634	0685	4408	0280	2007
9525	9086	8791	0973	6719	1562	8900	9343	5955	1649	6295	2928
0915	9140	6604	7365	4759	2270	0784	4276	8603	3133	1366	0002
7720	6298	8308	3167	4231	6882	3209	7320	5034	4323	0635	4903
3706	8108	5295	8802	5153	1704	3843	7720	1737	0942	0018	1633
9633	3103	1916	3571	4183	2958	0101	3980	2972	2014	5338	3906
5394	7204	4685	3270	7454	5295	4685	0453	0552	9233	0429	9477
2999	2702	9220	1000	3022	9133	7599	3399	2000	1415	0484	0175
6688	8560	1163	9939	9171	5572	0896	5228	3303	2768	6884	6390
6386	0802	7339	6813	4827	7643	2417	5714	2530	3755	9760	4769
0776	1730	3398	4820	8335	6629	4760	8901	0562	3267	4542	7852
6229	6709	4190	4758	0840	2216	5734	4465	5179	0893	8742	4422
7848	7293	3124	3108	0532	5223	6548	2280	4754	8001	5219	9305
8861	9420	6765	5814	3998	1660	3980	8939	7810	6411	8179	1375
4636	5440	0914	6526	0933	6865	2792	4969	4684	3387	8165	8505
7544	8718	4416	8035	8463	8463	4614	1513	7555	1711	2271	8229
8939	9570	6966	5670	1324	6915	9573	5205	5072	3582	5850	2857
4497	1268	7134	1393	4154	2382	6906	0001	7851	7102	1950	7785
9158	4885	6885	7351	2139	6676	0799	4711	1079	4075	4741	1767
7934	1706	8831	7625	6278	9036	7720	4992	0471	7901	3165	7885
8825	1981	2461	6941	9492	4485	1483	8532	7845	0282	1086	3978
4090	8738	5620	5073	9861	3507	2294	2199	2552	5522	0160	1263
6135	5445	7452	5713	7204	1812	6032	9884	5016	1140	1697	9921
4253	6230	9099	8529	9281	8924	0020	9802	8631	3573	3756	0381
8478	7445	8366	3189	3841	4348	1521	9994	6275	7700	9725	9053
6797	9301	4631	4079	2795	0064	5228	0787	7672	8946	4632	7277
1970	6328	0238	4480	4738	8103	5979	2947	3874	6719	5447	2205
4211	5421	4623	8947	2077	1944	2965	0297	5098	7915	1608	8409
5982	0209	7419	2635	9035	0497	1667	5528	8169	9260	2044	9822
5134	0502	6810	6338	6743	3410	9777	7970	9826	7227	4923	4497·
2674	5569	9350	5977	1708	6455	3360	2064	2143	4279	6386	9810
1380	9992	7536	5284	3883	5740	9491	5286	6294	0195	4520	5368
1527	0848	1347	0454	0598	9502	1632	4273	0946	7220	4809	3876
8870	5964	0084	6979	8548	7889	3995	6900	6419	3794	3884	9777
0188	3233	7708	7150	3523	6787	9018	3028	7001	4755	5526	0358
2414	1264	5859	3774	9913	5514	3866	3571	6633	7660	6267	8660
5557	5405	2415	5850	3364	7533	4917	1711	6009	0657	9861	3256
0786	5414	5406	3715	3633	8363	7482	9625	0411	5840	1345	5505
0925	6012	7744	2354	4429	5386	2451	6237	5358	6020	7893	3182
8055	9690	5648	6675	9222	5258	8549	3968	6867	5492	1151	7471

TABLE C

Logarithms

	0	1	2	3	4	5	6	7	8	9	1	2	3	4	5	6	7	8	9
100	0000	0004	0009	0013	0017	0022	0026	0030	0035	0039	0	1	1	2	2	3	3	3	4
101	0043	0047	0051	0056	0060	0064	0069	0073	0077	0081	1	1	2	2	3	3	3	4	4
102	0086	0090	0095	0099	0103	0107	0112	0116	0120	0124	0	1	1	2	2	2	3	3	4
103	0128	0133	0137	0141	0145	0149	0154	0158	0162	0166	0	1	1	2	2	3	3	3	4
104	0170	0174	0178	0182	0187	0191	0195	0199	0203	0207	1	1	2	2	3	3	3	4	4
105	0212	0216	0220	0224	0228	0233	0237	0241	0245	0249	0	1	1	2	2	2	3	3	4
106	0253	0257	0261	0265	0269	0273	0277	0281	0285	0289	1	1	2	2	2	3	3	4	4
107	0294	0298	0302	0306	0310	0314	0318	0322	0326	0330	0	1	1	2	2	3	3	3	4
108	0334	0338	0342	0346	0350	0354	0358	0362	0366	0370	1	1	1	2	2	3	3	3	4
109	0374	0378	0382	0386	0390	0394	0398	0402	0406	0410	1	1	1	2	2	3	3	3	4
11	0415	0454	0493	0531	0569	0607	0645	0682	0719	0755	3	7	11	15	19	22	26	30	34
12	0792	0828	0864	0899	0934	0969	1003	1037	1071	1105	4	7	11	14	18	21	25	28	32
13	1140	1173	1206	1239	1271	1303	1335	1367	1398	1430	3	6	10	13	16	19	23	26	29
14	1462	1493	1523	1553	1584	1614	1643	1673	1702	1731	3	6	9	12	15	18	21	24	27
15	1761	1790	1818	1847	1875	1903	1931	1958	1986	2013	3	6	9	12	14	17	20	23	26
16	2042	2069	2096	2122	2149	2175	2201	2227	2253	2279	2	5	8	10	13	16	18	21	23
17	2304	2330	2355	2380	2405	2430	2455	2479	2504	2528	3	5	8	10	13	15	18	20	23
18	2553	2577	2601	2625	2648	2672	2695	2718	2741	2764	2	5	7	9	12	14	16	19	21
19	2787	2810	2833	2855	2878	2900	2922	2944	2966	2988	3	5	7	9	12	14	16	18	20
20	3010	3032	3053	3075	3096	3117	3138	3159	3180	3201	3	5	7	9	11	13	15	17	19
21	3222	3243	3264	3284	3304	3324	3345	3365	3385	3404	2	4	6	8	10	12	14	16	18
22	3424	3444	3463	3483	3502	3521	3541	3560	3579	3598	2	4	6	8	10	12	14	16	18
23	3617	3636	3655	3673	3692	3710	3729	3747	3765	3784	2	4	6	8	10	11	13	15	17
24	3802	3820	3838	3856	3874	3892	3909	3927	3944	3962	2	4	5	7	9	11	13	14	16
25	3979	3997	4014	4031	4048	4065	4082	4099	4116	4133	2	4	5	7	9	10	12	14	16
26	4150	4166	4183	4199	4216	4232	4249	4265	4281	4297	2	3	5	7	8	10	12	13	15

N	0	1	2	3	4	5	6	7	8	9	1	2	3	4	5	6	7	8	9
27	4314	4330	4346	4362	4378	4394	4409	4425	4441	4456	1	3	4	6	8	9	11	12	14
28	4472	4488	4503	4518	4535	4549	4564	4579	4594	4609	1	3	4	6	7	9	10	12	13
29	4624	4639	4654	4669	4684	4698	4713	4728	4742	4757	1	3	4	6	7	9	10	12	13
30	4771	4785	4800	4814	4828	4843	4857	4871	4885	4899	2	3	5	6	8	9	10	12	13
31	4914	4928	4942	4956	4970	4983	4997	5011	5025	5038	1	2	4	5	7	8	9	11	12
32	5052	5065	5079	5092	5105	5119	5132	5145	5159	5172	1	3	4	5	7	8	9	11	12
33	5185	5198	5211	5224	5237	5250	5263	5276	5289	5302	2	3	4	5	7	8	9	11	12
34	5315	5328	5340	5353	5366	5378	5391	5403	5416	5428	1	2	4	5	6	7	9	10	11
35	5441	5453	5466	5478	5490	5502	5515	5527	5539	5551	1	2	3	5	6	7	8	10	11
36	5563	5575	5587	5599	5611	5623	5635	5647	5658	5670	1	2	4	5	6	7	8	10	11
37	5682	5694	5706	5717	5729	5741	5752	5764	5775	5787	1	2	3	4	5	7	8	9	10
38	5798	5809	5821	5832	5843	5855	5866	5877	5888	5899	1	2	3	5	6	7	8	9	10
39	5911	5922	5933	5944	5955	5966	5977	5988	5999	6010	1	2	3	4	5	6	8	9	10
40	6021	6032	6043	6053	6064	6075	6086	6096	6107	6118	1	2	3	4	5	6	7	8	9
41	6128	6139	6149	6160	6170	6181	6191	6202	6212	6222	1	2	3	4	5	6	7	8	9
42	6233	6243	6253	6264	6274	6284	6294	6304	6315	6325	1	2	3	4	5	6	7	8	9
43	6335	6345	6355	6365	6375	6385	6395	6405	6415	6425	1	2	3	4	5	6	7	8	9
44	6434	6444	6454	6464	6474	6483	6493	6503	6513	6522	1	2	3	4	5	6	7	8	9
45	6532	6542	6551	6561	6570	6580	6589	6599	6608	6618	1	2	3	4	5	6	7	8	9
46	6627	6637	6646	6656	6665	6674	6684	6693	6702	6711	1	2	3	4	5	6	7	8	9
47	6721	6730	6739	6748	6757	6767	6776	6785	6794	6803	1	2	3	4	5	6	7	8	9
48	6812	6821	6830	6839	6848	6857	6866	6875	6884	6893	1	2	3	4	5	6	7	8	8
49	6902	6911	6920	6929	6937	6946	6955	6964	6972	6981	1	2	3	3	4	5	6	7	8
50	6990	6998	7007	7016	7024	7033	7041	7050	7058	7067	1	2	3	4	5	6	7	8	9
51	7075	7084	7092	7101	7109	7118	7126	7135	7143	7151	1	2	3	4	5	5	6	7	8
52	7160	7168	7176	7185	7193	7201	7210	7218	7226	7234	1	2	3	4	4	5	6	7	8
53	7243	7251	7259	7268	7276	7284	7292	7300	7308	7316	1	1	2	3	4	5	5	6	7
54	7324	7332	7340	7348	7356	7364	7372	7380	7388	7396	1	2	2	3	4	5	5	6	7
55	7403	7411	7419	7427	7435	7443	7450	7458	7466	7474	1	2	3	3	4	5	6	7	7
56	7482	7490	7497	7505	7513	7520	7528	7536	7543	7551	1	2	2	3	4	5	5	6	7

SOURCE: Hald, A., *Statistical Tables and Formulas*, New York, John Wiley and Sons, and G.E.C. Gads Forlag, 1952, by permission of the publishers.

TABLE C (Continued)

Logarithms

	0	1	2	3	4	5	6	7	8	9	1	2	3	4	5	6	7	8	9
57	7559	7566	7574	7582	7589	7597	7604	7612	7619	7627	1	1	2	3	4	4	5	6	7
58	7634	7642	7649	7657	7664	7671	7679	7686	7694	7701	1	2	2	3	4	5	5	6	7
59	7708	7716	7723	7730	7738	7745	7752	7760	7767	7774	1	2	2	3	4	5	5	6	7
60	7782	7789	7796	7803	7810	7818	7825	7832	7839	7846	1	1	2	3	4	4	5	6	6
61	7854	7861	7868	7875	7882	7889	7896	7903	7910	7917	0	1	2	3	4	4	5	6	6
62	7924	7931	7938	7945	7952	7959	7966	7973	7980	7987	0	1	2	3	3	4	5	5	6
63	7993	8000	8007	8014	8021	8028	8034	8041	8048	8055	1	2	2	3	4	4	5	6	6
64	8062	8069	8076	8082	8089	8096	8103	8109	8116	8123	0	1	2	3	3	4	5	5	6
65	8129	8136	8142	8149	8156	8162	8169	8176	8182	8189	1	1	2	3	3	4	5	5	6
66	8195	8202	8208	8215	8221	8228	8234	8241	8247	8254	1	1	2	3	4	4	5	6	6
67	8261	8267	8274	8280	8287	8293	8300	8306	8312	8319	1	1	2	3	3	4	4	5	6
68	8325	8331	8338	8344	8350	8357	8363	8369	8376	8382	1	1	2	3	3	4	4	5	6
69	8389	8395	8401	8408	8414	8420	8426	8433	8439	8445	0	1	2	2	3	4	4	5	5
70	8451	8457	8463	8469	8476	8482	8488	8494	8500	8506	1	1	2	2	3	4	4	5	6
71	8513	8519	8525	8531	8537	8543	8549	8555	8561	8567	1	1	2	2	3	4	4	5	5
72	8573	8579	8585	8591	8597	8603	8609	8615	8621	8627	1	2	2	3	3	4	5	5	6
73	8633	8639	8645	8651	8657	8663	8669	8675	8681	8686	1	1	2	2	3	4	4	5	5
74	8692	8698	8704	8710	8716	8721	8727	8733	8739	8745	1	1	2	2	3	4	4	5	5
75	8751	8757	8763	8768	8774	8780	8786	8791	8797	8803	0	1	1	2	2	3	4	4	5
76	8808	8814	8819	8825	8831	8836	8842	8848	8853	8859	1	1	2	3	3	4	4	5	5

77	8865	8871	8876	8882	8888	8893	8899	8904	8910	8916	0	1	1	2	3	3	4	4	5
78	8921	8927	8932	8938	8943	8949	8954	8960	8965	8971	0	1	2	2	3	3	4	4	5
79	8976	8982	8987	8993	8998	9004	9009	9015	9020	9025	1	1	2	2	3	3	4	4	5
80	9031	9036	9042	9047	9052	9058	9063	9069	9074	9079	1	1	2	2	3	3	4	4	5
81	9085	9090	9095	9101	9106	9111	9117	9122	9127	9133	1	1	2	2	3	3	4	4	5
82	9138	9143	9149	9154	9159	9164	9170	9175	9180	9185	1	1	2	2	3	3	4	4	5
83	9191	9196	9201	9206	9212	9217	9222	9227	9232	9237	1	1	2	2	3	3	4	4	5
84	9243	9248	9253	9259	9264	9269	9274	9279	9284	9289	0	1	1	2	2	3	3	4	4
85	9294	9300	9305	9310	9315	9320	9325	9330	9335	9340	0	1	1	2	2	3	3	4	4
86	9345	9350	9355	9360	9365	9370	9375	9380	9385	9390	1	1	2	2	3	3	4	4	5
87	9395	9400	9405	9410	9415	9420	9425	9430	9435	9440	1	1	2	2	3	3	4	4	5
88	9445	9450	9455	9460	9465	9470	9475	9479	9484	9489	0	1	1	2	2	3	3	4	4
89	9494	9499	9504	9509	9514	9518	9523	9528	9533	9538	0	1	1	2	2	3	3	4	4
90	9543	9547	9552	9557	9562	9567	9571	9576	9581	9586	0	1	1	2	2	3	3	4	4
91	9590	9595	9600	9604	9609	9614	9619	9623	9628	9633	1	1	2	2	3	3	4	4	5
92	9638	9643	9647	9652	9657	9662	9666	9671	9676	9680	0	1	1	2	2	3	3	4	4
93	9685	9690	9694	9699	9704	9708	9713	9717	9722	9727	0	1	1	2	2	3	3	4	4
94	9731	9736	9741	9745	9750	9754	9759	9764	9768	9773	0	1	1	2	2	3	3	4	4
95	9777	9782	9786	9791	9796	9800	9805	9809	9814	9818	0	1	1	2	2	3	3	4	4
96	9823	9827	9832	9836	9841	9845	9850	9854	9859	9863	0	1	1	2	2	3	3	4	4
97	9868	9872	9877	9881	9886	9890	9895	9899	9904	9908	0	1	1	2	2	3	3	3	4
98	9912	9917	9921	9926	9930	9934	9939	9943	9948	9952	0	1	1	2	2	3	3	3	4
99	9956	9960	9965	9969	9974	9978	9982	9987	9991	9995	1	1	2	2	3	3	4	4	4

TABLE D

The Cumulative Normal Distribution Function

	.00	.01	.02	.03	.04	.05	.06	.07	.08	.09
−4.9	$.0^6 4792$	$.0^6 4554$	$.0^6 4327$	$.0^6 4112$	$.0^6 3906$	$.0^6 3711$	$.0^6 3525$	$.0^6 3348$	$.0^6 3179$	$.0^6 3019$
−4.8	$.0^6 7933$	$.0^6 7547$	$.0^6 7178$	$.0^6 6827$	$.0^6 6492$	$.0^6 6173$	$.0^6 5869$	$.0^6 5580$	$.0^6 5304$	$.0^6 5042$
−4.7	$.0^5 1301$	$.0^5 1239$	$.0^5 1179$	$.0^5 1123$	$.0^5 1069$	$.0^5 1017$	$.0^6 9680$	$.0^6 9211$	$.0^6 8765$	$.0^6 8339$
−4.6	$.0^5 2112$	$.0^5 2013$	$.0^5 1919$	$.0^5 1828$	$.0^5 1742$	$.0^5 1660$	$.0^5 1581$	$.0^5 1506$	$.0^5 1434$	$.0^5 1366$
−4.5	$.0^5 3398$	$.0^5 3241$	$.0^5 3092$	$.0^5 2949$	$.0^5 2883$	$.0^5 2682$	$.0^5 2558$	$.0^5 2439$	$.0^5 2325$	$.0^5 2216$
−4.4	$.0^5 5413$	$.0^5 5169$	$.0^5 4935$	$.0^5 4712$	$.0^5 4498$	$.0^5 4294$	$.0^5 4098$	$.0^5 3911$	$.0^5 3732$	$.0^5 3561$
−4.3	$.0^5 8540$	$.0^5 8163$	$.0^5 7801$	$.0^5 7455$	$.0^5 7124$	$.0^5 6807$	$.0^5 6503$	$.0^5 6212$	$.0^5 5934$	$.0^5 5668$
−4.2	$.0^4 1335$	$.0^4 1277$	$.0^4 1222$	$.0^4 1168$	$.0^4 1118$	$.0^4 1069$	$.0^4 1022$	$.0^5 9774$	$.0^5 9345$	$.0^5 8934$
−4.1	$.0^4 2066$	$.0^4 1978$	$.0^4 1891$	$.0^4 1814$	$.0^4 1737$	$.0^4 1662$	$.0^4 1591$	$.0^4 1523$	$.0^4 1458$	$.0^4 1395$
−4.0	$.0^4 3167$	$.0^4 3036$	$.0^4 2910$	$.0^4 2789$	$.0^4 2673$	$.0^4 2561$	$.0^4 2454$	$.0^4 2351$	$.0^4 2252$	$.0^4 2157$
−3.9	$.0^4 4810$	$.0^4 4615$	$.0^4 4427$	$.0^4 4247$	$.0^4 4074$	$.0^4 3908$	$.0^4 3747$	$.0^4 3594$	$.0^4 3446$	$.0^4 3304$
−3.8	$.0^4 7235$	$.0^4 6948$	$.0^4 6673$	$.0^4 6407$	$.0^4 6152$	$.0^4 5906$	$.0^4 5669$	$.0^4 5442$	$.0^4 5223$	$.0^4 5012$
−3.7	$.0^3 1078$	$.0^3 1036$	$.0^4 9961$	$.0^4 9574$	$.0^4 9201$	$.0^4 8842$	$.0^4 8496$	$.0^4 8162$	$.0^4 7841$	$.0^4 7532$
−3.6	$.0^3 1591$	$.0^3 1531$	$.0^3 1473$	$.0^3 1417$	$.0^3 1363$	$.0^3 1311$	$.0^3 1261$	$.0^3 1213$	$.0^3 1166$	$.0^3 1121$
−3.5	$.0^3 2326$	$.0^3 2241$	$.0^3 2158$	$.0^3 2078$	$.0^3 2001$	$.0^3 1926$	$.0^3 1854$	$.0^3 1785$	$.0^3 1718$	$.0^3 1653$
−3.4	$.0^3 3369$	$.0^3 3248$	$.0^3 3131$	$.0^3 3018$	$.0^3 2909$	$.0^3 2803$	$.0^3 2701$	$.0^3 2602$	$.0^3 2507$	$.0^3 2415$
−3.3	$.0^3 4834$	$.0^3 4665$	$.0^3 4501$	$.0^3 4342$	$.0^3 4189$	$.0^3 4041$	$.0^3 3897$	$.0^3 3758$	$.0^3 3624$	$.0^3 3495$
−3.2	$.0^3 6871$	$.0^3 6637$	$.0^3 6410$	$.0^3 6190$	$.0^3 5976$	$.0^3 5770$	$.0^3 5571$	$.0^3 5377$	$.0^3 5190$	$.0^3 5000$
−3.1	$.0^3 9676$	$.0^3 9354$	$.0^3 9043$	$.0^3 8740$	$.0^3 8447$	$.0^3 8164$	$.0^3 7888$	$.0^3 7622$	$.0^3 7364$	$.0^3 7114$
−3.0	$.0^2 1350$	$.0^2 1306$	$.0^2 1264$	$.0^2 1223$	$.0^2 1183$	$.0^2 1144$	$.0^2 1107$	$.0^2 1070$	$.0^2 1035$	$.0^2 1001$
−2.9	$.0^2 1866$	$.0^2 1807$	$.0^2 1750$	$.0^2 1695$	$.0^2 1641$	$.0^2 1589$	$.0^2 1538$	$.0^2 1489$	$.0^2 1441$	$.0^2 1395$
−2.8	$.0^2 2555$	$.0^2 2477$	$.0^2 2401$	$.0^2 2327$	$.0^2 2256$	$.0^2 2186$	$.0^2 2118$	$.0^2 2052$	$.0^2 1988$	$.0^2 1926$
−2.7	$.0^2 3467$	$.0^2 3364$	$.0^2 3264$	$.0^2 3167$	$.0^2 3167$	$.0^2 3072$	$.0^2 2890$	$.0^2 2803$	$.0^2 2718$	$.0^2 2635$
−2.6	$.0^2 4661$	$.0^2 4527$	$.0^2 4396$	$.0^2 4269$	$.0^2 4145$	$.0^2 4025$	$.0^2 3907$	$.0^2 3793$	$.0^2 3681$	$.0^2 3573$
−2.5	$.0^2 6210$	$.0^2 6037$	$.0^2 5868$	$.0^2 5703$	$.0^2 5543$	$.0^2 5386$	$.0^2 5234$	$.0^2 5085$	$.0^2 4940$	$.0^2 4799$

z	.00	.01	.02	.03	.04	.05	.06	.07	.08	.09
−2.4	$.0^2 8198$	$.0^2 7976$	$.0^2 7760$	$.0^2 7549$	$.0^2 7344$	$.0^2 7143$	$.0^2 6947$	$.0^2 6756$	$.0^2 6569$	$.0^2 6387$
−2.3	.01072	.01044	.01017	$.0^2 9903$	$.0^2 9642$	$.0^2 9387$	$.0^2 9137$	$.0^2 8894$	$.0^2 8656$	$.0^2 8424$
−2.2	.01390	.01355	.01321	.01287	.01255	.01222	.01191	.01160	.01130	.01101
−2.1	.01786	.01743	.01700	.01659	.01618	.01578	.01539	.01500	.01463	.01426
−2.0	.02275	.02222	.02169	.02118	.02068	.02018	.01970	.01923	.01876	.01831
−1.9	.02872	.02867	.02743	.02680	.02619	.02559	.02500	.02442	.02385	.02330
−1.8	.03593	.03515	.03438	.03362	.03288	.03216	.03144	.03074	.03005	.02938
−1.7	.04457	.04363	.04272	.04182	.04093	.04006	.03920	.03836	.03754	.03673
−1.6	.05480	.05370	.05262	.05155	.05050	.04947	.04846	.04647	.04648	.04551
−1.5	.06681	.06552	.06426	.06301	.06178	.06057	.05938	.05821	.05705	.05592
−1.4	.08076	.07927	.07780	.07636	.07493	.07353	.07215	.07078	.06944	.06811
−1.3	.09680	.09510	.09342	.09176	.09012	.08851	.08691	.08534	.08379	.08226
−1.2	.1151	.1131	.1112	.1093	.1075	.1056	.1038	.1020	.1003	.09853
−1.1	.1357	.1335	.1314	.1292	.1271	.1251	.1230	.1210	.1190	.1170
−1.0	.1587	.1562	.1539	.1515	.1492	.1469	.1446	.1423	.1401	.1379
−.9	.1841	.1814	.1788	.1762	.1736	.1711	.1685	.1660	.1635	.1611
−.8	.2119	.2090	.2061	.2033	.2005	.1977	.1949	.1922	.1894	.1867
−.7	.2420	.2389	.2358	.2327	.2297	.2266	.2236	.2206	.2177	.2148
−.6	.2743	.2709	.2676	.2643	.2611	.2578	.2546	.2514	.2483	.2451
−.5	.3085	.3050	.3015	.2981	.2946	.2912	.2877	.2843	.2810	.2776
−.4	.3446	.3409	.3372	.3336	.3300	.3264	.3228	.3192	.3156	.3121
−.3	.3821	.3783	.3745	.3707	.3669	.3632	.3594	.3557	.3520	.3483
−.2	.4207	.4168	.4129	.4090	.4052	.4013	.3974	.3936	.3897	.3859
−.1	.4602	.4562	.4522	.4483	.4443	.4404	.4364	.4325	.4286	.4247
−.0	.5000	.4960	.4920	.4880	.4840	.4801	.4761	.4721	.4681	.4641

SOURCE: Hald, A., *Statistical Tables and Formulas*, New York, John Wiley and Sons, 1952, by permission of the publisher.

TABLE D (Continued)

The Cumulative Normal Distribution Function

	.00	.01	.02	.03	.04	.05	.06	.07	.08	.09
.0	.5000	.5040	.5080	.5120	.5160	.5199	.5239	.5279	.5319	.5359
.1	.5398	.5438	.5478	.5517	.5557	.5596	.5636	.5675	.5714	.5753
.2	.5793	.5832	.5871	.5910	.5948	.5987	.6026	.6064	.6103	.6141
.3	.6179	.6217	.6255	.6293	.6331	.6368	.6406	.6443	.6480	.6517
.4	.6554	.6591	.6628	.6664	.6700	.6736	.6772	.6808	.6844	.6879
.5	.6915	.6950	.6985	.7019	.7054	.7088	.7123	.7157	.7190	.7224
.6	.7257	.7291	.7324	.7357	.7389	.7422	.7454	.7486	.7517	.7549
.7	.7580	.7611	.7642	.7673	.7703	.7734	.7764	.7794	.7823	.7852
.8	.7881	.7910	.7939	.7967	.7995	.8023	.8051	.8078	.8106	.8133
.9	.8159	.8186	.8212	.8238	.8264	.8289	.8315	.8340	.8365	.8389
1.0	.8413	.8438	.8461	.8485	.8508	.8531	.8554	.8577	.8599	.8621
1.1	.8643	.8665	.8686	.8708	.8729	.8749	.8770	.8790	.8810	.8830
1.2	.8849	.8869	.8888	.8907	.8925	.8944	.8962	.8980	.8997	.90147
1.3	.90320	.90490	.90658	.90824	.90988	.91149	.91309	.91466	.91621	.91774
1.4	.91924	.92073	.92220	.92364	.92507	.92647	.92785	.92922	.93056	.93189
1.5	.93319	.93448	.93574	.93699	.93822	.93943	.94062	.94179	.94295	.94408
1.6	.94520	.94630	.94738	.94845	.94950	.95053	.95154	.95252	.95352	.95449
1.7	.95543	.95637	.95728	.95818	.95907	.95994	.96080	.96164	.96246	.96327
1.8	.96407	.96485	.96562	.96638	.96712	.96784	.96856	.96926	.96995	.97062
1.9	.97128	.97193	.97257	.97320	.97381	.97441	.97500	.97558	.97615	.97670
2.0	.97725	.97778	.97831	.97882	.97932	.97982	.98030	.98077	.98124	.98169
2.1	.98214	.98257	.98300	.98341	.98382	.98422	.98461	.98500	.98537	.98574
2.2	.98610	.98645	.98679	.98713	.98745	.98778	.98809	.98840	.98870	.98899
2.3	.98928	.98956	.98983	$.9^{2}0097$	$.9^{2}0358$	$.9^{2}0613$	$.9^{2}0863$	$.9^{2}1106$	$.9^{2}1344$	$.9^{2}1573$
2.4	$.9^{2}1802$	$.9^{2}2024$	$.9^{2}2240$	$.9^{2}2451$	$.9^{2}2656$	$.9^{2}2857$	$.9^{2}3053$	$.9^{2}3244$	$.9^{2}3431$	$.9^{2}3613$

x	.00	.01	.02	.03	.04	.05	.06	.07	.08	.09
2.5	$.9^{2}3790$	$.9^{2}3963$	$.9^{2}4132$	$.9^{2}4297$	$.9^{2}4457$	$.9^{2}4614$	$.9^{2}4766$	$.9^{2}4915$	$.9^{2}5060$	$.9^{2}5201$
2.6	$.9^{2}5339$	$.9^{2}5473$	$.9^{2}5604$	$.9^{2}5731$	$.9^{2}5855$	$.9^{2}5975$	$.9^{2}6093$	$.9^{2}6207$	$.9^{2}6319$	$.9^{2}6427$
2.7	$.9^{2}6533$	$.9^{2}6636$	$.9^{2}6736$	$.9^{2}6833$	$.9^{2}6928$	$.9^{2}7020$	$.9^{2}7110$	$.9^{2}7197$	$.9^{2}7282$	$.9^{2}7365$
2.8	$.9^{2}7445$	$.9^{2}7523$	$.9^{2}7599$	$.9^{2}7673$	$.9^{2}7744$	$.9^{2}7814$	$.9^{2}7882$	$.9^{2}7948$	$.9^{2}8012$	$.9^{2}8074$
2.9	$.9^{2}8134$	$.9^{2}8193$	$.9^{2}8250$	$.9^{2}8305$	$.9^{2}8359$	$.9^{2}8411$	$.9^{2}8462$	$.9^{2}8511$	$.9^{2}8559$	$.9^{2}8605$
3.0	$.9^{2}8650$	$.9^{2}8694$	$.9^{2}8736$	$.9^{2}8777$	$.9^{2}8817$	$.9^{2}8856$	$.9^{2}8893$	$.9^{2}8930$	$.9^{2}8965$	$.9^{2}8999$
3.1	$.9^{3}0324$	$.9^{3}0646$	$.9^{3}0957$	$.9^{3}1260$	$.9^{3}1553$	$.9^{3}1836$	$.9^{3}2112$	$.9^{3}2378$	$.9^{3}2636$	$.9^{3}2886$
3.2	$.9^{3}3129$	$.9^{3}3363$	$.9^{3}3590$	$.9^{3}3810$	$.9^{3}4020$	$.9^{3}4230$	$.9^{3}4429$	$.9^{3}4623$	$.9^{3}4810$	$.9^{3}4991$
3.3	$.9^{3}5166$	$.9^{3}5335$	$.9^{3}5499$	$.9^{3}5658$	$.9^{3}5811$	$.9^{3}5959$	$.9^{3}6103$	$.9^{3}6242$	$.9^{3}6376$	$.9^{3}6505$
3.4	$.9^{3}6631$	$.9^{3}6752$	$.9^{3}6869$	$.9^{3}6982$	$.9^{3}7091$	$.9^{3}7197$	$.9^{3}7299$	$.9^{3}7398$	$.9^{3}7493$	$.9^{3}7585$
3.5	$.9^{3}7674$	$.9^{3}7759$	$.9^{3}7842$	$.9^{3}7922$	$.9^{3}7999$	$.9^{3}8074$	$.9^{3}8146$	$.9^{3}8215$	$.9^{3}8282$	$.9^{3}8347$
3.6	$.9^{3}8409$	$.9^{3}8469$	$.9^{3}8527$	$.9^{3}8583$	$.9^{3}8637$	$.9^{3}8689$	$.9^{3}8739$	$.9^{3}8787$	$.9^{3}8834$	$.9^{3}8879$
3.7	$.9^{3}8922$	$.9^{3}8964$	$.9^{4}0039$	$.9^{4}0426$	$.9^{4}0799$	$.9^{4}1158$	$.9^{4}1504$	$.9^{4}1838$	$.9^{4}2159$	$.9^{4}2468$
3.8	$.9^{4}2765$	$.9^{4}3052$	$.9^{4}3327$	$.9^{4}3593$	$.9^{4}3848$	$.9^{4}4094$	$.9^{4}4331$	$.9^{4}4558$	$.9^{4}4777$	$.9^{4}4988$
3.9	$.9^{4}5190$	$.9^{4}5385$	$.9^{4}5573$	$.9^{4}5753$	$.9^{4}5926$	$.9^{4}6092$	$.9^{4}6253$	$.9^{4}6406$	$.9^{4}6554$	$.9^{4}6696$
4.0	$.9^{4}6833$	$.9^{4}6964$	$.9^{4}7090$	$.9^{4}7211$	$.9^{4}7327$	$.9^{4}7439$	$.9^{4}7546$	$.9^{4}7649$	$.9^{4}7748$	$.9^{4}7843$
4.1	$.9^{4}7934$	$.9^{4}8022$	$.9^{4}8106$	$.9^{4}8186$	$.9^{4}8263$	$.9^{4}8338$	$.9^{4}8409$	$.9^{4}8477$	$.9^{4}8542$	$.9^{4}8605$
4.2	$.9^{4}8665$	$.9^{4}8723$	$.9^{4}8778$	$.9^{4}8832$	$.9^{4}8882$	$.9^{4}8931$	$.9^{4}8978$	$.9^{5}0226$	$.9^{5}0655$	$.9^{5}1066$
4.3	$.9^{5}1460$	$.9^{5}1837$	$.9^{5}2199$	$.9^{5}2545$	$.9^{5}2876$	$.9^{5}3193$	$.9^{5}3497$	$.9^{5}3788$	$.9^{5}4066$	$.9^{5}4332$
4.4	$.9^{5}4587$	$.9^{5}4831$	$.9^{5}5065$	$.9^{5}5288$	$.9^{5}5502$	$.9^{5}5706$	$.9^{5}5902$	$.9^{5}6089$	$.9^{5}6268$	$.9^{5}6439$
4.5	$.9^{5}6602$	$.9^{5}6759$	$.9^{5}6908$	$.9^{5}7051$	$.9^{5}7187$	$.9^{5}7317$	$.9^{5}7442$	$.9^{5}7561$	$.9^{5}7675$	$.9^{5}7784$
4.6	$.9^{5}7888$	$.9^{5}7987$	$.9^{5}8081$	$.9^{5}8172$	$.9^{5}8258$	$.9^{5}8340$	$.9^{5}8419$	$.9^{5}8494$	$.9^{5}8566$	$.9^{5}8634$
4.7	$.9^{5}8699$	$.9^{5}8761$	$.9^{5}8821$	$.9^{5}8877$	$.9^{5}8931$	$.9^{5}8983$	$.9^{6}0320$	$.9^{6}0789$	$.9^{6}1235$	$.9^{6}1661$
4.8	$.9^{6}2067$	$.9^{6}2453$	$.9^{6}2822$	$.9^{6}3173$	$.9^{6}3508$	$.9^{6}3827$	$.9^{6}4131$	$.9^{6}4420$	$.9^{6}4696$	$.9^{6}4958$
4.9	$.9^{6}5208$	$.9^{6}5446$	$.9^{6}5673$	$.9^{6}5889$	$.9^{6}6094$	$.9^{6}6289$	$.9^{6}6475$	$.9^{6}6652$	$.9^{6}6821$	$.9^{6}6981$

TABLE E

Fractiles of the Chi-Squared Distribution

F	.01	.02	.05	.10	.20	.30	.50	.70	.80	.90	.95	.98	.99	.999
							PROBABILITY							
1	$.0^3157$	$.0^3628$	.00393	.0158	.0642	.148	.455	1.074	1.642	2.706	3.841	5.412	6.635	10.827
2	.0201	.0404	.103	.211	.446	.713	1.386	2.408	3.219	4.605	5.991	7.824	9.210	13.815
3	.115	.185	.352	.584	1.005	1.424	2.366	3.665	4.642	6.251	7.815	9.837	11.345	16.268
4	.297	.429	.711	1.064	1.649	2.195	3.357	4.878	5.989	7.779	9.488	11.668	13.277	18.465
5	.554	.752	1.145	1.610	2.343	3.000	4.351	6.064	7.289	9.236	11.070	13.388	15.086	20.517
6	.872	1.134	1.635	2.204	3.070	3.828	5.348	7.231	8.558	10.645	12.592	15.033	16.812	22.457
7	1.239	1.564	2.167	2.833	3.822	4.671	6.346	8.383	9.803	12.017	14.067	16.622	18.475	24.322
8	1.646	2.032	2.733	3.490	4.594	5.527	7.344	9.524	11.030	13.362	15.507	18.168	20.090	26.125
9	2.088	2.532	3.325	4.168	5.380	6.393	8.343	10.656	12.242	14.648	16.919	19.679	21.666	27.877
10	2.558	3.059	3.940	4.865	6.179	7.267	9.342	11.781	13.442	15.987	18.307	21.161	23.209	29.588
11	3.053	3.609	4.575	5.578	6.989	8.148	10.341	12.899	14.631	17.275	19.675	22.618	24.725	31.264
12	3.571	4.178	5.226	6.304	7.807	9.034	11.340	14.011	15.812	18.549	21.026	24.054	26.217	32.909
13	4.107	4.765	5.892	7.042	8.634	9.926	12.340	15.119	16.985	19.812	22.362	25.472	27.688	34.528
14	4.660	5.368	6.571	7.790	9.467	10.821	13.339	16.222	18.151	21.064	23.685	26.873	29.141	36.123
15	5.229	5.985	7.261	8.547	10.307	11.721	14.339	17.322	19.311	22.307	24.996	28.259	30.578	37.697
16	5.812	6.614	7.962	9.312	11.152	12.624	15.338	18.418	20.465	23.542	26.296	29.633	32.000	39.252
17	6.408	7.255	8.672	10.085	12.002	13.531	16.338	19.511	21.615	24.769	27.587	30.995	33.409	40.790
18	7.015	7.906	9.390	10.865	12.857	14.440	17.338	20.601	22.760	25.989	28.869	32.346	34.805	42.312
19	7.633	8.567	10.117	11.651	13.716	15.352	18.338	21.689	23.900	27.204	30.144	33.687	36.191	43.820
20	8.260	9.237	10.851	12.443	14.578	16.266	19.337	22.775	25.038	28.412	31.410	35.020	37.566	45.315
21	8.897	9.915	11.591	13.240	15.445	17.182	20.337	23.858	26.171	29.615	32.671	36.343	38.932	46.797
22	9.542	10.600	12.338	14.041	16.314	18.101	21.337	24.939	27.301	30.813	33.924	37.659	40.289	48.268
23	10.196	11.293	13.091	14.848	17.187	19.021	22.337	26.018	28.429	32.007	35.172	38.968	41.638	49.728
24	10.856	11.992	13.848	15.659	18.062	19.943	23.337	27.096	29.553	33.196	36.415	40.270	42.980	51.179
25	11.524	12.697	14.611	16.473	18.940	20.867	24.337	28.172	30.675	34.382	37.652	41.566	44.314	52.620
26	12.198	13.409	15.379	17.292	19.820	21.792	25.336	29.246	31.759	35.563	38.885	42.856	45.642	54.052
27	12.879	14.125	16.151	18.114	20.703	22.719	26.336	30.319	32.912	36.741	40.113	44.140	46.963	55.476
28	13.565	14.847	16.928	18.939	21.588	23.647	27.336	31.391	34.027	37.916	41.337	45.419	48.278	56.893
29	14.256	15.574	17.708	19.768	22.475	24.577	28.336	32.461	35.139	39.087	42.557	46.693	49.588	58.302
30	14.953	16.306	18.493	20.599	23.364	25.508	29.336	33.530	36.250	40.256	43.773	47.962	50.892	59.703

Source: Fisher, R. A., and Yates, F., *Statistical Tables for Biological, Agricultural and Medical Research*, Table IV, published by Oliver and Boyd, Edinburgh. By permission of the authors and publishers.

TABLE F

Percentage Points,

df	.0005	.005	.01	P .025	.05	.10	.25
1	−636.619	−63.657	−31.821	−12.706	−6.314	−3.078	−1.000
2	−31.598	−9.925	−6.965	−4.303	−2.920	−1.886	−.816
3	−12.941	−5.841	−4.541	−3.182	−2.353	−1.638	−.765
4	−8.610	−4.604	−3.747	−2.776	−2.132	−1.533	−.741
5	−6.859	−4.032	−3.365	−2.571	−2.015	−1.476	−.727
6	−5.959	−3.707	−3.143	−2.447	−1.943	−1.440	−.718
7	−5.405	−3.499	−2.998	−2.365	−1.895	−1.415	−.711
8	−5.041	−3.355	−2.896	−2.306	−1.860	−1.397	−.706
9	−4.781	−3.250	−2.821	−2.262	−1.833	−1.383	−.703
10	−4.587	−3.169	−2.764	−2.228	−1.812	−1.372	−.700
11	−4.437	−3.106	−2.718	−2.201	−1.796	−1.363	−.697
12	−4.318	−3.055	−2.681	−2.179	−1.782	−1.356	−.695
13	−4.221	−3.012	−2.650	−2.160	−1.771	−1.350	−.694
14	−4.140	−2.977	−2.624	−2.145	−1.761	−1.345	−.692
15	−4.073	−2.947	−2.602	−2.131	−1.753	−1.341	−.691
16	−4.015	−2.921	−2.583	−2.120	−1.746	−1.337	−.690
17	−3.965	−2.898	−2.567	−2.110	−1.740	−1.333	−.689
18	−3.922	−2.878	−2.552	−2.101	−1.734	−1.330	−.688
19	−3.883	−2.861	−2.539	−2.093	−1.729	−1.328	−.688
20	−3.850	−2.845	−2.528	−2.086	−1.725	−1.325	−.687
21	−3.819	−2.831	−2.518	−2.080	−1.721	−1.323	−.686
22	−3.792	−2.819	−2.508	−2.074	−1.717	−1.321	−.686
23	−3.767	−2.807	−2.500	−2.069	−1.714	−1.319	−.685
24	−3.745	−2.797	−2.492	−2.064	−1.711	−1.318	−.685
25	−3.725	−2.787	−2.485	−2.060	−1.708	−1.316	−.684
26	−3.707	−2.779	−2.479	−2.056	−1.706	−1.315	−.684
27	−3.690	−2.771	−2.473	−2.052	−1.703	−1.314	−.684
28	−3.674	−2.763	−2.467	−2.048	−1.701	−1.313	−.683
29	−3.659	−2.756	−2.462	−2.045	−1.699	−1.311	−.683
30	−3.646	−2.750	−2.457	−2.042	−1.697	−1.310	−.683
40	−3.551	−2.704	−2.423	−2.021	−1.684	−1.303	−.681
60	−3.460	−2.660	−2.390	−2.000	−1.671	−1.296	−.679
120	−3.373	−2.617	−2.358	−1.980	−1.658	−1.289	−.677
%	−3.291	−2.576	−2.326	−1.960	−1.645	−1.282	−.674

Source: Fisher, R. A., and Yates, F., Table III (abridged), *Statistical Tables for Biological,* of the authors and publishers.

Note: Numbers at the head of each column indicate the percentage of random variates from a

Student's *t*-Distribution

				P				
.40	.60	.75	.90	.95	.975	.99	.995	.9995
-.325	.325	1.000	3.078	6.314	12.706	31.821	63.657	636.619
-.289	.289	.816	1.886	2.920	4.303	6.965	9.925	31.598
-.277	.277	.765	1.638	2.353	3.182	4.541	5.841	12.941
-.271	.271	.741	1.533	2.132	2.776	3.747	4.604	8.610
-.267	.267	.727	1.476	2.015	2.571	3.365	4.032	6.859
-.265	.265	.718	1.440	1.943	2.447	3.143	3.707	5.959
-.263	.263	.711	1.415	1.895	2.365	2.998	3.499	5.405
-.262	.262	.706	1.397	1.860	2.306	2.896	3.355	5.041
-.261	.261	.703	1.383	1.833	2.262	2.821	3.250	4.781
-.260	.260	.700	1.372	1.812	2.228	2.764	3.169	4.587
-.260	.260	.697	1.363	1.796	2.201	2.718	3.106	4.437
-.259	.259	.695	1.356	1.782	2.179	2.681	3.055	4.318
-.259	.259	.694	1.350	1.771	2.160	2.650	3.012	4.221
-.258	.258	.692	1.345	1.761	2.145	2.624	2.977	4.140
-.258	.258	.691	1.341	1.753	2.131	2.602	2.947	4.073
-.258	.258	.690	1.337	1.746	2.120	2.583	2.921	4.015
-.257	.257	.689	1.333	1.740	2.110	2.567	2.898	3.965
-.257	.257	.688	1.330	1.734	2.101	2.552	2.878	3.922
-.257	.257	.688	1.328	1.729	2.093	2.539	2.861	3.883
-.257	.257	.687	1.325	1.725	2.086	2.528	2.845	3.850
-.257	.257	.686	1.323	1.721	2.080	2.518	2.831	3.819
-.256	.256	.686	1.321	1.717	2.074	2.508	2.819	3.792
-.256	.256	.685	1.319	1.714	2.069	2.500	2.807	3.767
-.256	.256	.685	1.318	1.711	2.064	2.492	2.797	3.745
-.256	.256	.684	1.316	1.708	2.060	2.485	2.787	3.725
-.256	.256	.684	1.315	1.706	2.056	2.479	2.779	3.707
-.256	.256	.684	1.314	1.703	2.052	2.473	2.771	3.690
-.256	.256	.683	1.313	1.701	2.048	2.467	2.763	3.674
-.256	.256	.683	1.311	1.699	2.045	2.462	2.756	3.659
-.256	.256	.683	1.310	1.697	2.042	2.457	2.750	3.646
-.255	.255	.681	1.303	1.684	2.021	2.423	2.704	3.551
-.254	.254	.679	1.296	1.671	2.000	2.390	2.660	3.460
-.254	.254	.677	1.289	1.658	1.980	2.358	2.617	3.373
-.253	.253	.674	1.282	1.645	1.960	2.326	2.576	3.291

Agricultural and Medical Research, published by Oliver and Boyd, Edinburgh. By permission

population having Student's *t*-distribution, which will be less than the value in the table.

TABLE G

Confidence Intervals for ρ, Given r and the Number of Observations

r	NUMBER OF OBSERVATIONS								
	5	8	10	12	15	20	25	50	100
	.99	.98	.98	.97	.97	.97	.97	.97	.97
.95	.37	.75	.78	.82	.85	.87	.88	.92	.93
	.99	.96	.97	.96	.96	.96	.95	.94	.93
.90	.10	.50	.60	.65	.71	.75	.77	.83	.85
	.98	.96	.96	.94	.94	.94	.92	.91	.90
.85	−.10	.34	.45	.52	.58	.65	.67	.75	.79
	.97	.95	.94	.92	.92	.91	.90	.88	.86
.80	−.23	.20	.32	.40	.47	.55	.58	.68	.72
	.96	.94	.93	.91	.90	.88	.88	.85	.83
.75	−.32	.08	.21	.30	.37	.45	.49	.60	.65
	.96	.92	.91	.89	.88	.86	.85	.82	.79
.70	−.40	−.02	.12	.20	.28	.36	.41	.53	.58
	.95	.91	.89	.87	.86	.84	.83	.78	.75
.65	−.45	−.10	.03	.12	.20	.28	.34	.47	.52
	.94	.90	.88	.86	.84	.82	.80	.75	.71
.60	−.50	−.17	−.05	.04	.12	.20	.26	.40	.46
	.94	.88	.86	.84	.82	.79	.77	.72	.67
.55	−.55	−.24	−.12	−.03	.05	.13	.20	.34	.40
	.93	.87	.84	.82	.79	.76	.74	.68	.63
.50	−.58	−.30	−.19	−.10	−.02	.07	.13	.27	.34
	.92	.85	.82	.80	.77	.73	.71	.64	.59
.45	−.62	−.35	−.25	−.16	−.08	.00	.07	.20	.28
	.91	.83	.80	.77	.74	.70	.68	.61	.55
.40	−.65	−.40	−.30	−.22	−.14	−.05	.00	.14	.22
	.89	.82	.78	.75	.72	.68	.65	.57	.51
.35	−.68	−.44	−.35	−.27	−.20	−.11	−.05	.08	.16
	.88	.80	.76	.72	.69	.65	.61	.53	.47
.30	−.70	−.48	−.39	−.32	−.25	−.16	−.10	.02	.11
	.87	.78	.74	.70	.66	.62	.58	.49	.42
.25	−.73	−.52	−.43	−.36	−.30	−.21	−.15	−.03	.05
	.86	.76	.72	.67	.63	.58	.54	.45	.38
.20	−.75	−.55	−.47	−.40	−.34	−.26	−.20	−.08	.00
	.85	.74	.68	.65	.60	.55	.51	.41	.34
.15	−.76	−.58	−.51	−.45	−.38	−.31	−.25	−.13	−.05
	.84	.72	.66	.62	.57	.51	.47	.37	.29
.10	−.77	−.62	−.54	−.48	−.42	−.35	−.30	−.18	−.10
	.83	.69	.63	.58	.53	.47	.43	.33	.25
.05	−.80	−.64	−.57	−.52	−.46	−.39	−.35	−.23	−.15
	.82	.67	.60	.55	.50	.43	.39	.28	.20
.00	−.82	−.67	−.60	−.55	−.50	−.43	−.39	−.28	−.20

Note: For negative values of r, use the corresponding positive value in the column for r, then change the sign of the upper and lower limits.

TABLE H

Testing Hypotheses about ρ

	α	
n	.05	.01
3	.997	.999
4	.950	.990
5	.878	.958
6	.811	.917
7	.754	.875
8	.707	.834
9	.666	.798
10	.632	.765
11	.602	.735
12	.576	.708
13	.553	.684
14	.532	.661
15	.514	.641
22	.360	.537
27	.323	.487
32	.296	.449
37	.275	.418
42	.257	.393
47	.243	.372
52	.231	.354
62	.211	.325
72	.195	.302
82	.183	.283
92	.173	.267
102	.164	.254

TABLE I

Ranking of Three Population Means

DEGREES OF FREEDOM (n)	PROBABILITY (P)				
	0.50	0.75	0.90	0.95	0.99
1	0.867	2.225	5.881	11.850	59.385
2	.744	1.553	2.864	4.231	9.777
3	.708	1.395	2.333	3.161	5.812
4	.691	1.325	2.121	2.767	4.595
5	.681	1.286	2.008	2.566	4.028
6	0.674	1.261	1.938	2.444	3.706
7	.670	1.243	1.891	2.363	3.499
8	.666	1.231	1.857	2.305	3.355
9	.664	1.221	1.831	2.261	3.250
10	.662	1.213	1.811	2.228	3.169
11	0.660	1.207	1.794	2.201	3.106
12	.658	1.202	1.781	2.179	3.055
13	.657	1.197	1.770	2.160	3.012
14	.656	1.193	1.760	2.145	2.977
15	.655	1.190	1.752	2.131	2.947
16	0.654	1.187	1.745	2.120	2.921
17	.654	1.185	1.739	2.110	2.898
18	.653	1.183	1.733	2.101	2.879
19	.653	1.181	1.729	2.093	2.861
20	.652	1.179	1.724	2.086	2.846
21	0.652	1.178	1.720	2.080	2.832
22	.651	1.176	1.717	2.074	2.819
23	.651	1.175	1.714	2.069	2.808
24	.651	1.174	1.711	2.064	2.797
25	.650	1.173	1.708	2.060	2.788
26	0.650	1.172	1.750	2.056	2.779
27	.650	1.171	1.703	2.052	2.771
28	.649	1.170	1.701	2.049	2.764
29	.649	1.169	1.699	2.046	2.757
30	.649	1.168	1.697	2.043	2.750
33	0.648	1.166	1.692	2.035	2.734
36	.648	1.165	1.688	2.028	2.720
39	.648	1.163	1.685	2.023	2.708
42	.647	1.162	1.682	2.018	2.698
45	.647	1.161	1.679	2.014	2.690
48	0.647	1.160	1.677	2.011	2.683
51	.646	1.159	1.675	2.008	2.676
54	.646	1.159	1.674	2.005	2.670
57	.646	1.158	1.672	2.003	2.665
60	.646	1.157	1.671	2.001	2.661
75	0.645	1.155	1.666	1.993	2.643
90	.645	1.154	1.662	1.987	2.632
105	.645	1.153	1.660	1.983	2.624
120	.644	1.152	1.658	1.980	2.618
150	0.644	1.151	1.655	1.976	2.609
300	.643	1.149	1.650	1.968	2.593
600	.643	1.148	1.648	1.964	2.584
	0.64235	1.14630	1.64457	1.95993	2.57568

Source: Dunnett, C. W., and Sobel, M., "A Bivariate Generalization of Student's t-Distribution with Tables for Certain Special Cases," *Biometrika*, (1954), Vol. 41, parts 1 and 2, pp. 153–169.

TABLE J

Part 1. Values That Exceed 95 Percent

m \ ℓ	1	2	3	4	5	6	7	8	9
1	161.4	199.5	215.7	224.6	230.2	234.0	236.8	238.9	240.5
2	18.51	19.00	19.16	19.25	19.30	19.33	19.35	19.37	19.38
3	10.13	9.55	9.28	9.12	9.01	8.94	8.89	8.85	8.81
4	7.71	6.94	6.59	6.39	6.26	6.16	6.09	6.04	6.00
5	6.61	5.79	5.41	5.19	5.05	4.95	4.88	4.82	4.77
6	5.99	5.14	4.76	4.53	4.39	4.28	4.21	4.15	4.10
7	5.59	4.74	4.35	4.12	3.97	3.87	3.79	3.73	3.68
8	5.32	4.46	4.07	3.84	3.69	3.58	3.50	3.44	3.39
9	5.12	4.26	3.86	3.63	3.48	3.37	3.29	3.23	3.18
10	4.96	4.10	3.71	3.48	3.33	3.22	3.14	3.07	3.02
11	4.84	3.98	3.59	3.36	3.20	3.09	3.01	2.95	2.90
12	4.75	3.89	3.49	3.26	3.11	3.00	2.91	2.85	2.80
13	4.67	3.81	3.41	3.18	3.03	2.92	2.83	2.77	2.71
14	4.60	3.74	3.34	3.11	2.96	2.85	2.76	2.70	2.65
15	4.54	3.68	3.29	3.06	2.90	2.79	2.71	2.64	2.59
16	4.49	3.63	3.24	3.01	2.85	2.74	2.66	2.59	2.54
17	4.45	3.59	3.20	2.96	2.81	2.70	2.61	2.55	2.49
18	4.41	3.55	3.16	2.93	2.77	2.66	2.58	2.51	2.46
19	4.38	3.52	3.13	2.90	2.74	2.63	2.54	2.48	2.42
20	4.35	3.49	3.10	2.87	2.71	2.60	2.51	2.45	2.39
21	4.32	3.47	3.07	2.84	2.68	2.57	2.49	2.42	2.37
22	4.30	3.44	3.05	2.82	2.66	2.55	2.46	2.40	2.34
23	4.28	3.42	3.03	2.80	2.64	2.53	2.44	2.37	2.32
24	4.26	3.40	3.01	2.78	2.62	2.51	2.42	2.36	2.30
25	4.24	3.39	2.99	2.76	2.60	2.49	2.40	2.34	2.28
26	4.23	3.37	2.98	2.74	2.59	2.47	2.39	2.32	2.27
27	4.21	3.35	2.96	2.73	2.57	2.46	2.37	2.31	2.25
28	4.20	3.34	2.95	2.71	2.56	2.45	2.36	2.29	2.24
29	4.18	3.33	2.93	2.70	2.55	2.43	2.35	2.28	2.22
30	4.17	3.32	2.92	2.69	2.53	2.42	2.33	2.27	2.21
40	4.08	3.23	2.84	2.61	2.45	2.34	2.25	2.18	2.12
60	4.00	3.15	2.76	2.53	2.37	2.25	2.17	2.10	2.04
120	3.92	2.07	2.68	2.45	2.29	2.17	2.09	2.02	1.96
	3.84	3.00	2.60	2.37	2.21	2.10	2.01	1.94	1.88

Source: Fisher, R. A., and Yates, F., *Statistical Tables for Biological, Agricultural and Medical* and publishers.

of Observations from an F Distribution

10	12	15	20	24	30	40	60	120
241.9	243.9	245.9	248.0	249.1	250.1	251.1	252.2	253.3	254.3
19.40	19.41	19.43	19.45	19.45	19.46	19.47	19.48	19.49	19.50
8.79	8.74	8.70	8.66	8.64	8.62	8.59	8.57	8.55	8.53
5.96	5.91	5.86	5.80	5.77	5.75	5.72	5.69	5.66	5.63
4.74	4.68	4.62	4.56	4.53	4.50	4.46	4.43	4.40	4.36
4.06	4.00	3.94	3.87	3.84	3.81	3.77	3.74	3.70	3.67
3.64	3.57	3.51	3.44	3.41	3.38	3.34	3.30	3.27	3.23
3.35	3.28	3.22	3.15	3.12	3.08	3.04	3.01	2.97	2.93
3.41	3.07	3.01	2.94	2.90	2.86	2.83	2.79	2.79	2.71
2.98	2.91	2.85	2.77	2.74	2.70	2.66	2.62	2.58	2.54
2.85	2.79	2.72	2.65	2.61	2.57	2.53	2.49	2.45	2.40
2.75	2.69	2.62	2.54	2.51	2.47	2.43	2.38	2.34	2.30
2.67	2.60	2.53	2.46	2.42	2.38	2.34	2.30	2.25	2.21
2.60	2.53	2.46	2.39	2.35	2.31	2.27	2.22	2.18	2.13
2.54	2.48	2.40	2.33	2.29	2.25	2.20	2.16	2.11	2.07
2.49	2.42	2.35	2.28	2.24	2.19	2.15	2.11	2.06	2.01
2.45	2.38	2.31	2.23	2.19	2.15	2.10	2.06	2.01	1.96
2.41	2.34	2.27	2.19	2.15	2.11	2.06	2.02	1.97	1.92
2.38	2.31	2.23	2.16	2.11	2.07	1.03	1.98	1.93	1.88
2.35	2.28	2.20	2.12	2.08	2.04	1.99	1.95	1.90	1.84
2.32	2.25	2.18	2.10	2.05	2.01	1.96	1.92	1.87	1.81
2.30	2.23	2.15	2.07	2.03	1.98	1.94	1.89	1.84	1.78
2.27	2.20	2.13	2.05	2.01	1.96	1.91	1.86	1.81	1.76
2.25	2.18	2.11	2.03	1.98	1.94	1.89	1.84	1.79	1.73
2.24	2.16	2.09	2.01	1.96	1.92	1.87	1.82	1.77	1.71
2.22	2.15	2.07	1.99	1.95	1.90	1.85	1.80	1.75	1.69
2.20	2.13	2.06	1.97	1.93	1.88	1.84	1.79	1.73	1.67
2.19	2.12	2.04	1.96	1.91	1.87	1.82	1.77	1.71	1.65
2.18	2.10	2.03	1.94	1.90	1.85	1.81	1.75	1.70	1.64
2.16	2.09	2.01	1.93	1.89	1.84	1.79	1.74	1.68	1.62
2.08	2.00	1.92	1.84	1.79	1.74	1.69	1.64	1.58	1.51
1.99	1.92	1.84	1.75	1.70	1.65	1.59	1.53	1.47	1.39
1.91	1.83	1.75	1.66	1.61	1.55	1.50	1.54	1.35	1.25
1.83	1.75	1.67	1.57	1.52	1.46	1.39	1.32	1.22	1.00

Research, Table V, published by Oliver and Boyd, Edinburgh. By permission of the authors

TABLE J (Continued)

Part 2. Values That Exceed 99% c

m \ ℓ	1	2	3	4	5	6	7	8	9
1	4052	4999.5	5403	5625	5764	5859	5928	5982	6022
2	98.50	99.00	99.17	99.25	99.30	99.33	99.36	99.37	99.3
3	34.12	30.82	29.46	28.71	28.24	27.91	27.67	27.49	27.3
4	21.20	18.00	16.69	15.98	15.52	15.21	14.98	14.80	14.6
5	16.26	13.27	12.06	11.39	10.97	10.67	10.46	10.29	10.1
6	13.75	10.92	9.78	9.15	8.75	8.47	8.26	8.10	7.9
7	12.25	9.55	8.45	7.85	7.46	7.19	6.99	6.84	6.7
8	11.26	8.65	7.59	7.01	6.63	6.37	6.18	6.03	5.9
9	10.56	8.02	6.99	6.42	6.06	5.80	5.61	5.47	5.3
10	10.04	7.56	6.55	5.99	5.64	5.39	5.20	5.06	4.9
11	9.65	7.21	6.22	5.67	5.32	5.07	4.89	4.74	4.6
12	9.33	6.93	5.95	5.41	5.06	4.82	4.64	4.50	4.3
13	9.07	6.70	5.74	5.21	4.86	4.62	4.44	4.30	4.1
14	8.86	6.51	5.56	5.04	4.69	4.46	4.28	4.14	4.0
15	8.68	6.36	5.42	4.89	4.56	4.32	4.14	4.00	3.8
16	8.53	6.23	5.29	4.77	4.44	4.20	4.03	3.89	3.7
17	8.40	6.11	5.18	4.67	4.34	4.10	3.93	3.79	3.6
18	8.20	6.01	5.09	4.58	4.25	4.01	3.84	3.71	3.6
19	8.18	5.93	5.01	4.50	4.17	3.94	3.77	3.63	3.
20	8.10	5.85	4.94	4.43	4.10	3.87	3.70	3.56	3.4
21	8.02	5.78	4.87	4.37	4.04	3.81	3.64	3.51	3.4
22	7.95	5.72	4.82	4.31	3.99	3.76	3.59	3.45	3.
23	7.88	5.66	4.76	4.26	3.94	3.71	3.54	3.41	3.
24	7.82	5.61	4.72	4.22	3.90	3.67	3.50	3.36	3.2
25	7.77	5.57	4.68	4.18	3.85	3.63	3.46	3.32	3.2
26	7.72	5.53	4.64	4.14	3.82	3.59	3.42	3.29	3.
27	7.68	5.49	4.60	4.11	3.78	3.56	3.39	3.26	3.
28	7.64	5.45	4.57	4.07	3.75	3.53	3.36	3.23	3.
29	7.60	5.42	4.54	4.04	3.73	3.50	3.33	3.20	3.6
30	7.56	5.39	4.51	4.02	3.70	3.47	3.30	3.17	3.6
40	7.31	5.18	4.31	3.83	3.51	3.29	3.12	2.99	2.
60	7.08	4.98	4.13	3.65	3.34	3.12	2.95	2.82	2.7
120	6.85	4.79	3.95	3.48	3.17	2.96	2.79	2.66	2.
	6.63	4.61	3.78	3.32	3.02	2.80	2.64	2.51	2.4

>servations from an _F_ Distribution

10	12	15	20	24	30	40	60	120	
56	6106	6157	6209	6235	6261	6287	6313	6339	6366
99.40	99.42	99.43	99.45	99.46	99.47	99.47	99.48	99.49	99.5
27.23	27.05	26.87	26.69	26.60	26.50	26.41	26.32	26.22	26.1
14.55	14.37	14.20	14.02	13.93	13.84	13.75	13.65	13.56	13.4
10.05	9.89	9.72	9.55	9.47	9.38	9.29	9.20	9.11	9.0
7.87	7.72	7.56	7.40	7.31	7.23	7.14	7.06	6.97	6.8
6.62	6.47	6.31	6.16	6.07	5.99	5.91	5.82	5.74	5.6
5.81	5.67	5.52	5.36	5.28	5.20	5.12	5.03	4.95	4.8
5.26	5.11	4.96	4.81	4.73	4.65	4.57	4.48	4.40	4.3
4.85	4.71	4.56	4.41	4.33	4.25	4.17	4.08	4.00	3.9
4.54	4.40	4.25	4.10	4.02	3.94	3.86	3.78	3.69	3.6
4.30	4.16	4.01	3.86	3.78	3.70	3.62	3.54	3.45	3.3
4.10	3.96	3.82	3.66	3.59	3.51	3.43	3.34	3.25	3.1
3.94	3.80	3.66	3.51	3.43	3.35	3.27	3.18	3.09	3.0
3.80	3.67	3.52	3.37	3.29	3.21	3.13	3.05	2.96	2.8
3.69	3.55	3.41	3.26	3.18	3.10	3.02	2.93	2.84	2.7
3.59	3.46	3.31	3.16	3.08	3.00	2.92	2.83	2.75	2.6
3.51	3.37	3.23	3.08	3.00	2.92	2.84	2.75	2.66	2.5
3.43	3.30	3.15	3.00	2.92	2.84	2.76	2.67	2.58	2.4
3.37	3.23	3.09	2.94	2.86	2.78	2.69	2.61	2.52	2.4
3.31	3.17	3.03	2.88	2.80	2.72	2.64	2.55	2.46	2.3
3.26	3.12	2.98	2.83	2.75	2.67	2.58	2.50	2.40	2.3
3.21	3.07	2.93	2.78	2.70	2.62	2.54	2.45	2.35	2.2
3.17	3.03	2.89	2.74	2.66	2.58	2.49	2.40	2.31	2.2
3.13	2.99	2.85	2.70	2.62	2.54	2.45	2.36	2.27	2.1
3.09	2.96	2.81	2.66	2.58	2.50	2.42	2.33	2.23	2.1
3.06	2.93	2.78	2.63	2.55	2.47	2.38	2.29	2.20	2.1
3.03	2.90	2.75	2.60	2.52	2.44	2.35	2.26	2.17	2.0
3.00	2.87	2.73	2.57	2.49	2.41	2.33	2.23	2.14	2.0
2.98	2.84	2.70	2.55	2.47	2.39	2.30	2.21	2.11	2.0
2.80	2.66	2.52	2.37	2.29	2.20	2.11	2.02	1.92	1.8
2.63	2.50	2.35	2.20	2.12	2.03	1.94	1.84	1.73	1.6
2.47	2.34	2.19	2.03	1.95	1.86	1.76	1.66	1.53	1.3
2.32	2.18	2.04	1.88	1.79	1.70	1.59	1.47	1.32	1.0

APPENDIX K

PRGM1

The following is a program with three options:

1. Means, variances, standard deviations for several groups
2. Correlation coefficients between several measurements
3. One-way analysis of variance for several groups, same number of measurements in each group

APPENDIX K (*Continued*)

PRGM1

```
$JOB              PRGM1,KP=29,TIME=60,PAGES=20,LINES=48
      C
      C
      C     PRGM1: PROGRAM FOR CALCULATIONS TO BE PERFORMED
      C     EITHER ON ONE MEASUREMENT MADE ON SEVERAL GROUPSOF
      C     PEOPLE, OR ON SEVERAL MEASUREMENTS MADE ON THE
      C     SAME GROUP OF PEOPLE.
      C
      C     MEANS, VARIANCES AND STANDARD DEVIATIONS ARE CALCULATED
      C     FOR EACH GROUP OR MEASUREMENT. THE FOLLOWING OPTIONS
      C     ARE AVAILABLE:
      C         1. CORRECTIONS BETWEEN THE MEASUREMENTS
      C         2. ANALISIS OF VARIANCE BETWEEN GROUPS
      C
      C     LINES PRECEDED BY THE LETTER C ARE NOT PART OF THE
      C     PROGRAM, AND ARE INTENDED TO MAKE THE PROGRAM
      C     EASIER TO USE. ALL LINES WHICH ARE PART OF THE
      C     PROGRAM ARE ASSIGNED TO A NUMBER, ON THE LEFT-HAND
      C     SIDE OF THE PAGE. YOU NEED ONLY TYPE
      C     THE NUMBERED STATEMENTS, TO GET A USABLE PROGRAM.
      C
      C     INICIAL SYSTEMS CARDS, OFTEN CALLED JOB CARDS,
      C     GO AT THE BEGINNING OF YOUR DECK. THE ONE BEGINNING
      C     $JOB IS AN EXAMPLE, FOR A WATFIV FORTRAN COMPILER,
      C     USING IBM 360/44 EQUIPTMENT. IT IS ACTUALLY THE
      C     THIRD OF THREE PRELIMINARY JOB CARDS;
      C     THE OTHER TWO WERE NOT PRINTED.
      C
1           DATA HA,HB,HC/'END','FIN','   '/
2           DIMENSION FMT(18),SUM(7),SUMPR(7,7),AVE(7),
           *SUMSQ(7),XSUMSQ(7),STDEV(7),COR(7,7),X(7),HDG(20)
3         1 READ(5,100)HDG
4           READ(5,200)K,L,M
5           READ(5,100)FMT
      C     SET ALL STORAGE LOCATIONS TO ZERO, BEFORE
      C     BEGINNING PROCESSING.
6           DO 2 IA=1,K
7           SUM(IA)=0.
8           AVE(IA)=0.
9           SUMSQ(IA)=0.
10          XSUMSQ(IA)=0.
11          STDEV(IA)=0.
12          X(IA)=0.
13          DO 2 IB=1,7
14          SUMPR(IA,IB)=0.
15        2 COR(IA,IB)=0.
16          RAWSS=0.
17          TOTAL=0.
```

APPENDIX K (*Continued*)

PRGM1

```
        C
        C
18          TOTSS=0.
19          ERRSS=0.
20          XN=0.
        C   PRINT OUT CONTROL CARDS
21          WRITE(6,1900)HDG
22          WRITE(6,2200)
23          WRITE(6,2300)K,L,M
24          WRITE(6,2400)
25          WRITE(6,2500)FMT
        C   STORE THE DATA
26          WRITE(6,2000)
27          WRITE(6,2100)
28        3 XN=XN+1
        C   MAKE PRELIMINARY CALCULATIONS
29          READ(5,FMT)HC,(X(IB),IB=1,K)
30          WRITE(6,1700)HC,(X(IB),IB=1,K)
31          DO 4 IC=1,K
32          SUM(IC)=SUM(IC)+X(IC)
33          DO 4 ID=IC,K
34        4 SUMPR(IC,ID)=SUMPR(IC,ID)+X(IC)*X(ID)
35          IF(HC.NE.HA.AND.HC.NE.HB)GO TO 3
36          XN=XN-1.
37          N=XN
38          WRITE(6,1800)N
39          DO 5 IE=1,K
40          AVE(IE)=SUM(IE)/XN
41          SUMSQ(IE)=(SUMPR(IE,IE)-SUM(IE)*SUM(IE)/XN)
42          XSUMSQ(IE)=SUMSQ(IE)/(XN-1.)
43          HMSQ=XSUMSQ(IE)
        C   CALCULATE CORRELATION COEFFICIANTS
44          STDEV(IE)=SQRT(HMSQ)
45          DO 5 IT=1,IE
46        5 COR(IT,IE)=(SUMPR(IT,IE)-SUM(IT)*SUM(IE)/XN)/
           *(STDEV(IT)*STDEV(IE)*(XN-1.))
47          WRITE(6,300)
48          WRITE(6,800)(I,I=1,K)
49          WRITE(6,400)(AVE(IG),IG=1,K)
50          WRITE(6,401)(XSUMSQ(IH),IH=1,K)
        C   WRITE OUT THE CORRELATION COEFFICIANTS,
        C   IF OPTION CALLS FOR IT.
51          WRITE(6,402)(STDEV(II),II=1,K)
52          IF(L.EQ.0)GO TO 7
53          WRITE(6,900)
54          WRITE(6,1000)
55          WRITE(6,800)(IQ,IQ=1,K)
56          DO 6 IJ=1,K
```

APPENDIX K *(Continued)*

PRGM1

```
      C
      C
57       6 WRITE(6,700)IJ,(COR(IK,IJ),IK=1,IJ)
      C     CALCULATE ANALISIS OF VARIANCE TABLE, IF OPTION CALLS FOR IT
58       7 IF(M.EQ.0)GO TO 9
59         WRITE(6,1100)
60         WRITE(6,1200)
61         DO 8 IL=1,K
62         RAWSS=RAWSS+SUM(IL)*SUM(IL)
63         TOTAL=TOTAL+SUM(IL)
64         ERRSS=ERRSS+SUMSQ(IL)
65       8 TOTSS=TOTSS+SUMPR(IL,IL)
66         XK=K
67         TRTSS=RAWSS/XN-TOTAL*TOTAL/(XK*XN)
68         ADJSS=TOTSS-TOTAL*TOTAL/(XK*XN)
69         TRTDF=K-1
70         KTRDF=K-1
71         ERRDF=K*(N-1)
72         KERDF=K*(N-1)
73         KTODF=K*N-1
74         TRTMS=TRTSS/TRTDF
75         ERRMS=ERRSS/ERRDF
76         F=(TRTSS/TRTDF)/(ERRSS/ERRDF)
77         WRITE(6,1300)KTRDF,TRTSS,TRTMS,F
78         WRITE(6,1400)KERDF,ERRSS,ERRMS
79         WRITE(6,1500)KTODF,ADJSS
80       9 IF(HC.EQ.HA) GO TO 1
81         IF(HC.EQ.HB) GO TO 10
82      10 WRITE(6,101)
83         STOP
84     100 FORMAT(20A4)
85     200 FORMAT(3I5)
86     300 FORMAT(//24X,'GROUP OR MEASUREMENT NUMBER')
87     400 FORMAT('     AVERAGE',2X,7(1X,E15.7,2X)/)
88     401 FORMAT('    VARIANCE',1X,7(1X,E15.7,2X)/)
89     402 FORMAT('      SQRT',5X,7(1X,E15.7,2X)/)
90     700 FORMAT(10X,I2,2X,7(8X,F6.3,6X)//)
91     800 FORMAT(17X,7(8X,I1,11X)///)
92     900 FORMAT(//9X,'MEAS.',20X,'MEASUREMENT NO.')
93    1000 FORMAT(10X,'NO.')
94    1100 FORMAT(//24X,'ANALYSIS OF VARIANCE')
95    1200 FORMAT(5X,'SOURCE',4X,'DF',9X,'SS',17X,'MS',15X,'F')
96    1300 FORMAT(5X,'TRTSS',5X,I2,2X,E15.7,2X,E15.7,2X,E15.7)
97    1400 FORMAT(5X,'ERRORSS',3X,I2,2X,E15.7,2X,E15.7)
98    1500 FORMAT(5X,'TOTSS',5X,I2,2X,E15.7,2X,E15.7)
99    1700 FORMAT(5X,A3,7F10.5)
100   1800 FORMAT(5X,'NO. OF OBSERVATIONS=',I5)
101   1900 FORMAT('1',20A4//)
```

APPENDIX K (*Continued*)

PRGM1

```
      C
      C
102   2000 FORMAT(//'      PRINT-OUT OF INFORMATION')
103   2100 FORMAT('      ON DATA CARDS')
104   2200 FORMAT('      CONTROL CARD #2 READS AS FOLLOWS:')
105   2300 FORMAT(5X,3I5)
106   2400 FORMAT('      YOUR FIELD DESCRIPTORS (CONTROL CARD #3)',
          *' READ AS FOLLOWS:')
107   2500 FORMAT(5X,20A4)
108    101 FORMAT(1H1)
109        END
      C     EXAMPLE FOR MEANS, VARIANCES, STD. DEVIATIONS
      C  3
      C  (T78,A3,T4,F3.0,2F2.0)
      C  2521032
      C  2761259
      C  2781122
      C  259 642
      C  2631264
      C  252 348
      C  2521632
      C  2521638
      C  2553133
      C  250 648
      C  261 336
      C  25414 9
      C  257 625
      C  259 831
      C  2572652
      C                                                          END
      C             EXAMPLE FOR ANALYSIS OF VARIANCE
      C  3       1
      C  (T78,A3,T4,3F2.0)
      C  231011
      C  311511
      C   51713
      C  15 435
      C  1429 9
      C   41725
      C  3519 5
      C  14   5
      C  1426 5
      C  3220 1
      C  37 711
      C  30 640
      C  18 910
      C  2510 4
      C                                                          END
```

APPENDIX K *(Continued)*

PRGM1

```
C
C
C      EXAMPLE FOR CORRELATION COEFFICIENTS
C   3      1
C   (T78,A3,T4,F3.0,2F2.0)
C   2631264
C   252 348
C   2521032
C   2761259
C   2781122
C   259 642
C   2521632
C   2521638
C   2553133
C   260 648
C   261 336
C   25415 9
C   257 625
C   259 831
C   2572652
C                                                         FIN

   $ENTRY
```

APPENDIX K (*Continued*)

PRGM1

EXAMPLE FOR MEANS, VARIANCES, STD. DEVIATIONS

CONTROL CARD #2 READS AS FOLLOWS:
```
     3    0    0
```
YOUR FIELD DESCRIPTORS (CONTROL CARD #3) READ AS FOLLOWS:
    (T78,A3,T4,F3.0,2F2.0)

PRINT-OUT OF INFORMATION
ON DATA CARDS
```
        252.00000    10.00000    32.00000
        276.00000    12.00000    59.00000
        278.00000    11.00000    22.00000
        259.00000     6.00000    42.00000
        263.00000    12.00000    64.00000
        252.00000     3.00000    48.00000
        252.00000    16.00000    32.00000
        252.00000    16.00000    38.00000
        255.00000    31.00000    33.00000
        250.00000     6.00000    48.00000
        261.00000     3.00000    36.00000
        254.00000    14.00000     9.00000
        257.00000     6.00000    25.00000
        259.00000     8.00000    31.00000
        257.00000    26.00000    52.00000
END       0.00000     0.00000     0.00000
```
NO. OF OBSERVATIONS=   15

| | GROUP OR MEASUREMENT NUMBER | | |
	1	2	3
AVERAGE	0.2584666E 03	0.1200000E 02	0.3806667E 02
VARIANCE	0.7083928E 02	0.6314285E 02	0.2103524E 03
SQRT	0.8416607E 01	0.7946247E 01	0.1450353E 02

APPENDIX K (*Continued*)

PRGM1

EXAMPLE FOR ANALYSIS OF VARIANCE

CONTROL CARD #2 READS AS FOLLOWS:
   3   0   1
YOUR FIELD DESCRIPTORS (CONTROL CARD #3) READ AS FOLLOWS:
  (T78,A3,T4,3F2.0)

PRINT-OUT OF INFORMATION
ON DATA CARDS

23.00000	10.00000	11.00000
31.00000	15.00000	11.00000
5.00000	17.00000	13.00000
15.00000	4.00000	35.00000
14.00000	29.00000	9.00000
4.00000	17.00000	25.00000
35.00000	19.00000	5.00000
14.00000	0.00000	5.00000
14.00000	26.00000	5.00000
32.00000	20.00000	1.00000
37.00000	7.00000	11.00000
30.00000	6.00000	40.00000
18.00000	9.00000	10.00000
25.00000	10.00000	4.00000

END   0.00000   0.00000   0.00000
NO. OF OBSERVATIONS=   14

GROUP OR MEASUREMENT NUMBER

	1	2	3
AVERAGE	0.2121428E 02	0.1350000E 02	0.1321428E 02
VARIANCE	0.1161815E 03	0.7011537E 02	0.1392582E 03
SQRT	0.1077875E 02	0.8373491E 01	0.1180077E 02

ANALYSIS OF VARIANCE

SOURCE	DF	SS	MS	F
TRTSS	2	0.5767617E 03	0.2883809E 03	0.2657439E 01
ERRORSS	39	0.4232215E 04	0.1085183E 03	
TOTSS	41	0.4808977E 04		

APPENDIX K (Continued)

PRGM1

EXAMPLE FOR CORRELATION COEFFICIENTS

CONTROL CARD #2 READS AS FOLLOWS:
     3   1   0
YOUR FIELD DESCRIPTORS (CONTROL CARD #3) READ AS FOLLOWS:
    (T78,A3,T4,F3.0,2F2.0)

PRINT-OUT OF INFORMATION
ON DATA CARDS
         263.00000   12.00000   64.00000
         252.00000   3.00000   48.00000
         252.00000   10.00000   32.00000
         276.00000   12.00000   59.00000
         278.00000   11.00000   22.00000
         259.00000   6.00000   42.00000
         252.00000   16.00000   32.00000
         252.00000   16.00000   38.00000
         255.00000   31.00000   33.00000
         260.00000   6.00000   48.00000
         261.00000   3.00000   36.00000
         254.00000   15.00000   9.00000
         257.00000   6.00000   25.00000
         259.00000   8.00000   31.00000
         257.00000   26.00000   52.00000
FIN   0.00000   0.00000   0.00000
NO. OF OBSERVATIONS=   15

	GROUP OR MEASUREMENT NUMBER		
	1	2	3
AVERAGE	0.2591333E 03	0.1206667E 02	0.3806667E 02
VARIANCE	0.6541071E 02	0.6349524E 02	0.2103524E 03
SQRT	0.8087688E 01	0.7968390E 01	0.1450353E 02

MEAS. NO.	MEASUREMENT NO.		
	1	2	3
1	1.000		
2	-0.143	1.000	
3	0.207	-0.020	1.000

APPENDIX L

PRGM2—Regression Analysis

```
      $JOB            PRGM2,KP=29,TIME=120,PAGES=15,LINES=47
      C
      C
      C       PRGM2: PROGRAM TO BATCH PROCESS SETS OF REGRESSION DATA,
      C       EACH WITH A PRINTER PLOT
      C
      C       LINES PRECEDED BY THE LETTER C ARE NOT PART OF THE
      C       PROGRAM, AND ARE INTENDED TO MAKE THE PROGRAM
      C       EASIER TO USE. ALL LINES WHICH ARE PART OF THE
      C       PROGRAM ARE ASSIGNED TO A NUMBER, ON THE LEFT-HAND
      C       SIDE OF THE PAGE. YOU NEED ONLY TYPE
      C       THE NUMBERED STATEMENTS, TO
      C       GET A USABLE PROGRAM.
      C
      C       SYSTEMS CARDS, OFTEN CALLED JOB CARDS, GO AT THE
      C       BEGINNING OF YOUR DECK. THE ONE BEGINNING $JOB IS
      C       AN EXAMPLE, FOR A WATFIV FORTRAN COMPILER, USING
      C       THREE PRELIMINARY JOB CARDS; THE OTHER TWO
      C       WERE NOT PRINTED.
      C
1             DATA HA,HB,HC/'END','FIN','   '/
      C       THE NUMBER OF OBSERVATIONS NEED NOT BE THE SAME, IN DIFFERENT
      C       SETS OF DATA
2             DIMENSION X(101),Y(101),Z(101),HDG(20),FMT(20)
      C       SET STORAGE POSITIONS TO ZERO, PRIOR TO PROCESSING
3           1 SSX=0.
4             SSY=0.
5             SUMX=0.
6             SUMY=0.
7             SPXY=0.
8             DO 2 IA=1,101
9             Z(IA)=0.
10            X(IA)=0.
11          2 Y(IA)=0.
      C       READ IN CONTROL CARDS
      C       CONTROL CARD #1 IS VERBAL DESCRIPTION OF YOUR JOB
12            READ(5,200)HDG
      C       CONTROL CARD #2 IS FOR THE LEAST SQUARES FIT AND AOV OPTIONS
13            READ(5,1300)KT
      C       CONTROL CARD #3 IS FOR THE SET OF FIELD DESCRIPTORS
      C       WHICH LOCATE X AND Y
      C       IN THE DATA CARDS
14            READ(5,200)FMT
      C       PRINT OUT INFORMATION ON THE CONTROL CARDS
15          3 WRITE(6,400)HDG
16            WRITE(6,1302)
17            WRITE(6,1301)KT
```

APPENDIX L (*Continued*)

PRGM2

```
       C
       C
18         WRITE(6,700)
19         WRITE(6,401)FMT
       C   STORE THE DATA
20         WRITE(6,500)
21         WRITE(6,600)
22         I=1
23         READ(5,FMT)HC,X(1),Y(1)
24         WRITE(6,100)HC,X(1),Y(1)
25         XMIN=X(1)
26         XMAX=X(1)
27         YMIN=Y(1)
28         YMAX=Y(1)
29         SUMX=SUMX+X(1)
30         SUMY=SUMY+Y(1)
31         SSX=SSX+X(1)*X(1)
32         SSY=SSY+Y(1)*Y(1)
33         SPXY=SPXY+X(1)*Y(1)
34       4 I=I+1
35         READ(5,FMT)HC,X(I),Y(I)
36         WRITE(6,100)HC,X(I),Y(I)
37         IF(HC.EQ.HA.OR.HC.EQ.HB)GO TO 5
       C   INITIALIZE VALUES FOR MAXIMA AND MINIMA
       C   OF X AND Y IN THE PRINTER PLOT
38         IF(X(I).LT.XMIN)XMIN=X(I)
39         IF(X(I).GT.XMAX)XMAX=X(I)
40         IF(Y(I).LT.YMIN)YMIN=Y(I)
41         IF(Y(I).GT.YMAX)YMAX=Y(I)
       C   CALCULATE SUMS-OF-SQUARES AND PRODUCTS
42         SUMX=SUMX+X(I)
43         SUMY=SUMY+Y(I)
44         SSX=SSX+X(I)*X(I)
45         SSY=SSY+Y(I)*Y(I)
46         SPXY=SPXY+X(I)*Y(I)
47         GO TO 4
48       5 XN=I-1
49         N=I-1
50         XMIN=XMIN-(XMAX-XMIN)/20.
51         XMAX=XMAX+(XMAX-XMIN)/20.
52         YMIN=YMIN-(YMAX-YMIN)/20.
53         YMAX=YMAX+.25*(YMAX-YMIN)
54         SX=SSX-SUMX*SUMX/XN
55         SY=SSY-SUMY*SUMY/XN
56         SXY=SPXY-SUMX*SUMY/XN
57         R=SXY/(SQRT(SX)*SQRT(SY))
58         IF(KT.EQ.0)GO TO 9
```

APPENDIX L *(Continued)*

PRGM2

```
      C
      C
59          RSS=SXY*SXY/SX
60          DF=N-2
61          ESS=SY-RSS
62          EMS=ESS/DF
63          F=RSS/EMS
      C     CALCULATE CONSTANTS FOR THE EQUATION
64          B=SXY/SX
65          A=SUMY/XN-B*(SUMX/XN)
66          WRITE(6,300)A,B
      C     CALCULATE VALUES FOR THE 'FITTED' CURVE
67          H=(XMAX-XMIN)/50.
68          Z(1)=A+B*XMIN
69          XV=XMIN
70          DO 6 IB=2,50
71          XV=XV+H
72        6 Z(IB)=A+B*XV
      C     WRITE ANALYSIS OF VARIANCE TABLE
73          WRITE(6,900)
74          WRITE(6,1000)
75          WRITE(6,1100)RSS,RSS,F
76          WRITE(6,1200)DF,ESS,EMS
77        9 CONTINUE
78          CALL GRAPH(HDG,X,Y,N,Z,XMIN,XMAX,YMIN,YMAX,1)
79          IF(KT.EQ.0)WRITE(6,1303)R
80        7 IF(HC.EQ.HA)GO TO 1
81          IF(HC.EQ.HB)GO TO 8
82        8 WRITE(6,101)
83          STOP
84      100 FORMAT(' ',A3,2(F15.7,5X))
85      101 FORMAT('1')
86      200 FORMAT(20A4)
87      300 FORMAT(/' THE REGRESSION EQUATION IS:',4X,'Y=',
           *F10.5,' + ',F10.5,'X')
88      400 FORMAT('1',20A4)
89      401 FORMAT(' ',20A4)
90      500 FORMAT(/' PRINT-OUT OF INFORMATION')
91      600 FORMAT(' ON DATA CARDS')
92      700 FORMAT(/' YOUR FIELD DESCRIPTORS (CONTROL ',
           *'CARD #3)ARE:')
93      900 FORMAT(/25X,'REGRESSION ANALYSIS OF VARIANCE'/)
94     1000 FORMAT(3X,'SOURCE',5X,'DF',7X,'SS',14X,'MS',14X,'F')
95     1100 FORMAT(1X,'REGRESSION',3X,'1.',3(1X,E15.7))
96     1200 FORMAT(3X,'ERROR',5X,F3.0,2(1X,E15.7))
97     1300 FORMAT(I5)
98     1301 FORMAT(' ',I5)
```

APPENDIX L (*Continued*)

PRGM2

```
        C
        C
 99    1302 FORMAT(' CONTROL CARD #2 READS:')
100    1303 FORMAT(10X,'R= ',F6.3)
101         END

102         SUBROUTINE GRAPH (HEADNG,XX,YY,M,VARY,XMIN,XMAX,           GRAPH001
           *YMIN,YMAX,MPAGES)                                         GRAPH001
103         REAL LINE,BLANK/' '/,DOT/'.'/,X/'X'/,O/'O'/,              GRAPH002
           *Y/'Y'/,PLUS/'+'/                                          GRAPH002
104         REAL AST/'*'/                                             GRAPH003
105         DIMENSION LINE(112),XX(100),YY(100),YAXIS(20),XAXIS(101)
106         DIMENSION VARY(101), HEADNG(20)
107         WRITE (6,9) HEADNG
108      10 DYMXMN = YMAX - YMIN                                      GRAPH006
109         YAXIS(1) = YMIN                                           GRAPH007
110         GO TO (12,14), MPAGES                                     GRAPH008
111      12 XSPACE = 50.0                                            GRAPH009
112         MSPACE = 51                                               GRAPH010
113         GO TO 16                                                  GRAPH011
114      14 XSPACE = 100.0                                            GRAPH012
115         MSPACE = 101                                              GRAPH013
116      16 DO 20  K=2,11                                            GRAPH014
117      20 YAXIS(K) = YAXIS(K-1) + 0.1*DYMXMN                       GRAPH015
118      30 IF (DYMXMN - 1000.0) 40,100,100                          GRAPH016
119      40 IF (YMAX - 1000.0) 50,100,100                            GRAPH017
120      50 IF (YMIN + 100.0) 100,100,60                             GRAPH018
121      60 IF (ABS(YMIN) - (1.0E-02)) 70,70,80                      GRAPH019
122      70 IF (YMIN) 100,80,100                                     GRAPH020
123      80 IF (ABS(YMAX) - (1.0E-02)) 90,90,110                     GRAPH021
124      90 IF (YMAX) 100,110,100                                    GRAPH022
125     100 WRITE (6,1) (YAXIS(K), K=2,11)                           GRAPH023
126         GO TO 120                                                GRAPH024
127     110 WRITE (6,2) (YAXIS(K), K=2,11)                           GRAPH025
128     120 DO 130 J=1,112                                           GRAPH026
129     130 LINE(J) = BLANK                                          GRAPH027
130         WRITE (6,3) LINE                                         GRAPH028
131         KOUNT = 0                                                GRAPH029
132         IF (XMIN) 140,170,170                                    GRAPH030
133     140 IF (XMAX) 170,170,150                                    GRAPH031
134     150 DO 160 J=10,112                                          GRAPH032
135     160 LINE(J) = BLANK                                          GRAPH033
136         GO TO 200                                                GRAPH034
137     170 DO 180  J=10,110                                         GRAPH035
138     180 LINE(J) = DOT                                            GRAPH036
139         DO 190  J=10,110,10                                      GRAPH037
140     190 LINE(J) = PLUS                                           GRAPH038
                                                                     GRAPH039
```

APPENDIX L (*Continued*)

PRGM2

```
          C                                                                GRAPH
          C
141              LINE(111) = BLANK                                         GRAPH040
142              LINE(112) = Y                                             GRAPH041
143       200 DXMXMN = XMAX - XMIN                                         GRAPH042
144              XAXIS(1) = XMIN                                           GRAPH043
145              DO 210  KK=11,MSPACE,10                                   GRAPH044
146       210 XAXIS(KK) = XAXIS(KK-10) + (10.0/XSPACE)*DXMXMN             GRAPH045
147              KK = 1                                                    GRAPH046
148              XINVL = DXMXMN/XSPACE                                     GRAPH047
149              VARX = XMIN                                               GRAPH048
150       220 DO 770  L=1,MSPACE                                          GRAPH049
151              IF (YMIN) 230,260,260                                     GRAPH050
152       230 JY = (100.0/DYMXMN)*ABS(YMIN) + 9.5                         GRAPH051
153              IF (JY-110) 250,240,240                                   GRAPH052
154       240 JY = 9                                                      GRAPH053
155       250 LINE(JY+1) = DOT                                            GRAPH054
156              GO TO 270                                                 GRAPH055
157       260 LINE(10) = DOT                                              GRAPH056
158              JY = 9                                                    GRAPH057
159       270 IF (L-1) 280,330,280                                        GRAPH058
160       280 IF (L-11) 290,340,290                                       GRAPH059
161       290 IF (L-21) 300,340,300                                       GRAPH060
162       300 IF (L-31) 310,340,310                                       GRAPH061
163       310 IF (L-41) 320,340,320                                       GRAPH062
164       320 IF (L-51) 321,340,321                                       GRAPH063
165       321 GO TO (430,322),MPAGES                                      GRAPH064
166       322 IF (L-61) 323,340,323                                       GRAPH065
167       323 IF (L-71) 324,340,324                                       GRAPH066
168       324 IF (L-81) 325,340,325                                       GRAPH067
169       325 IF (L-91) 326,340,326                                       GRAPH068
170       326 IF (L-101) 430,340,430                                      GRAPH069
171       330 LINE(JY+1) = X                                             GRAPH070
172              GO TO 430                                                 GRAPH071
173       340 LINE(JY+1) = PLUS                                          GRAPH072
174              KK = L                                                    GRAPH073
175              IF (DXMXMN - 1000.0) 350,410,410                         GRAPH074
176       350 IF (XMAX -1000.0) 360,410,410                              GRAPH075
177       360 IF (XMIN + 100.0) 410,410,370                              GRAPH076
178       370 IF (ABS(XMIN) - (1.0E-02)) 380,380,390                     GRAPH077
179       380 IF (XMIN) 410,390,410                                      GRAPH078
180       390 IF (ABS(XMAX) - (1.0E-02)) 400,400,420                     GRAPH079
181       400 IF (XMAX) 410,420,410                                      GRAPH080
182       410 WRITE(6,4) XAXIS(KK)                                       GRAPH081
183              GO TO 430                                                 GRAPH082
184       420 WRITE (6,5) XAXIS(KK)                                      GRAPH083
185       430 IF ((VARX + XINVL/2.0) - ABS(VARX)) 480,440,440            GRAPH084
```

APPENDIX L (*Continued*)

PRGM2

```
                C
                C
186        440 KOUNT = KOUNT + 1                                    GRAPH085
187            IF (KOUNT - 1) 480,450,480                           GRAPH086
188        450 DO 460   J=10,110                                    GRAPH087
189        460 LINE(J) = DOT                                        GRAPH088
190            DO 470   J=20,110,10                                 GRAPH089
191        470 LINE(J) = PLUS                                       GRAPH090
192            LINE(111) = BLANK                                    GRAPH091
193            LINE(112) = Y                                        GRAPH092
194        480 K = 0                                                GRAPH093
195            KMAX = 0                                             GRAPH094
196            DO 530 I=1,M                                         GRAPH095
197            TRY = XX(I) - VARX                                   GRAPH096
198            TTRY = TRY - (XINVL/2.0)                             GRAPH097
199            IF (TTRY) 490,530,530                                GRAPH098
200        490 IF (TTRY + XINVL) 500,510,510                        GRAPH099
201        500 GO TO 530                                            GRAPH100
202        510 K = (YY(I) - YMIN)*100.0/DYMXMN + 9.5                GRAPH101
203            IF (K-111) 512,525,525                               GRAPH102
204        512 IF (8-K) 515,525,525                                 GRAPH103
205        515 LINE(K+1) = 0                                        GRAPH104
206            IF (KMAX - K) 520,530,530                            GRAPH105
207        520 KMAX = K                                             GRAPH106
208            GO TO 530                                            GRAPH107
209        525 K = 0                                                GRAPH108
210        530 CONTINUE                                             GRAPH109
211            J = (VARY(L) - YMIN)*100.0/DYMXMN + 9.5              GRAPH110
212            IF (J-111) 540,580,580                               GRAPH111
213        540 IF (8-J) 550,580,580                                 GRAPH112
214        550 IF (LINE(J+1) - 0) 570,560,570                       GRAPH113
215        560 LINE(J+1) = 0                                        GRAPH114
216            GO TO  590                                           GRAPH115
217        570 LINE(J+1) = AST                                      GRAPH116
218            GO TO 590                                            GRAPH117
219        580 J = 0                                                GRAPH118
220        590 J1 = J + 1                                           GRAPH119
221            K1 = KMAX + 1                                        GRAPH120
222            JY1 = JY + 1                                         GRAPH121
223            IF (LINE(112) - Y) 600,720,600                       GRAPH122
224        600 IF (JY - J) 620,610,610                              GRAPH123
225        610 IF (JY - K) 660,630,630                              GRAPH124
226        620 IF (J - K) 660,690,690                               GRAPH125
227        630 IF (L - KK) 640,650,640                              GRAPH126
228        640 WRITE (6,3) (LINE(JJ), JJ=10,JY1)                    GRAPH127
229            GO TO 750                                            GRAPH128
230        650 WRITE (6,6) (LINE(JJ), JJ=10,JY1)                    GRAPH129
```

APPENDIX L (Continued)

PRGM2

```
          C
          C
231           GO TO 750                                        GRAPH130
232     660 IF (L - KK) 670,680,670                            GRAPH131
233     670 WRITE (6,3) (LINE(JJ), JJ=10,K1)                   GRAPH132
234           GO TO 750                                        GRAPH133
235     680 WRITE (6,6) (LINE(JJ), JJ=10,K1)                   GRAPH134
236           GO TO 750                                        GRAPH135
237     690 IF (L - KK) 700,710,700                            GRAPH136
238     700 WRITE (6,3) (LINE(JJ), JJ=10,112)
239           GO TO 750                                        GRAPH138
240     710 WRITE (6,6) (LINE(JJ), JJ=10,112)
241           GO TO 750                                        GRAPH140
242     720 IF (L - KK) 740,730,740                            GRAPH141
243     730 WRITE (6,6) (LINE(JJ), JJ=10,112)                  GRAPH142
244           GO TO 750                                        GRAPH143
245     740 WRITE (6,3) (LINE(JJ), JJ=10,112)                  GRAPH144
246     750 DO 760  J=10,112                                   GRAPH145
247     760 LINE(J) = BLANK                                    GRAPH146
248           VARX = VARX + XINVL                              GRAPH147
249     770 CONTINUE                                           GRAPH148
250           IF (DXMXMN - 1000.0) 780,870,870                 GRAPH149
251     780 IF (XMAX - 1000.0) 790,870,870                     GRAPH150
252     790 IF (DYMXMN - 1000.0) 800,870,870                   GRAPH151
253     800 IF (YMAX - 1000.0) 810,870,870                     GRAPH152
254     810 IF (YMIN + 100.0) 870,870,820                      GRAPH153
255     820 IF (ABS(YMIN) - (1.0E-02)) 870,870,830             GRAPH154
256     830 IF (ABS(YMAX) - (1.0E-02)) 870,870,840             GRAPH155
257     840 IF (XMIN + 100.0) 870,870,850                      GRAPH156
258     850 IF (ABS(XMIN) - (1.0E-02)) 870,870,860             GRAPH157
259     860 IF (ABS(XMAX) - (1.0E-02)) 870,870,880             GRAPH158
260     870 WRITE (6,7) XMIN,XMAX,YMIN,YMAX                     GRAPH159
261           GO TO 900                                        GRAPH160
262     880 WRITE (6,8) XMIN,XMAX,YMIN,YMAX                     GRAPH161
263       1 FORMAT (/,16X,1PE9.2,9(1X,1PE9.2))                 GRAPH162
264       2 FORMAT (/,17X,F7.3,9(3X,F7.3))                     GRAPH163
265       3 FORMAT (1H ,9X,103A1)                              GRAPH164
266       4 FORMAT (' ',1PE9.2)                                GRAPH165
267       5 FORMAT (' ',F9.4)                                  GRAPH166
268       6 FORMAT ('+',9X,103A1)                              GRAPH167
269       7 FORMAT (/,14X,'XMIN = ',1PE12.5,5X,'XMAX = ',1PE12.5, GRAPH168
              1 /,14X,'YMIN = ',1PE12.5,5X,'YMAX = ',1PE12.5)  GRAPH169
270       8 FORMAT (/,14X,'XMIN = ',F10.6,5X,'XMAX = ',F10.6,  GRAPH170
              1 /,14X,'YMIN = ',F10.6,5X,'YMAX = ',F10.6)      GRAPH171
271       9 FORMAT ('1',20A4)                                  GRAPH172
272     900 RETURN                                             GRAPH173
273           END                                              GRAPH174
```

APPENDIX L (*Continued*)

PRGM2

```
C
C
C   SYSTEMS CARDS (SOMETIMES ONLY ONE) COME
C   IMMEDIATELY AFTER THE END CARD
C   $ENTRY WAS USED WITH A WATFIV COMPILER,
C   USING IBM 360/44 EQUIPMENT, FOR THE OUTPUT IN THIS BOOK.
C
C   CONTROL CARD #1 IS FOR THE VERBAL DESCRIPTION OF JOB
C   '1' IN COL. 5 OF CARD #2, IF REGRESSION IS DESIRED.
C   CONTROL CARD #3 PROVIDES FIELD DESCRIPTORS FOR
C   THE DATA. IT SHOULD BEGIN WITH T78,A3 - SEESECTION
C   THE DATA. IT SHOULD BEGIN WITH T78,A3 - SEE THE
C   SECTION ON DATA PROCESSING FOR LINEAR REGRESSION,
C   CHAPTER EIGHT.
C
C   THE DATA MUST FOLLOW CONTROL CARD #2
C
C   FIRST CARD FOLLOWING THE DATA DECK SHOULD BE BLANK,
C   EXCEPT FOR 'END' OR 'FIN' IN THE LAST THREE
C   COLUMNS. 'END', IF ANOTHER SET OF CONTROL AND DATA
C   CARDS FOLLOWS; 'FIN' IF THE SET IS THE LAST ONE.
C
C   TWO SAMPLE SETS OF DATA FOLLOW, IN EXACTLY THE FORM
C   USED IN PROCESSING, EXCEPT FOR THE C IN COLUMN ONE.
C   THESE SETS MAY BE USED FOR TRIAL RUNS OF THE PROGRAM,
C   IF THEY ARE PUNCHED EXACTLY AS HEREIN, EXCEPT FOR THE C.
C
C
C   EXAMPLE: SCATTER DIAGRAM FOR MATH SCORES VS. SCIENCE SCORES
C   0
C   (T78,A3,T4,2F3.0)
C   269254
C   271253
C   258238
C   287263
C   254245
C   251249
C   273253
C   259249
C   276272
C   262251
C   271254
C   238238
C   266251
C   283269
C   250236
C   255262
```

APPENDIX L *(Continued)*

PRGM2

```
C
C
C     267247
C     244231
C     262253
C     260251
C     261253
C     258243
C     263253
C     244231
C                                                                  END
C     APPENDIX N - EXAMPLE: REGRESSION OF MATH SCORES ON SCIENCE SCORES
C     EXAMPLE: REGRESSION OF MATH SCORES ON SCIENCE SCORES
C     1
C     (T78,A3,T4,2F3.0)
C     269254
C     271253
C     258238
C     287263
C     254245
C     251249
C     273253
C     259249
C     276272
C     262251
C     271254
C     238238
C     266251
C     283269
C     250236
C     255262
C     267247
C     244231
C     262253
C     260251
C     261253
C     258243
C     263253
C     244231
C                                                                  FIN
C     POSSIBLE SOURCES OF ERROR, IF THE PROGRAM
C     DOESN'T RUN PROPERLY:
C              1. CONTROL CARDS IN ORDER? IF NOT, YOUR
C                 ERROR MESSAGES WILL INDICATE SOME
C                 FORMAT (FIELD DESCRIPTOR) ERROR, AND YOUR
C                 CONTROL CARD PRINT-OUT WILL BE UNUSUAL
C              2. DATA PUNCHED ON CARDS CONSISTENTLY
```

APPENDIX L (Continued)

PRGM2

```
C
C
C                    WITH FIELD DESCRIPTORS? IF NOT, YOU
C                    WILL GET WILD NUMERICAL RESULTS
C           3. NUMBER OF DATA CARDS CORRECT?
C                    THE PROGRAM WILL NOT DETECT THIS TYPE
C                    OF ERROR; IT SIMPLY RECORDS IN THE OUTPUT
C                    HOW MANY OBSERVATIONS PER GROUP WERE
C                    READ IN, BEFORE AND 'END' (OR 'FIN')
C                    CARD WAS ENCOUNTERED
C           4. DO YOU HAVE YOUR 'END' (OR 'FIN')
C                    CARD FOLLOWING YOUR DATA?
C                    IF NOT, THE NEXT DATA SET WILL BE READ AS
C                    PART OF THE PRECEDING SET, AND THE
C                    CONTROL CARDS OF THE NEXT SET WILL GENERATE
C                    AN ERROR. INDICATING IMPROPER DATA.
C           5. IF THE CARDS FOR A DATA SET ARE NOT
C                    PUNCHED PROPERLY, THE DATA SETS WHICH
C                    FOLLOW IT WILL HAVE TO BE RE-RUN.
C
C     THE FINAL SET OF SYSTEMS CARDS COMES AFTER THE
C     'FIN' CARD.

$ENTRY
```

APPENDIX L (*Continued*)

PRGM2

EXAMPLE:SCATTER DIAGRAM FOR MATH SCORES VS. SCIENCE SCORES
CONTROL CARD #2 READS:
   0

YOUR FIELD DESCRIPTORS (CONTROL CARD #3)ARE:
  (T78,A3,T4,2F3.0)

PRINT-OUT OF INFORMATION
ON DATA CARDS

269.0000000	254.0000000
271.0000000	253.0000000
258.0000000	238.0000000
287.0000000	263.0000000
254.0000000	245.0000000
251.0000000	249.0000000
273.0000000	253.0000000
259.0000000	249.0000000
276.0000000	272.0000000
262.0000000	251.0000000
271.0000000	254.0000000
238.0000000	238.0000000
266.0000000	251.0000000
283.0000000	269.0000000
250.0000000	236.0000000
255.0000000	262.0000000
267.0000000	247.0000000
244.0000000	231.0000000
262.0000000	253.0000000
260.0000000	251.0000000
261.0000000	253.0000000
258.0000000	243.0000000
263.0000000	253.0000000
244.0000000	231.0000000

END   0.0000000   0.0000000

PRGM2

EXAMPLE:SCATTER DIAGRAM FOR MATH SCORES VS. SCIENCE SCORES

XMIN = 235.549900   XMAX = 289.572200
YMIN = 228.949900   YMAX = 282.762400

R= 0.808

APPENDIX L (*Continued*)

PRGM2

EXAMPLE: REGRESSION OF MATH SCORES ON SCIENCE SCORES
CONTROL CARD #2 READS:
    1

YOUR FIELD DESCRIPTORS (CONTROL CARD #3)ARE:
    (T78,A3,T4,2F3.0)

PRINT-OUT OF INFORMATION
ON DATA CARDS

269.0000000	254.0000000
271.0000000	253.0000000
258.0000000	238.0000000
287.0000000	263.0000000
254.0000000	245.0000000
251.0000000	249.0000000
273.0000000	253.0000000
259.0000000	249.0000000
276.0000000	272.0000000
262.0000000	251.0000000
271.0000000	254.0000000
238.0000000	238.0000000
266.0000000	251.0000000
283.0000000	269.0000000
250.0000000	236.0000000
255.0000000	262.0000000
267.0000000	247.0000000
244.0000000	231.0000000
262.0000000	253.0000000
260.0000000	251.0000000
261.0000000	253.0000000
258.0000000	243.0000000
263.0000000	253.0000000
244.0000000	231.0000000
FIN 0.0000000	0.0000000

THE REGRESSION EQUATION IS: Y= 64.26971 +   0.70941X

REGRESSION ANALYSIS OF VARIANCE

SOURCE	DF	SS	MS	F
REGRESSION	1.	0.1652221E 04	0.1652221E 04	0.4145724E 02
ERROR	22.	0.8767793E 03	0.3985359E 02	

APPENDIX L (Continued)

PRGM2

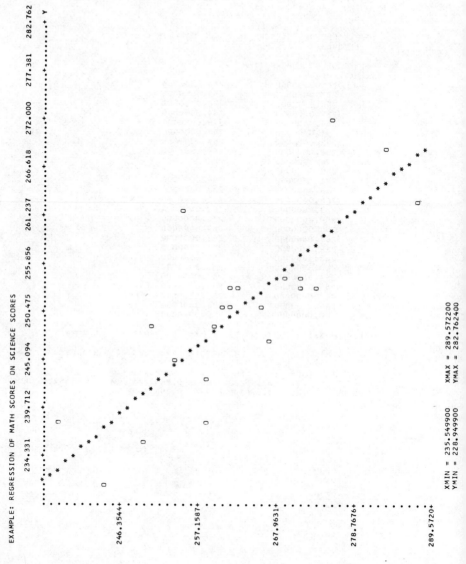

EXAMPLE: REGRESSION OF MATH SCORES ON SCIENCE SCORES

XMIN = 235.549900   XMAX = 289.572200
YMIN = 228.949900   YMAX = 282.762400

APPENDIX M

PRGM3—Analysis of Two-Way Contingency Table (Chi-Square)

```
$JOB              PRGM3,KP=29,TIME=60,PAGES=10,LINES=48
          C
          C
          C   PRGM3: PROGRAM FOR CALCULATION OF CHI-SQUARE IN A
          C   TWO-WAY CONTINGENCY TABLE
          C
          C   LINES PRECEEDED BY THE LETTER C ARE NOT PART OF THE
          C   PROGRAM, AND ARE INTENDED TO MAKE THE PROGRAM
          C   EASIER TO USE. ALL LINES WHICH ARE PART OF THE
          C   PROGRAM ARE ASSIGNED A NUMBER, ON THE LEFT-HAND
          C   SIDE OF THE PAGE. YOU NEED ONLY PUNCH THE NUMBERED
          C   CARDS, TO GET A USEABLE PROGRAM.
          C
          C   INITIAL SYSTEMS CARDS, OFTEN CALLED JOB CARDS,
          C   GO AT THE BEGINNING OF YOUR DECK. THE ONE BEGINNING
          C   $JOB IS AN EXAMPLE, FOR A WATFIV FORTRAN COMPILER,
          C   USING IBM 360/44 EQUIPMENT; IT IS ACTUALLY THE
          C   THIRD OF THREE PRELIMINARY JOB CARDS;
          C   THE OTHER TWO WERE NOT PRINTED.
          C
  1           DATA HA,HB/'END','FIN'/
  2           DIMENSIONO(20,20),OR(20),OC(20),P(20,20),PR(20),
             *PC(20),E(20,20),HDG(20)
  3       7 DO 6 IP=1,20
  4           PR(IP)=0.
  5           PC(IP)=0.
  6           OR(IP)=0.
  7       6 OC(IP)=0.
          C READ IN PARAMETER CARD
          C I IS NO. OF ROWS-J IS NO. OF COLUMNS
  8           READ(5,101)HDG
  9           WRITE(6,104)HDG
 10           READ(5,100)I,J
 11           WRITE(6,1100)I,J
 12           XN=0.
 13           NDF=(I-1)*(J-1)
 14           XSQ=0.
          C READ IN DATA CARDS
 15           WRITE(6,1200)
 16           DO 1 IA=1,I
 17           READ(5,200)(O(IA,JA),JA=1,J)
 18         1 WRITE(6,1000)(O(IA,JA),JA=1,J)
 19           DO 2 IB=1,I
 20           DO 2 JB=1,J
 21           OR(IB)=OR(IB)+O(IB,JB)
 22           OC(JB)=OC(JB)+O(IB,JB)
 23         2 XN=XN+O(IB,JB)
 24           WRITE(6,1300)XN
```

APPENDIX M *(Continued)*

PRGM3

```
        C
        C
25              DO 3 IC=1,I
26              DO 3 JC=1,J
27              P(IC,JC)=O(IC,JC)/XN
28              PR(IC)=PR(IC)+P(IC,JC)
29              PC(JC)=PC(JC)+P(IC,JC)
30           3  E(IC,JC)=OR(IC)*OC(JC)/XN
31              H=0.
32              DO 4 ID=1,I
33              DO 4 JD=1,J
34              IF(P(ID,JD).EQ.0.)GO TO 4
35              H=H+P(ID,JD)*ALOG(P(ID,JD)/SQRT(PR(ID)*PC(JD)))
36              XSQ=XSQ+(O(ID,JD)-E(ID,JD))**2/E(ID,JD)
37           4  CONTINUE
38              XK=EXP(H)
39              XMRSQ=1./(I*J)
40              WRITE(6,300)
41              WRITE(6,400)
42              WRITE(6,401)
43              WRITE(6,402)
44              WRITE(6,500)(JE,JE=1,J)
45              DO 5 IG=1,I
46           5  WRITE(6,600)IG,(P(IG,JG),JG=1,J),PR(IG)
47              WRITE(6,700)(PC(JG),JG=1,J)
48              WRITE(6,1400)
49              WRITE(6,800)XSQ,NDF
50              WRITE(6,900)XK,XMRSQ
51              READ(5,102)HC
52              IF(HC.EQ.HA)GO TO 7
53              IF(HC.EQ.HB)GO TO 8
54           8  WRITE(6,103)
55              STOP
56         100  FORMAT(3X,2I2)
57         101  FORMAT(20A4)
58         102  FORMAT(T78,A3)
59         103  FORMAT('1')
60         104  FORMAT('1',20A4)
61         200  FORMAT(3X,20F2.0)
62         300  FORMAT(30X'CONTINGENCY TABLE',//)
63         400  FORMAT(40X'COLUMN')
64         401  FORMAT(60X,'ROW')
65         402  FORMAT(60X,'TOTALS')
66         500  FORMAT(20X,'ROW',5X,20(7X,I2))
67         600  FORMAT(//21X,I2,5X,20(2X,F6.3))
68         700  FORMAT(//20X,'COL.',3X,20(2X,F6.3))
69         800  FORMAT(///10X,'TEST FOR INDEPENDENCE(CHI-SQUARE)=',
               *E15.7,4X,'DF=',I3)
```

APPENDIX M (*Continued*)

PRGM3

```
       C
       C
70        900 FORMAT(//5X,'RSQ=',E15.7,4X,'MINIMUM VALUE FOR RSQ=',E15.7)
71       1000 FORMAT(' ',20F3.0)
72       1100 FORMAT(' NO. OF ROWS=',I2,4X,'NO. OF COLUMNS=',I2)
73       1200 FORMAT(' THE INFORMATION ON YOUR DATA CARDS IS AS FOLLOWS:')
74       1300 FORMAT(' TOTAL SAMPLE SIZE=',F6.1)
75       1400 FORMAT(19X,'TOTALS')
76            END
       C
       C   A SYSTEMS CARD COMES IMMEDIATELY AFTER THE END CARD
       C   $ENTRY WAS USED WITH A WATFIV FORTRAN COMPILER,
       C   IBM 360/44 EQUIPMENT.
       C
       C   CONTROL CARD #1 IS FOR THE VERBAL DESCRIPTION OF THE JOB
       C   CONTROL CARD #2 IS TO RECORD THE NUMBER OF ROWS
       C   AND COLUMNS, EACH LESS THAN 99, IN THE TABLE.
       C   THE NUMBER OF ROWS IS ENTERED IN COLUMNS 4 AND 5;
       C   THE NUMBER OF COLUMNS SHOULD BE ENTERED
       C   IN COLUMNS 6 & 7 OF CONTROL CARD #2.
       C
       C   DATA CARDS FOLLOW CONTROL CARD #2.  EACH CARD
       C   HAS THE ENTRIES  OF ONE ROW OF THE CONTINGENCY TABLE.
       C   THE FIRST DATA CARD HAS THE ENTRIES OF ROW ONE,
       C   THE SECOND CARD IS FOR THE SECOND ROW, AND SO ON.
       C   THE COUNTS FOR THE CELLS OF A GIVEN ROW ARE PUNCHED
       C   IN COLUMNS 5&6, 7&8, 9&10, AND SO ON.
       C
       C   FIRST CARD FOLLOWING THE DATA DECK SHOULD BE BLANK,
       C   EXCEPT FOR 'END' OR 'FIN' IN THE LAST THREE
       C   COLUMNS. 'END', IF ANOTHER SET OF CONTROL AND DATA
       C   CARDS FOLLOWS; 'FIN' IF THE SET IS THE LAST ONE.
       C
       C   FOLLOWING IS A SET OF DATA CARDS, EXACTLY AS THEY
       C   ARE PROCESSED, EXCEPT FOR THE C IN COLUMN ONE.
       C
       C      CONTINGENCY TABLE EXAMPLE
       C      3 4
       C      1 91812
       C      1126 4
       C      1 610 2
       C                                                    FIN
       C
       C   POSSIBLE SOURCES OF ERROR, IF THE PROGRAM
       C   DOESN'T RUN PROPERLY:
       C             1. CONTROL CARDS IN ORDER? IF NOT, YOUR
       C                ERROR MESSAGES WILL INDICATE SOME
       C                FORMAT(FIELD DESCRIPTOR) ERROR, AND YOUR
```

APPENDIX M *(Continued)*

PRGM3

```
C
C
C                 CONTROL CARD PRINT-OUT WILL BE UNUSUAL
C              2. DATA PUNCHED IN THE CORRECT COLUMNS?
C                 IF NOT, YOU WILL OBTAIN SOME WILD
C                 NUMERICAL RESULTS.
C              3. NUMBER OF DATA CARDS CORRECT?
C                 IF NOT,  THE PROGRAM WILL BE OUT OF PHASE
C                 WITH THE 'END' OR 'FIN' CARD, AND INCORRECT
C                 VALUES WILL BE ENTERED IN THE PRINT-OUT
C                 OF THE CONTINGENCY TABLE.
C              4. IS THE 'END' OR 'FIN' CARD IN PLACE?
C                 IF NOT, THE PROGRAM WILL BE OUT OF PHASE
C                 WITH THE CONTROL CARDS OF THE NEXT DATA SET,
C                 AND WILD RESULTS WILL BE OBTAINED FOR
C                 THE REMAINING DATA SETS.
C              5. IF THE CARDS FOR A DATA SET ARE NOT
C                 PUNCHED PROPERLY, THE DATA SETS WHICH
C                 FOLLOW IT WILL HAVE TO BE RE-RUN.
C
C   THE FINAL SET OF SYSTEMS CARDS COMES AFTER THE
C   'FIN' CARD.

$ENTRY
```

APPENDIX M (*Continued*)

PRGM3

```
CONTINGENCY TABLE EXAMPLE
NO. OF ROWS= 3     NO. OF COLUMNS= 4
THE INFORMATION ON YOUR DATA CARDS IS AS FOLLOWS:
  1. 9.18.12.
  0.11.26. 4.
  1. 6.10. 2.
TOTAL SAMPLE SIZE= 100.0
```

CONTINGENCY TABLE

ROW	COLUMN 1	2	3	ROW TOTALS 4
1	0.010	0.090	0.180	0.120	0.400
2	0.000	0.110	0.260	0.040	0.410
3	0.010	0.060	0.100	0.020	0.190
COL. TOTALS	0.020	0.260	0.540	0.180	

TEST FOR INDEPENDENCE(CHI-SQUARE)= 0.8105497E 01   DF= 6

RSQ= 0.3633956E 00   MINIMUM VALUE FOR RSQ= 0.8333331E-01

APPENDIX N

PRGM4—Analysis of Variance for Cluster Sampling

```
$JOB                PRGM4,KP=29,TIME=60,PAGES=20,LINES=48
   C
   C
   C
   C   PRGM4: THIS PROGRAM PROVIDES ANALYSIS OF
   C   VARIANCE FOR TWO-STAGE CLUSTER SAMPLING
   C   WITH UNEQUAL NUMBERS OF PSU'S IN EACH
   C   POPULATION, AND UNEQUAL NUMBERS OF SAMPLING
   C   UNITS WITHIN EACH PSU.
   C
   C   THE F TEST MAY NOT BE VALID, IF THE SAMPLE
   C   SIZES DIFFER GREATLY.
   C
   C   LINES PRECEEDED BY THE LETTER C ARE NOT PART OF THE
   C   PROGRAM, AND ARE INTENDED TO MAKE THE PROGRAM
   C   EASIER TO USE. ALL LINES WHICH ARE PART OF THE
   C   PROGRAM ARE ASSIGNED A NUMBER, ON THE LEFT-HAND
   C   SIDE OF THE PAGE. YOU NEED ONLY PUNCH THE
   C   NUMBERED STATEMENTS, TO GET A USABLE PROGRAM.
   C
 1          DATA HA,HB,HC/'END','FIN','    '/
 2          DIMENSION XT(25),N(25,25),XPSU(25,25),J(25),NT(25),
            *XMT(25),XNT(25),SN(25,25),FMT(20),HDG(20),XM(25)
   C   SET ALL STORAGE POSITIONS TO ZERO
   C   I IS THE NUMBER OF POPULATIONS
   C   XT(IA) IS THE TOTAL OF OBSERVATIONS FROM POPULATION IA
   C   XMT(IA) IS THE MEAN OF OBSERVATIONS FROM POPULATION IA
   C   XNT(IA) IS THE SAMPLE SIZE FOR POPULATION IA
   C    N(IA,JA) IS THE SAMPLE SIZE FOR PSU JA WITHIN
   C   POPULATION IA. XPSU(IA,JA) IS THE TOTAL OF OBSERVATIONS
   C   FROM PSU JA WITHIN POPULATION IA. HC IS
   C   ALPHAMERIC STORAGE POSITION TO STORE 'END' OR 'FIN',
   C   WHICH IS WRITTEN IN COLUMNS 78 - 80 OF THE CARD
   C   IMMEDIATELY AFTER THE LAST DATA CARD. 'END' SIGNIFIES
   C   THAT THE NEXT CARD WILL BE A CONTROL CARD FOR THE
   C   NEXT SET OF DATA. A 'FIN' CARD REPLACES THE 'END'
   C   CARD FOR THE LAST SET OF DATA.
 3        1 I=0
 4          DO 2 IA=1,25
 5          XT(IA)=0.
 6          XMT(IA)=0.
 7          XNT(IA)=0.
 8          J(IA)=0.
 9          DO 2 JA=1,25
10          N(IA,JA)=0.
11        2 XPSU(IA,JA)=0.
12          RS=0.
13          XB=0.
14          RSXT=0.
```

SOURCE: From *An Introduction to Linear Statistical Models*, Vol. I, Tables 16.9 and 16.10, pp. 358–359, by F. Graybill. Copyright 1961. Used with permission of McGraw-Hill Book Company.

APPENDIX N (*Continued*)

PRGM4

```
       C
       C
15         RSPSU=0.
16         XNTO=0.
17         XTO=0.
18         READ(5,200)HDG
19         WRITE(6,102)HDG
       C READ IN FIELD SPECIFICATIONS FOR THE CARDS BEING USED
20         READ(5,200)FMT
21         WRITE(6,2000)
22         WRITE(6,100)FMT
       C  READ IN HC, AND THE POPULATION AND PSU NUMBERS
       C  WITH AN OBSERVATION CORRESPONDING TO THESE NUMBERS,
       C  ON THE NEXT CARD.
23         WRITE(6,1800)
24         WRITE(6,1900)
25       3 READ(5,FMT)HC,IB,JB,X
       C  LIST THE DATA CARDS, TO ALLOW CHECKING FOR ERRORS
26         WRITE(6,300)HC,IB,JB,X
       C  CHECK FOR 'END' OR 'FIN' CARD
27         IF(HC.EQ.HB.OR.HC.EQ.HA)GO TO 4
       C  COUNTER FOR NUMBER OF CARDS IN EACH COMBINATION OF
       C  POPULATION AND PSU.
28         N(IB,JB)=N(IB,JB)+1
       C  SUB-TOTAL FOR EACH PSU WITHIN EACH POPULATION
29         XPSU(IB,JB)=XPSU(IB,JB)+X
       C  COUNTER FOR NUMBER OF CARDS IN EACH POPULATION
30         XNT(IB)=XNT(IB)+1
31         XNTO=XNTO+1
       C  SUB-TOTAL FOR POPULATION IB
32         XT(IB)=XT(IB)+X
       C  GRAND TOTAL
33         XTO=XTO+X
       C  TOTAL RAW SS
34         RS=RS+X*X
       C COUNTER FOR NUMBER OF PSU'S IN EACH POPULATION-
       C PSU'S MUST BE NUMBERED CONSECUTIVELY
35         IF(JB.GT.J(IB))J(IB)=JB
       C  COUNTER FOR NUMBER OF POPULATIONS
       C  THE POPULATIONS MUST BE NUMBERED CONSECUTIVELY
36         IF(IB.GT.I)I=IB
       C  READ ANOTHER CARD
37         GO TO 3
       C  WRITE OUT NUMBER OF PSU'S IN EACH POPULATION,
       C  AND SAMPLE SIZE FOR EACH PSU.
38       4 WRITE(6,102)HDG
39         WRITE(6,400)
40         WRITE(6,500)(IC,IC=1,I)
```

APPENDIX N *(Continued)*

PRGM4

```
      C
      C
41          WRITE(6,501)
42          WRITE(6,502)(J(ID),ID=1,I)
43          WRITE(6,600)
      C  OBTAIN NO. OF PSU'S IN EACH POPULATION.
44          MAXP=J(1)
45          DO 5 ID=2,I
46        5 IF(J(ID).GT.MAXP)MAXP=J(ID)
      C  WRITE OUT SAMPLE SIZE FOR EACH COMBINATION
      C  OF POPULATION AND PSU.
47          WRITE(6,1500)
48          WRITE(6,2100)
49          WRITE(6,500)(IT,IT=1,I)
50          WRITE(6,503)
51          DO 6 JE=1,MAXP
52        6 WRITE(6,700)JE,(N(IE,JE),IE=1,I)
      C  CALCULATE AND FLOAT ALL PERTINENT SAMPLE SIZES
53          DO 7 II=1,I
54          NT(II)=XNT(II)
55        7 XB=XB+J(II)
56          WRITE(6,2101)(NT(IJ),IJ=1,I)
      C  XB IS TOTAL NO. OF PSU'S IN THE EXPERIMENT
      C  XNTO IS THE TOTAL NO. OF OBSERVATIONS IN THE EXPERIMENT
      C  CALCULATE RAW SS
57          RSTO=XTO*XTO/XNTO
58          DO 8 IG=1,I
59          RSXT=RSXT+XT(IG)*XT(IG)/XNT(IG)
60          XMT(IG)=XT(IG)/XNT(IG)
61          NJ=J(IG)
62          DO 8 JG=1,NJ
63          XN=N(IG,JG)
64        8 RSPSU=RSPSU+XPSU(IG,JG)*XPSU(IG,JG)/XN
      C  CALCULATE DEGREES OF FREEDOM FOR POPULATION, PSU,
      C  AND SSU SUMS-OF-SQUARES, RESPECTIVELY.
65          TDF=I-1
66          KTDF=TDF
67          XI=I
68          PSUDF=XB-XI
69          KPSUDF=PSUDF
70          SSUDF=XNTO-XB
71          KSSUDF=SSUDF
      C  CALCULATE CORRECTED SS,MS,F
72          TOSS=RS-RSTO
73          TSS=RSXT-RSTO
74          PSUSS=RSPSU-RSXT
75          SSUSS=RS-RSPSU
76          TMS=TSS/TDF
```

APPENDIX N (*Continued*)

PRGM4

```
        C
        C
77          PSUMS=PSUSS/PSUDF
78          SSUMS=SSUSS/SSUDF
79          F=TMS/PSUMS
        C   CALCULATE EXPECTED MEAN SQUARES
80          VO=0.
81          V1=0.
82          V2=0.
83          DO 9 II=1,I
84          KT=XNT(II)
85          V2=V2+KT*KT/XNTO
86          DO 9 JI=1,KT
87          SN(II,JI)=N(II,JI)
88          VO=VO+SN(II,JI)*SN(II,JI)/XNT(II)
89        9 V1=V1+SN(II,JI)*SN(II,JI)/XNTO
90          QO=(XNTO-VO)/PSUDF
91          Q1=(VO-V1)/TDF
92          Q2=(XNTO-V2)/TDF
        C   WRITE OUT ANALYSIS OF VARIANCE TABLE
93          WRITE(6,800)
94          WRITE(6,900)
95          WRITE(6,1000)KTDF,TSS,TMS,Q2,Q1
96          WRITE(6,1100)KPSUDF,PSUSS,PSUMS,QO
97          WRITE(6,1200)KSSUDF,SSUSS,SSUMS
98          WRITE(6,1201)F
99          WRITE(6,1202)
100         WRITE(6,1203)
101         WRITE(6,1204)
102         WRITE(6,1300)
103         WRITE(6,1400)
        C WRITE OUT TABLE OF MEANS
104         DO10 IH=1,I
105      10 WRITE(6,1700)IH,XMT(IH)
106         IF(HC.EQ.HA)GO TO 1
107         WRITE(6,101)
108         STOP
109     100 FORMAT(' ',20A4/)
110     101 FORMAT('1')
111     102 FORMAT('1',20A4/)
112     200 FORMAT(20A4)
113     300 FORMAT(' ',A3,2(2X,I2),E15.7)
114     400 FORMAT(' ',24X,'POPULATION NUMBER')
115     500 FORMAT(12X,7(7X,I1,8X)/////)
116     501 FORMAT(' NO. OF PSUS')
117     502 FORMAT(' IN EACH',10X,7(I2,14X))
118     503 FORMAT(' ')
119     600 FORMAT(' POPULATION',5(6X,I3,7X))
```

APPENDIX N *(Continued)*

PRGM4

```
        C
        C
120       700 FORMAT(10X,I2,7(6X,I2,8X)////)
121       800 FORMAT(///25X,'ANALYSIS OF VARIANCE',//)
122       900 FORMAT(6X,'SOURCE',2X,'DF',9X,'SS',12X,'MS',16X,
          *'EMS'//)
123      1000 FORMAT(1X,'POPULATIONS',1X,I3,2X,2(E13.7,2X),
          *E13.7,'SA + ',E13.7,'SB + SC')
124      1100 FORMAT(5X,'PSU',5X,I3,2X,2(E13.7,2X),E13.7,
          *'SB + SC'//)
125      1200 FORMAT(5X,'SSU',5X,I3,2X,2(E13.7,2X),'SC'////)
126      1201 FORMAT(' ','F = ',E13.7)
127      1202 FORMAT(' THE F REPORTED HERE IS POPULATIONS',
          *' MEAN-SQUARE DIVIDED BY')
128      1203 FORMAT(' PSU MEAN-SQUARE. THE STANDARD F TABLES',
          *' CAN BE USED')
129      1204 FORMAT(' IF THE SAMPLE SIZES ARE EQUAL,',
          *' OR ALMOST SO.')
130      2101 FORMAT(/9X,'TOTAL',4X,7(I2,14X))
131      1300 FORMAT(10X,'POPULATION',25X,'SAMPLE')
132      1400 FORMAT(12X,'NUMBER',29X,'MEAN')
133      1500 FORMAT(////' TABLE OF SAMPLE SIZES FOR COMBINATIONS',
          *' OF POPULATION AND PSU')
134      1700 FORMAT(14X,I2,24X,E15.7)
135      1800 FORMAT(' PRINT-OUT OF INFORMATION')
136      1900 FORMAT(' ON DATA CARDS')
137      2000 FORMAT(' ','YOUR FIELD DESCRIPTORS ARE')
138      2100 FORMAT(10X,'PSU',12X,'POPULATION NUMBER')
139          END
        C
        C   THE NUMBER OF POPULATIONS (OR TREATMENTS)
        C   IS LIMITED TO 25. ALSO, THE NUMBER OF PSU'S
        C   PER POPULATION IS LIMITED TO 25. IF THIS CAPACITY
        C   IS INSUFFICIENT, THE CORRESPONDING NUMBERS IN THE
        C   DIMENSION STATEMENTS CAN BE CHANGED, ALONG WITH
        C   THE CORRESPONDING NUMBERS IN THE PROGRAM.
        C
        C   IF MORE TREATMENTS OR POPULATIONS ARE DESIRED,
        C   CHANGE ALL VARIABLES WITH A SINGLE SUBSCRIPT
        C   IN THE DIMENSION STATEMENT WHOSE VALUES ARE
        C   NOW 25, TO THE NUMBER OF POPULATIONS DESIRED.
        C   ALSO CHANGE THE 25 IN STATEMENT 4 TO THE
        C   APPROPRIATE LARGER NUMBER.
        C
        C   IF MORE PSU'S PER POPULATION ARE DESIRED,
        C   CHANGE THE SECOND SUBSCRIPT OF THE DOUBLE SUB-
        C   SCRIPTED VARIABLES IN THE DIMENSION STATEMENT
        C   TO THE APPROPRIATE NUMBER. ALSO CHANGE THE 25
```

APPENDIX N (*Continued*)

PRGM4

```
C
C
C    IN STATEMENT 9 TO THE LARGER VALUE DESIRED.
C    ONE OR MORE SYSTEMS CARDS WILL FOLLOW
C    THE END CARD, BEFORE THE FIRST CONTROL CARD.
C
C    CONTROL CARD #1 IS THE VERBAL
C    DESCRIPTION OF YOUR JOB
C    CONTROL CARD #2 PROVIDES THE
C    FIELD DESCRIPTOR FOR YOUR DATA.
C    IT SHOULD BEGIN WITH (T78,A3,
C    EACH CARD IS TO HAVE A SINGLE OBSERVATION ON IT, WITH
C    THE FIELD DESCRIPTORS FOR READING (A) 'END' OR 'FIN',
C    (B) THE PSU NUMBER, (C) THE SSU NUMBER WITHIN THE PSU,
C    AND (D) THE OBSERVATION--GIVEN ON CONTROL CARD #1
C    IN THAT ORDER.
C            A. THE 'A3' IS FOR 'END' OR 'FIN', AND IS
C               REQUIRED TO BE IN COLUMNS 78-80, AS PER
C               THE INITIAL ENTRIES IN CONTROL CARD #1.
C               THIS CAN BE CHANGED TO ANY OTHER
C               THREE COLUMNS, IF DESIRED.
C            B&C. PSU AND SSU NUMBERS MUST BE IN THE
C               'I' FIELD DESCRIPTOR CODE.
C            D. THE OBSERVATION IS TO BE SPECIFIED USING
C               THE 'F' FIELD DESCRIPTOR CODE.
C
C    DATA MUST FOLLOW CONTROL CARD #2
C
C    FIRST CARD FOLLOWING THE DATA DECK SHOULD BE BLANK,
C    EXCEPT FOR 'END' OR 'FIN' IN COLUMNS 78 - 80.
C    'FIN' IS FOR THE LAST DATA SET.
C
C    FOLLOWING ARE TWO SETS OF DATA EXACTLY AS PUNCHED FOR
C    PRGM4, EXEPT FOR THE C IN COLUMN ONE.  THESE SETS
C    MAY BE USED TO TEST THE PROGRAM AT YOUR COMPUTING
C    CENTER. THE SECOND SET OF DATA HAS UNEQUAL NUMBERS OF
C    PSU'S IN EACH POPULATION. ALTHOUGH THIS CASE IS NOT
C    TREATED IN THE TEXT, THE USE OF THE PROGRAM IS
C    ILLUSTRATED, IN CASE MISSING OBSERVATIONS ARE OBTAINED
C    IN PRACTICE. THE UNEQUAL NUMBERS CASE IS FROM PAGE
C    358, GRAYBILL(1961).
C
C    EXAMPLE FOR BALANCED AOV WITH CLUSTER SAMPLING
C    (T78,A3,T4,I1,1X,I1,1X,F2.0)
C    1 1 18
C    1 1 30
C    1 1 33
C    1 1 42
```

APPENDIX N (Continued)

PRGM4

```
C
C
C    1 1 66
C    1 2 29
C    1 2 12
C    1 2 23
C    1 2 30
C    1 2 31
C    1 3 40
C    1 3 30
C    1 3 72
C    1 3 06
C    1 3 51
C    2 1 23
C    2 1 66
C    2 1 43
C    2 1 35
C    2 1 15
C    2 2 04
C    2 2 36
C    2 2 19
C    2 2 20
C    2 2 01
C    2 3 00
C    2 3 16
C    2 3 53
C    2 3 62
C    2 3 41
C                                                              END
C    EXAMPLE FOR UNBALANCED AOV WITH CLUSTER SAMPLING
C    (T78,A3,T4,2I1,F2.0)
C    1132
C    1131
C    1123
C    1126
C    1230
C    1226
C    1229
C    1228
C    1218
C    1334
C    1330
C    1326
C    1334
C    1332
C    1331
C    1326
C    2126
```

APPENDIX N (*Continued*)

PRGM4

```
C
C
C    2120
C    2118
C    2222
C    2231
C    2220
C    2221
C    2323
C    2321
C    2324
C    2326
C    2318
C    2421
C    2421
C    2430
C    3116
C    3120
C    3132
C    3214
C    3218
C    3216
C    3217
C    4131
C    4134
C    4141
C    4140
C    4242
C    4243
C    4240
C    4235
C    4229
C    4326
C    4325
C    4329
C    4340
C    4337
C                                                              FIN
C    POSSIBLE SOURCES OF ERROR, IF THE PROGRAM DOESN'T
C    RUN PROPERLY:
C        1. CONTROL CARDS IN ORDER? IF NOT, YOUR ERROR
C    MESSAGES WILL INDICATE SOME FORMAT (FIELD DESCRIPTOR)
C    ERROR, OR YOU WILL GET SOME STRANGE PRINT-OUTS FOR
C    YOUR CONTROL CARDS, IN THE OUT-PUT.
C        2. DATA PUNCHED ON CARDS CONSISTENTLY WITH FIELD
C    DESCRIPTOR? IF NOT, YOU WILL GET SOME WILD OUTPUT.
C        3. NUMBER OF DATA CARDS CORRECT? THE PROGRAM WAS
C    NOT WRITTEN TO DETECT THIS TYPE OF ERROR. IT SIMPLY
```

APPENDIX N (*Continued*)

PRGM4

```
C
C
C    RECORDS IN THE OUTPUT HOW MANY OBSERVATIONS WERE READ
C    IN, BEFORE AN 'END' OR 'FIN' CARD WAS ENCOUNTERED.
C        4. DO YOU HAVE YOUR 'END' (OR 'FIN') CARD FOLLOWING
C    YOUR DATA? IF NOT, YOU WILL GET SOME KIND OF MESSAGE
C    TO THE EFFECT THAT AN ATTEMPT TO STORE DATA WAS MADE,
C    AND A SYSTEMS CARD WAS ENCOUNTERED. IF SEVERAL SETS
C    OF DATA WERE STACKED TOGETHER, THE NEXT CARD
C    WILL BE THE HEADING FOR THE NEXT JOB. AN ATTEMPT WILL
C    BE MADE TO STORE THE INFORMATION AS THOUGH IT WERE
C    DATA, AND YOU WILL GET AN ERROR MESSAGE, INDICATING
C    THAT THE DATA IS NOT CONSISTENT WITH YOUR
C    FORMAT SPECIFICATIONS.
C        5. ALL DATA SETS AFTER THE SET THAT WAS
C    IMPROPERLY PUNCHED WILL HAVE TO BE RE-RUN.
C
C    THE FINAL SET OF SYSTEMS CARDS COMES
C    AFTER THE 'FIN' CARD.

$ENTRY
```

APPENDIX N (*Continued*)

PRGM4

EXAMPLE FOR BALANCED AOV WITH CLUSTER SAMPLING

YOUR FIELD DESCRIPTORS ARE
    (T78,A3,T4,I1,1X,I1,1X,F2.0)

PRINT-OUT OF INFORMATION
ON DATA CARDS

```
            1   1   0.1800000E 02
            1   1   0.3000000E 02
            1   1   0.3300000E 02
            1   1   0.4200000E 02
            1   1   0.6600000E 02
            1   2   0.2900000E 02
            1   2   0.1200000E 02
            1   2   0.2300000E 02
            1   2   0.3000000E 02
            1   2   0.3100000E 02
            1   3   0.4000000E 02
            1   3   0.3000000E 02
            1   3   0.7200000E 02
            1   3   0.6000000E 01
            1   3   0.5100000E 02
            2   1   0.2300000E 02
            2   1   0.6600000E 02
            2   1   0.4300000E 02
            2   1   0.3500000E 02
            2   1   0.1500000E 02
            2   2   0.4000000E 01
            2   2   0.3600000E 02
            2   2   0.1900000E 02
            2   2   0.2000000E 02
            2   2   0.1000000E 01
            2   3   0.0000000E 00
            2   3   0.1600000E 02
            2   3   0.5300000E 02
            2   3   0.6200000E 02
            2   3   0.4100000E 02
END         0   0   0.0000000E 00
```

APPENDIX N (Continued)

PRGM4

EXAMPLE FOR BALANCED AOV WITH CLUSTER SAMPLING

POPULATION NUMBER

	1	2
NO. OF PSUS IN EACH POPULATION	3	3

TABLE OF SAMPLE SIZES FOR COMBINATIONS OF POPULATION AND PSU

POPULATION NUMBER

PSU	1	2
1	5	5
2	5	5
3	5	5
TOTAL	15	15

ANALYSIS OF VARIANCE

SOURCE	DF	SS	MS	EMS
POPULATIONS	1	0.2080313E 03	0.2080313E 03	0.1500000E 02SA + 0.4999998E 01SB + SC
PSU	4	0.1909328E 04	0.4773320E 03	0.5000000E 01SB + SC
SSU	24	0.8966008E 04	0.3735835E 03	SC

F = 0.4358208E 00
THE F REPORTED HERE IS POPULATIONS MEAN-SQUARE DIVIDED BY
PSU MEAN-SQUARE. THE STANDARD F TABLES CAN BE USED
IF THE SAMPLE SIZES ARE EQUAL, OR ALMOST SO.

POPULATION NUMBER	SAMPLE MEAN
1	0.3420000E 02
2	0.2893332E 02

APPENDIX N *(Continued)*

PRGM4

EXAMPLE FOR UNBALANCED AOV WITH CLUSTER SAMPLING

YOUR FIELD DESCRIPTORS ARE
(T78,A3,T4,2I1,F2.0)

PRINT-OUT OF INFORMATION
ON DATA CARDS

1	1	0.3200000E 02
1	1	0.3100000E 02
1	1	0.2300000E 02
1	1	0.2600000E 02
1	2	0.3000000E 02
1	2	0.2600000E 02
1	2	0.2900000E 02
1	2	0.2800000E 02
1	2	0.1800000E 02
1	3	0.3400000E 02
1	3	0.3000000E 02
1	3	0.2600000E 02
1	3	0.3400000E 02
1	3	0.3200000E 02
1	3	0.3100000E 02
1	3	0.2600000E 02
2	1	0.2600000E 02
2	1	0.2000000E 02
2	1	0.1800000E 02
2	2	0.2200000E 02
2	2	0.3100000E 02
2	2	0.2000000E 02
2	2	0.2100000E 02
2	3	0.2300000E 02
2	3	0.2100000E 02
2	3	0.2400000E 02
2	3	0.2600000E 02
2	3	0.1800000E 02
2	4	0.2100000E 02
2	4	0.2100000E 02
2	4	0.3000000E 02
3	1	0.1600000E 02
3	1	0.2000000E 02
3	1	0.3200000E 02
3	2	0.1400000E 02
3	2	0.1800000E 02
3	2	0.1600000E 02
3	2	0.1700000E 02
4	1	0.3100000E 02
4	1	0.3400000E 02
4	1	0.4100000E 02

APPENDIX N (*Continued*)

PRGM4

	4	1	0.4000000E	02
	4	2	0.4200000E	02
	4	2	0.4300000E	02
	4	2	0.4000000E	02
	4	2	0.3500000E	02
	4	2	0.2900000E	02
	4	3	0.2600000E	02
	4	3	0.2500000E	02
	4	3	0.2900000E	02
	4	3	0.4000000E	02
	4	3	0.3700000E	02
FIN	0	0	0.0000000E	00

APPENDIX N (*Continued*)

PRGM4

EXAMPLE FOR UNBALANCED AOV WITH CLUSTER SAMPLING

POPULATION NUMBER

	1	2	3	4
NO. OF PSUS IN EACH POPULATION	3	4	2	3

TABLE OF SAMPLE SIZES FOR COMBINATIONS OF POPULATION AND PSU

PSU	POPULATION NUMBER			
	1	2	3	4
1	4	3	3	4
2	5	4	4	5
3	7	5	0	5
4	0	3	0	0
TOTAL	16	15	7	14

ANALYSIS OF VARIANCE

SOURCE	DF	SS	MS	EMS
POPULATIONS	3	0.1669941E 04	0.5566470E 03	0.1267948E 02SA + 0.4409548E 01SB + SC
PSU	8	0.2503086E 03	0.3128857E 02	0.4269497E 01SB + SC
SSU	40	0.9498086E 03	0.2374521E 02	SC

F = 0.1779074E 02
THE F REPORTED HERE IS POPULATIONS MEAN-SQUARE DIVIDED BY
PSU MEAN-SQUARE. THE STANDARD F TABLES CAN BE USED
IF THE SAMPLE SIZES ARE EQUAL, OR ALMOST SO.

POPULATION NUMBER	SAMPLE MEAN
1	0.2850000E 02
2	0.2279999E 02
3	0.1900000E 02
4	0.3514285E 02

GLOSSARY OF SYMBOLS USED IN THE TEXT

This glossary is designed to be used when the reader encounters a symbol or other mathematical term he is unfamiliar with or has forgotten. Given the brief description in the Glossary, the reader can then turn to the page in the text where the term is explained in greater detail.

		sides of the symbol. The value next to the point is taken to be smaller than that next to the wide side; $x > y$ means "x is greater than y."
20	$<$	The inequality sign reversed; $x < y$ means "x is less than y."
20	$\geq$ or $\leq$	The element next to the point is taken to be "less than or equal to" that next to the open end.
38	$\bar{x}$	Pronounced "x-bar." The sample mean— average of all observations in a sample of size n.
38	$\bar{x} = \dfrac{1}{n} \sum\limits_{i=1}^{n} x_i$	Formula for the sample mean.
23	$\log x$	Pronounced "log of x." The logarithm of x, to the base 10.
25	$\sqrt[n]{c}$	The nth root of c. The value which when multiplied by itself n times, gives c.
38	μ	Pronounced "mew." The population mean— average of all the elements in the same population. . .
	$\mu = \dfrac{1}{N} \sum\limits_{i=1}^{N} x_i$	where x_i is the ith element in the population, and there are N elements in the population.
41	σ^2	Pronounced "sigma squared." The population variance.
	$\sigma^2 = \dfrac{1}{N-1} \sum\limits_{i=1}^{N} (x_i - \mu)^2$	
41	σ	Pronounced "sigma." Standard deviation of the elements in a population.
	$\sigma = \sqrt{\dfrac{1}{N-1} \sum\limits_{i=1}^{N} (x_i - \mu)^2}$	
43	$\mu_{\bar{x}}$	Pronounced "mew sub x bar." The population mean of the sample means. Average of all possible sample means, each sample being selected from the same population.
44	$\sigma_{\bar{x}}^2$	Pronounced "sigma squared sub x bar."

TEXT
PAGE

		The population variance of the sample means. Variance of all possible sample means, each sample being selected from the same population.
44	$\cong$	Is approximately equal to; $x \cong y$ means "x is approximately equal to y."
44	s^2	The sample variance—variance calculated from a random sample of size n.
45	μ_{s^2}	Pronounced "mew sub s squared." The population mean of the sample variances—average of the variances of all possible samples selected from the same population.
57	$\chi^2_{(k)1-\alpha}$	Pronounced "ki-squared sub k, 1 minus alpha." The value that is greater than $(1 - \alpha) \cdot 100$ percent of the observations from a chi-square distribution with k degrees of freedom. Appendix Table E gives a table of these values.
69	$\sim$	"Comes from a population." The random variable appears on the left; the description of the population goes on the right. For example, $x \sim (\mu, \sigma^2)$ means "x comes from a population with mean μ and variance σ^2."
72	$P(E)$	The probability of the event E.
75	α	The Greek letter alpha; usually used to denote small probabilities, although it is sometimes used for the constant term in a linear equation.
73	$Z_{1-\alpha}$	Pronounced "z sub 1 minus alpha." The value that is greater than $(1 - \alpha) \cdot 100$ percent of the observations from a normal distribution with zero mean and unit variance. Appendix Table D gives a table of these values.
81	$t_{(k)1-\alpha}$	Pronounced "t sub k, 1 minus alpha." The value that is greater than $(1 - \alpha) \cdot 100$ percent of the observations from a t-distribution with k degrees of freedom. Appendix Table F gives a table of these values.
84	K_p	Pronounced "k sub p." The value that is greater than $p \cdot 100$ percent of the observations from an arbitrary distribution.
244	β	The Greek letter beta (pronounced "bayta"). The coefficient of x in a linear equation.

91   s_x, s_y When the relationship between x and y in a random sample is being considered, then s_x (pronounced "s sub x") is the sample variance for the x's; s_y (pronounced "s sub y") is the same for the y's. That is,

$$s_x = \sqrt{\frac{1}{n-1} \sum_{i=1}^{n} (x_i - \bar{x}.)^2}$$

$$s_y = \sqrt{\frac{1}{n-1} \sum_{i=1}^{n} (y_i - \bar{y}.)^2}$$

91   s_{xy} Pronounced "s sub x, y." The mean of the product of the deviation of x from its mean, with the deviation of y from its mean.

$$s_{xy} = \frac{1}{n-1} \sum_{i=1}^{n} (x_i - \bar{x}.)(y_i - \bar{y}.)$$

91   r The sample correlation coefficient.

$$r = \frac{s_{xy}}{s_x s_y}$$

92   μ_x Pronounced "mew sub x." The population mean for the x values.

92   μ_y Pronounced "mew sub y." The population mean for the y values.

93   σ_x Pronounced "sigma sub x." The population standard deviation for the x values.

93   σ_y Pronounced "sigma sub y." The population standard deviation for the y values.

93   σ_{xy} Pronounced "sigma sub x, y."

$$\sigma_{xy} = \frac{1}{N-1} \sum_{i=1}^{N} (x_i - \mu_x)(y_i - \mu_y)$$

This is the population value for s_{xy}.

92   ρ The population correlation coefficient; the Greek letter rho, pronounced "row."

$$\rho = \frac{\sigma_{xy}}{\sigma_x \sigma_y}$$

93   μ_r Pronounced "mew sub r." The population mean of the sample correlation coefficient.

94     $\neq$ Means "is unequal to"; $x \neq y$ means "x is unequal to y."

131   ϵ Greek letter epsilon. Usually used in this text to denote the degree to which the member of a population deviates from an assumed model—the "error" component. For example,

$$y_{ij} = \mu_i + \epsilon_{ij}$$

135   x_{ij} Pronounced "x sub i, j." A doubly subscripted variable. This is a measurement which is classified in two ways—the j may indicate the person the measurement was made on, and the i may specify the population from which the person was selected, for instance.

136     $X_{i\cdot}$ Pronounced "cap x, sub i dot." Let $i = 1, 2, \ldots, k; j = 1, 2, \ldots, n$. Then

$$X_{i\cdot} = \sum_{j=1}^{n} x_{ij} = \sum_{j} x_{ij}$$

That is,

$$X_{i\cdot} = x_{i1} + x_{i2} + \cdots + x_{in}$$

Summing over a single subscript can be indicated by capitalizing the variable and replacing the subscript over with a dot.

136     $X_{\cdot\cdot}$ Pronounced "cap x, sub dot dot."

$$X_{\cdot\cdot} = \sum_{i=1}^{k} \sum_{j=1}^{n} x_{ij} = \sum_{i} \sum_{j} x_{ij} = \sum_{i,j} x_{ij}$$

$$= (x_{11} + x_{12} + \cdots + x_{1n}$$
$$+ x_{21} + x_{22} + \cdots + x_{2n}$$
$$+ \cdots$$
$$+ x_{k1} + x_{k2} + \cdots + x_{kn})$$

137     $\bar{x}_{i\cdot}$ Pronounced "x sub i dot bar." The *average* of all terms having the first subscript equal to i. That is,

$$\bar{x}_{i\cdot} = \frac{1}{n} \sum_{j=1}^{n} x_{ij}$$

as compared with

$$X_{i.} = \sum_{j=1}^{n} x_{ij}$$

146	n_0	Pronounced "*n* sub zero." Used in this text to denote the initial sample in a sampling plan consisting of two successive random samples selected from the same population.
165	U	Represents the set of all possible characteristics for a sampling unit. Example: all possible eye colors may include blue, grey, hazel, green, brown, albino, so that U would be the collection of all these events.
72	E	Represents some property of a sampling unit such as, The person selected has blue eyes, or the student has an IQ greater than 110. E is termed an "event."
165	$N(E)$	The number of sampling units with property E.
165	$P(E) = N(E)/N(U)$	The probability that event E will occur.
166	$\cap$	If X,Y are events (in the same sense as E), then $X \cap Y$ is called "the intersection of X and Y" and denotes the set of all events which have both characteristics X and Y.
166	ϕ	The Greek letter phi. Denotes the set having no events in it; corresponds to zero in the number system.
167	$\cup$	If X,Y are events, then $X \cup Y$ is called "the union of X and Y" and denotes the set of all events which have either characteristic X *or* Y, but not necessarily both.
169	$P(X\|Y)$	The probability that event X will occur when it is known that event Y has occurred $P(X\|Y) = N(X \cap Y)/N(Y)$.
173	p_{ij}	Is the probability that a person selected at random will be in the cell corresponding to row i and column j of a contingency table.
172	n_{ij}	Is the number of people in a random sample who were classified in the cell corresponding to row i and column j of a contingency table.

$i = 1, 2, \ldots, r$ (r = number of rows)

$$j = 1, 2, \ldots, c \ (c = \text{number of columns})$$

172

$$n_{i.} = \sum_{j=1}^{c} n_{ij}$$

$$n_{.j} = \sum_{i=1}^{r} n_{ij}$$

$$n_{..} = \sum_{i=1}^{r} \sum_{j=1}^{c} n_{ij}$$

174	O_{ij}	Defined as n_{ij}—"the 'observed' number of sampling units in row i and column j." Used for consistency with terminology used in some other texts.
174	E_{ij}	Defined as $E\{n_{ij}\}$—the "expected" number of sampling units in row i, column j.
224	ˆ	Pronounced "alpha-hat," "beta-hat," etc. Called a caret, it is placed over some constant value (usually represented by a Greek symbol), to indicate an estimate of that value; as $\hat{\alpha}$, $\hat{\beta}$, etc.
177	H	A measure of the degree of relationship between the rows and the columns in a two-way contingency table. The formula is

$$\log H = \sum_{i=1}^{r} \sum_{j=1}^{c} \hat{P}(A_i \cap B_j) \log \hat{P}(A_i \cap B_j)$$

$$- \tfrac{1}{2} \sum_{i=1}^{r} \hat{P}(A_i) \log \hat{P}(A_i)$$

$$- \tfrac{1}{2} \sum_{j=1}^{c} \hat{P}(B_j) \log \hat{P}(B_j)$$

where $\hat{P}(A_i \cap B_j) = \dfrac{n_{ij}}{n_{..}}$

$$\hat{P}(A_i) = \dfrac{n_{i.}}{n_{..}}$$

$$\hat{P}(B_j) = \dfrac{n_{.j}}{n_{..}}$$

r = number of rows
c = number of columns

191         $E\{\ \}$ Stands for the population mean of whatever statistic is in the brackets. For example,

$$E\{s^2\} = \mu_s{}^2$$

(The same symbol was used previously for an event, but here it is followed by curly brackets.)

197         $F_{(k,l)1-\alpha}$ Pronounced "F sub k, l, 1 minus alpha." The value that is greater than $(1 - \alpha) \cdot 100$ percent of the observations from an F-distribution, with k degrees of freedom in the numerator and l degrees of freedom in the denominator. Appendix J gives a table of these values.

199   τ The Greek letter tau used to denote the treatment component in an analysis of variance model, as

$$y_{ij} = \mu + \tau_i + \epsilon_{ij}$$

where

$$\sum_{i=1}^{k} \tau_i = 0$$

228   MS_R Pronounced "regression mean-square," or "mean-square sub r." The sum-of-squares due to regression, divided by the degrees of freedom ($= 1$). Term used in Table 8–3:

$$MS_R = SS_R/1 = SS_R$$
$$= [\Sigma(x_i - \bar{x}.)(y_i - \bar{y}.)]^2/\Sigma(x_i - \bar{x}.)^2$$

228   MS_E Pronounced "error mean-square." The "error" sum-of-squares divided by the degrees of freedom. The term is first used in Table 8–3 in the regression model. It is used to estimate the variance of the error term (denoted by ϵ with subscripts) in many situations, each time with a different formula.

228   SS_R Pronounced "regression sum-squares" or "sum-squares sub r." The sum-of-squares due to regression in an analysis of variance table for regression.

$$SS_R = [\Sigma(x_i - \bar{x}.)(y_i - \bar{y}.)]^2/\Sigma(x_i - \bar{x}.)^2$$

228   SS_E Pronounced "error sum-of-squares." Sum-of-squares due to error. In the analysis of variance for regression, this is

$$SS_E = \Sigma(y_i - \bar{y}.)^2 - \frac{[\Sigma(x_i - \bar{x}.)(y_i - \bar{y}.)]^2}{\Sigma(x_i - \bar{x}.)^2}$$

246   SS_T, SS_C, SS_E Pronounced "T sum-of-squares, C sum-of-squares," etc. Sums-of-squares corresponding to various components in the analysis of variance table for cluster sampling. Formulas are in Table 9–3.

BIBLIOGRAPHY

Baker, F. B., and **Collier, R. B.** (1968). An Empirical Study into Factors Affecting the *F-test* Under Permutation for the Randomized Block Design. *Jour. Amer. Stat. Assoc.,* *63,* 323, 902–911.

Bechhofer, F. E., Dunnett, C. W., and **Sobel, M.** (1954). A Two-Sample Multiple Decision Procedure for Ranking Means of Normal Populations with a Common Unknown Variance. *Biometrika, 41,* 170–176.

Borg, W. R. (1965). Ability Grouping in the Public Schools. *Jour. Exp. Educ., 34,* 2, 1–97.

Dunnett, C. W., and **Sobel, M.** (1955). Approximations to the Probability Integral and Certain Percentage Points of a Multivariate Analogue of Student's *t* Distribution. *Biometrika, 42,* 258–260.

Eisenhart, C. (1947). The Assumptions Underlying the Analysis of Variance. *Biometrics, 3,* 1–21.

Fraser, D. A. S., and **Guttman, I.** (1956). Tolerance Regions. *Ann. Math. Statist., 27,* 1, 162–179.

Graybill, F. A. (1961). *An Introduction to Linear Statistical Models,* Vol. I. New York, McGraw-Hill Book Co.

Kempthorne, O. (1952). *Design and Analysis of Experiments.* New York, John Wiley and Sons.

Kempthorne, O., Zuskind, G., Addleman, S., Throckmorton, T. N., and **White, R. F.** (1961). *Analysis of Variance Procedures.* U.S.A.F. Aeronautical Research Lab. Report 149.

Kullback, S. (1968). *Information Theory and Statistics.* New York, Dover.

Scheffe, H. (1958). *The Analysis of Variance.* New York, John Wiley and Sons.

INDEX